THE Marriage Compass

Using Gospel Principles and Relationship Science to Navigate the Course of Dating, Engagement, & Marriage

Jason S. Carroll Ph.D.

"Everything" by Lifehouse
Songwriters: Kate Holmes / Sarah Blackwood
Everything lyrics © Sony/ATV Music Publishing LLC

Layout and design by Kent Minson
Illustrations by April Martin

Copyright © 2018 Brigham Young University School of Family Life and BYU Academic Publishing

All rights reserved. This work is not an official publication of The Church of Jesus Christ of Latter-day Saints. The views expressed herein are the responsibility of the authors and do not necessarily represent the position of the Church or Brigham Young University.

For more information or permission to use material from this text contact:

BYU Academic Publishing
3995 WSC
Provo, UT 84606
Tel. (801) 422-6231
Fax (801) 422-0070
Academic publishing@byu.edu

To report ideas or text corrections email:

Jason S. Carroll, Ph.D. is a Professor of Marriage and Family Studies in the School of Family Life and a Fellow of the Wheatley Institution at Brigham Young University. He received his Ph.D. in Family Social Science from the University of Minnesota. Dr. Carroll is an internationally-recognized researcher and educator in the areas of marriage fragmentation, sexual intimacy, marriage readiness among young adults, the effectiveness of marriage education, and modern threats to marriage (such as pornography, delayed age at marriage, materialism, premarital sexuality, and non-marital childbirth). Dr. Carroll's work has been featured in the Economist, the Wall Street Journal, the New York Times, the LA Times, Newsweek, USA Today, Psychology Today Magazine, National Public Radio, the Tonight Show with Jay Leno, and other popular media and news outlets. In 2014, Dr. Carroll received the *Berscheid-Hatfield Award for Distinguished Mid-Career Achievement,* a biennial award given for distinguished scientific achievement by the International Association for Relationship Research.

Dr. Carroll has authored over 100 scientific articles, book chapters, and pubic scholarship pieces; and has presented numerous papers at national and international conferences. He is a professional member of the *International Association for Relationship Research* (IARR) and the *Society for the Study of Emerging Adulthood* (SSEA). Dr. Carroll's research has appeared in leading scientific journals such as the *Journal of Family Psychology, Archives of Sexual Behavior, Journal of Sex Research, Aggressive Behavior, Journal of American College Health,* and the *Journal of Adolescent Research*. He recently authored a chapter entitled, "Marriage and Emerging Adulthood" in the *Oxford Handbook of Emerging Adulthood* and previously authored a chapter, entitled "Theorizing About Marriage" in the *Sourcebook of Family Theories and Research*. Most recently, Dr. Carroll was the research director and co-author of a highly publicized report entitled "*Knot Yet: The Benefits and Costs of Delayed Marriage in America*" (www.twentysomethingmarriage.org).

Dr. Carroll served as a visiting scholar and was a research advisor for a national media campaign on healthy marriage targeting young adults that was commissioned by the U.S. Department of Health and Human Services (DHHS).In 2003, Dr. Carroll was commissioned by the Administration for Children and Families (ACF) to co-author a guiding report for the National Healthy Marriage Initiative entitled: *A Comprehensive Framework for Marriage Education*. Dr. Carroll currently serves on the editorial board for three journals: *Emerging Adulthood, Family Relations*, and the *Journal of Couple and Relationship Therapy*.

Dr. Carroll is a popular instructor at BYU where he teaches courses on marriage and family relationships to thousands of students each year. He and his wife Stefani have been married for 25 years and are the blessed parents of five children, Garret, Austin, Lindsey, Caleb and Hailey.

For Stefani
My everything

You are the light,
That's leading me,
To the place,
Where I find peace again.

You are the strength,
That keeps me walking.
You are the hope,
That keeps me trusting.

You calm the storms,
And you give me rest.
You hold me in your hands,
You won't let me fall.

You are the light,
To my soul.
You are my purpose,
You're everything.

Contents

Shadow Modeling — 1
Preface

Healthy Marriage Relationships — 5
Introduction
- The Purpose of this Book — 6
- What the Book Contains — 7
- Summary of the Volume — 8

The Divine Institution of Marriage — 13
Chapter 1
- Three Views of Marriage — 14
- Marriage and the Great Plan of Happiness — 18

Discipleship—The Foundation of Marriage — 24
Chapter 2
- The Joy of Christ — 25
- The First Principles of the Gospel — 27
- The Challenge to Become — 34

Charity (Love) — 36
Chapter 3
- What Is Love? — 37
- The Science of Love — 40

Cleaving (Commitment) — 44
Chapter 4
- The Ordinance of Marriage — 45
- Marriage as a Covenant — 48
- Research on Commitment in Marriage — 51
- Cleaving — 53

Equal Partnership (Equality) — 57
Chapter 5
- The Divine Design — 58
- Equal Partnership — 58
- Distinguish Between Leadership & Decision Making — 62
- Equal Partnership: Summary — 67

Family Stewardships (Unity) — 68
Chapter 6
- Family Stewardships — 69
- The Sacred Responsibilities of Fathers — 70
- The Sacred Responsibilities of Mothers — 74
- Family Stewardships—Key Principles — 76
- It Takes Two — 78
- Why Do These Principles Matter? — 81

Chastity (Intimacy) — 82
Chapter 7
- Metaphors of Sexual Purity — 83
- A Third Option: Sexual Wholeness in Marriage — 87
- Three Guiding Doctrines — 94
- Chastity in Marriage — 96
- Repentance from Sexual Sin — 97

Modern Threats to Marriage — 99
Chapter 8
- The Deinstitutionalization of Marriage — 100
- The Benefits of Marriage — 104
- Selection Versus Causation? — 105
- Marriage Benefits for Men and Women — 107
- Paradigms of Modernity — 109
- Modern Threats to Marriage — 111

Becoming and Creating — 115
Chapter 9

Approaches to Dating 116
Marriage as a Couple Relationship 118
The Ecology of Marriage 119

Family of Origin — 121
Chapter 10

The Generational Nature of Married Life . . 122
Two Key Tasks of Marriage Readiness . . . 123
Stability—"Going With the Flow" 123
Change—"Altering the Flow" 127
Coming to Terms—Intentionality 128

Personal Security — 132
Chapter 11

Amae: Our True Nature 133
Belonging: The Basis of Self-Worth 134
Personal Security is Needed in Dating and Marriage 136
How Can You Strengthen Your Personal Security? 137

Other Centeredness — 141
Chapter 12

Marital Virtues 141
Conclusion 147

Effective Communication — 148
Chapter 13

Effective Communication 149
Clear-Sending Communication 153

When to Wed? — 159
Chapter 14

A Deep and Abiding Concern 164

Who to Wed? — 165
Chapter 15

Eight Traps of Soulmate Thinking 169
Compatibility and Attraction 171
Physical Attraction 174

The Power of Pairing and the Stages of Dating — 178
Chapter 16

The Erosion of Traditional Dating and Courtship 179
Principles of Dating 182
Stages of Dating 183
Wedding Planning 190
Key Principles to Remember 192
Conclusion 193

Chastity in Dating — 194
Chapter 17

Three Levels of Chastity in Dating 195
Three Types of Intimacy 198
Where is the Line? 203
Research on Sexual Restraint in Dating . . 205
Pornography in Dating 207

Couple Differences — 209
Chapter 18

Differences in Marriage 210
Patterns of Couple Conflict 212
Conflict Patterns 213
Covert Conflict 216
Learn to Handle Differences Constructively 216
Managing Differences 217

Protecting Marital Resources — 220
CHAPTER 19

It's About Time 220
Marital Rituals 223
Extended Family Relationships 223
Money Issues and Marriage 226

Intimacy in Marriage — 231
CHAPTER 20

Intimacy in Marriage. 232
Moving From Sexual Response to a Sexual Relationship 233
The Anatomy of the Sexual Response . . . 236
Sexual Conditioning 241
Key to Marital Intimacy: Managing Differences 243
Proper Sources of Revelation 244
Sexual Decision Making in Marriage . . . 246
Becoming One 247

Two Become Three — 248
CHAPTER 21

Marriage as a Co-Parenting Stewardship . . 249
Child-Centeredness and Parenting Principles 252
The Transition to Parenthood 254

Marital Distress — 257
CHAPTER 22

Prophetic Teachings about Divorce 258
At the Crossroads 260
Seek to Heal Your Marriage 265

Shadow Modeling
PREFACE

> The LDS scholar has his citizenship in the kingdom, but carries his passport into the professional world—not the other way around.
>
> *Elder Neal A. Maxwell*

Many years ago when I was in graduate school at the University of Minnesota, I became close friends with a classmate of mine named John. He is still a dear friend and we enjoy the opportunity from time to time to catch up with each other when we attend professional conferences. John is from Eastern Canada and when we were first introduced to each other he had never meet a Latter-day Saint before. John grew up in a very religious Christian home and was a devout reader of the Bible. In fact, he had completed a Masters of Divinity degree before coming to the United States to pursue his doctoral degree in Family Studies. In between our classes, John and I would often eat lunch together and our conversations frequently turned to the subject of religion. He was very curious about the Church and would sometimes ask me about my beliefs and the doctrines of the Church.

One day, John and I were eating lunch in the student union building on campus. During this conversation, John asked me a question: "Jason, do Latter-day Saints believe in male headship?" My initial response was, "Well, I need a better understanding of what you mean by 'male headship' to answer your question." His response was, "It is when the father is the leader and ultimate decision maker in the home." I thought for a moment and my mind reflected on the phrase "to help one another as equal partners" that is found in the Proclamation on the Family that President Gordon B. Hinckley had shared with the world just a few years earlier. I then replied, "No, that's not quite right—we believe that husbands and wives are equal partners and should make family decisions together." John and I then launched into one of our memorable conversations as we discussed the differences between the two patterns of decision making in marriage. Oh, how I loved those conversations.

The interactions I had with John and my other classmates and professors during graduate school have always stayed with me. In fact, as I reflect back I have come to see that those conversations shaped me significantly. As I was studying research studies on families and learning the best knowledge the relationship sciences had to offer in my classes and in my work as a research assistant, John's sincere inquires also pushed me to deepen my study of the Lord's revelations on

marriage and family relationships. Those years were truly a time in my life that fit the Lord's plea to each of us—"seek ye out of the best books words of wisdom; seek learning even by study and also by faith" (D&C 88:118).

As I commenced my career as a researcher and professor, I committed myself to always try to integrate my scholarly work with spiritual truths. The quote from Elder Neal A. Maxwell at the first of this chapter is posted on the wall in my office and I have reflected many times on its implications for my work. Over the years, as I have developed theories and conducted studies I have developed a process that I call *shadow modeling*. What this means is that as I develop a "scholarly model" or theory I always strive to also develop the "spiritual model" of the concepts as well—a shadow model so to speak. Also, as I come to better understand spiritual truths, whether through study, prayer, or lived experiences with my wife and children, I try to "shadow model" these principles in the language and concepts of the relationship sciences.

At its core, shadow modeling is a bilingual experience. The learning that comes by study and the learning that comes by faith are often articulated in different languages, rely on different forms of evidence, and communicate with different audiences. And while many concepts and principles overlap, there are almost always some eternal spiritual understandings that scientific theory cannot replicate. In trying to do this type of scholarship, I have found that I usually develop three shadows models of any given principle or process: a *restored gospel model*, articulated in the doctrines of the restoration and faith language familiar to Latter-day Saints; a *faith-based spiritual model*, articulated in broader understandings of world religions and the ecumenical language of spirituality and divine providence; and a *scholarly model*, articulated in the theories of the social sciences and the conceptual language of academic studies. I try to move from model to model depending on the audience of a particular presentation or paper.

Why am I telling you about shadow modeling? Because this book is full of shadow models and mixed language systems. I believe that all of us live in a very blessed time when it comes to marriage and family life. I do not believe it is an overstatement to say that we now live in a time when we know more about how to establish and maintain a loving and lasting marriage than at any other time in the history of the world. In the ongoing process of the restoration of the gospel in the latter days, the Lord has revealed many great and marvelous principles about His divine institution of marriage and its centrality in His plan of happiness for each of us. When added to the sacred teachings of ancient scriptures we can truly see that we live in the "fullness of times" in our understanding of our Father in Heaven's "divine design" of marriage and family life (The Family: A Proclamation to the World, 1995, ¶ 7).

At the same time, we can all be the beneficiaries the truths discovered by the last 80 plus years of relationship science. Marriage research has advanced greatly during the last 40 years and marriage scholars have identified many of the factors that help couples form loving and lasting marriages. In fact, marriage scholars

can predict marriage outcomes now with very high levels of accuracy. So in a time when everyone seems to be talking about how unpredictable marriage is, marriage research is actually showing that marriage outcomes are highly predictable. And the good news is that the factors that matter can be changed and improved for anyone who wants to improve themselves and their marriages.

Recently, President Russell M. Nelson visited the campus at Brigham Young University to dedicate the new Life Sciences building. In his remarks, President Nelson talked about the nature of truth and our quest to understand truth in our lives. He said,

This university is committed to search for truth and teach the truth. All truth is part of the gospel of Jesus Christ. Whether truth comes from a scientific laboratory or by revelation from the Lord, it is all compatible, conflict only arises from an incomplete knowledge of either science or religion, or both (http://universe.byu.edu/2015/04/10/life-sciences-building-dedicated-by-elder-russell-m-nelson/)

This view of truth is the foundation for shadow modeling, striving to integrate revealed truth with scientific truth—and learning to bring those truths into our everyday lives.

Healthy Marriage Relationships
INTRODUCTION

Considering the enormous importance of marriage, it is rather astonishing that we don't make better preparation for success... too many people are inadequately prepared for this lofty responsibility.

Elder David B. Haight

President Gordon B. Hinckley introduced and read *The Family: A Proclamation to the World* in September of 1995 in the General Meeting of the Relief Society. It was only the fifth proclamation issued by the First Presidency and the Quorum of the Twelve Apostles of the Church of Jesus Christ of Latter-day Saints during its nearly 200-year history. Elder Merrill J. Bateman said about the Proclamation, "the statement is an extraordinary document outlining Church doctrine concerning the family and the relationships between husband and wife, parents and children" (BYU Speeches, January 6, 1998).

One of the central teachings of the Proclamation on the Family is the importance of marriage in our Heavenly Father's plan and the priority each of us should give, both as individuals and as couples, to strengthening our capacity to form and maintain loving and lasting marriage relationships. In the Proclamation, our prophetic leaders "solemnly proclaim that marriage between a man and a woman is ordained of God and that the family is central to the Creator's plan for the eternal destiny of His children" (¶ 1).

Explaining the centrality of marriage in the gospel plan, Elder Bruce R. McConkie taught:

From the moment of birth into mortality to the time we are married in the temple, everything we have in the whole gospel system is to prepare and qualify us to enter that holy order of matrimony which makes us husband and wife in this life and in the world to come.... There is nothing in this world as important as the creation and perfection of family units (Improvement Era, June 1970, p. 43–44).

Not only have our prophetic leaders emphasized the need for intentional marriage preparation, but leading educators and scholars have also pointed out a deficiency in relationship training in our culture as well. Leading marriage educator Dr. David Olson has remarked, "Too many couples spend more time preparing for a wedding than they do preparing for a

marriage." The goal of this book is to help teens, young adults, and married couples learn about healthy marriages and strengthen their preparation for marriage in their lives—now or in the future.

The Purpose of This Book

This book is primarily intended to be helpful to two groups of people. First, students at Brigham Young University as well as students at other Church colleges and institutes. This book attempts to respond faithfully to a call by President Boyd K. Packer in his inaugural address at the creation of the School of Family Life at Brigham Young University. President Packer called for School of Family Life faculty to produce textbooks on marriage and family relationships that would be worthy of a great university, that would be filled with moral and spiritual truths in full harmony with the restored gospel, and that would help students be good spouses and parents.

This volume was created to be a textbook for the "Preparation for Marriage" class and other courses taught in the School of Family Life on BYU's campus. These classes teach students the doctrines in the Proclamation on the Family; as well as providing them with a "Marriage Prep" experience to prepare them for marriage and family life. This course is offered by the School of Family Life with the aim to assist students in becoming better prepared to form and maintain loving and lasting marriage relationships.

The focus of this course is personal application, rather than professional or disciplinary training. This course is offered to students from all across campus in any major. These courses are taken by young single adults who are not currently dating, people who are seriously dating, engaged couples, and individuals who are already married. The emphasis of these classes is on personal preparation for the *vocation of marriage*—regardless of a person's current marital status.

The second, and largest, audience for this volume is the general Latter-day Saint reader who is interested in gaining deeper insights into how to form or maintain an enduring marriage. Similar to the Preparation for Marriage course on campus, this volume was designed to be applicable to a wide range of people—young single adults, engaged couples preparing for their wedding, newlyweds navigating the early years of marriage, or long-time spouses looking to strengthen their marriage.

The overarching purpose of this book is two-fold. First, to increase readers' testimonies of the importance of the divine institution of marriage in Heavenly Father's plan, and second, to increase readers' confidence in their ability to establish and maintain their

own eternal marriages. The specific goals of this book include:

1. To increase readers' understanding of the Lord's "divine design" (The Family: A Proclamation to the World, 1995, ¶ 7) for marriage relationships (e.g., the importance of discipleship, the nature of the marriage covenant, the importance of true equal partnership, stewardships of husbands and wives, etc).
2. To increase readers' awareness of the benefits that come from viewing marriage as a divine institution and not only a couple relationship.
3. To sensitize readers to the "paradigms of modern society" (secularism, individualism, materialism, and hedonism) and how to safeguard their current or future marriages from the modern threats to marriage created by these paradigms.
4. To increase readers' awareness of the factors that relationship science has shown to contribute to the formation and maintenance of healthy and stable marriages.
5. To enhance readers' spiritual awareness and academic understanding in order to help them weigh scholarly and contemporary ideas about marriage relationships and use both faith and scholarship to "hold fast to that which is good" (1 Thessalonians 5:21).

WHAT THE BOOK CONTAINS

There are many books about marriage, including self-help books, research monographs, and doctrinal volumes. This volume draws from both sacred and scholarly sources and attempts to provide both principle-based and practical information on dating and marriage relationships. The most unique and important contribution of this volume is the *integration* of scriptures and prophetic teachings with relationship science research related to dating, courtship, and marriage. Our goal is to "seek learning by study and also by faith" (D&C 88:118).

This volume uses a type of instruction called *principle based learning*. This means that each chapter focuses on principles (doctrines) and precepts (practices) of personal competence for marriage and couple formation (dating, engagement, and early marriage) that can be applied to many different types of personal situations. This is similar to the pattern established by the Prophet Joseph Smith who said, "I teach them correct principles, and they govern themselves" (Teachings of Presidents of the Church: Joseph Smith, 2007, p. 284). As you study the volume, you will need to prayerfully consider how the principles and practices presented can be incorporated in your personal life. As you do this, the principles will become alive and have the power to transform you and your relationships with others.

A reasonable question may be asked, "Why include scholarship in addition to scripture and prophetic teachings since this mixes human wisdom with eternal truth?" The following quote from President Brigham Young is instructive on this matter. He said:

> "Mormonism," so called, embraces every principle pertaining to life and salvation, for time and eternity. No matter who has it. . . . All that is good, lovely, and praiseworthy belongs to this Church and Kingdom. "Mormonism" includes all truth. There is no truth but what belongs to the Gospel . . . .It is the business of the Elders of the Church. . .*to gather up all the truths in the world pertaining to life and salvation,* to the Gospel we preach, . . . to the sciences, and to philosophy, wherever it may be found in every nation, kindred, tongue, and people *and bring it to Zion* (Teachings of Presidents of the Church: Brigham Young, 1997, p. 16, emphasis added).

Notice how President Young uses a gathering metaphor in referring to truth. While Latter-day Saints have a missionary message that needs to be shared with the entire world, there are also many truths we need to "bring to Zion." Indeed, the School of Family Life at Brigham Young University, at least in part, exists to facilitate a process of gathering truth. Thus, one of the purposes of this book is to gather some of the most helpful ideas and understandings that have emerged from the best scholarship on marriage relationships. Many important insights about marriage have been learned by scholars over the years and an understanding of these ideas, in concert with revealed truth, can be helpful in establishing lasting marriages.

Summary of the Volume

This book has been organized into three sections. The first section is a *Marriage Foundations Section* that focuses on some core doctrines and principles related to dating, courtship, and marriage. In this section, you will be introduced to what it means to view marriage as a *divine institution*, rather than just a *couple relationship*. This type of perspective will help you see why incorporating divinely prescribed principles and practices into your relationship with your spouse is essential to developing a disciple marriage in this life and an eternal marriage in the life to come. In this section you will also be introduced to five foundation principles (Charity, Cleaving, Equal Partnership, Family Stewardships, and Chastity) that both social science experts and sacred teachings emphasize as essential attributes of healthy marriages.

With these foundation principles in place, the next two sections of this book are intended to help you in your efforts to *become* a right person for marriage and to *create* a right relationship for marriage. These sections are organized according to the major scientific insights of marriage prediction research which have found that the personal characteristics of spouses (i.e., their level of maturity and growth) and couple interaction patterns (i.e., how spouses communicate and manage differences) are the two strongest predictors of marital happiness and success.

The *Becoming Section* will help you evaluate your personal strengths and improvement areas related to dating and marriage with chapters discussing family background experiences, personal security and self-worth, authenticity and differentiation, developing marital virtues, effective communication skills, and growth versus destiny approaches to couple relationships.

The *Creating Section* will discuss principles of healthy couple interaction. Chapters in this section will discuss couple compatibility and physical attraction, stages of dating and pace of courtship, creating deep emotional intimacy, sexuality prior to marriage, and managing couple differences. This section also discusses how spouses can safeguard their marriages from modern threats to marriage, such as emotional distance between spouses, debt and financial stress, and sexual problems in marriage, when they commit to living in certain ways. Therefore, this section also includes chapters on establishing marital rituals, principles of wise money management, sexuality in marriage, the transition to parenthood, and healing distressed marriages.

It should be noted that this book gives particu-

lar attention to the topic of healthy sexuality and the development of sexual wholeness in marriage. While teaching courses on marriage for many years now, I have noted that many Latter-day saints do not feel confident or prepared for this important part of marriage. Three chapters in this book provide the foundation readings for what is referred to as the *Lecture Series on Healthy Sexuality* presented in my Marriage Preparation and Eternal Family courses at Brigham Young University. Students and others are also encouraged to supplement and expand their learning related to this topic beyond the course by reading the book *Sexual Wholeness in Marriage: An LDS Perspective on Integrating Sexuality and Spirituality in Our Marriages* (Busby, Carroll, & Leavitt, 2014; Forward Press Publishing).

It may also be helpful for readers to know that students of the Preparation for Marriage course at Brigham Young University are typically required to complete an assignment that involves having them complete the online *RELATionship Evaluation Questionnaire (RELATE)* and evaluate their personal feedback report (https://relateinstitute.com). The RELATE survey was developed myself and other scholars in the School of Family Life at BYU and helps couples evaluate strengths and improvement areas in their relationship. For dating and engaged couples RELATE guides them to have meaningful discussions about issues proven to effect later marital satisfaction. Identifying trouble spots and common ground often helps premarital couples determine whether to continue, deepen, or end the relationship.

For married couples, RELATE acts as a "relationship checkup" and helps spouses understand specific ways they can improve their relationship. For single adults, a version of the survey called READY helps individuals assess their personal strengths and improvement areas as they date and prepare for marriage. There is a cost associated with completing these surveys. This price includes the complete questionnaire, a full-color report you can download and print from your printer, and technical support during your assessment.

SECTION 1

Marriage Foundations

In this section, we seek to deepen our collective understanding and testimonies of marriage as a divine institution created by our Father in Heaven. This stands in stark contrast to the dominant perspective of the broader culture that views marriage as simply a personal relationship created by couples. Viewing marriage as a divine institution involves learning more about the centrality of marriage in God's plan for our progression and happiness. It involves striving to emulate our Heavenly Parents so that we can return to their presence and participate in eternal life. Your focus in this first section should be on deepening your vision of marriage. As you come to better understand what type of relationship you are trying to create in an eternal marriage, it will give you a core vision of marriage to build on as we discuss specific aspects of couple relationships in later sections.

Our goal in this section is to enhance our understanding of the Lord's foundations for loving and lasting marriage. In particular, we will examine the principle of discipleship and discuss how committing to live a disciple's life provides each of us with the foundation for successful marriage and family life. We will discuss how active discipleship that is expressed in faith, consecration, and repentance has the ability to transform not only our individual lives, but also our relationships.

Following our discussion of discipleship, you will be introduced to five foundation principles for marriage – Charity (Love), Cleaving (Commitment), Equal Partnership (Equality), Family Stewardships (Unity), and Chastity (Intimacy). These principles each have two labels – a sacred label that draws from revealed patterns of eternal marriage and a science label that draws from the terminology used in relationship science research. Because these principles are founded on divine revelation, and are supported by studies on healthy marriage relationships, you can have confidence that these principles will give you a sound foundation for evaluating and strengthening relationships during dating, courtship, and marriage (cue the Primary song - "the wise man built his house upon a rock..."). These foundation principles will help you understand the Lord's "divine design" (Proclamation, ¶ 7) and give you confidence that you are building your marriage relationship according to the pattern our Father in Heaven has given us; and that He will bless and strengthen your marriage in important ways throughout your life. These foundation principles provide you with broad perspectives, insights, and understandings that should give you guidance in becoming a right person for marriage and in creating a right relationship before and after you marry.

The Divine Institution of Marriage

CHAPTER 1

The eternal nature and importance of marriage can be fully understood only within the overarching context of the Father's plan for His children.

Elder David A. Bednar

As you set out to improve your readiness for marriage, there are some key questions you should consider. These include:

- What is marriage?
- What are the purposes of marriage?
- How do you know if a marriage is a "good marriage"?
- Who are the "stakeholders of marriage" or the people who are influenced by the quality and stability of a marriage?

How you answer these questions reveals a lot about how you are thinking about marriage. Your answers also reveal the aspects of marriage that are most important to you and the vision you have for marriage. How you answer these questions will also greatly impact the types of preparation you engage in before marriage and will influence who you are attracted to while dating. In fact, how you answer these questions will impact the type of marriage relationship you have in your life and whether or not your marriage will last.

As you ponder on these questions, ask yourself: *How would my grandparents answer these questions*? Would your grandmother answer them the same way you do? Would her view of what makes a "good marriage" be different than yours? Perspectives of marriage have changed over time—some of these changes have been for the better and others have been for the worse.

Now ask yourself, *How would the popular culture of our time answer these questions*? What messages do we receive from the media and broader culture about what makes marriages work and what are the key parts of a "good marriage"?

Now consider the most important question, *How would our Father in Heaven answer these questions*? What is the Lord's view of marriage? What are the purposes and reasons for marriage in His plan? What are

Three Views of Marriage

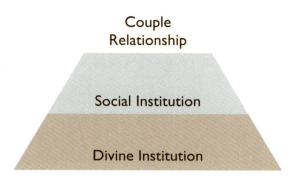

the key ingredients of a "good marriage" according to God? In the Lord's plan, who are the people that marriage is intended to bless? Is it just the spouses themselves or are there other people who are influenced by the quality and permanence of our marriages?

In this chapter, we step back for a moment and consider marriage from a broad perspective. We will look at *three views of marriage*—three different ways to think about marriage that should influence how you and me answer the questions above. In particular, we will consider what it means to view marriage as a "divine institution" and not just a couple relationship. This chapter sets the focus for the *Marriage Foundations* section—which will deepen your understanding of the Lord's pattern for eternal marriage. Your goal in this section of the book should be to better understand how eternal marriages are different from other types of marriages so that in the later sections you have a core vision of marriage to build upon.

THREE VIEWS OF MARRIAGE

It is helpful to distinguish between three views of marriage. Each of these views emphasizes certain parts of marriage and what is needed to be ready for marriage. These three views include (see figure at top of page):

1. Marriage as a couple relationship
2. Marriage as a social institution
3. Marriage as a divine institution

MARRIAGE AS A COUPLE RELATIONSHIP

In our modern society, marriage is viewed almost exclusively as a *couple relationship*. When viewed as a *couple relationship*, marriage is seen as a personal expression of love between two people who want to share their lives together. This view of marriage typically emphasizes personal happiness, emotional gratification, physical attraction, good communication, satisfying sexual intimacy, and couple compatibility as the essential elements of a good marriage.

As you look at this list, you are probably thinking, *well yeah, those look pretty good to me.* And I hope you do desire a marriage that has good communication and helps make you happy. All of us agree that these are parts of the marriage relationship we hope to have some day. However, for many people this "couple relationship view" is as deep as their perspective of marriage goes. Marriage is seen as a relationship that is created by the couple for themselves—ultimately their relationship is of the couple, by the couple, for the couple. "It's just about us" is the modern mantra of couple relationships. Is this how you think about dating and marriage relationships?

If you only see marriage as a couple relationship, you will miss out on other ways to view marriage that emphasize the need for commitment, sacrifice, caring for others, and the benefits of marriage for children.

Marriage as a "Couple Relationship"

Emphasizes
- Personal Happiness
- Emotional Closeness
- Lasting Attraction
- Good Communication
- Sexual Satisfaction
- Couple Compatibility

Lacks
- Commitment
- Sacrifice / Forgiveness
- Manage Adversity
- Other Stakeholders
- Sacred Meanings
- The Lord's Purposes

Most importantly, if you see marriage as only a couple relationship, you will lack the needed foundation of the Lord's purposes for marriage that ground two people's relationship with each other in the principles of discipleship, covenants, cleaving, equal partnership, the sacred responsibilities of husbands and wives, and the eternal purposes of marriage.

To be clear, viewing marriage as a couple relationship is not wrong—it is just incomplete. It is a foundation-less way to think about marriage. It emphasizes the "fruits" of marriage that we all desire to experience, but it does not tie these outcomes to the true "roots" that create loving and lasting marriages. Put another way, a couple relationship view of marriage emphasizes the *outcomes of marriage*, but does not link them with the *principles and practices of marriage*.

By strengthening your understanding and testimony of marriage as a *divine institution* you will have a deeper foundation of *true doctrine* upon which to build effective skills related to communication, intimacy, and other parts of couple relationships that will help you form a successful marriage relationship. Plus, you will come to see that eternal marriages are not created by the couple themselves, but rather they are created together with the Lord.

Marriage as a Divine Institution

In the Book of Moses in the Pearl of Great Price we learn some important insights into how our Father in Heaven views marriage. In the creation account referring to Adam and Eve's placement within the Garden of Eden, we read:

> And I the Lord God, commanded of the man, saying: Of every tree of the garden thou mayest freely eat. But of the tree of the knowledge of good and evil, thou shalt not eat of it, nevertheless, thou mayest choose for thyself, for it is given unto thee; but remember that I forbid it, for in the day thou eatest thereof thou shalt surely die. And I, the Lord God, said unto mine Only Begotten, *that it was not good that the man should be alone*; wherefore, I will make a helpmeet for him. (Moses 3:16–18, emphasis added)

What does it mean when our Father in Heaven says that it is "not good that the man should be alone?" Not good for whom? Not good for Adam? Not good for Eve? Why was it so important that Adam be married and have a helpmeet like Eve? (We will discuss the full meaning of the term *helpmeet* in Chapter 5—Equal Partnership). Like most questions that come up while reading the scriptures, the answer to these questions is found elsewhere in the scriptures. In the Doctrine and Covenants, the Prophet Joseph Smith received a revelation from the Lord stating:

> And again, verily I say unto you, that whoso forbiddeth to marry is not ordained of God, for marriage is ordained of God unto man. Wherefore, it is lawful that he should have one wife, and they twain shall be one flesh, and all this that the earth might answer the end of its creation. (D&C 49:15–16)

From this scripture, it is clear that the Lord's statement that it is "not good that the man should be alone" is making reference to much more than just the personal wellbeing of Adam and Eve. Yes, it would not have been good for Adam himself to be alone (or Eve too for that matter), but the Lord was making reference to the essential place of marriage within His divine plan.

The very purposes of the plan of our Father in Heaven's are intertwined with marriage. In this sense, marriage is viewed by our Father in Heaven as a *divine institution*. An institution is defined in Webster's Dictionary as "*an established law, custom, practice, or system*" and "*an organization or society having a public character.*" Therefore, when marriage is viewed as a divine institution it is seen as a sacred system established by our Father in Heaven, with divinely decreed laws and practices, which are intended to bring about His eternal purposes. The divine institution of marriage is intended to not only contribute to the personal wellbeing of the spouses themselves, but is also intended to have a public character that contributes to the building of eternal families and the kingdom of God, thus providing for the collective good of all of God's children.

Can you see how different this view of marriage is from the notion that marriage is just a couple relationship? With the *divine institution view*, the practices and patterns of marriage are not created or defined by the spouses themselves. This view teaches us that one of the keys to lasting marriage is to seek not just compatibility with one's spouse, but also to seek alignment with God. When we build our marriages according to the Lord's pattern and seek to contribute to His divine purposes our relationship with our spouse can be endowed with the Holy Spirit of Promise—which blesses us with greater love for our spouse, deeper meaning in our lives, and an enduring sense of oneness with God. This is why the divine institution view of marriage should be our foundational perspective of marriage.

Marriage as a Social Institution

In addition to viewing marriage as a divine institution, Figure 1.1 also depicts how marriage can be seen as a *social institution*. Our Father in Heaven created and ordained marriage as not only the basic building block of the family and the kingdom of God, but also as the foundational institution of society. In paragraph nine of the Proclamation on the Family we read:

> We call upon responsible citizens and officers of government everywhere to promote those measures designed to maintain and strengthen the family as the fundamental unit of society. (The Family: A Proclamation to the World, 1995, ¶ 9)

What makes the family the "fundamental unit of society?" Families are fundamental because they are uniquely designed to provide all of the most basic needs of a community, including: procreation, child care, education, health-

Marriage as a "Divine Institution"

When marriage is viewed as a divine institution it is seen as a sacred system established by our Father in Heaven, with divinely decreed laws and practices, which are intended to bring about His eternal purposes.

care, economic support, caregiving of the elderly, and many other functions critical to the wellbeing of society. In a recent statement, Church leaders taught:

> Marriage is far more than a contract between individuals to ratify their affections and provide for mutual obligations. Rather, marriage is a vital institution for rearing children and teaching them to become responsible adults. Throughout the ages, governments of all types have recognized marriage as essential in preserving social stability and perpetuating life. Regardless of whether marriages were performed as a religious rite or a civil ceremony, in almost every culture marriage has been protected and endorsed by governments primarily to preserve and foster the institution most central to rearing children and teaching them the moral values that undergird civilization. (The Divine Institution of Marriage, p. 2, ¶ 2 & 3; http://www.mormonnewsroom.org/article/the-divine-institution-of-marriage)

In a time when many are seeking to redefine marriage in our society, it is critical for us to consider the implications of such changes on the welfare of children and our communities. Numerous social trends, such as the intentional delay of marriage, non-marital cohabitation, out-of-wedlock childbirth, divorce, and the legalization of same-sex partnership, are redefining the significance and practice of marriage in modern society (we will discuss these social trends in detail in Chapter 8—Modern Threats to Marriage).

Recently, scholars have also begun to label the collective impact of these trends as the *Deinstitutionalization of Marriage*. Expressing concern about these trends, one team of scholars noted:

Marriage is a social institution and a legal contract between two individuals to form a sexual, productive and reproductive union. Through the marriage, this union is recognized by family, society, religious institutions and the legal system. Marriage defines the relationship of the two individuals to each other, to any children they might have, to their extended families, to shared property and assets, and to society generally. It recognizes the paternity of the father and defines his responsibilities to the mother and child. It also defines the relationship of others, including social institutions, toward the married couple. (Doherty, Carroll, and Waite, 2007, Supporting the Instruction of Marriage, p. 21)

Marriage scholars have also spent the last two decades investigating the impact of social trends such as out-of-wedlock childbirth and divorce on the welfare of children. After conducting a review of all of the research findings in this area, one leading scholar concluded:

> Over the past 20 years, a body of research has developed on how changes in patterns of family structure affect children. Most researchers now agree that, on average, children who grow up in families with both their biological parents in a low-conflict marriage are better off in a number of ways than children who grow up in single-, step- or cohabiting-parent households. Compared to children who are raised by their married parents, children in other family types are more likely to achieve lower levels of education, to become teen parents, and to experience health, behavior, and mental health problems. And children in single- and cohabiting-parent families are more likely to be poor. (Parke, 2003, Are Married Parents

Really Better for Children?, Center For Law and Social Policy, p. 1)

While our focus in this book is not on marriage as a social institution, it is important for us to see how such a view of marriage encourages us to emphasize aspects of marriage that go beyond our own personal happiness and emotional gratification. Such a perspective reminds us that children and others are stakeholders of our marriages and a "*good marriage*" is not just one that works for the spouses, but is one that also contributes to the wellbeing of others and society.

Marriage and the Great Plan of Happiness

What are the Lord's purposes of marriage and how specifically does marriage fit into our Father in Heaven's plan? Let's return to the Book of Moses to see if we can deepen our understanding of the divine institution of marriage. When Moses went to the mount to commune with the Lord, he was shown a vision of the inhabitants of the whole earth (Moses 1:27–29). When he saw these things, he asked the Lord two questions: *And it came to pass that Moses called upon God, saying: Tell me, I pray thee, why these things are so, and by what thou madest them?* (Moses 1:30).

So Moses' first question was "why"—why have you created this earth and set forth your great plan of happiness? His second question was "how"—how do you make this plan come to pass? The Lord answered Moses' first question with what is one of the most well known scriptures to Latter-day Saints, saying: "Behold this is my work and my glory, to bring to pass the *immortality* and *eternal life* of man" (Moses 1:39, emphasis added). The Lord's overarching purpose in all that He does is to bring about immortality and eternal life of us, His beloved chidlren. If these are the two key purposes of our Father's plan, it is essential that we develop a sound understanding of the nature of *immortality* and *eternal life*.

What Is Immortality?

What is immortality? The most common answer to this question is that immortality means to live forever. This is a correct answer, but an incomplete one. Immortality involves not just living forever, but living forever as a resurrected being—with an inseparable body and spirit. We are taught in the Book of Mormon and in other prophetic sources that immortality is a gift of grace to all of God's children born on this earth through the Atonement and Resurrection of Jesus Christ (see Mosiah 15:19–23). Therefore, since the Atonement of Christ has already been completed, this purpose of our Father in Heaven has been accomplished.

What Is Eternal Life?

What is eternal life? The most common answer to this question is that eternal life means to return to live again with our Father in Heaven. Again, this is a

correct answer, but it is also an incomplete one. Eternal life involves not only living *with* our Father in Heaven, but also living *like* Him. President Henry B. Eyring has taught, "Eternal life means to *become like the Father* and to *live in families* in happiness and joy forever" (The Family, Ensign, February 1998). This means that eternal life is more about lifestyle than location. Eternal life pertains more to *how* we will live, than *where* we will live. While the physical environment of the celestial kingdom will undoubtedly be most beautiful and pleasing to our senses, it will be how we treat each other and care for each other that will make the celestial kingdom glorious. In this sense, we will "*create*" celestial glory as much as we "*partake*" of it. In the Doctrine and Covenants we read:

> When the Savior shall appear we shall see him as he is. We shall see that he is a man like ourselves. And that same sociality which exists among us here will exist among us there, only it will be coupled with eternal glory, which glory we do not now enjoy. (D&C 130:1–2)

The phrase, "that same sociality which exists among us here will exist among us there," teaches us that the relationships and patterns of interacting we develop in this life will be a central part of life in the eternities. This places an incomparable importance on how we learn to treat others and care for one another's needs, particularly our family members, in this life.

Eternal Life Is Family Life

If our purpose in this life is to learn how to live like our Heavenly Parents, it becomes very important for us to understand how they live. While the scriptures and other prophetic sources do not give us much detail about the specific activities of eternal life, they do teach us the foundational principles of what makes up the celestial lifestyle. President Henry B. Eyring once said,

> We can understand why our Heavenly Father commands us to reverence life and to cherish the powers that produce it as sacred. If we do not have those reverential feelings in this life, how could our Father give them to us in the eternities? Family life here is the schoolroom in which we prepare for a family life

> there. And to give us the opportunity for family life there was and is the purpose of creation (The Family, Ensign, February 1998).

Notice that President Eyring stresses that eternal life involves *family life*. Eternal life is familial—it is centered on living together as eternal families, particularly in eternal marriages. Elder Hugh B. Brown taught,

> The family concept is one of the major and most important of the whole theological doctrine. In fact, our very concept of heaven is the projection of the home into eternity. Salvation, then, is essentially a family affair; and full participation in the plan of salvation can be had only in family units. (Conference Report, October 1966, p. 103)

If eternal life is the "projection of the home into eternity"—then only homes that are *heavenly* will continue in the eternities. This does not mean that our marriages and families must be perfect in this life, but we should be striving for them to be celestial in nature. Marriage and family relationships, not just individuals, need to be redeemed through the Atonement of Jesus Christ. The scriptures teach us that "no unclean thing can dwell with God" (1 Ne 10:21). Therefore, both individuals, in their desires and behaviors, and families, in their interactions and associations, need to be eternal in nature to one day be a part of eternal life. If our efforts are sincere and dedicated, the Savior will redeem our marriages, just as he will redeem our souls.

Each of us has probably heard some of the radio or TV ads that the Church uses in its missionary efforts. One of the popular themes has been, "*Family—It's*

About Time." The ads are touching, and sometimes humorous, as they depict scenes of families talking, working, and playing together. Do you remember those ads? Many people do, both inside and outside of the church. In fact, for many people outside of the church they have come to know the "Mormon Church" as the "Family Church." It is not uncommon to hear people say something like, *Aren't Mormons the ones who talk about families all the time?* or *I know Mormons put a lot of importance on family relationships.* Each of these statements are true. But, it is important to remember that the emphasis Church leaders and members place on marriage and family life is not just a cultural matter, it is a doctrinal one. Family is our theology, not just our culture.

What Do We Mean When We Say—"Families Are Forever?"

Latter-day Saints are fond of the phrase "*families are forever*." This mantra captures our vision of eternal life and helps us focus on what matters most in this life. However, we need to make sure that we have the correct vision in our mind when we envision a "forever family." The Proclamation on the Family teaches us that, "*. . .marriage between a man and a woman is ordained of God and that the family is central to the Creator's plan for the eternal destiny of His children*" (The Family: A Proclamation to the World, 1995, ¶ 1). President Joseph F. Smith also taught:

> God instituted marriage in the beginning. He made man in his image and likeness, male and female, and in their creation it was designed that they should be united together in sacred bonds of marriage, and one is not perfect without the other. (Conference Report, April 1913, p. 118–119)

How do these teachings help us better understand the nature and configuration of eternal families? It reminds us that eternal families are ultimately eternal marriages.

While growing up, we may envision our family of parents and siblings as our *forever family*. However, while sealing ties to parents are very important, the image of a father and mother with children as a forever family is incomplete. What is missing? According to President Smith, the missing part of this vision of a *forever family* is marriage—children need marriages of their own to emulate their Heavenly Parents.

Sometimes we use the metaphor of a chain to refer to how the sealing ordinances of the temple can link the generations together. Within this metaphor, we need to understand that the links of the chain are eternal marriages. As spouses are sealed together by the Holy Spirit of Promise, they form the fundamental unit of eternal life. Therefore, when we speak of form-

ing forever families we need to remember that this in its essence means forming celestial marriages, for both parents and children.

How Is This Accomplished?

Earlier we noted that Moses asked the Lord two questions on the mount. The first question was "why" and the answer was *immortality and eternal life*. The second question was "how"—how is this plan brought to pass? While the first question was largely answered in one verse of scripture (Moses 1:39), the Lord's answer to Moses' second question is found in the remainder of the Book of Moses (chapters 2 through 8). These chapters contain an account of the creation of the earth and detail some of the specific parts of the plan for *how* our Father in Heaven has set out to help His children receive eternal life.

Prophets have long taught that there are three core doctrines of our Father in Heaven's "great plan of happiness" (Alma 42:8): the *Creation* of the earth; the *Fall* of all humankind, and the *Atonement* of Jesus Christ. Elder Bruce R. McConkie called these doctrines the "three pillars of eternity" (A New Witness for the Articles of Faith, 1985, p. 84). Professor Dan Judd and his colleagues observed:

> The Creation, Fall, and Atonement are historic events. They have direct application to our physical creation, separation from God, mortal experience, death, and resurrection. They have metaphoric or interpretive application to many of the significant events in our lives, characterized by periods of creation followed by the fall or opposition and eventual achievement of reconciliation. They apply directly to our personal and family lives. (Judd, Dorius, and Dollahite, Families and the Great Plan of Happiness, 2000, p. 8)

Elder Russell M. Nelson also taught:

> Before we can comprehend the atonement of Christ, however, we must first understand the fall of Adam. And before we can understand the Fall of Adam, we must first understand the Creation. These three crucial components of the plan of salvation relate to each other. (Ensign, November 1996, p. 33)

These doctrines were revealed to help us see our marriages and families as more than just a part of this life. Elder David A. Bednar taught:

> As we look beyond mortality and into eternity, it is easy to discern that the counterfeit alternatives the adversary advocates can never lead to the completeness that is made possible through the sealing together of a man and a woman, to the happiness of righteous marriage, to the joy of posterity, or to the blessing of eternal progression. (Ensign, June 2006, p. 82)

Take time to ponder on the beauty of our Father in Heaven's plan for you and me. It is glorious and beautiful. Speaking about the plan of salvation in our lives, Elder Neal A. Maxwell remarked:

> Conversationally, we reference this great design almost too casually at times; we even sketch its rude outlines on chalkboards and paper as if it were the floor plan for an addition to one's house. However, when we really take time to ponder the Plan, it is breathtaking and overpowering! Indeed, I, for one, cannot decide which creates in me the most awe—

its very vastness or its intricate, individualized detail. (Ensign, July 1982, p. 5)

Historic Event or Living Process?

Although the Creation, Fall, and Atonement are "historic events" in the plan of our Father in Heaven, we must be careful to not only see these key doctrines as a part of our history. They must also be understood and acted upon in ways that make them "living processes" in our lives. In short, they must be in our present and future as well! Typically, when we talk about these doctrines we place the same word in front of them—*the*—and refer to them as *the* Creation, *the* Fall, and *the* Atonement. By so doing, we may inadvertently limit our view of these doctrines. If we only see these doctrines as historic events, we may view ourselves as merely historic observers of their occurrence.

Properly understood, these doctrines have application to the most significant aspects of our personal lives. The doctrines of the Creation, Fall, and Atonement of Jesus Christ are also living processes that we are invited to participate in our current lives. Think for a moment. Has the creation ceased? If you say yes, then I invite you to come visit my ward's sacrament meeting each Sunday. I currently live in a ward where the sounds of the creation ring out, and sometimes cry out, with amazing volume! The chapel pews are alive with little, wiggling bodies, that are munching cereal and coloring in books on the floor. Oh, yes—the creation is ongoing and we are invited to participate! We are invited to be co-creators with God in His plan.

The Fall is also ongoing. We all "come short of the glory of God" (Rom 3:23) and, thereby, separate ourselves from our Father in Heaven's presence. And most importantly, the Atonement of Christ is intended to be a living, ongoing process in our lives. While it was Christ's acts in the garden, on the cross, and at the tomb that make repentance, forgiveness, and reconciliation possible; it is the embracing of His Atonement in our day-to-day lives now that makes it real and transformative. We worship our Savior by keeping His commandments, sincerely partaking of the sacrament, keep the Sabbath day holy, serving others, and repenting of our sins. This brings the grace of the Lord into our lives and purifies our motives and actions. We should never forget that it is the Atonement of our Savior Jesus Christ that makes eternal marriages and families possible.

What Do These Living Processes Provide?

In reference to the core doctrines of our Father in Heaven's plan, Elder Merrill J. Bateman said:

> There are three major purposes for the earth's creation and the mortal experience. The first is to obtain a physical body (see Abraham 3:26). The second is to grow spiritually by keeping the Lord's commandments (see Abraham 3:25). The third is to initiate an eternal family (see D&C 131:1–4; 132:19). Thus, the physical body, spiritual growth, and family are the grand prizes of mortality. (BYU Devotional, January 14, 2003, p. 3)

These three "grand prizes" of mortal life are made possible within the context of marriage and family relationships. They are the *hows* that Moses was asking about—the ways that we can become like our Heavenly Parents and be ready to live the life that they live—eternal life. What then is the meaning of life? Simply put, it is to become like our Heavenly Parents in these three ways—in body, in spirit, and in marriage.

Marriage as a Divine Means and a Divine End

When properly understood, marriage and family life become indistinguishable from our Father in Heaven's plan. Eternal marriage is not only an end, or desired outcome, of the plan; it is also the means, mechanism, and institution by which our Father brings about His divine plan (see figure on next page). This is why marriage and family life are the focus of the plan, because in deeply meaningful ways they *are* the plan.

President Boyd K. Packer taught:

> I invoke the blessings of the Lord upon you, all of you here, with reference to your home and your families. It is the choicest of all life's experiences. I urge you to put it first. The center core of the Church is not the

Marriage = A Divine Means and Divine End

A Divine Means

"That by which something is done or obtained—a method, process, or mechanism to accomplish an intended goal."

Institution

Marriage

A Divine Means

"The reason why something is done; the final goal—the culmination, objective, or purpose of an activity or process"

Purpose of Life

As you read the remaining chapters in this book carefully ponder on your personal views of marriage. Have you been viewing marriage as a divine institution or as just a couple relationship? Our Father in Heaven has ordained marriage as both a *divine end* (i.e., a purpose of life) and as a *divine means* (i.e., the way that His plan is brought about).

stake house; it is not the chapel; that is not the center of Mormonism. And, strangely enough, the most sacred place on earth may not be the temple, necessarily. The chapel, the stake house, and the temple are sacred as they contribute to the building of the most sacred institution in the Church–the home–and to the blessing of the most sacred relationships in the Church, the family. (BYU Devotional, 1963, p. 1)

As you prayerfully consider the divine institution of marriage, you will be better prepared to date and marry so that you are aligned with God's plan and purposes for your life. Remember that "*it is upon the rock of our Redeemer, who is Christ, the Son of God, that ye must build your foundation. . .a foundation whereon if men build they cannot fail*" (Helaman 5:12).

WE MUST LOOK BEYOND MORTALITY...

As we look beyond mortality and into eternity, it is easy to discern that the counterfeit alternatives the adversary advocates can never lead to the completeness that is made possible through the sealing together of a man and a woman, to the happiness of righteous marriage, to the joy of posterity, or to the blessing of eternal progression

—ELDER DAVID A. BEDNAR

Discipleship—The Foundation of Marriage

CHAPTER 2

> Happiness in family life is most likely to be achieved when founded upon the teachings of the Lord Jesus Christ.
>
> *Proclamation on the Family, ¶ 7*

Within gospel circles we often speak of finding happiness in this life. This makes sense given the fact that the Proclamation on the Family refers to our Father in Heaven's plan as "the divine plan of happiness" (Proclamation ¶ 2) and we are taught in the Book of Mormon that "men are that they might have joy" (2 Ne 2:25). And perhaps nowhere in our Father's divine plan is happiness more intended to be a part of our lives than in our marriage and family relationships. However, the peace and joy promised to us by Christ is quite different than the types of happiness offered by this world. This is particularly true when we speak of finding joy within the sacred relationship of marriage.

We all desire to have a happy marriage in this life. But, if this is the case, why do some couples struggle to find happiness in their marriage relationship? Is there a way to be certain that we will be happy in our marriages? The simple answer to this question is yes. Our Father in Heaven would not call His plan the "divine plan of happiness" if this was not the case. However, the Lord has also emphasized: *For my thoughts are not your thoughts, neither are your ways my ways, saith the Lord. For as the heavens are higher than the earth, so are my ways higher than your ways, and my thoughts than your thoughts* (Isaiah 55:8). Therefore, a critical part of what will determine if you and I will find true and lasting happiness in our marriages is whether or not we will trust in our Father's pattern of happiness or if we will seek happiness in our own ways.

Our goal in this chapter is to better understand

the Lord's foundation for happiness in marriage. In particular, we will examine the doctrine of *discipleship* and discuss how committing to live the disciple's life provides each of us with the foundation for successful marriage and family life. We will discuss how active discipleship that is expressed in faith, consecration, and repentance has the ability to transform not only individual lives, but also relationships.

THE JOY OF CHRIST

In the Proclamation on the Family we are taught how to establish and maintain a happy marriage. We read:

> Happiness in family life is most likely to be achieved when founded upon the teachings of the Lord Jesus Christ. Successful marriages and families are established and maintained on principles of faith, prayer, repentance, forgiveness, respect, love, compassion, work, and wholesome recreational activities. (The Family: A Proclamation to the World, 1995, ¶ 7)

In order to fully receive Christ's promised joy in our marriage relationships, we must first understand the true nature of joy and how it comes into our lives. What is joy? Is it a feeling? Is it an emotion? Is it something we can only experience when life is going well? In everyday conversation we talk about joy in these ways—a personal feeling of satisfaction or happiness that is typically experienced when life is free from stressful or unpleasant events. If this is how we think about happiness in our lives, then happiness can seem fleeting and unstable—something that ebbs and flows in our life based on our fortunes and circumstances.

If we view happiness in marriage this way, then having a happy marriage someday feels like something we cannot count on—something that is elusive and unstable. From this view, a happy marriage is something we hope for, but we do not feel we can count on it. Do you feel this way? How confident are you that you can have a loving and lasting marriage?

RECEIVING CHRIST'S JOY IN OUR MARRIAGES

The Lord wants us to feel confident in our ability to form a lasting marriage. He has given us a sure way to feel true joy and peace in our family relationships. Consider what the Savior taught us about true happiness or joy when He was with his disciples in Jerusalem. In chapter 14 of John's testimony in the New Testament, we read an account of Christ's final discussions at the Last Supper with his apostles before leaving for the Mount of Olives and eventually to the Garden of Gethsemane. Sensing the Apostles' anxiety at his impending departure, Jesus taught them about the Comforter and explained to them the divine pattern of finding peace in this life. He said,

> Peace I leave with you, my peace I give unto you: *not as the world giveth, give I unto you.* Let not your heart be troubled, neither let it be afraid. (John 14:27, emphasis added)

At this time, the Savior also told his apostles, "these things have I spoken unto you, that my joy might remain in you, and that your joy might be full" (John 15:11, emphasis added).

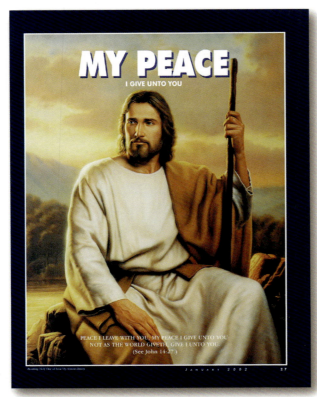

Notice how the Savior describes His peace and joy with the phrase—*not as the world giveth*. In these simple, yet deeply profound pronouncements, Christ teaches us that true and lasting happiness is best understood as an endowed gift from the Spirit—something that only the Lord can give unto us. From these scriptures, we also learn that there are different *types* of happiness and that the "Joy of Christ" must be carefully distinguished from the "Happiness of the World." Christ's promised joy is experienced through our spiritual senses—it is something that can "remain in us." The happiness of the world is experienced through our physical senses—it is something that only lasts as long as the physical experience that creates it. Also, the happiness of the world is often illusory—we believe we are happy because we excel in some worldly criteria such as beauty, achievement, or wealth; but ultimately these accomplishments do not meet our true needs.

The Joy of Christ also differs from the Happiness of the World in that we can experience it during the anticipated, enjoyable, and positive times in our lives; as well as during the unexpected, stressful, and negative events in our lives. The world's happiness is only available to us when life is going well, but Christ's peace and joy are accessible to us even in times of adversity or trial. In Philippians, chapter 4 verse 7 we read, "And the peace of God, which passeth all understanding, shall keep your hearts and minds through Christ Jesus." This scripture teaches us that only Christ knows the true path of happiness in our lives. We do not know the path, only He knows the path. In fact, He is the path. Jesus taught, "I am the way, the truth, and the life: no man cometh unto the Father, but by me" (John 14:6). Therefore, the peace and joy we all seek in this life must be grounded in following Christ and often we will need the Holy Spirit to reveal unto us the path that we must follow to fully receive of the Lord's peace and joy.

With these divine teachings as your foundation, you are better prepared to contemplate the happiness we all seek in our dating and marriage relationships. In our efforts to form a joyful marriage, the cornerstone questions each of us must answer are:

1. "Am I striving to pattern my dating and marriage according to the gospel of Jesus Christ?"
2. "Do I have my heart set on the type of joy that Christ promises can be mine in marriage?"

Far too often couples lack the joy of Christ in their relationship because they have built their marriage according to the blueprint for happiness offered by the world. Marriage is too frequently seen as a means to worldly ends, such as personal gratification, social status, or material accumulation. While incorporating some elements of the gospel, couples who view their marriage these ways ultimately reduce marriage to a relationship aimed at personal ends and selfishly make personal happiness the primary criteria of a good marriage.

This way of viewing marriage stands in contrast to the pattern Christ has revealed to us for our marriages. We are to strive to cast our marriages in Christ's image and follow His example of charity and other-centeredness. As we approach marriage this way, peace and joy are more clearly seen as by-products of loving and serving one another, not as the focal purpose of our marriage. Paradoxically, the more we directly seek after

our own happiness, the less joyful our life will likely be. However, when we cultivate an anxious concern for the wellbeing of our spouse and seek to follow the will of the Lord, we are endowed with a fuller meaning in our lives and are filled with a measure of joy that transcends any happiness offered in this world.

The First Principles of the Gospel

So, how do we seek after the joy of Christ in our lives and one day in our marriages? The answer is quite simple—we strive to be true disciples of our Savior Jesus Christ. We commit ourselves to the life of the disciple and follow after the principles and patterns of the gospel of Jesus Christ. While this may sound like the "seminary answer" to the question, it's the right one. Discipleship is truly the foundation of successful and happy marriages. Nearly all unhappiness in marriage can be traced back to where one or both spouses have adopted patterns of living that are not in harmony with God's plan for the divine institution of marriage.

As we set out to deepen our discipleship, it is important to make sure we are setting our foundation on true doctrines and principles. In the Articles of Faith, the Prophet Joseph Smith taught that the core doctrines of the gospel are Faith in the Lord Jesus Christ and Repentance:

> We believe that the first principles and ordinances of the Gospel are: first, *Faith in the Lord Jesus Christ;* second, *Repentance;* third, Baptism by immersion for the remission of sins; fourth, Laying on of hands for the gift of the Holy Ghost. (The Fourth Article of Faith, emphasis added)

Thus, true discipleship must be based in faith in the Lord Jesus Christ and repentance. Now, I am sure that this is not the first time that any of you have heard about these principles. But, if your experience is like mine, you have probably learned about faith and repentance as *individual principles*—principles that pertain to your inner personal life. For example, most lessons on repentance emphasize how sincere repentance can change a person's behaviors and transform his or her life. This is a correct understanding of repentance. However, faith and repentance are also *relationship principles*. This means that they can change relationships and transform marriages too. As you study the principles of this chapter, I encourage you to prayerfully consider the role of these principles in forming and maintaining a happy marriage.

Faith in the Lord Jesus Christ

In Chapter 1 (The Divine Institution of Marriage), we discussed the nature of eternal life and how

we must prepare ourselves to one day not only live *with* our Father in Heaven, but also to live *like* Him. The prophet Joseph Smith taught that only individuals with unshakable faith in the Lord Jesus Christ will be able to enjoy eternal life. *Faith* is a necessary foundation of discipleship in this life and eternal life in the next. So, how then does one obtain such faith? Are there specific things we can do develop this degree of faith?

Joseph Smith taught that our faith is directly tied to the depth of our discipleship—the degree to which we strive to follow God's will for our lives versus following after our own paths. Through devout discipleship we can obtain a confidence that we are living according to God's will—a needed part of having faith. Prayerfully consider the following quotes from the prophet Joseph Smith's Lectures on Faith:

> A religion that does not require *the sacrifice of all things* never has power sufficient *to produce the faith* necessary to lead unto life and salvation; for, from the first existence of man, the faith necessary unto the enjoyment of life and salvation never could be obtained without the sacrifice of all earthly things. It was through this sacrifice, *and this only*, that God has ordained that men should enjoy eternal life. (Joseph Smith, Lectures on Faith, 7.7, emphasis added)

> It is in vain for persons to fancy to themselves that they are heirs with those, or can be heirs with them, who have offered their all in sacrifice, and by this means obtain faith in God and favor with him so as to obtain eternal life, unless they, in like manner, offer unto him the same sacrifice, and through that offering obtain the knowledge that they are accepted of him. (Joseph Smith, Lectures on Faith, 7.8, emphasis added)

> Those, then, who make the sacrifice, will have the testimony that their course is pleasing in the sight of God; and those who have this testimony will have faith to lay hold on eternal life, and will be enabled, through faith, to endure unto the end, and receive the crown that is laid up for them that love the appearing of our Lord Jesus Christ. But those who do not make the sacrifice cannot enjoy this faith, because men are dependent upon this sacrifice in order to obtain this faith: therefore, they cannot lay hold upon eternal life, because the revelations of God do not guarantee unto them the authority so to do, and without this guarantee faith could not exist. (Joseph Smith, Lectures on Faith, 7.10, emphasis added)

> But those who have not made this sacrifice to God do not know that the course which they pursue is well pleasing in His sight; for whatever may be their belief or their opinion, it is a matter of doubt and uncertainty in their mind; and where doubt and uncertainty are, there faith is not, nor can it be. For doubt and faith do not exist in the same person at the same time; so that persons whose minds are under doubts and fears cannot have unshaken confidence; and *where unshaken confidence is not there faith is weak*; and where faith is weak the persons will not be able to contend against all the opposition, tribulations, and afflictions which they will have to encounter in order to be heirs of God, and joint heirs with Christ Jesus; and they will grow weary in their minds, and the adversary will have power over them and destroy them. (Joseph Smith, Lectures on Faith, 7.12, emphasis added)

How then do we obtain the faith necessary to lay hold of eternal life? According to the prophet Joseph Smith we must dedicate ourselves to a course in life that is pleasing to our Father in Heaven. Only when we repeatedly and consistently align our lives with His

DISCIPLESHIP PRODUCES FAITH

Those, then, who make the sacrifice, will have the testimony that their course is pleasing in the sight of God; and those who have this testimony will have faith to lay hold on eternal life...

But those who have not made this sacrifice to God do not know that the course which they pursue is well pleasing in His sight; for whatever may be their belief or their opinion, it is a matter of doubt and uncertainty in their mind; and where doubt and uncertainty are - there faith is not, nor can it be. For doubt and faith do not exist in the same person at the same time; so that persons whose minds are under doubts and fears cannot have unshaken confidence; and where unshaken confidence is not there faith is weak...

—Joseph Smith, Lectures on Faith, 7.10 & 7.12

---

plan will we have the confidence that He will bless our lives and guide our paths back to His presence.

The *Core of Discipleship* consists of three primary principles:

Obedience—An unwavering commitment to live the commandments of our loving Father in Heaven.

Consecration—A willingness to dedicate our time, talents, and resources to the building up of the kingdom of God.

Sacrifice—A willingness to give up "all earthly things" in order to pattern our lives after the divine plan of our Father in Heaven.

The essence of faith is trust. Trusting Christ involves turning to Him and seeking His grace through the power of His atonement. It involves remembering that He knows you, loves you, and desires to bless you. As Sister Linda Reeve's taught,

> I testify that He has not forgotten you! Whatever sin or weakness or pain or struggle or trial you are going through, He knows and understands those very moments. He loves you! And He will carry you through those moments, just as He did Mary and Martha. He has paid the price that He might know how to succor you. Cast your burdens upon Him. Tell your Heavenly Father how you feel. Tell Him about your pain and afflictions and then give them to Him. Search the scriptures daily. There you will also find great solace and help. (October 2012, The Lord Has Not Forgotten You)

Unshaken Confidence in Marriage

For some of us, the thoughts of becoming ready for marriage, finding someone to marry, and making a marriage work are somewhat scary. In fact, for some of us, the thought of getting married feels simply overwhelming. As I have talked with thousands of young adults over the years about marriage readiness, I have found that fears about dating and marriage are quite common. Sometimes these fears are grounded in troubling family experiences while growing up that leave individuals feeling unprepared or poorly taught about healthy marriage. Maybe your parents divorced and you are worried about repeating the pattern. For others, they have anxiety about attracting a quality spouse and fear that their efforts at dating will not be successful.

Most of us are quite aware of our personal faults and we worry that no one will want to marry us for eternity. Others of us fear the responsibilities of marriage—particularly marriages entered into during the young adult years. Matters of schooling, employment, and economics create an anxiety that suggest that marriage must be pushed further and further down the life path. Whatever the reasons may be, there seems to be a growing fear among some young people that forming a

> ### SAVE HE SHALL PREPARE A WAY
>
> Spirituality yields two fruits. The first is inspiration to know what to do. The second is power, or the capacity to do it. These two capacities come together. That's why Nephi could say, "I will go and do the things which the Lord hath commanded" (1 Ne 3:7). He knew the spiritual laws upon which inspiration and power are based. Yes, God answers prayer and gives us spiritual direction when we live obediently and exercise the required faith in Him.
>
> —RICHARD G. SCOTT, "TO ACQUIRE SPIRITUAL GUIDANCE," ENSIGN, NOV 2009, 6–9

loving and lasting marriage relationship may be something that will not happen for them.

If you have any of these types of thoughts about marriage, you are not alone. Whether it be serving a mission, getting married, serving in a Church calling, or becoming a parent, there are many parts of the gospel plan that can feel beyond out capacity to accomplish. At these times in your life, the principle of discipleship and faith in the Lord Jesus Christ are particularly important ones for you to practice. In Nephi 3:7 we read:

> . . .I will go and do the things which the Lord has commanded, for I know that the Lord giveth no commandments unto the children of men, save he shall prepare a way for them to accomplish the thing which he commandeth them.

Have you ever thought of this as a scripture about marriage? I hope you will think of it that way. The Lord will prepare a way for you to follow His commandments. He will endow you with what you need in order to live His divine plan of happiness. But, you and I need the faith to trust in His plan and the discipleship to do all that we can to follow His will. In 2 Nephi 25:23 we are taught that "…it is by grace that we are saved, after all that we can do." This pattern is true for marriage and all of God's commandments. If you do your part, the Lord will bless you and stand by you to bring about His purposes. Marriage is central to our Father in Heaven's plan. Our Father cares deeply about your dating and future marriage. Place your faith in His plan and in His ability to bless your life—He will prepare a way for you. While none of us know the exact timing of these blessings in our lives (in Chapter 14 we will discuss more about the timing of marriage), each of us can trust in the promise of the Lord that eternal marriage will be a part of celestial glory that awaits all true disciples of Jesus Christ.

COMING TO KNOW CHRIST

An important part of strengthening our faith is to deepen our worship of Jesus Christ. In the New Testament, the apostle John taught: "And this is life eternal, that they might know thee the only true God, and Jesus Christ, whom thou hast sent" (John 17:3). What does it mean "*to know*" God and Jesus Christ? I learned something about this when I was a young missionary preparing to serve my full-time mission in central Chile. As I entered the Missionary Training Center, I was feeling very overwhelmed with the prospect of

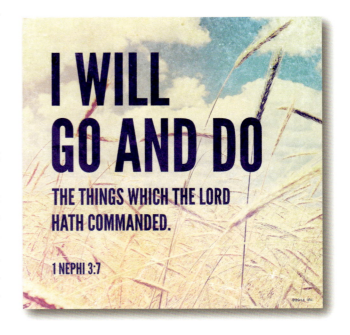

teaching the gospel in Spanish. I had made a sincere effort to read the scriptures prior to my mission and had come to love spending time studying and pondering the scriptures. But, in the early weeks of my mission I was struggling to have a spiritual experience while reading the scriptures in another language.

However, this changed one night in the MTC when I read John 17:3 in my Spanish scriptures. We had just had a lesson in our language class that week about the verb *to know* in Spanish. We learned that in the Spanish language there are two verbs that both mean *to know*—*saber* and *conocer*. The verb *saber* is used when someone wants to say that they know facts or information about someone or something. So, if I said to you "I *saber* (know) Abraham Lincoln," you would assume that I had read a book about him or maybe did a report for school about his life and presidency. In contrast, the verb *conocer* is used when someone wants to convey that they know someone personally and he or she is an acquaintance or friend—it implies a personal relationship. So, if I said to you "I *conocer* (know) Abraham Lincoln," you would have to assume that either I am crazy or that I have a time machine!

As I read John 17:3 in my Spanish scriptures the Spirit taught me something very profound. In that verse, which Spanish verb do you think is used when we are told that eternal life is to come to know God and Jesus Christ? The verb used is conocer—meaning that we need to come to know Our Father in Heaven and Jesus Christ through personal experience, to develop a real relationship with them, through the sanctifying influence of the Holy Spirit. That was the first time I felt the spirit while reading my Spanish scriptures, and even more importantly I felt a tender reassurance that my Father in Heaven loved me and was aware of me as I was feeling overwhelmed by my mission call.

While it is helpful to study the life of the Savior in the scriptures and to read about the events of His earthly ministry, coming to know the Lord involves much more than learning facts or historical information. Our Father in Heaven and the Savior are living persons. We can communicate and build a relationship with them in this life. Yes, our communication at this time is predominantly through prayer and experiences with the Spirit. But, when properly sought and understood, such forms of communication can be as real and meaningful as talking with someone face to face. Seek to know Christ and develop a relationship with Him through the spirit. As you date, seek a future spouse who likewise is striving to come unto Christ. As you do this, the Lord will walk with you in this life and will be a part of your future marriage relationship. This is the true rock upon which to build a happy and successful marriage.

Repentance

The second center principle of the gospel is repentance. Most of us have been taught about this principle—but not typically as a principle for forming and maintaining an eternal marriage. What is repentance? Typically we emphasize that repentance is the process by which we seek forgiveness from the Lord for things we have done wrong and the Lord then cleanses us from our sins—making us pure again. While this understanding of repentance is correct, repentance applies to much more than being made clean again after we have sinned. In the original Hebrew version of the Old Testament, the Hebrew word *Shub* is the root word that is translated as "repentance" in English. Literally translated, the term *shub* means—"to turn away." Most of the New Testament was originally written in Greek, which uses the word *Metanoeo* for the term "repentance." Literally translated this word means *a change of mind, thought, or thinking so powerful that it changes one's very way of life.*

Repentance does involve being cleansed from our sins, but it also is a process of becoming more like Christ. It involves a transformation of our actions (bodies) and desires (spirit). Repentance involves a changing of our souls, not just a change in our behaviors. This is what makes repentance a critical part of happy and lasting marriages. Repentance is a lifelong process of change that transforms us as individuals, and these changes can change us as couples.

More Than Clean

Elder Dallin H. Oaks used an analogy of a tree in a storm to help us understand the full nature of true repentance. He says:

> We tend to think of the results of repentance as simply cleansing us from sin. But that is an incomplete view of the matter. A person who sins is like a tree that bends easily in the wind. On a windy and rainy day, the tree bends so deeply against the ground that the leaves become soiled with mud, like sin. If we focus only on cleaning the leaves, the weakness in the tree that allowed it to bend and soil its leaves may remain. Similarly, a person who is merely sorry to be soiled by sin will sin again in the next high wind. The susceptibility to repetition continues until the tree has been strengthened.
>
> When a person has gone through the process that results in what the scriptures call a broken heart and a contrite spirit, the Savior does more than cleanse that person from sin. He also gives him or her new strength. That strengthening is essential for us to realize the purpose of the cleansing, which is to return to our Heavenly Father. *To be admitted to his presence, we must be more than clean. We must also be changed from a morally weak person who has sinned into a strong person with the spiritual stature to dwell in the presence of God.* We must, as the scripture says, "[become] a saint through the atonement of Christ the Lord" (Mosiah 3:19.) This is what the scripture means in its explanation that a person who has repented of his sins will "forsake them" (D&C 58:43). Forsaking sins is more than resolving not to repeat them. Forsaking involves a fundamental change in the individual. (BYU Speeches, August 1990, p. 5, emphasis added)

From this analogy, we see that repentance is the central focus of the true disciple of Jesus Christ. Each of us must be committed to an ongoing process of repentance and change. Each of us must monitor our lives for any degree of not being properly aligned with the Lord's divine plan and seeking to change to be on the proper path. Such a process cleanses us and strengthens us—transforms who we are. This is a developmental process and takes time and patience; but it is the means by which we reach our fullest potential and greatest happiness—as individuals and as married couples.

Repentance and Consecration

Elder Neal A. Maxwell also taught members of the church that in order to take full advantage of repentance in our lives we must broaden our understanding of what types of actions require repentance. He said:

Whenever Church members speak of consecration, it should be done reverently while acknowledging that each of us "come[s] short of the glory of God," some of us far short (Rom 3:23). Even the *conscientious* have not arrived, but they sense the shortfall and are genuinely striving. Consolingly, God's grace flows not only to those "who love [Him] and keep all [His] commandments," but likewise to those "that [seek] so to do" (D&C 46:9).

A second group of members are *"honorable" but not "valiant."* They are not really aware of the gap nor of the importance of closing it (see D&C 76:75). These "honorable" individuals are certainly not miserable nor wicked, nor are they unrighteous and unhappy. It is not what they have done but what they have left undone that is amiss.

In a third group are those who are *grossly entangled with the "ungodliness" of the world*, reminding us all, as Peter wrote, that if "[we are] overcome" by something worldly, "[we are] brought in bondage" (2 Pet. 2:19). ("Swallowed Up in the Will of the Father," 1995, p.1, emphasis added)

Notice how Elder Maxwell divides the members of the Church into three groups according to their levels of consecration and efforts at repentance (see the figure below). The first group he labels as the "conscientious." The second group he calls "honorable but not valiant" and the third group he labels as those "grossly entangled with the ungodliness of the world." What is it that distinguishes these three groups?

Levels of Consecration

Conscientious

Honorable, but not valiant

Entangled with ungodliness

In another address on this same topic Elder Maxwell answered this question further, he explained:

Repentance requires both turning away from evil and turning to God. When "a mighty change" is required, full repentance involves a 180-degree turn, and without looking back! Initially, this turning reflects prog-

ress from telestial to terrestrial behavior, and later on to celestial behavior. As the sins of the telestial world are left behind, the focus falls ever more steadily upon the sins of omission, which often keep us from full consecration. (Repentance, Ensign, November 1991)

From this explanation we see that what distinguishes the third group from the second group are *Sins of Commission*—thoughts or behaviors we commit that are wrong. When we break the word of wisdom, violate our covenants of chastity, or partake of other forms of ungodliness, we are engaging in these types of sins. They are what Elder Maxwell labels as "telestial behavior." We must repent of these behaviors by confessing and forsaking them in our lives if we are to join the second group and live the terrestrial standard.

For most of us, repenting of our wrong actions is what we typically think about when we think about repentance in our lives. However, Elder Maxwell expands this understanding by teaching us that there is another level of repentance—the type that distinguishes the second group from the first group of church members. What distinguishes the second group from the first group are *Sins of Omission*—the righteous deeds or behaviors that we leave undone. These are times in our lives when the Spirit prompts us to do something, but we do not do it. There are also times when we have been taught a correct pattern that we do not fully follow or dedicate ourselves to. Perhaps we do not complete our visiting teaching on a regular basis or we do not share the gospel with someone when the spirit prompts us to, or we do not provide service to others.

In order to progress to celestial behavior, we must use the process of repentance and the atonement of Jesus Christ to bring change to the areas of life where we fall short of God's will for us. So, the first level of repentance involves a *turning away* from unrighteousness and the second level of repentance involves a *turning toward* righteousness. The first process involves a cleansing, the second process involves a strengthening. Both types of repentance are needed during the course of a marriage.

The Challenge to Become

Each of us must decide in our lives if we believe in the *Gospel of Doing* or the *Gospel of Becoming*. Far too often, some people allow the gospel of Jesus Christ to become a list of behaviors to follow in their lives, devoid of true worship. Viewed this way, righteous individuals are simply defined as those who choose the right actions, while unrighteous individuals are those who choose wrong behaviors. Elder Dallin H. Oaks taught that a form of discipleship that focuses only on behaviors is not enough. He said:

> . . .the final judgment is not just an evaluation of a sum total of good and evil acts—what we have done. It is an acknowledgement of the final effects of our acts and thoughts—what we have become. It is not enough for anyone to go through the motions. The commandments, ordinances, and covenants of the gospel are not a list of deposits required to be made in some heavenly account. The gospel of Jesus Christ is a plan that shows us how to become what our Heavenly Father desires us to become. (Ensign, November 2000, p. 32)

He also emphasized that our efforts to be disciples in our marriage and family relationships are a particularly important part of our efforts to become.

> . . .we should remember that our family relationships—even more than our Church callings—are the setting in which the most important part of that development can occur. The conversion we must achieve requires us to be a good husband and father or a good wife and mother. . .exaltation is an eternal family experience, and it is our mortal family experiences that are best suited to prepare us for it. (Ensign, November 2000, p. 34)

Are you living the *Gospel of Doing* or the *Gospel of Becoming*? Do you ever feel that you are just going through the motions? Striving to become is an essential part of being prepared for marriage. As you strive to become the person your Father in Heaven wants you to become, you will increase your readiness for marriage and family life in the future. Elder Jeffry R. Holland has taught:

> You want capability and safety in dating and romance, in married life and eternity? Be a true disciple of Jesus. Be a genuine, committed, word-and-deed Latter-day Saint. Believe that your faith has everything to do with your romance, because it does. You separate dating from discipleship at your peril. Or to phrase that more positively, Jesus Christ, the Light of the World, is the only lamp by which you

can successfully see the true path of love and happiness for you and your sweetheart. (New Era, October 2003, p. 4)

There is nothing you can do to better prepare for marriage than strengthening your discipleship of the Lord Jesus Christ. As you complete this chapter I invite you to prayerfully consider an important question—in what ways do you need to become a fuller and more complete disciple of Jesus Christ? Your prayerful and humble answers to this question are the most important things you can do to improve your marriage readiness.

Charity (Love)

The True Nature of Love in Marriage
CHAPTER 3

> ...charity is the pure love of Christ, and it endureth forever...
> pray unto the Father with all the energy of heart, that ye may be
> filled with this love, which he hath bestowed upon all who
> are true followers of his Son, Jesus Christ...
>
> *Moroni 7:47–48*

How important is love in marriage? Most people would almost instinctually answer this question by saying that love is of course a *very* important to successful marriage. In fact, in our culture today many would say that love is the only true reason for a couple to come together and stay together in marriage. (I know some of you are thinking about the movie *The Princess Bride* right now—"Wuv, Twue Wuv!")

However, such an answer assumes that you and I know what is meant by the word *love*. Although we use the word love all the time when we talk about dating and marriage relationships, people are rarely very clear about what exactly they mean when they say that someone is *in love* or *loves someone*.

In fact, it has been my experience that many young adults today struggle in their dating efforts because love is seen as some sort of state of existence or intense feeling that they cannot quite explain, but they are sure they will know it when they see it—or, better said, when they feel it.

But is it really true that love is what matters most? Should love be the primary reason we come together and stay together in our marriages? The answers to these questions completely depends on what you believe love is and how it works in a couple's relationship. Properly understood, true love is indeed the foundation for lasting and loving marriage. But, improper understandings of love—which are very common in our culture today—

are responsible for many of the struggles some couples have in coming together and staying together.

In this chapter, we discuss the true nature of love in marriage and how couples can make sure they are building their relationships on proper understandings of love. This chapter explores how prophetic teachings on marriage differ from many of the *perspectives* of marriage that exist in the world today and discusses how gospel *principles* offer spouses a unique way to maintain a loving, lasting marriage. Specifically, we will consider how couples can be endowed with charity during dating and marriage. We will also look at relationship science that helps distinguish between mature and immature forms of love and teaches the importance of agency in fostering lasting love and other-centeredness in marriage.

What is Love?

In C.S. Lewis's "The Screwtape Letters," we follow the correspondence between two devils. The first, Uncle Screwtape, is a master devil, and the second, Wormwood, is his nephew and is an apprentice devil still learning the trade. One area of training discussed involves how to ruin marriages. Uncle Screwtape admonishes young nephew Wormwood that:

> Humans can be made to infer the false belief that the blend of affection, fear, and desire, which they call "being in love" is the only thing that makes marriage either happy or holy. (C.S. Lewis. The Screwtape Letters, p. 91)

Uncle Screwtape explains that this form of deception keeps men and women from recognizing the deeper nature and purposes of marriage that involve "the intention of loyalty to a partnership for mutual help, for the preservation of chastity, and for the transmission of life." Promoting the delusion that the personal emotions of *being in love* are the foundation of marriage is the primary means by which these devils keep spouses from realizing that when God "described a married couple as 'one flesh' he did not say 'a happily married couple' or a couple who married because they were in love." (C.S. Lewis. The Screwtape Letters, p. 94–95)

But isn't *being in love* the key factor of a successful marriage? Aren't love, romance, and happiness the cornerstones of good marriage? If not, what are the key aspects of a healthy and strong marriage? How we answer these questions largely depends on our understanding of marriage and the nature of love in marriage and family relationships. More specifically, the answers to these questions depend on whether or not we seek after the Lord's intended purposes for marriage or if we embrace the popular culture's view of love and romance.

Charity—It Endureth Forever

Uncle Screwtape's tactic of leading people to believe that marriage should be primarily based on the emotional state of *being in love* seems to be particularly effective with couples today. Living in a individualistic, consumer-driven, media-saturated, divorce-prone culture, many people at this point in history seem to believe that being in love, which is understood as an

emotional state, is the only rationale for a couple to come together and stay together in marriage.

While it is natural for each of us to desire the emotional closeness and intimacy that can be a part of marriage, many of the ideas about marriage in society today are drifting away from God's intended purposes of marriage. By understanding and living according to gospel perspectives of love, we are better prepared to avoid the relationship snares set in this world and to pattern our marriages after the principles taught to us in prophetic counsel.

Consider the following quote from Jeffry R. Holland about love in couple relationships:

> . . .Christlike staying power in romance and marriage requires more than we naturally have. It requires an endowment from heaven. Remember Mormon's promise—that such love, the love we each yearn for and cling to, is bestowed upon true followers of Christ. (BYU Speeches, February 2000, p. 6)

What does it mean when Elder Holland says that "staying power" in marriage will require "more than we naturally have"? Quite simply it means that on our own none of us will naturally have enough love to keep our marriage going strong through the natural ups and downs of life. We will need to become more than we naturally are.

Elder Holland then points out a crucial and comforting truth—each of us can be endowed with the love we will need. He then references the Prophet Mor-

mon's teachings on charity—a unique and different type of love.

> . . .charity is the pure love of Christ, and it endureth forever. . . Wherefore, my beloved brethren, pray unto the Father with all the energy of heart, that ye may be filled with this love, which he hath bestowed upon all who are true followers of his Son, Jesus Christ. (Moroni 7:47–48)

TRUE LOVE

...Christlike staying power in romance and marriage requires more than we naturally have. It requires an endowment from heaven. Remember Mormon's promise— that such love, the love we each yearn for and cling to, is bestowed upon true followers of Christ.

—ELDER HOLLAND, *How Do I Love Thee?*, p. 4

> **Charity is the pure love of Christ, and it endureth forever... Wherefore, ...pray unto the Father with all the energy of heart, that ye may be filled with this love, which he hath bestowed upon all who are true followers of his Son, Jesus Christ; that ye may become the sons [and daughters] of God; that when he shall appear we shall be like Him, for we shall see him as he is; ...that we may be purified even as he is pure.**
>
> –Moroni 7:47–48

Every couple that marries would love to have the assurance that their relationship will endure forever and Mormon teaches us how that can happen—each spouse must dedicate themselves to being a true follower of Christ so they can be endowed throughout their lives with charity for their spouse and others. This is what true love is and it is a gift from God.

This is why Elder Holland made the following promise to single adults and newly married couples:

> You want capability and safety in dating and romance, in married life and eternity? Be a true disciple of Jesus. Be a genuine, committed, word-and-deed Latter-day Saint. Believe that your faith has everything to do with your romance, because it does. You separate dating from discipleship at your peril. Or to phrase that more positively, Jesus Christ, the Light of the World, is the only lamp by which you can successfully see the true path of love and happiness for you and your sweetheart. (BYU Speeches, February 2000, p. 4)

President Gordon B. Hinckley similarly taught:

> Love is the very essence of life. It is the pot of gold at the end of the rainbow. Yet it is more than the end of the rainbow. Love is the beginning also, and from it springs the beauty that arches across the sky on a stormy day. Love is the security for which children weep, the yearning of youth, the adhesive that binds marriage, and the lubricant that prevents devastating friction in the home; it is the peace of old age, the sunlight of hope shining through death. How rich are those who enjoy it in their associations with family, friends, church, and neighbors ... love like faith, is a gift of God. (Ensign, March 1984, p. 44)

Elder Holland also emphasized that the endowment of charity is a process that is possible because of the atonement of Jesus Christ, which enables our Savior to uplift and change our feelings, motivations, and understandings; which can prompt us to act in more loving ways. Christ also provided an example for each of us of true charity and loving care for others. Elder Holland taught,

> True charity, the absolutely pure, perfect love of Christ, has really been known only once in this world—in the form of Christ Himself, the living Son of the living God... Christ is the only one who got it all right, did it all perfectly, loved the way we are all to try to love. (Elder Jeffrey R. Holland, How Do I Love Thee? p. 4)

Sister Jean Bingham further taught:

> Of course, Jesus Christ is the perfect embodiment of charity. His premortal offering to be our Savior, His interactions throughout His mortal life, His supernal gift of the Atonement, and His continual efforts to bring us back to our Heavenly Father are the ultimate expressions of charity. He operates with a singular focus: love for His Father expressed through His love for each of us. When asked about the greatest commandment, Jesus answered: "Thou shalt love the Lord thy God with all thy heart, and with all thy soul, and with all thy mind. This is the first and great commandment. And the second is like unto it, Thou shalt love thy neighbour as thyself." (Oct. 2016, I Will Bring the Light of the Gospel Into My Home).

President Dieter F. Uchtdorf further taught that the full example of Christ's love is found in his sacrifice and atonement for us. He said:

> The Savior's Atonement cannot become commonplace in our teaching, in our conversation, or in our hearts. It is sacred and holy, for it was through this "great and last sacrifice" that Jesus the Christ brought "salvation to all those who shall believe on his name."
>
> I marvel to think that the Son of God would condescend to save us, as imperfect, impure, mistake-prone, and ungrateful as we often are. I have tried to understand the Savior's Atonement with my finite mind, and the only explanation I can come up with is this: God loves us deeply, perfectly, and everlastingly. I cannot even begin to estimate "the breadth, and length, and depth, and height ... [of] the love of Christ. (April 2015, The Gift of Grace)

Agency and Love

The word "love" appears five times in the Proclamation on the Family, each time the word is linked with action words such as *"to love and care"* or *"to love and serve."* What does this teach us about nature of love? What does this teach us about the kind of love that is needed to foster and nurture a strong and healthy marriage relationship?

The Proclamation on the Family teaches us that sustained love in marriage is based upon a mature type of love. The language of the Proclamation suggests that love falls within the scope of our agency. *Love* is something *we do*, something *we can control*, and ultimately something *we can choose*—if not, God could not command us to love one another (John 13:34).

The scriptures teach us that love is a multifaceted aspect of relationships—not simply an emotion or feeling. This makes it agentive and controllable. Dr. Howard Bahr, a family sociologist at BYU, has commented,

> God commands us to love in language that teaches us that love is more than an interior feeling, that heart, might, mind, and strength are united in love. . . genuine love requires each aspect of self, not just part of us. The heart is essential, as is the mind, and so is the "might" of physical activity, of doing as the love-filled heart directs. . .in our marriages and families we must love with our heart, our mind, our spirit, and our hands. (Strengthening Our Families, 2000, p. 168)

Elder Lynn G. Robbins has also taught:

> Many popular songs and films make reference to loving forever or to an everlasting love. For the world, these lyrics are simply poetic; for us, they are genuine expressions of our divine potential. We believe that eternal love, eternal marriages, and eternal families are "central to the Creator's plan for the eternal destiny of his children" (Proc. ¶ 1). However, every couple will encounter some struggles on their journey toward this glorious destiny. There are no perfect marriages in the world because there are no perfect people. But our doctrine teaches us how to nurture our marriages toward perfection and how to keep the romance in them along the way. No one need ever "fall out of love." Falling out of love is a cunning myth which causes many broken hearts and homes. (Ensign, October 2000)

The Science of Love

Part of the complexity of understanding love comes from the fact that there are different types of love. We use the term "love" to describe our relationship to our spouse, but we also use the term "love" in referring to our grandma and our newborn baby daughter. We also say that we "love" double fudge chocolate ice-cream and getting a foot massage. Clearly our relationship with our spouse should involve a different type of love than our love for ice-cream or the "love" we felt for that pretty girl in our math class in 9th grade.

In order to better understand love, we need to appreciate that there are different types of love. Furthermore, we must understand that some types of love are better than others in forming and maintaining a strong marriage relationship. In fact, the type of love your marriage is based in will be one of the most important determinants of whether your relationship will last or not. Marriages based on mature love will

last. Marriages built upon immature love will not. It is as simple as that.

What Is Mature Love?

While fuzzy definitions of love are problematic in everyday conversation, they are an extreme problem in social science research. In order to conduct meaningful research, scholars must have clear definitions of what they are studying in order to measure the phenomenon in a meaningful way. In a landmark article by a leading family psychologist Dr. Patricia Noller, she defined, on the basis of theorizing and research, the particular type of love that supports marriage and family relationships.

In particular, Dr. Noller sets out to define the type of "*mature love*" that is related to high levels of satisfaction in relationships, to the psychological well-being of family members, and to stable family relationships. While her goal was to give scholars a clearer definition of love for their research studies on marriage and family relationships, her definition offers some insights into how you can distinguish mature from immature forms of love in your own dating and marriage experience.

From her extensive review of research on love, Dr. Noller concludes that in couple relationships:

> . . . mature love may be best conceptualized as creating an environment in which both the lovers and those that depend on them can grow and develop. (What is This Thing Called Love? 1996, p. 97)

She also concludes from her review that love is an attitude toward a particular person that has *emotional, cognitive, and behavioral* components; and all three of these aspects of love can be mature or immature in nature. Dr. Noller explains,

> The way these three aspects of love are manifested in each individual will determine whether an experience of love involves a stable, healthy, growth promoting relationship or an immature, over-dependent, and growth-stifling relationship. (What is This Thing Called Love? 1996, p. 100)

Mature Love vs. Immature Love

Three Aspects of Mature Love

- Cognitive (attitudes - mind)
- Emotions (feelings - heart)
- Behavior (actions – strength)

The first thing we can learn from Dr. Noller's definition is that *love is multidimensional*. Love involves our feelings, attitudes, and actions. This definition is very similar to what we observed in scriptural teachings about love—the way the Lord commands us to love and serve him with all of our "heart, might, mind, and strength" (D&C 4:2).

Typically when we use the term *falling in love* we are referring to the emotional aspects of love. While there needs to indeed be an intense emotional connection between two people in their courtship and marriage, there are other parts of love that are needed for their love to be mature. In addition to falling in love,

> **Although immature love is a reality in our world, mature love is possible and is sustained by beliefs that love involves acknowledging and accepting differences and weaknesses; that love involves an internal decision to love another person and a long-term commitment to maintain that love; and finally that love is controllable and needs to be nurtured and nourished by the lovers.**
>
> -Dr. Patricia Noller, What is this thing called love?, p. 112

and a long-term commitment to maintain that love; and finally that love is controllable and needs to be nurtured and nourished by the lovers.. (What is This Thing Called Love, 1996, p. 112)

each of us needs to be *choosing in love* and *doing in love* as well. These distinctions are important, because the emotional aspect of love is the most unstable. Emotions by their nature ebb and flow and go up and down. Our attitudes and behaviors, on the other hand, can be stable and consistent. Plus, when we feel the emotional feelings of love waning in a relationship or strained because of conflict, a mature view of love recognizes that we can continue to choose to love our partner and to restore our feelings of love by doing loving behaviors and giving loving service.

In addition to distinguishing love into three components, Dr. Noller provides examples of mature and immature emotions, attitudes, and behaviors in couple relationships. Dr. Noller concludes,

> . . . although immature love is a reality in our world, mature love is possible and is sustained by beliefs that love involves acknowledging and accepting differences and weaknesses; that love involves an internal decision to love another person

Mature Love = Divine Love

Dr. Noller's description of *mature love* is very similar to the concept of *divine love* taught by President Spencer W. Kimball.

Divine love is not like that association of the world which is misnamed love, but which is mostly physical attraction. . .The love of which the Lord speaks is not

How Can We Strengthen Our Love?

Choosing Love – "Selfless Attitude"

- Be Humble ~ Forgiving
- Be Optimistic ~ Positive
- Focus on solutions rather than problems

Doing Love – "Selfless Action"

- Service and Sacrifice
- Obedience and Repentance
- Pray for Love – a gift from God

Feeling Love

CHAPTER 3: Charity (Love) 43

only physical attraction, but also faith, confidence, understanding, and partnership. It is devotion and companionship, parenthood, common ideals and standards. It is cleanliness of life and sacrifice and unselfishness. This kind of love never tires nor wanes. It lives on through sickness and sorrow, through accomplishment and disappointment, through time and eternity. You must treat each other in a manner that your love will grow. Today it is a demonstrative love, but in the tomorrows of ten, thirty, fifty years it will be a far greater and more intensified love, grown quieter and more dignified with the years of sacrifice, suffering, joys, and consecration to each other, to your family, and to the Kingdom of God. (The Teachings of Spencer W. Kimball, 1982, p. 248)

Elder Marvin J. Ashton also taught:

True love is a process. True love requires personal action. Love must be continuing to be real. Love takes time. Too often expediency, infatuation, stimulation, persuasion, or lust are mistaken for love. How hollow, how empty if our love is no deeper than arousal of momentary feelings or the expression in words of what is no more lasting than the time it takes to speak them .(Ensign, November 1975, p. 108)

As you seek to become ready for marriage or to strengthen your current marriage, you should strive to develop the capacity for this type of divine love. This requires selflessness and attention to the needs of others. The more you seek to serve others, the more you will feel your love for them grow. This is why missionaries come home from their missions and often say how much they "came to love the people." Their love grew as their service for them deepened. Also, while there is much that each of us can do to refine our capacity to love, do not forget that a fullness of charity is ultimately an endowed spiritual gift (Moro 7:48). As you seek to be a true disciple of Christ and to worship Him, this type of love will be more fully bestowed upon you and will bless you in dating and marriage.

Cleaving (Commitment)

THE NATURE OF THE MARRIAGE COVENANT
CHAPTER 4

> Therefore shall a man leave his father and his mother, and shall cleave unto his wife: and they shall be one flesh.
>
> *Genesis 2:24*

We live in the era of disposable marriages. We frequently hear about celebrity marriages that end in divorce after only a few months or years of marriage. The news is filled with other famous people who avoid the commitments of marriage altogether—moving from "relationship to relationship" as easily as they change their clothes or hairstyles. Far too often these "here-today-gone tomorrow" relationships produce children who grow up in an ever-changing landscape of parent figures and caregivers.

Unfortunately, these patterns of easy divorce and uncommitted relationships are not limited to famous people or movie stars. Even in common circles, many people are coming to view marriage as a less than permanent relationship. A few years ago, a newspaper writer wrote about an experience he had while attending a wedding for a friend. While the congregation was waiting for the ceremony to begin, he overheard a conversation of some family members of the groom. Referring to the bride, one family member said to the other, "Don't you just love Megan?—she is a wonderful girl." The other family member replied, "Oh yes, she is a delightful girl—I'm certain she'll make a wonderful *first wife* for John." Needless to say, the newspaper writer was stunned.

In his article, the writer expressed concern about a culture that is beginning to view marriage much like we do homes. Similar to the notion of a "starter home" that a young couple moves into with plans to move into a nicer home when they are more established, some people accept the notion that some marriages are "starter marriages." The writer asked, "Have we really come to the point where we accept the notion of someone being our 'starter wife' or our 'starter husband?'" He expressed concern for the future of marriages if individuals approach them with such a disposable mindset.

44

CHAPTER 4: *Cleaving (Commitment)* 45

In this chapter, we examine the nature of the marriage covenant as the Lord intends it to be. Specifically, we study the doctrine of *cleaving* and what it means to "become one" in marriage. Your goal with this chapter should be to better understand what types of commitments you will take upon yourself as you enter into the covenant of marriage and to understand the role that the Holy Spirit of Promise can have in helping you keep those commitments. In particular, we set out to answer three key questions:

- What does it mean when we say that marriage is an *ordinance*?

- What does it mean when we say that marriage is a *covenant*?

- How does embracing marriage as an ordinance and a covenant change the meaning and nature of marriage in our *current* lives?

As you read this chapter, I invite you to focus on how embracing marriage as a divine ordinance and sacred covenant can change your relationship with your spouse *in this life*—not just in the eternities. There is a significant difference between couples who view their marriage as a covenant with each other and their Father in Heaven and those who see their marriage as merely a contract or agreement between two people. Covenant marriages are not only deeper in their commitment to stay together, but they are also a fundamentally different type of relationship that is endowed with strength and support from the Lord—making life richer, happier, and more meaningful.

THE ORDINANCE OF MARRIAGE

Ordinances are a central part of the restored gospel of Jesus Christ. Both ancient and living prophetic leaders have long taught that our spiritual progression in this life, and in the eternities, is linked to our willingness to make and keep sacred promises with our Father in Heaven through gospel ordinances. Ordinances may be once in a lifetime events, such as baptism or being ordained to the priesthood; or they may be repeated rites or rituals, such as partaking of the sacrament each week on the sabbath or receiving a priesthood blessing when we are ill or troubled.

IN THE ORDINANCES...THE POWER OF GODLINESS IS MANIFEST

All ordinances are intended to connect each of us with the divine support and power of our loving Father in Heaven. In a revelation on the priesthood given to the Prophet Joseph Smith, the Lord taught that:

> And this greater priesthood administereth the gospel and holdeth the key of the mysteries of the kingdom, even the key of the knowledge of God. Therefore, in the ordinances thereof, the power of godliness is manifest. And without the ordinances thereof, and the authority of the priesthood, the power of godliness is not manifest unto men in the flesh. (D&C 84:19–21)

Sister Carole Stephens explained:

> These priesthood ordinances and covenants provide access to the fulness of the blessings promised

Continuing this line of teaching, Sister Linda Burton taught:

> We need to study and understand temple ordinances and covenants. The temple holds a place at the very center of our most sacred beliefs, and the Lord asks that we attend, ponder, study, and find personal meaning and application individually. We will come to understand that through the ordinances of the temple, the power of godliness is manifest in our lives— and that because of temple ordinances, we can be armed with God's power, and His name will be upon us, His glory round about us, and His angels have charge over us.— I wonder if we are fully drawing upon the power of those promises. (Oct, 2016, Rise Up in Strength Sisters in Zion).

When we worthily participate in priesthood ordinances we open the door for God's spirit to be poured out in our homes and relationships. Ordinances are one of the primary means by which the power of the priesthood can be manifest in our lives. When properly honored, ordinances are developmental milestones in our spiritual progression that mark a deeper commitment to and connection with our Father in Heaven and His son Jesus Christ.

The Most Holy and Sacred Ordinance

So what does it mean to say that marriage is an ordinance? To properly answer this question, we must first understand that marriage is not just another ordinance in the gospel plan—it is a unique and particularly important ordinance. President Spencer W. Kimball taught that:

> Marriage according to the law of the Church is the most holy and sacred ordinance. It will bring to the husband and wife, if they abide in their covenants, the fullness of exaltation in the Kingdom of God. (Conference Report, October 1962, p. 57–59)

Marriage is the "most holy and sacred ordinance" because it is the doorway to exaltation and the fullness of eternal life. Elder Bruce R. McConkie taught:

> Baptism is the gate to the celestial kingdom; celestial marriage is the gate to exaltation in the highest heaven within the celestial world (D&C 131:1–4). . . . Celestial marriage is a holy and an eternal ordi-

to us by God, which are made possible by the Savior's Atonement. They arm sons and daughters of God with power, God's power, and provide us with the opportunity to receive eternal life—to return to God's presence and live with Him in His eternal family. (October 2013, Do We Know What We Have?).

nance. . .its importance in the plan of salvation and exaltation cannot be overestimated. (Mormon Doctrine, 1978, p. 118)

The description of ordinances in the "Gospel Topics" library on the Church website (www.lds.org) can help us better understand what it means to say that marriage is an ordinance. The Church website says:

> In the Church, an ordinance is a sacred, formal act performed by the authority of the priesthood. Some ordinances are essential to our exaltation. These ordinances are called saving ordinances. They include baptism, confirmation, ordination to the Melchizedek Priesthood (for men), the temple endowment, and the marriage sealing. With each of these ordinances, we enter into solemn covenants with the Lord.
>
> Other ordinances, such as naming and blessing children, consecrating oil, and administering to the sick and afflicted, are also performed by priesthood authority. While they are not essential to our salvation, they are important for our comfort, guidance, and encouragement.
>
> Ordinances and covenants help us remember who we are. They remind us of our duty to God. The Lord has provided them to help us come unto Him and receive eternal life. When we honor them, He strengthens us spiritually. (www.lds.org, Gospel Library, Gospel Topics, Ordinances)

By applying this statement to marriage, we learn at least three critical truths of what it means to say that marriage is an ordinance:

1. First, all ordinances are performed by the authority of the priesthood. This means that when a couple is sealed in the temple by a temple sealer who holds special priesthood keys, their marriage is authorized and recognized by the Lord. In short, their marriage becomes a divinely enforceable union that is legitimate both in this life and in the world to come. Temple marriages are meant to be eternal in nature and duration—there is no "for as long as we both shall live" or "until death do us part" clause in the Lord's pattern of marriage.

2. Second, marriage is a saving ordinance. In order to become like our Heavenly Parents, we need to enter into the new and everlasting covenant of marriage and maintain a marriage relationship that is compatible with eternal life.

3. Third, celestial marriage is a means to enter into a sacred and unique covenant with our Father in Heaven. Elder Dennis B. Neuenschwander of the Presidency of the Seventy taught that "sacred gospel ordinances are the gateway to solemn covenants with God. . .our important steps toward God are introduced by sacred ordinances and are governed by the conditions of the covenants associated with those ordinances" (Ensign, Aug 2001, p. 20).

4. Fourth, this statement also teaches us that God strengthens us spiritually through ordinances. Elder Neuenschwander also taught that "sacred ordinances provide an endowment of divine power in our lives. . .worthy participation in sacred gospel ordinances changes our lives and brings blessings

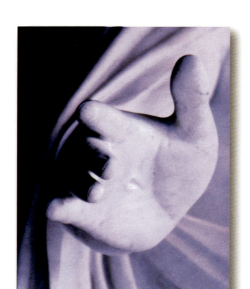

and power to us we would otherwise not enjoy. The power of the Atonement itself is unlocked by sacred gospel ordinances that are performed under the keys of the priesthood" (Ensign, Aug 2001, p. 20).

Marriage as a covenant

What does it mean when we say that marriage is a covenant? To fully answer this question, each of us needs to understand three aspects of the marriage covenant. First, we need to understand who are the people involved in the celestial marriage covenant. In short, we need to know with whom we are making the covenant. Second, we need to understand what we are promising to do when we enter into the marriage covenant. Third, we need to understand what the Lord is promising us in return as we strive to fulfill the marriage covenant to Him and our spouse.

With Whom Do We Covenant When We Marry?

Typically, we define a covenant as a sacred agreement between ourselves and God. In Primary classes throughout the Church, children are taught that a covenant is a *two-way promise with God*—perhaps that is how you were taught about covenants too. This is an accurate description of nearly all of the covenants we make with our Father in Heaven in this life. When we are baptized, confirmed, ordained to the priesthood, and receive our temple endowments we enter into a two-person covenant with our Father in Heaven. However, this definition of a covenant does not fully fit the covenant involved in celestial marriage.

The marriage covenant is unlike any other gospel ordinance or covenant. This is because the marriage covenant involves three people, rather than just two, who have covenanted themselves to each other. The marriage covenant is a triangle covenant—it is a three-way promise and commitment involving the two spouses and God. Viewing marriage as a *divine triangle* (see figure below) expands our understanding of the nature and meaning of the marriage covenant.

The Divine Triangle

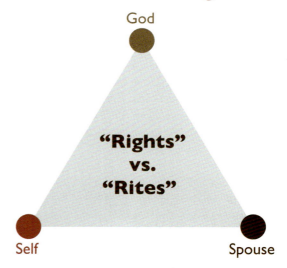

In all covenants, we make sacred promises to those we make the covenant with. In marriage then, we make promises to both God and our spouse. This should shift our view of marriage from what we expect to *receive* from our spouse to what we have promised to *give* in our marriage.

A temple sealer once taught me an important way to think about the promises we make when we are married. While I was attending the sealing ceremony of one of my cousins to his sweet bride, this temple sealer cautioned this couple, and all of us in attendance, to make sure we listened to the sealing ordinance correctly. He taught us that during the ordinance the couple would covenant to observe and keep the "rites" associated with the celestial order of marriage. He cautioned us to not hear this phrase as the "rights" associated with marriage. When we think of the *rights* of marriage we may be tempted to focus on what we believe we are entitled to in our marriage—what we think our spouse should be doing for us. A *rite* however, is an observance or practice—it is something we do and keep, it is not something we are entitled to or receive.

This wise temple sealer then counseled this couple to always remember what they were promising to do for each other and their marriage that day in the temple. He also emphasized that when they were struggling or feeling a lack of love toward one another are the times when their covenant to practice the rites of marriage is most needed. What an important lesson! When you and I feel least like being loving and taking care of our spouses are the times we most need to remember our covenant to do just that.

Viewing marriage as a divine triangle also reminds us that happiness in marriage is at its fullest when all three members of the triangle are in alignment with each other. We must seek to be unified with both our spouse and with God. Sister Susan W. Tanner, former Young Women General President taught:

> The marriage commitment is a three-way commitment. Husbands and wives are committed to each other, but they are also definitely committed to our Father in Heaven. The binding force in this marriage relationship is charity, the pure love of Christ. As we have this charity for one another, it draws us closer to our Father in Heaven and, therefore, closer to each other in the marriage relationship. (Worldwide Leadership Training Meeting, February 2008, p. 11)

What Do We Covenant To Do When We Marry?†

The Proclamation on the Family gives a beautiful description of what husbands and wives promise to do for each other when they enter into the marriage covenant. The Proclamation reads, "husband and wife have a solemn responsibility to love and care for each other . . ." (Proclamation on the Family, ¶ 6). In its simplest form, this is what we promise in the marriage covenant—to love our spouse and to care for his or her needs throughout our lives.

In the Doctrine and Covenants, the Lord teaches us that the love we should express for our spouse should exceed all others, except the Lord Himself. The Lord taught, "Thou shalt love thy wife [husband] with *all* thy heart, and shalt cleave unto her [him] and none else (D&C 42:22, emphasis added). In all the scriptures,

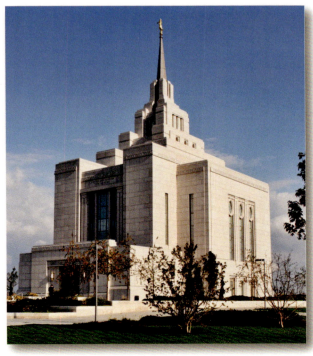

there is only one other person that we are commanded to love with *all* our heart—that is our Father in Heaven Himself. That is how the Lord views the divine triangle of marriage—it is the covenant relationship in which all three people promise to love each other with all their hearts—holding nothing back.

Shepherd or Hireling?

In his book, Covenant Hearts, Elder Bruce C. Hafen compares the Parable of the Good Shepherd in the New Testament to the marriage covenant—emphasizing that this passage of scripture may be our best description of the nature of commitment the Lord intends for us to have in our marriages. Elder Hafen emphasizes that if each of us will strive to emulate the Savior's commitment to us personally in our devotion to our spouse, we will come closer to the type of love the Lord expects of us in the marriage covenant. The Lord taught:

> I am come that they might have life, and that they might have it more abundantly. I am the good shepherd: the good shepherd giveth his life for the sheep. But he that is an hireling, and not the shepherd, whose own the sheep are not, seeth the wolf coming, and leaveth the sheep, and fleeth: and the wolf catcheth them, and scattereth the sheep. The hireling fleeth, because he is an hireling, and careth not for the sheep. I am the good shepherd, and know my sheep, and am known of mine. As the Father knoweth me, even so know I the Father: and I lay down my life for the sheep. (John 10:10–15)

The insight we can gain about the marriage covenant from this parable is truly transformative. I encourage you to pay special attention to this portion of the chapter—it can truly change the nature of your marriage relationship now and in the future. Reflecting on these scriptures, Elder Hafen taught that:

> The parable of the Good Shepherd contains many clues for understanding covenant marriage. The parable is not only about Christ's love for us. It is also about the love of marriage partners or parents who give themselves to others in covenants so deep that they may fairly think of the other as their "own" and "mine"—even though their companion's freedom

and personal growth are, paradoxically, as precious to them, perhaps more precious, than their own. (Covenant Hearts, 2005, p. 85)

Covenant vs. Contract

Elder Hafen also taught that the Parable of the Good shepherd can help us appreciate the difference between viewing marriage as a "covenant" versus as a "contract." Prayerfully ponder on these statements from Elder Hafen:

> *Covenant marriage* is unconditional, unlimited, and eternal—a reflection of the kind of love and commitment on which it is based. *Contractual marriage*, by contrast, is subject to conditions and limited in the breadth of its demands as well as expected duration. (Covenant Hearts, 2005, p. 80)

The partners in a covenant marriage also give their lives for each other, a day or an hour at a time. They sacrifice and hearken to each other as equal partners. Each gives wholly to the other; each receives the other fully to himself or herself. They belong to each other—never as property but as souls willingly entrusted to each other's keeping. By caring passionately about their partner's personal spiritual growth, a central part of their life's work is to help their partner develop a more abundant life. (Covenant Hearts, 2005, p. 85–86)

Contractual attitudes, on the other hand, rest on very different assumptions. A contract is always limited in its scope and duration. It never involves a contracting party's "whole life or even its greater part." Moreover, people enter contracts for reasons of self-interest, "uniting with the other party only so far as this provides him with an advantage (profit, pleasure, or service). Today's society wrongfully but fully expects the contracting parties to interpret their marital differences according to what is in their personal interest—like a hireling. (Covenant Hearts, 2005, p. 82)

Research on Commitment in Marriage

Marriage researchers have been studying commitment in couple's relationships for some time now and what they have found in their studies has some very interesting parallels to Elder Hafen's observations about the difference between covenant and contract-based couples.

According to Dr. Scott Stanley at the University of Denver, the world's foremost expert on couple commitment, there are two key components to commitment: personal dedication and constraint.

Personal dedication speaks to how internally committed partners are to one another, whereas constraints are the outside pressures that might keep couples together when partners would rather leave. *Constraints* are the things that accumulate as relationships grow and make it hard to break up, such as financial considerations, responsibilities for children, social pressure, and a lack of foreseeable alternatives.

Dr. Stanley emphasizes that despite the negative connotation of "constraints" in a culture like ours that emphasizes personal freedoms, constraints can actually have a positive function in the lives of couples because they can help prevent one or both partners from making drastic decisions that unravel investment during periods of temporary unhappiness. However, constraints do not lead to happy marriages in the long run. They mostly put the brakes on impulsive, destabilizing behaviors at critical times for many couples. Of course, when someone is really unhappy for a long time in a marriage, constraints can lead to a sense of feeling trapped.

Devotion vs. Constraint
Dr. Scott Stanley

Devotion
Want To = Interpersonal Commitment

"...motivation to build and maintain the quality of the relationship, having a couple identity, and willingness to sacrifice for the partner or relationship."

Constraint
Have To – Institutional Commitment

"...factors that reinforce staying in a relationship even if satisfaction and dedication wane, such as financial or other tangible investments, concern for one's partner, or a sense of moral obligation to stay."

Personal dedication, on the other hand, refers to interpersonal and more intrinsic commitment processes, particularly in commitment to the partner and the relationship. When partners are committed to each other and their relationship together, this creates a type of safety and security that people need to have to thrive in life together as a couple.

According to Dr. Stanley's research with couples, there are four important components of personal dedication:

1. A desire for a future together.
2. A sense of "us" or "we"—or as being part of a team.
3. A high sense of priority for the relationship.
4. A sense of satisfaction with sacrificing for the other.

Dr. Stanley explains,

> Marriage can be fundamentally construed as a long-term investment, and in many ways, functions like one. It is the expectation of longevity that makes the day-to-day investment rational. People require a sense of security about the future of the relationship in order to fully invest in the present for that future. This is the nature of commitment in marriage, in which some options are given up in favor of the richer possibilities of building a life together.
>
> In contrast, relationships with no clear sense of a future favor pressure for performance in the present (because there is no guarantee that the partner will stay), with score-keeping about levels of effort and investment, and anxiety about continuance, being the logical outgrowth. Simply put, couples do best when they have a clear sense of couple identity and a long-term view. (The Power of Commitment, 2005, p. 12)

Although commitment is often thought of as an attitude or cognitive part of a relationship, it can also be thought of as a behavior. In fact, leading marriage scholar Dr. Paul Amato emphasizes that commitment in relationships is best measured as partners' behaviors in times the relationship may be threatened or in trouble. He explains,

> Trying to measure commitment is akin to measuring a construct such as bravery. Imagine a questionnaire in which people responded to items such as "I don't become afraid in dangerous situations." As long as people are not threatened, it is easy for them to imagine that they will react to danger with courage. But a researcher studying bravery cannot predict how a person will react until a threat is present. This is why the military hands out medals after the battle and not before . . .although bravery and commitment may have intrapsychic components, they are demonstrated through behavior. (Alone Together, 2007, p. 65)

What type of commitment does the Good Shepherd have? Linking scriptures to research on commitment reveals that the primary difference between a shepherd and a hireling is the type of commitment that motivates their involvement with the sheep. A *hireling* fits the pattern of *constraint commitment*—only doing what is needed when they have to and being far more concerned about himself or herself than the wellbeing of the sheep. Unfortunately, too many spouses fit this pattern as well—becoming primarily concerned about their own wants and needs and resenting the needs of their spouse. *Shepherds*, on the other hand, demonstrate *devotion commitment*—concerning themselves with the needs of their spouse. Loving and caring for their spouse because they want to not because they have to.

What Does the Lord Promise to Do for Us in the Marriage Covenant?

As with all sacred ordinances and covenants, the Lord promises to endow us with special blessings as we are faithful to our covenants. The Lord has said: "I, the Lord, am bound when ye do what I say: but when ye do not what I say, ye have no promise" (D&C 82:10).

Thus, if we are worthy as we participate in the ordinance of marriage and then strive with all our hearts to keep our covenants to God and our spouse, the Lord will walk with us in marriage. He will bless us and our relationship. He will guide our paths and change our hearts—He will bring us home to Him to share in eternal happiness and progression. President James E. Faust taught:

> When the covenant of marriage for time and eternity, the culminating gospel ordinance, is sealed by the Holy Spirit of promise, it can literally open the windows of heaven for great blessings to flow to a married couple who seek for those blessings. Such marriages become rich, whole, and sacred. Though each party can maintain his or her separate identity, yet together in their covenants they can be two vines wound inseparably around each other. Each thinks of his or her companion before thinking of self. (Ensign, May 1989)

Far too often, we only think of the Holy Spirit of Promise sealing a couple together in the eternities—a blessing we can receive after this life. Notice how President Faust emphasizes how such blessings are available to us now in our day-to-day lives. The *Holy Spirit of Promise* is best understood as the *Gift of the Holy Ghost* for couples. Just as we understand how the Gift of the Holy Ghost is intended to bless us throughout our lives, so too should we understand the Holy Spirit of Promise as an ongoing resource and blessing through our married lives.

Can you see why approaching marriage as an ordinance and covenant is so important? It changes the very nature of our marriage relationship. Such covenant marriages differ significantly from marriages based on contract, self-interest, or worldly designs. President Faust also gives us a beautiful metaphor to understand the nature of the marriage covenant—"two vines wound inseparably around each other." Such devotion to each other and to the Lord is the foundation to having the windows of heaven open upon our marriages.

Cleaving

How Does Embracing Marriage as an Ordinance and a Covenant Change the Meaning and Nature of Marriage in Our Lives?

As we approach marriage as a holy ordinance and covenant we learn several *principles* and *practices* that can guide our actions in dating, courtship, and early marriage. As we incorporate these principles and practices into our actions, the meaning and nature of marriage will change in our lives. In this final section we will discuss two principles connected with the marriage covenant—*cleaving* and *spousal preeminence*; and we will discuss several practices that couples can engage in to strengthen their marriage covenant and create a strong marital identity.

Principles: Cleaving and Spousal Preeminence

Cleaving in marriage was one of the first principles of the gospel given to Adam and Eve when they were in the Garden of Eden. In the Old Testament, we read, "Therefore shall a man leave his father and his mother, and shall cleave unto his wife" (Genesis 2:24). The principle of cleaving has been restored in the Latter-days as well. Returning to a scripture we previously read in the Doctrine and Covenants, the Lord taught, "Thou shalt love thy wife [or husband] with all thy heart, and shalt *cleave* unto her [him] and none else (D&C 42:22, emphasis added).

In modern usage, the term "to cleave" means "to remain attached, devoted, or faithful to" (Oxford Dictionary). President Spencer W. Kimball taught that cleaving is an important part of successful marriage and is particularly important for engaged and newly-married couples in the early years of their relationship. Prayerfully read the following statements from President Kimball.

> Frequently, people continue to cleave unto their mothers and their fathers. . .sometimes mothers will not relinquish the hold they have upon their children, and husbands as well as wives return to their mothers and fathers to obtain advice and counsel and to confide, whereas *cleaving should be to the [spouse] primarily*. . .
>
> Couples do well to immediately *find their own home, separate and apart from that of the in-laws on either side.* The home may be very modest and unpretentious, but still it is an independent domicile. *Your married life should become independent of her folks and his folks.* . .
>
> . . .you love them (parents) more than ever; you cherish their counsel; you appreciate their association; *but you live your own lives,* being governed by your decisions, by your own prayerful considerations after you have received the counsel of those who should give it. To cleave does not mean merely occupy the same home; it means to adhere closely, to stick together.
>
> [Speaking to men] She, the woman, occupies the first place. She is preeminent, even above parents who are so dear to us. Even the children must take their proper but significant place. I have seen some women who give their children that spot, that preeminence, in their affection and crowd out the father. That is a serious mistake. (Ensign, October 2002, emphasis added)

The doctrine of cleaving is inseparably connected to the principle of *spousal preeminence* or the idea that our relationship with our spouse becomes preeminent over *all other relationships* in our life. Notice how President Kimball teaches that all other relationships—including parents, children, siblings, and other family members and friends—need to be prioritized in ways that support the preeminence of our relationship with our spouse.

Practices of Cleaving

Cleaving in marriage requires more than just saying that your spouse is the most important person in your life. Your actions must show that you place your spouse as the top priority in your lives. Likewise, Elder Robert D. Hales taught: "An eternal bond doesn't just happen as a result of the sealing covenants we make in

Practices of Cleaving

- Nurture the sacred in your marriage
- Confide in & counsel w/ your spouse
- Seek and consider outside counsel together – prayerfully
- Respect the "inner fence of marriage"
- Practice the "rites of marriage"
- Allow the atonement to be active in your marriage

the temple. How we conduct ourselves in this life will determine what we will be in all the eternities to come" (Ensign, Nov. 1996). Drawing from the teachings of our living prophets there are several practices that couples can commit to that will *strengthen* their marital bond and covenant. Similarly, there are a number of things that fiancée's and spouses can do to *weaken* that bond and trust in their relationship. These practices include:

Confide in and Counsel With Your Spouse

Prophets have repeatedly warned that many spouses continue to cleave to their parents and others more than they do their spouse. Often times this involves turning to others to confide in with our troubles and to seek advice and counsel. The proper pattern is for spouses to confide in and counsel with each other primarily. Spouses should make decisions together and work through whatever problems may arise in the course of their marriage. Elder Dallin H. Oaks recently said,

> I like to tell a young couple who are being married that in the marriage relationship they ought to look first to each other, as they do across the altar during their marriage—not first to their parents, not first to their siblings, not first to their friends, but in solving all their problems they should look first to one another. (Worldwide Leadership Training Meeting, February 2008, p. 12)

Seek and Consider Outside Counsel Together—Prayerfully

At times, a couple may feel that they would like to get some advice from someone outside their marriage for a decision they are making or a situation they are confronting. How we seek such counsel is a key distinguisher of whether or not we are cleaving in our marriage. The best pattern for seeking outside counsel from a bishop, parent, family member, or anyone else is to *go together* as a couple to talk with that person. This way, both spouses are present and the couple acts in unity in seeking and considering any outside advice. If it is not possible to go together, then the spouse seeking the outside advice should make sure that their spouse knows that such advice is being sought and should convey to the outside counselor, parent, or family member that he or she is acting on behalf of the couple. Any counsel received in these circumstances should be prayerfully considered by both spouses before making a decision.

Respect the Sacred Ground of Inner-Marriage Life

In married life, we become aware of intimate and private details about our partner's character and habits. We become very aware of their strengths, talents, and virtues. We also become aware of their shortcomings,

weaknesses, and sins. What do we do with such intimate information? We must remember that we are only aware of such things because our spouse has opened up to us and shared their soul with us. Private details about our spouse are very vulnerable and sensitive topics. We stand on sacred ground when we share the intimacies of inner-married life. Expect for some very rare circumstances, we should never share information with others that our spouse would desire to be kept private.

There should be an "invisible fence" around this part of our marriage. We should never engage in conversations that start with the statements like, "My husband would kill me if he knew I was telling you this, but. . ." or "Don't tell my wife I told you this. . ." In our conversations with others we should always safeguard the sacred trust given to us by our spouse.

Establish Your Own Home

President Kimball also taught that newly married couples should make every effort to seek out and maintain a separate home from their parents on either side. This home or apartment may be very modest and small, but this type of living arrangement best safeguards the principles of cleaving and spousal preeminence. At times, true economic needs may require that married couples live with their parents or other extended families for a short time. However, such arrangements should be seen as temporary and couples should seek as soon as possible to reestablish an independent home and living space.

Nurture the Sacred in Your Marriage

The Lord has counseled couples and families to constantly engage in spiritual practices that will invite the Spirit of the Lord to be present in their relationships. Married couples should develop a pattern of regular couple prayer, scripture reading, church attendance, tithe paying, service, and temple worship. In young adulthood and while dating, individuals should establish personal patterns of these practices—which will set the pattern for couple patterns in later courtship and marriage. These sacred practices recognize the divine triangle of marriage and seek to invite the presence of the Lord into our homes and relationships.

Equal Partnership (Equality)

THE DIVINE PATTERN FOR MAKING DECISIONS IN MARRIAGE

CHAPTER 5

> In the marriage companionship there is neither inferiority nor superiority. The woman does not walk ahead of the man; neither does the man walk ahead of the woman. They walk side by side as a son and daughter of God on an eternal journey.
>
> *President Gordon B. Hinckley*

To this point, you have been introduced to several principles that should help you better understand what it means to view marriage as a divine institution. Specifically, we have discussed how eternal marriage is the centerpiece of the Lord's plan of happiness and that this pattern for marriage is based on the doctrines of discipleship, covenants, and cleaving. These foundation principles provide you with broad perspectives, insights, and understandings that should give you guidance in becoming a right person for marriage and in finding a right person to marry.

In the next two chapters (Chapter 5 and Chapter 6), we build on these foundation principles and discuss the *divine design of marriage*. The divine design of marriage consists of two *core principles—equal partnership* and *family stewardships* or the sacred responsibilities of husbands and wives. These principles are labeled as "core principles" because they teach couples the Lord's pattern for successfully handling two central aspects of marriage and family life. *Equal partnership* is the Lord's pattern for how husbands and wives should *make decisions and resolve differences* in their marriage relationship. *Family stewardships* come from prophetic teachings on the sacred responsibilities of fathers and mothers and teach us how to *organize our marriages* to fulfill our divine stewardship to meet the needs of children in our families. In this chapter we will discuss the principle of equal partnership and in the next chapter we will discuss family stewardships.

The Divine Design

Our focus for this chapter comes from paragraph seven of the Proclamation on the Family, which reads:

> By *divine design*, fathers are to preside over their families in love and righteousness and are responsible to provide the necessities of life and protection for their families. Mothers are primarily responsible for the nurture of their children. In these sacred responsibilities, fathers and mothers are obligated to help one another as equal partners. (The Family: A Proclamation to the World, 1995, ¶ 7)

When properly understood, these lines of prophetic instruction summarize the essence of what it means to live according to the divine design of marriage and family life. The first three words are particularly noteworthy: "By divine design." What does this mean? Simply stated, it means that our loving Father in Heaven has a pattern for each of us to follow in organizing and structuring our marriages and families. The divine design of marriage is a blueprint or template to teach us the proper pattern for marriage in this life and in the eternities. It should be noted that the divine design of marriage taught in the Proclamation on the Family blends the stewardships of marriage and parenting (e.g., husbands/fathers and wives/mothers). While our focus here is on marriage, the divine design also provides core principles for the stewardship of parenting together as fathers and mothers.

The Proclamation on the Family teaches us that God's pattern for marriage consists of specific sacred responsibilities that have been divinely given primarily to husbands/fathers, specifically to preside, to provide, and to protect; and primarily to wives/mothers to nurture—and that all of these are to be intertwined and united by the practice of equal partnership in marriage. It is in the proper *integration of these principles* that the power and purposes of God are fully manifest. Each of the principles discussed in this and the next chapter, such as equal partnership, presiding, and nurturing, can only be properly understood in relation to one another. You should study them as an *interconnected and interdependent eco-system*. Each principle must be understood in a way that supports and upholds the other principles.

Unfortunately, some individuals, couples, and cultures misunderstand these principles or do not fully appreciate how they must support and reinforce one another. In particular, I have found that many individuals struggle to describe how *equal partnership* and *presiding* can be integrated in the divine design of marriage. Is it possible to have both equal partnership and a presider in a family? The answer to this question is yes. But how is this done? Our objective in this chapter is to answer that very question.

Equal Partnership

Let's return to the conversation I told you about in the preface. When I was a graduate student at the

University of Minnesota many years ago, I became close friends with a classmate of mine named John. He is still one of my closest friends and we always try to get together when we attend professional conferences. John is from Eastern Canada and when we were first introduced to each other he had never met a member of the Church before. John grew up in a very religious Christian home and was a devout reader of the Bible. In fact, he had completed a Masters of Divinity degree before coming to the United States to pursue his doctoral degree in family studies. John and I would often eat lunch together and our conversations frequently turned to the subject of religion. He was very curious about the Church and would sometimes ask me about our beliefs and doctrines.

One day, John and I were eating lunch in the student union building on campus. The weather was snowy and about 10 degrees below zero, so neither of us had much desire to venture outside.

During this conversation, John asked me a question:

"Do Latter-day Saints believe in male headship?"

My initial response was,

"Well, I need a better understanding of what you mean by 'male headship' to answer your question."

His response was,

"It is when the father is the leader and ultimate decision maker in the home."

I thought for just a moment and then replied,

"If you put it that way, my answer is no."

I share this experience with you because the way my friend defined his question makes a very important distinction that can help you better understand how equal partnership needs to be distinguished from, and intertwined with, the sacred responsibilities of husbands and wives in marriage. My friend's question provides an important starting point for our exploration of the doctrine of equal partnership in marriage. Let's explore some principles and then we'll return to my conversation with John.

Why did I tell John no? Ultimately it is because

the notion of "male headship" he described does not fit the divine principle of equal partnership. *Equal partnership* is the overarching principle within the divine design of marriage which must always be preserved and strengthened by how we fulfill our stewardships as husbands and wives. Put another way, presiding and nurturing are done in service to equal partnership, not the other way around. *Presiding cannot eclipse equal partnership*. Let me say that again, presiding cannot eclipse equal partnership. If a husband's pattern of presiding does not foster and strengthen his wife's sense of equal partnership within the marriage, something is not right.

Equal Partners: Equality, Not Hierarchy

The Lord intends for marriage to be one of true equality and partnership. As we just read in the Proclamation on the Family, "fathers and mothers are obligated to help one another as equal partners" (¶ 7).The apostle Paul declared, "Neither is the man without the

women, neither the women without the man, in the Lord" (1 Cor. 11:11). President Gordon B. Hinckley taught,

> In the marriage companionship there is neither inferiority nor superiority. The woman does not walk ahead of the man; neither does the man walk ahead of the woman. They walk side by side as a son and daughter of God on an eternal journey. (Ensign, May 2002, p. 52)

The notion of hierarchy, where one spouse is put above or ahead of the other is contrary to God's design for marriage.

Equal Partnership and the Divine Triangle

Previously, when we discussed the nature of the marriage covenant (see Chapter 4), you were introduced to the concept of the *Divine Triangle of Marriage*. This is an important principle to bring into our discussion here. The divine triangle captures the fact that the ordinance of marriage involves two interdependent covenants—a covenant with God and a covenant with our spouse. This *triangle covenant* helps us envision how true equal partnership can be maintained in marriage. The source of authority resides outside both the husband and the wife. It resides with God and within the principles of the gospel.

...reciprocal service requires husbands and wives to stand as equals in their homes; neither husbands nor wives should exercise authority over the other. . .righteous husbands and wives do not try to rule over each other; rather, each submits to the principles of the gospel and allows these principles to govern. (Hawkins et al., Strengthening Our Families, 2000, p. 65).

President James E. Faust taught how the divine triangle in marriage helps couples make decisions as equal partners. In the General Relief Society Meeting of the Church he taught,

> Now a word to you sisters who are married. In a very substantial way, you sisters make our homes a refuge of peace and happiness in a troubled world. A righteous husband is the bearer of the priesthood, which priesthood is the governing authority of the home. But he is not the priesthood; he is the holder of the priesthood. His wife shares the blessings of the priesthood with him. He is not elevated in any way above the divine status of his wife. (Ensign, November 2002, p. 110)

Notice how President Faust distinguishes between "the priesthood" and a "priesthood holder." What does he mean by this? In an effort to help us better understand a true doctrine, President Faust is explaining how decision-making should be done within the divine triangle of marriage. The *priesthood* is the governing

---

Equal Partners: Side by Side

In the marriage companionship there is neither inferiority nor superiority. The woman does not walk ahead of the man; neither does the man walk ahead of the woman. They walk side by side as a son and daughter of God on an eternal journey.

—Pres. Gordon B. Hinckely, Ensign, May 2002, p. 52

authority in the home—which authority belongs to and comes from the Lord. It is the revealed word of the Lord and the principles of the gospel that should govern in the home. A *priesthood holder* has a divine commission to preside in the home, but he is not the governing authority—God is. Together, husbands and wives should prayerfully seek the will of the Lord as they make unified decisions.

Equal Counsel and Equal Consent

John listened intently as I explained to him that Latter-day Saints believe that God intends for husbands and wives to be true partners, without hierarchy or one placed above the other. It was clear from my response that John was worried that he had not explained himself very well. After my response, he rephrased his question,

"Do Latter-day Saints believe in benevolent male headship?"

Once again I asked for a clarification of what he meant by "benevolent" male headship. He explained that benevolent male headship is a pattern where a husband counsels with his wife before he personally makes important family decisions. He emphasized that a benevolent husband is seeking to do the will of the Lord and follow the pattern of Christ in sacrificing himself for the wellbeing of his wife and children. It is within this context that a husband is the leader and ultimate decision maker in the home.

I thanked John for his explanation. I admired my friend for his deep understanding of the New Testament which was evident in his explanation of benevolent male headship. Then I looked at him and said: "If in the end, the husband is the ultimate decision maker in the home—then my answer is still no."

Why would I tell John no? Is it not the responsibility of husbands to be a leader in their families and seek after the model of Christ? Of course it is. But the trouble with the notion of benevolent male headship is that even though it calls for benevolent or kind motives, it still implies a hierarchy between husbands and wives in decision making in their marriage. The wife is still viewed as a counselor or consultant, not a full-fledged equal decision maker. Wives have an equal responsibility to be leaders in their homes. Put another way, the pattern of benevolent male headship introduces the concept of *equal counsel* to marital decision making (i.e., a husband should consult with his wife), but it does not include prophetic teachings about *equal consent* in marriage (i.e., a husband and wife prayerfully coming to a unified decision). The divine design of marriage calls upon husbands and wives to be equal partners who make decisions with *both* equal counsel and equal consent.

Prayerfully Come to a Unified Decision

President Howard W. Hunter taught a pattern of decision making in marriage that involves both equal counsel and equal consent when he taught,

> A man who holds the priesthood accepts his wife as a partner in the leadership of the home and family *with full knowledge of and full participation in all decisions relating thereto.* Of necessity there must be in the Church and in the home a presiding officer. By divine appointment, the responsibility to preside in the home rests upon the priesthood holder. The Lord intended that the wife be a helpmeet for man (meet means equal)—that is, *a companion equal and necessary in full partnership.* Presiding in righteousness necessitates a shared responsibility between husband and wife; together you act with knowledge and participation in all family matters. (Ensign, November 1999, p. 49, emphasis added)

Notice how President Hunter emphasizes "*full* knowledge," "*full* participation," and "*full* partnership"

between husbands and wives in "*all* decisions" relating to family matters. He also taught that a "helpmeet" is very different than a "help mate." Meet means equal and this equality is the essence of equal partnership.

Other prophetic leaders have also stressed the need for both equal counsel and equal consent in the marriage partnership. Speaking to husbands, President Boyd K. Packer taught,

> When there is a family decision to be made that affects everyone, you and your wife together will seek whatever counsel you might need, and *together you will prayerfully come to a unified decision*. If you ever pull priesthood rank on her you will have failed. (Quoted by C. Broderick, In "One Flesh, One Heart: Putting Celestial Love Into Your Temple Marriage," 1986, p. 32, emphasis added)

In a recent general conference, Elder Dallin H. Oaks quoted President Spencer W. Kimball who said,

> When we speak of marriage as a partnership, let us speak of marriage as a full partnership. We do not want our LDS women to be silent partners or limited partners in that eternal assignment! Please be a contributing and full partner. (Ensign, November 2005, p. 24)

The Lord's pattern of marital decision making involves husbands and wives prayerfully coming to unified decisions—unified with each other and unified with the Lord. Elder Richard G. Scott taught this pattern when he said:

> The family proclamation states that a husband and wife should be equal partners. I feel assured that every wife in the Church would welcome that opportunity and support it. Whether it occurs or not depends upon the hus-

band. Many husbands practice equal partnership with their companion to the benefit of both and the blessing of their children. However, many do not. I encourage any man who is reluctant to develop an equal partnership with his wife to obey the counsel inspired by the Lord and do it. *Equal partnership yields its greatest benefit when both husband and wife seek the will of the Lord in making important decisions for themselves and for their family.* (Ensign, November 2008, p. 45–46, emphasis added)

Distinguish between Leadership & Decision Making

As I noted previously, one area of possible confusion for Latter-day Saint couples is they do not understand how to integrate the counsel within the Proclamation on the Family that calls upon fathers to "preside over their families in love and righteousness," with the teaching that "fathers and mothers are obligated to help one another as equal partners" (The Family: A Proclamation to the World, 1995, ¶ 7). Is it possible to have one preside in the home, yet truly live a pattern of equal partnership? The answer is simply yes. This is exactly what the Lord holds as the divine pattern of oneness in marriage (Gen 2:2–24; D&C 42:22).

The key to understanding these principles is to distinguish between leadership and decision-making. Family decision-making is something the prophets have counseled us should happen together as spouses—with *both* husband and wife seeking inspiration and revelation for their mutually shared family stewardship. Because it is a shared stewardship, both wives and husbands have *equal access to revelation* for their marriage and family. This is the essence of equal partnership. Husbands/fathers have the divine responsibility to preside over and lead their families according to the decisions that have already been prayerfully made together as a couple. If situations arise that require new decisions, husbands and wives should come together again to prayerfully make a new unified decision. Once that decision has been made, the father/husband has the responsibility to provide leadership in helping the family follow the mutually agreed upon course of action. This is the way that our prophets have taught us that husbands can *preside in equal partnership.*

The Metaphor of the Canoe

The metaphor of a couple in a canoe can help us envision how presiding in equal partnership functions in married life. Imagine a couple launching their canoe into a lake with the intention of paddling to the other side. As they get settled into the canoe, the couple must decide which point on the other side of the lake is their targeted destination. The question may be: *Should we paddle toward the big rock at the north end of the shore or for the fallen log at the south end of the shore?*

Understanding that they need to work together to reach the other side, this is a time when the couple should take their paddles out of the water and turn to face each other in their canoe. Together they should seek the counsel of the Lord as they prayerfully decide what course of action is best for them. When agreement is reached, the couple is ready to work as a team as they set out to reach the other side of the lake.

As the couple begins to paddle toward their chosen destination on the other side of the lake, each spouse will need to focus on his or her specific responsibilities for paddling on one side of the canoe. Without this balance, it will be easy for the canoe to veer off course or to even spin in circles. Circumstances will require that spouses frequently help each other by rowing together on the same side. Also, their progress needs to be constantly monitored to stay on course and, from time to time, steering corrections will be needed. This is where the need for a presider or leader comes in. As the priesthood holder, the husband is called upon to provide leadership in guiding the canoe towards the previously determined destination on the other side of the lake. He does not guide the canoe along a course of *his* choosing; rather he helps the couple steer toward the destination *they decided* upon together with the counsel of the Lord. A husband's efforts to look ahead and monitor the course allows his wife to give full attention to her sacred responsibilities and enables the couple to coordinate their efforts. Along the journey, couples will frequently be faced with new decisions about how things should be done or what course should be followed. Sometimes a new course will need to be set. When this occurs, couples should always huddle together to prayerfully come to a unified decision before they head off again in their marriage canoe.

The Example of the Eyrings

A number of years ago, President Henry B. Eyring was called to serve as a counselor in the First Presidency. Soon after this calling, a biographical article was written and published in the Ensign by Elder Robert

D. Hales on the life of President Eyring. In this article, we learn about a living example of equal partnership in President Eyring's marriage relationship with his wife, Kathleen. Elder Hales wrote:

> Nine years later Hal was enjoying tenure at Stanford and serving as bishop of the Stanford First Ward. With his in-laws living nearby, "things were set," he recalls. But in the middle of the night in 1971, Kathleen woke him with two unusual questions: "Are you sure you are doing the right thing with your life?" Wondering how they could be any happier, Hal asked, "What do you mean?" Kathleen replied, "Couldn't you be doing studies for Neal Maxwell?"
>
> Neal A. Maxwell had just been appointed Commissioner of the Church Educational System. Neither Hal nor Kathleen knew him, but Kathleen felt that perhaps her husband could be doing more to change lives.
>
> "Doing studies for Neal Maxwell—at my stage of my career?" Hal responded. After all, he thought, 'Doing studies' was something a young graduate student might do. Following a pause, Kathleen said, "Will you pray about it?"
>
> At that stage in his marriage, Hal knew better than to ignore his wife's counsel. He got out of bed, knelt, and uttered a prayer. "I got no answer," he says, "and I felt terrific about it because I didn't want to go anywhere."
>
> The following day during bishopric meeting, a voice that Hal has come to know well came to his mind and rebuked him for treating lightly his wife's prompting. "You don't know what way is up in your career," he was told. "If you ever get another job offer, you bring it to me."
>
> Hal was shaken by the experience and immediately returned home. "We've got a problem," he told Kathleen. He feared he had made a mistake by passing up several job offers he had received while at Stanford. "I had never prayed over any of them," he says.
>
> Humbled, he began praying about his future. Less than a week after Kathleen's late-night questions, Commissioner Maxwell called and invited Hal to be the president of Ricks College.
>
> "I went to Ricks knowing a couple of things," he says. "One is that I wasn't as much of a big shot as I thought I was in terms of my great position at Stanford. Another is that I knew my wife had received

> revelation before I did." (Ensign, July 2008, pp. 8–15)

Another experience from the marriage of President Eyring and his wife Kathleen also illustrates the Lord's pattern of presiding in equal partnership. Before being called as an apostle, President Eyring served for several years as the president of Ricks College (now BYU-Idaho). During his time as president, he was offered an executive position with a prestigious company that would require him to leave his position at the college and move his family to another part of the country. He recently described this experience:

> I considered the offer and prayed about it and even discussed it with the First Presidency. They responded with warmth and a little humor but certainly not with any direction. President Spencer W. Kimball listened to me describe the offer I had received from a large corporation and said: "Well, Hal, that sounds like a wonderful opportunity! And if we ever needed you, we'd know where to find you." They would have known where to find me, but my desires for professional success might have created a

pavilion that would make it hard for me to find God and harder for me to listen to and follow His invitations. My wife, sensing this, had a strong impression that we were not to leave Ricks College. I said, "That's good enough for me." But she insisted, wisely, that I must get my own revelation. And so I prayed again. This time I did receive direction, in the form of a voice in my mind that said, "I'll let you stay at Ricks College a little longer." (Ensign, October 2012 "Where is the Pavilion?)

These experiences are wonderful examples of shared decision making and equal partnership in marriage. Notice how President Eyring never acted as if this decision was *his decision*, rather it was viewed as a *shared decision* for his wife and him to make together. He fully recognized and embraced his wife's ability to seek revelation for their shared stewardship. As partners they sought the will of the Lord and without coercion or hierarchy they mutually followed His will.

The Patriarchal Priesthood and Marital Partnership

A few days after my initial conversation with John, I mentioned his questions to a member of my ward at that time. As we talked about the notion of male headship and how it differs from equal partnership, this ward member asked me two questions that highlighted some areas of possible confusion that members of the church may have when it comes to correctly understanding and applying the doctrine of equal partnership.

Although this ward member agreed with my responses to John's questions, he did have some concerns about how we should reconcile the doctrine of equal partnership with other teachings in the church. His first question was:

"But, don't we believe in the patriarchal priesthood?"

Of course we believe in the patriarchal nature of the priesthood, but what exactly does that mean? Similar to John's questions, a definition of terms is critical here. In our modern culture, the words "patriarchy"

and "patriarchal" have come to mean "of men" or being controlled by men. They clearly convey a system or pattern of hierarchy, not one of equity. However, this is not the meaning of the word connected to the priesthood in the scriptures. The root word *patri* in Latin means "father." Therefore, the literal translation of the phrase "patriarchal priesthood" is *the priesthood of the fathers*. This is a more accurate meaning that fits the gospel use of the term.

The patriarchal priesthood is not so called to imply a hierarchy between men and women. Instead, as President Ezra Taft Benson taught, it is called patriarchal because in ancient days it was handed down from faithful father to faithful son, and today frequently still is (see D&C 107:40–42). President Benson also taught that the patriarchal order is the family order of government, presided over by mothers and fathers (Ensign, August 1985, p. 61). President James E. Faust taught that "every father is to his family a patriarch and every mother a matriarch as co-equals in their distinctive parental roles" (Ensign, May 1996, p. 6). Therefore, the patriarchal priesthood is a reference to the *generational nature* of the priesthood—not the *gendered nature* of the priesthood. Properly understood and practiced, the priesthood unifies men and women; it does not separate them.

Presiding vs. Presiding

The next questions my fellow ward member asked were:

"Doesn't the gospel teach that there is a line of authority in how the church functions?"

"Isn't a marriage like a missionary companionship with a senior and junior companion or a bishop and his counselors?"

These questions capture a key way in which some individuals become confused about the true nature of equal partnership in marriage. Some of the confusion stems from the fact that we use the term "*preside*" within the church to refer to positions where individuals with priesthood keys have been called to serve in an authoritative stewardship over others. Because of this, some have interpreted 'presiding' to mean that after equal counsel, equal consent is not necessary because the husband, the presider, has the right to the final say. However, it is an error to infer that the principle of presiding in marriage and family life means the same thing that it does within the church. President Boyd K. Packer explained,

> In the Church there is a distinct line of authority. We serve where called by those who preside over us. In the home it is a partnership with husband and wife equally yoked together, sharing in decisions, always working together. (Ensign, May 1998, p. 73)

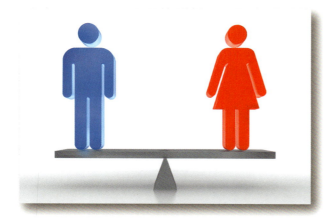

Marriage is a unique co-stewardship relationship that requires a unique form of presiding and partnership. Elder Dallin H. Oaks has also taught,

A most important difference in the functioning of priesthood authority in the family and in the Church results from the fact that the government of the family is *patriarchal*, whereas the government of the Church is *hierarchical*. The concept of partnership functions differently in the family than in the Church. The family proclamation gives this beautiful explanation of the relationship between a husband and a wife: While they have separate responsibilities, "in these sacred responsibilities, fathers and mothers are obligated to help one another as equal partners." (Ensign, November 2005, p. 24, emphasis added)

Presiding vs. Presiding

> A most important difference in the functioning of priesthood authority in the family and in the Church results from the fact that the government of the family is patriarchal, whereas the government of the Church is hierarchical. The concept of partnership functions differently in the family than in the Church. The family proclamation gives this beautiful explanation of the relationship between a husband and a wife: While they have separate responsibilities, "in these sacred responsibilities, fathers and mothers are obligated to help one another as equal partners.
>
> —Elder Dallin H. Oaks, Ensign, November 2005, p. 24, emphasis added

Although we use the term *preside* in both the church and in the home, they do not have the same meaning. A presiding officer in a ward or stake of the church follows the pattern of equal counsel with their counselors in making decisions, but he or she does not necessarily follow the principle of equal consent.

A Bishop or Relief Society president has been given a stewardship and authority that is above his or her counselors—their callings are *hierarchical*. The hierarchical nature of the stewardship means that a Bishop or Relief Society president has access to revelation above and beyond what is available to their counselors or to others in their ward. This pattern fosters order in the church in that only those with properly ordained authority will receive the revelation needed for the church, a stake, or a ward.

As we have noted previously, the marriage stewardship is shared between husbands and wives—their callings are *patriarchal*. President Boyd K. Packer taught,

> We find in that an equality of the brethren who hold the priesthood and the women who stand at their side. We work together, and we are organized first as families. We all have the right to inspiration and revelation, and oh, how we need it in this world, especially in the great challenge of raising a family. (Worldwide Leadership Training Meeting: Building Up a Righteous Posterity, February 2008, p. 4)

Because husbands and wives are co-equals in this stewardship, both have access to the same level of revelation and guidance for their marriage and families. Thus, the pattern of presiding in the home differs from the pattern of presiding in the church.

Equal Partnership: Summary

How then does a couple live in equal partnership and still honor the sacred responsibility fathers have to preside over their families? Our prophetic leaders in both word and example have shown us that the key is for spouses to make a distinction between *decision making* and *leadership*. With decisions made together as co-equals in the home, wives and husbands are then prepared to support and assist one another in their interdependent, yet distinct primary responsibilities. Following Christ's example, husbands should preside over their families and provide leadership that will guide the family towards the decisions the couple has made in unity with one another. This type of leadership toward mutually-determined goals fosters a sense of partnership and unity between spouses, rather than a sense of competition or mistrust. Similarly, this type of approach honors:

1. The mutual stewardship of marriage,
2. The revealed truth that both spouses are entitled to divine revelation for their family, and
3. Fosters oneness in marriage as spouses mutually seek the will of the Lord for their marriage.

Family Stewardships (Unity)

Meeting Children's Needs in Eternal Families
CHAPTER 6

> In the Lord's plan, it takes two—a man and a woman—
> to form a whole. Indeed, a husband and wife are not two
> identical halves, but a wondrous, divinely determined combination
> of complementary capacities and characteristics.
>
> *Elder Richard G. Scott*

As you studied in the previous chapter, equal partnership is the Lord's pattern for how husbands and wives should make decisions and resolve differences in their marriage relationship. It is one of two core principles in understanding the Lord's divine design for marriage. However, this principle does not stand alone in the Lord's plan of husband and wife relationships. Within the divine institution of marriage, husbands and wives have each been given sacred responsibilities to fulfill as spouses and parents. Our purpose in this chapter is to better understand what those family stewardships are and how they are interdependent within marriage.

Remember that our focus for this chapter comes from paragraph seven of the Proclamation on the Family, which reads:

By divine design, fathers are to preside over their families in love and righteousness and are responsible to provide the necessities of life and protection for their families. Mothers are primarily responsible for the nurture of their children. In these sacred responsibilities, fathers and mothers are obligated to help one another as equal partners (1995, ¶ 7).

As you begin this chapter, remember that the Proclamation on the Family teaches us that God's pattern for marriage consists of specific sacred responsibilities that have been divinely given to husbands/fathers (to preside, to provide, and to protect) and wives/mothers (to nurture) which are to be intertwined and united by the practice of equal partnership in marriage. It is in the proper *integration of these principles* that the power and purposes of God are fully manifest. Each of the principles discussed in this chapter (e.g., presiding, nurturing, etc.) can only be properly understood in relation to one

another. You should study them as an interconnected and interdependent eco-system. Each principle must be understood in a way that supports and upholds the other principles.

FAMILY STEWARDSHIPS

In the previous chapter, I introduced you to conversations I had years ago with a friend named John and a member of my ward. The day after my conversation with the member of my ward, I again ate lunch with John. We were joined this time by another friend who would eat lunch with us from time to time. I had found some quotes from church leaders that I wanted to share with John about our previous conversation. Our friend listened intently to our conversation for a couple of minutes and then she interjected with two questions that furthered the conversation. Her first question was descriptive in nature, she asked:

"What do Latter-day Saints believe are the roles of husbands and wives?"

Now, before we answer this question, note that my friend used the term *roles* of husbands and wives. The Proclamation on the Family uses the phrase "sacred responsibilities" to describe family stewardships. This distinction is important. A role assumes a status or position, possibly conveying what a person is entitled to receive because of their status. A role is also the term we use for someone acting in a play or movie—suggesting that we can play our role even if it is not who we are or a representation of our true self. Also, the term role focuses on tasks or duties rather than principles and responsibilities. The use of the term *sacred responsibilities* in the Family Proclamation reminds us that being a husband or wife is a stewardship—something we commit to do (similar to our previous discussion of rites vs. rights in Chapter 4). Also, this term from the Proclamation on the Family reminds us that these stewardships are sacred in nature—not just a personal ideology about who does what chores when it comes to housework. They are part of the Lord's divine design for marriage.

MEETING THE NEEDS OF CHILDREN

To correctly understand why our Father in Heaven has designated primary family stewardships in marriage, we need to consider again what it means to view marriage as a divine institution, rather than just a couple relationship. In God's plan, marriage exists to bring about divine ends or purposes. The primary purpose of marriage is to create eternal families that allow each of us to return to the presence of our Heavenly Parents so we can emulate the eternal life they live. So, in the divine plan of happiness, marriage is linked to the creation of families.

When we appreciate the inherent link between marriage and family formation, we recognize the essential role of marriage in the procreation and nurturance of children. President Gordon B. Hinckley taught:

> Every individual in the world is a child of a mother and a father. Neither can ever escape the consequences of their parenthood. Inherent in the very act of creation is responsibility for the child who is created. None can with impunity run from that responsibility. It is not enough simply to provide food and shelter for the physical being. There is an equal responsibility to provide nourishment and direction to the spirit and the mind and the heart.
>
> . . . The very structure of our society is now threatened by broken homes and the tragic consequences of those homes. I believe that with effort we can change this course. We must begin with parents. We must provide understanding on the part of every man and woman of the eternal purposes of life, of the obligations of marriage, and of the responsibilities of

parenthood. (Ensign, 1993, Bring Up a Child in the Way He Should Go)

Family stewardships focus on husbands and wives unifying to meet the needs of their children and provide for them that which they cannot provide for themselves. This unity in purpose has a unique way to connect spouses to a cause greater than themselves, which enriches their marriage and gives them a shared vision of the good life.

Three Ps and One N

So what are the sacred responsibilities of husbands/fathers and wives/mothers in marriage and parenting? According to the Proclamation on the Family, these responsibilities can be primarily summarized as the three "*Ps*" of the primary stewardship of husbands/fathers and the one "*N*" of the priamry stewardship of wives/mothers. The three Ps of husbands and fathers include: to *preside*, to *provide*, and to *protect;* while wives and mothers are instructed to take a primary stewardship in the *nurturing* of their children.

Thinking about the stewardships of parents in these terms can give us some important insights. If you'll think back to your math classes in junior high and high school you may remember the experience of balancing equations (I know high school math is not the best memory for some of you—sorry!). If we turn this part of the Proclamation into a math equation, we get:

$$3P = 1N$$

Now, we know that the sign in the middle of the equation must be an equals sign, right? In Chapter 5 we discussed in detail how husbands and wives are intended to be equal partners in marriage. So, an equal sign is needed in the middle of our equation—not a "greater than" or "lesser than" sign (there are no alligators turning to eat one of the numbers here!).

So, what does the equation 3P = 1 N tell us about the nature and value of N? We know immediately that N is large and significant. This is an important starting point for us in understanding the interdependent nature of the stewardships given to husbands and wives. The three "*Ps*" of husbands' primary stewardships only have meaning and purpose in the context of the *"N"*—in fact, all three are intended to create and foster an environment where nurturing can optimally take place.

The sacred responsibilities of fathers

In the Proclamation on the Family, we learn that husbands/fathers have a multi-pronged primary stewardship in their families. By divine design, fathers are called upon to *preside* in their families, to *provide* the necessities of life, and to *protect* their families.

Preside in Love and Righteousness

The primary family stewardship of husbands and fathers is to "preside in love and righteousness" in their homes. In our previous chapter, we discussed the principle of presiding extensively in relation to equal partnership and decision making in marriage. In that chapter, we noted the need to distinguish *decision making* from *leadership* in the principle of presiding. Decision making is a shared stewardship for the couple, whereas presiding is a form of leadership and ties to sacred responsibilities given to fathers as priesthood holders in their home. It is important to note that presiding isn't the only form of leadership in a family. In fact, a good way to view all of these family stewardships is as forms or areas of leadership. The primary stewardship to nurture is as much a form of leadership as is presiding.

CHAPTER 6: Family Stewardships (Unity) 71

There are at least three key aspects of presiding in marriage and family life:

1. First, Christ should be a husband's model for providing leadership in the home. Presiding should *emulate the perfect love of the Savior* and seek the wellbeing of one's spouse and children. Presiding should be a process where fathers seek to know and do the will of God, rather than to use their leadership to impose or enforce their will or desires.

2. The Lord's pattern of leadership was one of *servant leadership*. The Savior taught his disciples, ". . . but whosoever will be great among you, let him be your minister; And whosoever will be chief among you, let him be your servant. Even as the Son of man came not to be ministered unto, but to minister . . ." (Matt 20:25–27). The term *minister* means to serve and care for others. This type of leadership involves continual service, often at significant personal sacrifice.

3. As a priesthood holder, husbands and fathers have the divine commission to lead their families in family worship activities and to administer the ordinances and covenants of the gospel to their families. This involves leading out in family prayer, scripture reading, church attendance, temple attendance, church service, community service, and other forms of worshiping and serving as a couple and family. As presiders, fathers also act as a liaison with church leaders and other outside institutions that the family interacts with. By overseeing the boundaries and interactions *between* the family and others, mothers are better able to oversee and monitor the boundaries and interactions *within* the family.

Elder L. Tom Perry emphasized these principles when he taught Priesthood holders that:

Fatherhood is leadership, the most important kind of leadership. . . Your leadership in the home must include leading in family worship. You preside at the meal table, at family prayer. You preside at family home evening; and as guided by the Spirit of the Lord, you see that your children are taught correct principles. . . You give father's blessings. You take an active part in establishing family rules and discipline. As a leader in your home you plan and sacrifice to achieve the blessing of a unified and happy family. To do all of this requires that you live a family-centered life.

Remember, brethren, that in your role as leader in the family, your wife is your companion. Since the beginning, God has instructed mankind that marriage should unite husband and wife together in unity. Therefore, there is not a president or a vice president in a family. The couple works together eternally for the good of the family. They are united together in word, in deed, and in action as they lead, guide, and direct their family unit. They are on equal footing. They plan and organize the affairs of the family jointly and unanimously as they move forward. (Ensign, May 2004, p. 69)

Provide the Necessities of Life and Protection

By divine design, husbands/fathers are also primarily responsible to provide for the temporal needs of their wives and children. This includes providing for all aspects of physical care such as sheltering, feeding, educating, clothing, and providing for healthcare needs. Because of this lofty responsibility, young men in the Church are encouraged in the Duties of the Aaronic Priesthood to "obtain as much education as possible" in their teen and young adult years in order to increase their capacity as a provider. This kind of preparation has always been important, but is becoming even more important in our modern economy that places a value on professional services and technology training, as well as skilled-labor skills in various trades.

In addition to presiding and providing, fathers are responsible to provide protection for their wives and children. While this part of a man's family stewardship may evoke images of Captain Moroni and the Title of

Liberty, more often than not it involves providing temporal and spiritual safeguards for one's family. Temporally, husbands and fathers should make preparations to provide in times of plenty and in times of adversity. You cannot afford to assume that life will always go according to your plans. Safeguards such as: financial savings, health insurance, life insurance, food storage, emergency preparedness, and other aspects of family readiness all fall under a father's divine stewardship to provide and protect his family. Think of how important life insurance would be to a young mother whose husband passes away or the difference a well-prepared food storage would make to a family if the husband/father loses his job for a season. Young men should make a point of learning about these aspects of family provisioning and make themselves ready to provide as much as possible in all of these aspects of family life. We will discuss family finances and principles of provident living in Chapter 19.

Spiritually, fathers can provide safeguards to their families such as priesthood blessings, administering sacred ordinances, and leading in family worship. There is divine protection for all people who worthily make and keep gospel ordinances in their lives. Social science research has also shown that fathers can protect their children spiritually by spending time with them and being involved in their lives. Numerous studies have found that children and teens that grow up with highly involved fathers are less likely to use drugs, be sexually permissive, struggle in school, have children out-of-wedlock, or engage in delinquent and criminal behavior. A father's loving presence can provide protection, both physically and spiritually, for his family.

Sometimes young men feel that preparing for the three-pronged stewardship of marriage and family life

Primary Sacred Responsibilities of Fathers and Mothers

Fathers

Preside in Love and Righteousness

- Christ is the model: perfect love, seek the will of God
- Servant leadership/minister: continual service, often at significant personal sacrifice
- Priesthood holder responsibilities: lead family worship, administer blessings and ordinances, liaison with church and outside institutions

Provide the Necessities of Life and Protection

- Provide temporal support: readiness to provide, obtain as much education as possible
- Safeguards: savings, insurance, family preparedness, etc.
- Spiritual and physical protection: spending time, sacred covenants and ordinances, safe neighborhood and family environment

Mothers

Nurture of Their Children

- Meeting the personal needs of each child
- Nurturance of their physical bodies, their mental education, their social development, and the spiritual progression
- Development of a testimony of Christ and using their agency to make and keep covenants with their Father in Heaven
- Foster the well-being of society as the accumulative effect of mothering directs the course of communities and societies

providing for a family. As you prepare for marriage, partner with the Lord and he will work together with you to meet your sacred responsibilities as a husband and father. Also, finding balance between the interconnected stewardships of presiding, providing, and protecting can be challenging, particularly for young husbands and fathers who are trying to finish schooling and get established in their careers.

However, providing for one's family should never eclipse a father's primary stewardship of presiding in their families. How can a husband and father know if he is devoting too much time to providing? Simply put, if a father does not have the time and energy to

is overwhelming and scary. If you ever feel this way, remind yourself that these stewardships are part of the Lord's divine design for marriage. He will provide a way for you to fulfill His divine purposes, which includes

meaningfully preside in his home, then he is spending too much time providing. Of course, work, church, and other commitments are important and will require the sacrifice of marriage and family time occasionally, but we should be mindful to not set the pattern of letting important matters take precedence over essential ones.

The sacred responsibilities of mothers

In the Proclamation on the Family, we are taught that, "mothers are primarily responsible for the nurture of their children" (¶ 7). As we mentioned, all of a father's stewardships only have meaning and purpose in relation to the nurturing of children. They are to provide a context in which nurturing can occur. So what exactly is meant by the term nurturing and why has God given this sacred primary stewardship to women? President Spencer W. Kimball taught:

> To be a righteous woman is a glorious thing in any age. To be a righteous woman during the winding up scenes on this earth, before the second coming of our Savior, is an especially noble calling. The righteous woman's strength and influence today can be tenfold what it might be in more tranquil times. (New Era, January 1979, p. 42)

More recently, Elder D. Todd Christofferson further taught:

> "Women bring with them into the world a certain virtue, a divine gift that makes them adept at instilling such qualities as faith, courage, empathy, and refinement in relationships and cultures. . .most

sacred is a woman's role in the creation of life. We know that our physical bodies have a divine origin and that we must experience both a physical birth and a spiritual rebirth to reach the highest realms in God's celestial kingdom. Thus, women play an integral part in God's work and glory "to bring to pass the immortality and eternal life of man." (Ensign, 2013, The Moral Force of Women)

In our Father in Heaven's plan, nurturance is a broad term. It refers to a number of parenting behaviors including attachment, warmth, support, and attending to children's needs. Nurturance is far more than just caring for a child's physical needs. Nurturance involves the development of children's bodies, minds, and spirits. In 1942, the First Presidency of the Church taught,

> Motherhood becomes a holy calling, a sacred dedication for carrying out the Lord's plans, a consecration of devotion to the uprearing and fostering, the nurturing in body, mind, and spirit, of those who kept their first estate and who come to this earth for the second estate "to see if they will do all things whatsoever the Lord their God shall command them" (Abraham 3:25). To lead them to keep their second estate is the work of motherhood, and they who keep their second estate shall have glory added upon their heads forever and ever. (Conference Report, October 1942, pp. 759, 761)

Our Father in Heaven has declared that His work and purpose is to bring to pass the eternal life of His children. This is the same purpose of wives and mothers—to bring to pass eternal life is the essence of nurturing. Elder M. Russell Ballard taught:

> The proclamation teaches that mothers are primarily responsible for the nurture of their children. Nurtur-

ing refers to parenting behaviors such as warmth, support, bonding, attachment, recognizing each child's unique abilities, and attending to children's needs. Nurturing in and of itself is more important in the development of a child than is any particular method or technique of child rearing. It hardly needs saying that nurturing is best carried out in a stable, safe, family context...

A mother's nurturing love arouses in children, from their earliest days on earth, an awakening of the memories of love and goodness they experienced in their premortal existence. Because our mothers love us, we learn, or more accurately remember, that God also loves us. (Ensign, March 2006, pp. 26–33)

One particular line of thought argues that this dedication to home and family limits a woman's opportunities and constrains her development. This way of thinking disconnects a mother's wellbeing from the wellbeing of her child. In recent years, thousands of studies have validated what is called the *Attachment Theory* of child development. This theory suggests that children come into the world biologically pre-programmed to form attachments with others, because this will help them to survive. The studies using this theory have proven that both infants <u>and</u> mothers have evolved a biological need to stay in contact with each other and that children need an attachment figure, primarily their mothers, to act as a secure base for exploring the world. This attachment relationship acts as a prototype for all future social relationships, what child development experts call our "internal working model." Studies have shown that disrupting the attachment bond by not giving sustained and dedicated nurturance to a child can have severe consequences for children—and therefore their mothers as well.

The idea that women are limited by motherhood devalues the types of growth and progression that are possible in the divine stewardship of nurturing. Nurturing a child can be one of the most profoundly transformative experiences in a woman's life. Sister Neill F. Marriott, explains:

> The Lord's Church needs Spirit-directed women who use their unique gifts to nurture, to speak up, and to defend gospel truth. Our inspiration and intuition are necessary parts of building the kingdom of God, which really means doing our part to bring salvation to God's children. We build the kingdom when we nurture others. However, the first child of God we must build up in the restored gospel is ourselves. Love is making space *in* your life for someone else.
>
> Mothers literally make room in their bodies to nurture an unborn baby—and hopefully a place in their hearts as they raise them—but nurturing is not limited to bearing children. Eve was called a "mother" before she had children. I believe that "to mother" means "to give life." Think of the many ways you give life. It could mean giving emotional life to the hopeless or spiritual life to the doubter. With the help of the Holy Ghost, we can create an emotionally healing place for the discriminated against, the rejected, and the stranger. In these tender yet powerful ways, we build the kingdom of God. Sisters, all of us came to earth with these life-giving, nurturing, maternal gifts because that is God's plan.
>
> When we ask ourselves, "What shall we do?" let's ponder this question: "What does the Savior do continually?" He nurtures. He creates. He encourages growth and goodness. Women and sisters, we can do these things! Primary girls, is there someone in your family who needs your love and kindness? You build the kingdom by nurturing others too.
>
> Our high responsibility is to become women who follow the Savior, nurture with inspiration, and live truth fearlessly. As we ask Father in Heaven to

make us builders of His kingdom, His power will flow into us and we will know how to nurture, ultimately becoming like our heavenly parents. (What Shall We Do?, April 2016)

Maternal nurturing is very important in our Father in Heaven's plan. It is important to the well-being of children and all of society. It is also important to the well-being of wives, husbands, and marriages. Perhaps this is why our prophetic leaders have always taught that motherhood is near to divinity. We live in a time when maternal nurturing is diminished in the eyes of many. In our efforts to form disciple marriages, women, and men, need to develop and maintain a testimony of the sacred stewardship of nurturing—and pattern their families according to this divine design of marriage.

Family Stewardships—Key Principles

There are several principles that we need keep in mind as we strive to properly understand and live these family stewardships.

Principle #1—These Are Personal Stewardships

One of the biggest misunderstandings of the family stewardships taught in the Proclamation on the Family is the mistaken belief that they create a one-size fits all pattern for families. While these family stewardships teach principles and priorities, they do not determine the specific practices families will engage in to meet their family's needs. This is why these dimensions of family life need to be seen as stewardships, not roles or positions. The stewardships are interconnected and are about meeting family needs. Families involve unique people and unique circumstances. Parents should prayerfully seek direction from the Lord in finding their path.

Principle #2—Primarily Does Not Mean Exclusively

While divine family stewardships invite fathers and mothers to provide leadership in specific domains of family life, they should not create a sense of exclusive or rigidly divided patterns. The Proclamation of the Family uses the phrase "primarily responsible," not "exclusively responsible" or "solely responsible." Of course, fathers should also nurture their children, and mothers will need to provide for and protect their children in various ways.

Understanding that primary stewardships are not exclusive or sole stewardships is a particularly important one when responding to the concern that the stewardship of motherhood limits or constrains women. Our prophetic leaders have taught that we need to have a broad and inclusive vision of motherhood and the various decisions women and their spouses make in balancing family and other pursuits in their lives. President HInckley taught this when he said,

> In this day and time, a girl needs an education. She needs the means and skills by which to earn a living should she find herself in a situation where it becomes necessary to do so. The whole gamut of human endeavor is now open to women. There is not

The Whole Gamut of Human Endeavor

In this day and time, a girl needs an education. She needs the means and skills by which to earn a living should she find herself in a situation where it becomes necessary to do so. The whole gamut of human endeavor is now open to women. There is not anything that you cannot do if you will set your mind to it. I am grateful that women today are afforded the same opportunity to study for science, for the professions, and for every other facet of human knowledge. You are as entitled as are men to the Spirit of Christ, which enlightens every man and woman who comes into the world.

You can include in the dream of the woman you would like to be a picture of one qualified to serve society and make a significant contribution to the world of which she will be a part. Set your priorities in terms of marriage and family, but also pursue educational programs which will lead to satisfying work and productive employment in case you do not marry, or to a sense of security and fulfillment in the event you do marry.

—Pres. Gordon B. Hinckley, 2007, Seek Learning

---

anything that you cannot do if you will set your mind to it. I am grateful that women today are afforded the same opportunity to study for science, for the professions, and for every other facet of human knowledge. You are as entitled as are men to the Spirit of Christ, which enlightens every man and woman who comes into the world. You can include in the dream of the woman you would like to be a picture of one qualified to serve society and make a significant contribution to the world of which she will be a part. Set your priorities in terms of marriage and family, but also pursue educational programs which will lead to satisfying work and productive employment in case you do not marry, or to a sense of security and fulfillment in the event you do marry. (2007, Seek Learning)

Principle #3—These Stewardships Vary Across the Seasons of Life

As the needs of children and families evolve through the stages of life, so do these stewardships. This means that individuals and couples make many ongoing decisions about how to balance family, work, and church responsibilities—not just one decision at one time. President James E. Faust taught that we should view these stewardships, particularly the stewardship of nurturing within the principle of *sequential living*. He said,

> Women today are being encouraged by some to have it all—generally all simultaneously: money, travel, marriage, motherhood, and separate careers in the world. . .doing things sequentially—filling roles one at a time at different times—is not always possible,

as we know, but it gives a woman the opportunity to do each thing well in its time and to fill a variety of roles in her life. . . A woman may fit more than one career into the various seasons of her life. She need not try to sing all the verses of her song at the same time. (Ensign, September 1986, p. 18)

The amount of time it takes to nurture a two year old is different than the time it takes to nurture a twenty-two year old. As the times and seasons of life change, so will the nature and demands of nurturing, providing and presiding. By allowing their lives to have "*multiple verses,*" wives and husbands will be able to bless the lives of their children, their spouses, and individuals outside their family.

Principle #4—Specific Patterns Are Difficult to Determine Ahead of Time

If we seek to be truly "needs-focused," then we must stay humble and adaptable as specific needs arise with our children and families. While each of us can make preparations, none of us will know ahead of time what the specific needs will be for our families. The key is to commit ourselves to living these stewardships and then prayerful approaching the various needs and circumstances that present themselves during the seasons of our life. At their core, these stewardships are about our priorities. Using Elder Oaks's oft-quoted phrase they teach us—"Good, Better, Best"—Put your family above the rest!

It Takes Two

Returning to my conversation with my friends, after I explained the sacred stewardships of husband/fathers and wives/mothers to my friends, she asked me a follow-up question. With a ridiculing tone in her voice she said:

> "How can you believe in 'equal partnership' if you believe that women and men have distinct responsibilities?"

It was obvious from my friend's question that she believed that equality can only occur when two peo-

Family Stewardships – Key Principles

- ■ **Personal Stewardships**
  Families involve unique people and unique circumstances; prayerfully seek direction from the Lord in finding your path.

- ■ **Primarily Does Not Mean Exclusively**
  Leadership in specific domains of family life does not mean exclusive or rigidly divided patterns.

- ■ **Seasons of Life**
  As the needs of children and families evolve through the stages of life, so do these stewardships; many decisions, not just one.

- ■ **Difficult to Determine Ahead of Time**
  If we seek to be truly "needs-focused," then we must stay humble and adaptable as specific needs arise with our children and families.

- ■ **Priorities**
  "Good, Better, Best" – Put your family above the rest!

ple are the same. But this is not the Lord's pattern of equality. The Lord's plan for marital equality lies in recognizing the unique and irreplaceable purposes both husbands and wives have in family life and that these divine responsibilities can only be fully accomplished in a marriage of equals. Elder Richard G. Scott said:

> In the Lord's plan, it takes two—a man and a woman—to form a whole. Indeed, a husband and wife are not two identical halves, but a wondrous, divinely determined combination of complementary capacities and characteristics .(Ensign, November 1996, p. 73)

Dr. Alan Hawkins and colleagues commented:

> One of the most revolutionary aspects of the restored gospel is its ability to help us envision difference without hierarchy, distinctiveness without inequality. This is what the Proclamation calls upon us to hold as the ideal relationship between husbands and wives. (Strengthening Our Families, 2001, p. 66)

Research on equality in marriage supports the principles of the Proclamation on the Family. Studies have shown that when spouses report that they are respected and listened to in their marriages there is increased couple intimacy, higher relationship satisfaction, and better mental health among the spouses. Conversely, in contexts of marital inequality research has found that spouses have less self-esteem, feelings of hostility towards their spouse, less satisfying intimacy, and less satisfaction with marriage in general.

Gender Ideologies

One of the primary ways you can prepare to live the divine design of marriage is to develop proper perspectives about the role of gender in marriage. Adherence to any ideology that is out of tune with the gospel will result in some degree of disharmony in your future marriage and family life. Dr. Hawkins and his colleagues have identified four common gender ideologies in current society and how they differ from God's divine design for marriage. These four ideologies include:

Independence vs. Interdependence

An independence view of gender asserts that mothers and fathers operate as individual units with mutually exclusive, non-overlapping functions. This is the classic notion of "women's work" and "men's work" in the home. This independence ideology stands in contrast to the interdependent view espoused in the Proclamation on the Family that states that fathers and mothers should work together as equal partners. An interdependent view of gender emphasizes over-lapping stewardships that emphasize shared purpose, joint responsibility, and collaboration between spouses.

Separateness vs. Oneness

One of the best selling self-help book of all time is entitled, *Men are From Mars, Women are From Venus*. This book and other sources in society proclaim a separate gender ideology that holds that men and women are fundamentally different from one another and that their natures are alien to one another. This type of perspective of gender often places men and women at odds

with each other, competing for whose needs and desires win out in relationships. This is in contrast to the oneness God intends in marriage. Although there are some difference between men and women, these differences are intended to be complementary in their expression and use.

Mistrust vs. Trust

A particularly prominent version of the separate gender ideology that is espoused these days is a mistrusting view of gender. This view holds that it is unwise for men and women to rely on each other in marriage because you can never fully trust in that person. Perhaps the most common form of this thinking is in the falsehood that marital equality cannot exist in marriages in which husbands trust wives to contribute to the family with full-time homemaking for a season and wives trust husbands to contribute to the family with full-time employment. Hence, from this perspective, married mothers should be engaged continuously in paid work in order to maintain economic independence and equality. Touching directly on this subject, President Henry B. Eyring said:

> It takes courage and faith to plan for what God holds before you as the ideal rather than what might be forced upon you by circumstances. (Ensign, February 1998, p. 66)

Trusting one's spouse is an essential part of righteous marriage. Spouses may prayerfully determine to have the mother work outside of the home to meet family needs, but this is very different than choosing that pattern because spouses don't trust each other. When spouses place complete trust in each other it stretches their faith in each other and in God.

Irrelevant vs. Divine Gender

The Proclamation on the Family makes it clear that gender is eternal; it predates and continues beyond mortality. Although we do not fully understand the eternal nature of gender, we should acknowledge its meaning and purpose, and humbly seek to understand and appreciate the nature of divine gender distinctions in God's plan for His children.

> "All human beings—male and female—are created in the image of God. Each is a beloved spirit son or daughter of heavenly parents, and, as such, each has a divine nature and destiny. Gender is an essential characteristic of individual premortal, mortal, and eternal identity and purpose."
>
> -The Family: A Proclamation to the World, paragraph 2

The idea that gender is eternal contrasts with modern ideas that gender is *socially-constructed* and, therefore, irrelevant to how a couple organizes their marriage. An irrelevant view of gender sees men and women as the same and, therefore, interchangeable in roles and responsibilities. Whereas an eternal view of gender recognizes that God has ordained divine gender distinctions. Therefore, men and women are not interchangeable as "parents"—mothers are not fathers, and fathers are not mothers. Mothers and fathers have divinely determined complementary capacities and characteristics that make them unique, and together they form a distinct type of parenting partnership. Children are entitled to this type of family. The First Presidency has taught:

> The special status granted marriage is nevertheless closely linked to the inherent powers and responsibilities of procreation and to the innate differences between the genders. By contrast, same-sex marriage is an institution no longer linked to gender—to the biological realities and complementary natures of male and female. Its effect is to decouple marriage from its central role in creating life, nurturing time-honored values, and fostering family bonds across generations. . . social science evidence supports the idea that gender differentiated parenting is important for human development and that the contribution of fathers to child rearing is unique and irreplaceable. . . The complementarity of male and female parenting styles is striking and of enormous importance to a child's overall development. (The Divine Institution of Marriage, p. 2, ¶ 4 & 6)

Why do these principles matter?

Why do the principles of the divine design of marriage matter so much? Why is it so crucial that we embrace and live the principles of equal partnership and the sacred stewardships of husbands and wives? There are two primary reasons for the importance of these principles. First, by governing and organizing our marriage according to God's pattern, we position ourselves to fully partner with the Lord in our marriages. In a sense, the divine design is the organizational pattern of the divine triangle of marriage. It places God's purposes and power at the center of our marriage and family life.

Second, the principles that make up the divine design of marriage help us avoid two myths about marriage. The first myth is the *Traditional Myth* that believes that there should be a hierarchy between men and women in marriage. This pattern erodes marital partnership and impedes true intimacy between spouses. The second myth is the *Modern Myth* that is espoused today that equality can only exist in marriages where men and women are the same. God's purposes are brought about by equal, but distinct, family stewardships for His beloved sons and daughters.

A Marital Metaphor

In conclusion, I would like to share a metaphor with you to help you remember the divine design of marriage. The true nature of marriage is like scissors—with two interdependent shears or blades. It doesn't make much sense to ask which shear is most important in a pair of scissors, does it? Without either one of the shears you are just pushing paper. It takes both blades for the scissors to accomplish their purpose and design.

If you take the analogy further, you'll see that most scissors also represent the sacred stewardships of fathers and mothers too. The handle of one shear is meant for three fingers, just like the three Ps of a husband's primary stewardship and the other handle is meant for one finger, just like the one N of a wife's primary stewardship. The two blades are not the same—but they are equally valuable to what can be created when they come together as one.

President Kimball taught,

> If two people love the Lord more than their own lives and then love each other more than their own lives, working together in total harmony with the gospel program as their basic structure, they are sure to have great happiness. When a husband and wife go together frequently to the holy temple, kneel in prayer together in their home with their family, go hand in hand to their religious meetings...and both are working together for the building up of the Kingdom of God, then happiness is at its pinnacle. (Ensign, March 1977, p. 3)

Throughout your life, whenever you see a pair of scissors, you can be reminded of the true nature and pattern of marriage that the Lord has revealed—His divine design for marriage.

Chastity (Intimacy)

Becoming One in Marriage
CHAPTER 7

> The Bible celebrates sex and its proper use, presenting it as God-created, God-ordained, God-blessed.... His commandment to the first man and woman to be "one flesh" was as important as his command to "be fruitful and multiply."
>
> Pres. Spencer W. Kimball

Brother Robert L. Millet, former Dean of the College of Religious Education at Brigham Young University, once related the following experience during a scripture discussion he participated in on BYUTV (I paraphrase the experience here to the best of my memory). This experience occurred while Brother Millet was serving as the bishop of a student ward at BYU. A young woman in his ward had come to him to confess sexual transgression. Bishop Millet related that as he counseled with her it become clear that she did not understand some fundamental doctrines related to the nature of sexual intimacy in God's plan for His children.

Bishop Millet asked her, "Why is it that what you have done is wrong?"

She replied, "Well, my parents always taught me that sex before marriage is wrong."

"That is correct," replied Bishop Millet, "Why did you think your parents taught you that?"

"Well, the Church teaches that sexual sin is wrong," she replied.

"That is correct," replied Bishop Millet, "Why does the church teach us that sexual sin is wrong?"

A little perplexed, the young woman continued, "Well, the scriptures teach that it's wrong."

"That is correct," replied Bishop Millet, "Why do the scriptures say that?"

"Well, I guess it is because Heavenly Father wants us to know that sex before marriage is wrong?" she replied with an increasingly puzzled voice.

"That is correct," replied Bishop Millet, "And why do you think Father in Heaven wants us to know that?"

That question was followed by a long pause. The young women did not know what else to say. Brother Millet went on to explain that this young woman's understanding was limited because she had only learned the *precepts* of the law of chastity, but she did not have a testimony of the *principles* behind the precepts. Put another way, she knew *what* constituted an unchaste behavior, but she did not have a testimony of *why* sexual purity is so important and *how* living the law of chastity would bless her life. Nor did she fully comprehend the possible *consequences* that her actions could have on her future marriage and family life.

Brother Millet went on to explain that this young woman's experience is not unique. In fact, its quite common as many young people come to understand chastity in this limited way. He went on to explain how the repentance process of this dear sister was not only about stopping unchaste behaviors, but also developing a chaste heart that understood and loved the doctrine of sexual purity and its role in forming and maintaining a lasting marriage.

In this chapter we examine the importance of chastity and the proper expression of sexual intimacy within God's plan for us. Our primary focus in this chapter is to answer one extremely important question—*why be chaste*? In order to answer this question, we will discuss foundation principles of chastity and sexuality and how these principles give us guidance for becoming one in marriage with our spouse. This chapter sets the foundation for later chapters on chastity during dating and engagement and sexual intimacy in marriage.

Metaphors of Sexual Purity

Many people have collections of various types. Some people collect stamps, others collect coins, and some people collect spoons. I have a collection too—but it is a little bit different than most people's collections. I have a collection of metaphors of personal purity. For the past several years, I have asked students and others to share with me how they learned about chastity, purity, and sexuality while growing up. In particular, I have been intrigued by parents' and church members' use of object lessons to teach young people about these topics. I discussed these metaphors in detail in my book "Sexual Wholeness in Marriage."

As I have collected these personal accounts about the ways young people in the Church learned about sexual intimacy, I have been struck by how nearly all of the object lessons in these lessons can be grouped into two types or categories. As I share these accounts with you, reflect on your own learning experiences with the topics of chastity and sexuality. Does your experience fit any of those described here?

Fear-Based Metaphors

Many of the object lessons that have been shared with me over the years fall into a group I call *Fear-Based Metaphors*. This label is not meant to imply that the parents or ward leaders who have used these examples were trying to scare their young learners. In fact, I believe that all of the individuals who have used these types of object lessons over the years were well-intending people who were trying to impress an important lesson upon the minds of their children or class members. However, nearly all of the students who told me about these object lessons told me that these experiences created unintended side effects of fear, anxiety, and negative messages about sexual intimacy.

What are some examples of fear-based metaphors? Typically, they are lessons that involve something being damaged or being made unclean. For example, a seminary teacher once showed a class a wrapped cupcake and asked the class members if any of them would like to eat it. After the students enthusiastically said they wanted the treat, the teacher unwrapped the cupcake and asked the class members to pass it around the room. After the members of the class had each handled the cupcake, the seminary teacher then asked—"who would like to eat the cupcake now?" The point of the lesson was clear, the "handled" cupcake was now unclean and undesirable. The instructor then drew a comparison between the cupcake and sexual involvement before marriage.

Other young people have told me about similar lessons where flowers were used and after the class members had all touched the petals of the flower they would wilt and turn brown. Again, the parallel was drawn that such inappropriate *touching* spoiled a beautiful thing—leaving it wilted and damaged.

Another young woman told me about an object lesson that was used at a Girls Camp where leaders taught the girls about the importance of sexual purity before marriage. As the young women gathered for a fireside, a beautiful wedding dress was brought out and held up as an example of what it means to be clean. During the lesson, as examples of unworthy and unclean behaviors were discussed, portions of the dress were cut out and thrown into the campfire.

Perhaps the most dramatic fear-based object lesson I have been told about occurred in a young women's lesson. A young women leader was comparing personal purity to a beautiful china plate. As she showed the girls the plate, she commented on its beauty and fine craftsmanship. She discussed its value and mentioned that it is worth a very high price. Then without warning, the leader turned and threw the plate against the wall, shattering it into pieces! The leader then told the girls that to be sexually impure before marriage was similar to throwing their "purity plate" against a wall.

Now, not all fear-based metaphors involve shattering plates or burning wedding dresses. A more common form of this type of fear-based teaching about sexual intimacy is found in the tone of the message, rather than the content conveyed by parents and others. Numerous young people have told me about finding chastity pamphlets under their pillow when they go to bed or discovering other materials that parents left for them to read, rather than discussing the topic face-to-face. Others shared experiences of parents who would become very uncomfortable with the topic of chastity; often changing the topic of conversation when it would come up. Sometimes parents follow a strict gender pattern with conversations about chastity, with moms being the only parent to talk to daughters and dads being the only parent who talk to sons. Time and again, I have had teens and young adults in the church tell me that many of their parents and leaders were anxious and uncomfortable with discussing the topic of sexual intimacy.

So, what are the consequences of these types of object lessons? The consequences of fear-based learning about chastity include:

A Negative Portrayal of Sexual Intimacy

Fear-based lessons present a negative portrayal of sexual intimacy, often unintentionally conveying to young minds that sex is a bad thing that damages or harms us. While sexual sin can clearly have a negative effect on someone's life, fear-based object lessons often are not embedded in a balanced lesson about the potential positive consequences of sexual intimacy. And, even if a balanced view of sexuality is presented, many young people have told me that the negative emotions associated with these object lessons are sometimes so powerful that they struggle to internalize any other messages from the lesson.

Feelings of Fear and Anxiety

Over the years, many young people have told me that when parents and leaders were anxious about

teaching them about chastity, they began to feel anxious about the topic themselves. In fact, many students report that they feel parents and leaders often use object lessons because they are anxious about the topic and this form of teaching allows them to *talk about sex, without talking about sex.* If young people internalize these anxious emotions, this type of negative conditioning about sex can have long term consequences in later marriages as young couples struggle to re-program their thinking about modesty and sexuality.

DISCOURAGES DIALOGUE ABOUT SEXUAL MATTERS

Fear-based metaphors discourage dialogue between young people and their parents or leaders about chastity. Often in this context, young people feel that if they ask questions or show interest in the topic of sex they will be labeled as "bad" or "dirty." When this happens young people turn to friends, the media, or other sources to learn about these issues—often with values that are not in harmony with the gospel.

TEACHES PRECEPTS, BUT NOT PRINCIPLES

Similar to the experience related by Brother Millet, fear-based metaphors teach precepts (i.e., premarital sex is wrong), but they rarely teach young people the principles or reasons behind these prescriptions. This often leaves young people without the needed motivations to stay pure, particularly in a world that is encouraging them to be unchaste.

DISTORTS THE ATONEMENT OF CHRIST

Many young people have also commented that fear-based metaphors made them feel that there was no way they could repent of any sexual sins they had committed. To young minds, images of burned dresses and wilted flower petals appear irreparable and permanent. In sum, they leave some young people feeling like damaged goods that no one, including their Father in Heaven, will ever want or desire. We will discuss the topic of repentance in more detail later in the chapter.

ABSTINENCE-BASED METAPHORS

While fear-based metaphors are sometimes used by parents and leaders to teach young people about chastity, my experience is that the most commonly used types of object lessons in current church circles fit into a group I call *Abstinence-Based Metaphors.* These metaphors convey a *worth-waiting-for* message to young people as sexual intimacy is portrayed as a positive aspect of life when experienced in the context of marriage.

Metaphors of Sexual Purity

Fear-Based

Negative portrayal of sexual intimacy, discourages dialogue, precept vs. principle

- Undesirable food
- Wilted flower
- Broken Plate

Abstinence-Based

Added emphasis on context, correct but incomplete, behavioral/individual, marriage finish line

- Cookies on fast Sunday
- Chocolate candy trade-in

What are some examples of abstinence-based metaphors? For some reason, I have found that many of them involve desirable food (there is a problem with this that I'll point out in a minute). For example, a bishopric counselor once brought warm chocolate chip cookies to a combined youth lesson about chastity on a Fast Sunday. As the aroma of the cookies permeated the room, he asked the youth how many of them would like to have a cookie. After they all eagerly indicated they would love to have one of the cookies, the counselor reminded the youth group that it was Fast Sunday. After a series of groans from the youth, this counselor made the comparison between waiting to eat the cookies at the right time and saving sexual intimacy for marriage.

Another young man told me about an object lesson that was used in a deacon's quorum lesson. The advisor gave each of the young men two chocolate candies and told them, "If you bring these two chocolates back next week, I'll give you ten chocolates." The following week the boys who brought their candies back were rewarded with the additional chocolates. Then the advisor told them, "If you bring all ten chocolates back next week, I'll give you a whole bag of chocolates." You can see where the advisor was going with this, right? At the end of the third week, the advisor used the example to teach the boys that delayed gratification brings greater rewards and greater satisfactions.

Now, some of you may be thinking—*what's wrong with these metaphors*? The error in these metaphors is rooted in what they *don't teach* rather than what they *do teach*. In short, *they are correct, but incomplete.* They appropriately teach that the consequences related to sexual intimacy will vary according to the context of these experiences. They appropriately teach that sexual intimacy is a desirable part of life and that it is good and normal to have interest in sexual matters. However, these abstinence-based lessons can also have some unintended negative side-effects, such as:

CHASTITY IS PORTRAYED AS BEING SIMPLY A PHYSICAL MATTER

Abstinence-based lessons unintentionally present the view that chastity is only a physical or behavioral law. The focus in these lessons is on the *behaviors of intimacy* and the *timing* of such behaviors. While behaviors are a part of the law of chastity, they are not at the heart of the matter. Chastity is first and foremost a spiritual law that is lived in our hearts and in our minds, before it is expressed in our behaviors. Abstinence-based object lessons often assume that all expressions of sexuality are similar in intent, motivation, and purpose. There is typically no discussion of the difference in *loving* versus *lustful* approaches to sexuality, both before and after marriage. The attitudes and motives for *why* we seek sexual contact with our spouse is the primary definer of whether our behaviors are chaste or not.

CHASTITY IS PORTRAYED AS AN INDIVIDUAL MATTER

Abstinence-based perspectives also tend to discuss chastity as a personal condition—something that involves only our personal choices and worthiness. What is often missing is an appreciation of the relational nature of chastity. All sexual actions are either done for another person or for our self. How we conduct ourselves sexually always has consequences for current and future relationships. This is why using food in a metaphor about chastity is inherently misleading, particularly to young minds. When sexual intimacy is compared to one person consuming an inanimate object such as food or candy, it conveys the notion that sexual fulfillment comes from receiving, not from giving. The sharing and other-centered aspects of intimacy are missing; and these are the parts of sexual intimacy that are so important to forming and maintaining a healthy marriage.

They Teach That Chastity Has a "Marriage Finish Line"

Perhaps the most problematic aspect of abstinence-based messages is that they mistakenly convey the idea that the need for chastity ends at marriage. If young people can "just hold out" until they are married they will not have to worry about chastity any more. Perhaps this is why some couples rush their engagements to hurry and get married before they "make a mistake." Nothing could be further from the truth. There is no "marriage finish line" when it comes to chastity and personal purity. Chastity is one of the foundation principles of healthy and lasting marriage. Couples need to be chaste in their thoughts and actions on their honeymoon and on into their marriages. When understood correctly, marriage is the beginning, not the end, of chastity and personal purity.

A THIRD OPTION: SEXUAL WHOLENESS IN MARRIAGE

Our focus for the remainder of this chapter is to understand a third option, beyond fear-based or abstinence-based perspectives, for understanding (and teaching others about) the need for chastity in our personal lives and marriages. I call this perspective *Sexual Wholeness in Marriage* because a true understanding of personal purity can only be had when we understand the purposes of sexual intimacy within the divine institution of marriage. Even teens and young adults need to understand personal purity through the lens of marriage, because their choices about sexuality will assuredly impact their readiness for marriage.

Dr. Terrance Olson, a professor in the School of Family Life at BYU, captured the essence of sexual wholeness in marriage when he said:

> Chastity and fidelity are more than sexual abstinence before marriage and physical fidelity after marriage. This is because human sexuality is not simply a physical matter, as the world invites us to believe. *Chastity and fidelity begin in the spirit, not in the body*, and involve the giving of our hearts—our broken hearts, our softened hearts—to our mates unequivocally. (Chastity and Fidelity in Marriage and Family Relationships. In D. C. Dollahite (Ed), Strengthening Our Families, 2000, p. 56, emphasis added)

This quote highlights the spiritual and relationship aspects of true chastity. A good starting point for understanding sexual wholeness in marriage is to reconsider all of the foundation principles we have already discussed in this section of the book as principles of sexual intimacy. Each principle, such as discipleship, covenant, equal partnership, cleaving, spousal preeminence, and the divine triangle is a principle of marital intimacy. Being true partners and demonstrating spousal preeminence in the sexual aspects of marriage will give us true insight into how God intends us to handle this part of marriage.

To better understand sexual wholeness in marriage

we will look at several key principles, including: (a) the divine origins of our sexual nature, (b) the true purposes of sexual intimacy, (c) the true nature of sexual intimacy, and (d) the three guiding doctrines of why we should be chaste. We conclude with a discussion of the expression of chastity in marriage and perspectives of repentance related to sexual transgression.

The Divine Origins of Our Sexual Nature

A beginning question for our discussion is—*Are we sexual beings*? An extension of this question would be—*Is our Father in Heaven a sexual being*? If you have internalized negative messages about sexuality you may feel hesitant or uncertain about how to answer these questions. Is our sexual desire something divine and righteous or is it a part of the "natural man" (Mosiah 3:19) that needs to be overcome? President John Taylor taught,

> Well, He (God) has planted, in accordance with this, a natural desire in woman towards man, and in man towards woman and a feeling of affection, regard, and sympathy exists between the sexes. We bring it into the world with us, but that, like everything else, has to be sanctified. An unlawful gratification of these feelings and sympathies is wrong in the sight of God, and leads down to death, while a proper exercise of our functions leads to life, happiness, and exaltation in this world and the world to come. (Gospel Kingdom, 2002, p. 61)

A Parent's Guide, a manual published by the Church teaches,

> We would do well to remind ourselves of our first mortal parents. Instructing them, Heavenly Father commanded them to give attention to the whole range of their powers and passions. They were to subdue the earth, create and nurture posterity, become one flesh physically, cleave unto each other socially and emotionally, and learn to serve the purposes of God. They, as we, were endowed with bodies, parts, and passions after the image of the Creator. This implies that as we, the children of God, develop virtuously within marriage we will discover ever more profound enjoyments of all his creations, including our own emotions, bodies, and spiritual capacities. (A Parent's Guide, 1985, p. 49)

President Ezra Taft Benson stated, "Sex was created and established by our Heavenly Father for sacred, holy, and high purposes" (The Teachings of Ezra Taft Benson, 1988, p. 409). So, the clear answer to our ques-

Two Contrasting Views of Sexuality
2 Nephi 9:39

Carnal-Minded Sexuality
- Self-centered
- Present moment
- Satisfies a "drive"
- Physical
- Body focused
- Light-minded, casual

Likely Outcomes
Estrangement, disappointment, unfilled (contrary to true nature)

Spiritually-Minded Sexuality
- Other-centered
- Past/present/future
- Meets needs and fulfills divine purposes
- Spiritual, emotional, physical, and relational
- Body+Spirit=Soul
- Indicator of our spiritual condition

Likely Outcomes
Connection, intimacy, confidence, peace, (in harmony with true nature)

tions is yes—we are sexual beings. We are created in the image of our Father in Heaven, which includes our spiritual motivations and desires, as well as our physical bodies. Any confusion surrounding these questions comes from the fact that we live in a society that presents distorted images and messages about sex. This creates two contrasting views of our sexuality.

THE VIEW OF THE WORLD

The View of the World teaches us that sex is primarily about physical pleasure and self-gratification. This perspective teaches that it is natural and normal for teens and young adults to be sexually active, even outside of the committed relationship of marriage. In fact, a "hook-up" culture exists among young people today that involve physical intimacy outside of any relationship at all (i.e., "friends with benefits"). Young people are encouraged in the media and from other sources to "live in the moment" and enjoy being single and uncommitted in their expressions of affection and sexuality.

THE VIEW OF THE LORD

The View of the Lord, however, teaches us that sex is primarily about marital unity and other-centeredness. This perspective teaches that while our sexual desires are natural and normal, true sexual fulfillment can only come within the covenant relationship of marriage. The gospel of Jesus Christ encourages young people to live for the future, not just the present. In the Book of Mormon we read:

> O, my beloved brethren, remember the awfulness in transgressing against that Holy God, and also the awfulness of yielding to the enticings of that cunning one. Remember, to be carnally-minded is death, and to be spiritually-minded is life eternal (2 Nephi 9:39).

THE DIMENSIONS OF HUMAN SEXUAL NATURE

One of the most profound understandings found in the restored Gospel is the revealed truth that "the spirit and the body are the soul of man" (D&C 88:15) and that when the spirit and body are separated, men and women "cannot receive a fullness of joy" (D&C 93:34). The doctrine of the soul teaches us that all sexual experiences in this life involve both our bodies and our spirits—and have consequences for both. It also teaches us that if we are going to experience sexual fulfillment in our marriages, we must appreciate how the emotions, feelings, and thoughts of our spirits are integrated with the physical reactions of our bodies and vice versa (see the figure below). My colleagues and I discussed these dimensions of our sexual nature in our recent book, *Sexual Wholeness in Marriage*. I overview these dimensions here.

Dimensions of Our Sexual Nature

Spiritual Dimension
Meaning, purpose, progression
- Need: sexual meaning
- Attributes: positive and faithful

Emotional Dimension
Security, attachment, validation
- Need: sexual belonging
- Attributes: secure and authentic

Sexual Wholeness

Physical Dimension
Attraction, pleasure, health
- Need: sexual satisfaction
- Attributes: knowledgeable and aware

The Spiritual Dimension

Because we are spiritual beings it is our nature to seek meaning and purpose in our lives. The Proclamation on the Family teaches that each of us "is a beloved spirit son or daughter of heavenly parents, and, as such, each has a divine nature and destiny" (¶ 2). Because of our divine nature, a desire for progression permeates all aspects of our lives. When we live according to God's will and have faith in His divine plan, this desire is fulfilled and we feel contentment and peace because we are meeting "the measure of our creation" (D&C 88:5). However, when we feel a lack of progression in our lives, our divine nature tells us that something is amiss and we feel restless and frustrated. When our lack of progression is tied to sin and being out of alignment with God's commandments, we feel a sense of unworthiness, shame, and a decrease in faith.

Our innate desire for progression is also a part of our sexual nature. Because of this, each of us has an abiding desire for *sexual meaning*. When sexual expression in our lives is in alignment with God's purposes, we sense that sex has meaning and purpose in our lives. It becomes inseparably linked to our feelings of love for our spouse and for God. This endows us with a sense of worthiness and an appreciation for the positive role sex can play in our lives. At times, however, individuals and couples express their sexuality in meaningless ways that are not in alignment with God's divine purposes for sex. Whenever this happens our spiritual nature reacts to this and we will feel less fulfilled and content in our lives.

The Physical Dimension

Much of the current discussion about human sexuality in both popular and professional circles centers on the size of body parts, sexual techniques, and products to enhance the physical response of our bodies. In fact, for many people these days even sexual desire is seen as emerging from physical origins. This view of sexual desire is reflected in now popular notions of "libido," "sex drive," or "horniness" that equate sexual expression as a physical appetite. This view of sexual desire has its professional origins in Freud's psychoanalytic theory that viewed humans as having an involuntary, physically-generated sexual energy that must be expressed or repressed. The notion of human's having an involuntary physical sex drive is often used as the rationale for inappropriate sexual expression before and during marriage. Such perspectives are clearly not in harmony with the spiritual and emotional dimensions of our sexual nature, which emphasize the voluntary and controllable nature of sexual expression. This expression of love and commitment is not just an expression of genes or hormones.

While spiritual perspectives caution us to not embrace lustful perspectives and practices that can lead to body-only fragmentation, we must not discount the significance of the physical dimension of our sexual nature. The doctrine of the soul teaches us that our physical bodies are essential to our happiness, both in this life and in the world to come. In fact, a central tenant of the restored Gospel is that one of the major purposes of this life is for the children of God to receive physical bodies and that through the power of the resurrection we can live like our Heavenly Parents after this life with an immortal tangible body. Living a virtuous life does not require us to reject the joy of our physical senses, rather it provides a full and satisfying enjoyment of them.

While sexual desire and satisfaction are not solely physical phenomenon, husbands and wives do have physical desires connected to their bodies that are fulfilled through sex. Our innate desires to experience physical touch, closeness, and arousal are also a fundamental part of our sexual nature. We each have an

innate desire for *sexual satisfaction*. The bodies of both men and women are endowed with divinely created "arousal systems" that are linked to the natural processes of attraction, attachment, and touch. Because of our physical nature, humans innately desire and respond to physical closeness and touch in ways that can provide deep feelings of pleasure and satisfaction. The fullest expression of this need is found as husbands and wives become "one flesh" (Gen 2:4), thus uniting both their sprits and their bodies.

THE EMOTIONAL DIMENSION

Each of us has a fundamental need to be deeply connected to others. This need for attachment and belonging is a core part of our spiritual nature and is shared by all people. Elder Bruce C. Hafen explains, "People simply desire to be connected with others, especially in close relationships. They are feeling the longing to belong.. . .Both our theology and the feelings of our hearts make us want to belong, now and eternally, to the father of our Spirits, to his Son, and to those we love on earth" (Elder Bruce Hafen, The Belonging Heart, pp. 9–11). In a sense, this universal need is the desire to be loved. Through the fulfillment of this need we find security and happiness, as well as true freedom to trust, love, and sacrifice for others. It is through this belonging and investment in others that we develop a true sense of happiness and well-being.

Our innate need for emotional attachment is also a part of our sexual nature. We each have an innate need for *sexual belonging*. When sexual intimacy fosters a sense of understanding and appreciation between spouses, emotional attachments in marriage become secure and stable. This type of secure attachment reduces anxiety in spouses and gives each a sense of emotional security within the relationship. This can become reinforcing in the relationship as secure attachment fosters satisfying sexual intimacy and satisfying sexual intimacy in turn fosters secure attachment. However, the opposite can also occur as emotional insecurity leads to struggles with sexual intimacy, which in turn heightens spouses' feelings of insecurity. These patterns help us appreciate the critical role that commitment, attachment, and exclusivity play in sexual wholeness in marriage.

Emotional security is the foundation for several key principles that are needed in couple relationships. These include courage, vulnerability, and a willingness to trust your spouse. Without emotional security, the vulnerability in close relationships becomes threatening and fear of rejection will often dictate how people behave in intimate situations. When this happens, there is less authenticity, disclosure, and mutual reliance in couple relationships—all necessary ingredients to forming an intimate and supportive relationship. In fact, vulnerability is the gateway to both intimacy and pain. We can choose to minimize our pain by avoiding vulnerability in marriage, but we will also minimize the intimacy we experience. This is why emotional security is such an important part of the personal maturity needed to form and maintain a loving and lasting marriage relationship.

While the physical dimension of our sexual nature creates within us an innate desire to personally experience sexual satisfaction, the emotional dimension of our sexual nature also provides us with the capacity to experience profound fulfillment in the sexual satisfaction we provide for our spouse. Our emotional nature makes us relational beings. Interconnected with our needs for belonging and becoming is our need to be endowed with charity and to express true concern for the wellbeing of others. It is because of this part of our natures that Christ taught that "he that findeth his life shall lose it, and whosoever will lose his life for my sake shall find it" (Matt 16:25). Happiness cannot be found in simply seeking after our desires and needs, it must involve meeting the needs of others and fulfilling their need to be loved—in marriage this involves meeting our spouse's needs.

TRUE PURPOSES OF SEXUAL INTIMACY

As we come to appreciate that we are sexual beings and that this part of our nature is divine; we are prompted to consider why we were created this way. In God's plan, sexual intimacy is "purposeful." Which means it is intended to create and produce divine ends.

In fact, from an eternal perspective *sexual intimacy is always a "means" to divine ends, not the "end" in and of itself.* So, what are the divine purposes of sexual intimacy? According to President Spencer W. Kimball there are two divine purposes for sexuality in God's plan. In his April 1974 General Conference address, President Kimball quoted a popular evangelist, Billy Graham:

> The Bible celebrates sex and its proper use, presenting it as God-created, God-ordained, God-blessed. It makes plain that God himself implanted the physical magnetism between the sexes for two reasons: for the propagation of the human race, and for the expression of that kind of love between man and wife that makes for true oneness. His commandment to the first man and woman to be "one flesh" was as important as his command to "be fruitful and multiply." (Ensign, May, 1974)

Procreation

The first purpose for sexual intimacy in God's plan is to participate in the ongoing creation of bodies for God's spirit children. In paragraph four of the Proclamation on the Family we read,

> The first commandment that God gave to Adam and Eve pertained to their potential for parenthood as husband and wife. We declare that God's commandment for His children to multiply and replenish the earth remains in force. We further declare that God has commanded that the sacred powers of procreation are to be employed only between man and woman, lawfully wedded as husband and wife. (1995, ¶ 4)

Elder D. Todd Christofferson further taught:

> If, then in the course of our mortal experience, we chose to "do all things whatsoever the Lord [our] God [should] command [us]," we would have kept our "second estate." This means that by our choices we would demonstrate to God (and to ourselves) our commitment and capacity to live His celestial law while outside His presence and in a physical body with all its powers, appetites, and passions. Could we bridle the flesh so that it became the instrument rather than the master of the spirit? Could we be trusted both in time and eternity with godly powers, including power to create life? Would we individually overcome evil? Those who did would "have glory added upon their heads for ever and ever"—a very significant aspect of that glory being a resurrected, immortal, and glorified physical body. No wonder we "shouted for joy" at these magnificent possibilities and promises. (April 2015, Why Marriage, Why Family)

As we discussed in an chapter lesson, the ongoing process of creation is one of the pillars of eternity and one of the central focuses of God's plan. Marriage is the divinely decreed institution to bring about this creative process—and sexual union of spouses is the divinely decreed process to bring this about.

Expression of Love

The second, and most common, purpose for the expression of sexuality is to unify spouses with each other and with God. Latter-day Saint leaders have taught that sexual intimacy in marriage is for spouses to express love for one another, to attach and bond with one another, and to experience pleasure and joy. President Spencer W. Kimball taught,

> Sex is for procreation and expression of love. It is the destiny of men and women to join together to make eternal family units. In the context of lawful marriage, the intimacy of sexual relations is right and divinely approved. There is nothing unholy or degrading about sexuality in itself, for by that means men and women join in a process of creation and in an expression of love. (The Teachings of Spencer W. Kimball, 1995, p. 312)

More recently, Elder David A. Bednar taught:

The Church of Jesus Christ of Latter-day Saints has a single, undeviating standard of sexual morality: intimate relations are proper only between a man and a woman in the marriage relationship prescribed in God's plan. Such relations are not merely a curiosity to be explored, an appetite to be satisfied, or a type of recreation or entertainment to be pursued selfishly. They are not a conquest to be achieved or simply an act to be performed. Rather, they are in mortality one of the ultimate expressions of our divine nature and potential and a way of strengthening emotional and spiritual bonds between husband and wife. We are agents blessed with moral agency and are defined by our divine heritage as children of God—and not by sexual behaviors, contemporary attitudes, or secular philosophies. (April 2013, We Believe in Being Chaste)

The True Nature of Sexual Intimacy

With an understanding of our divine sexual natures and the true purposes of sexual intimacy in God's plan, we are able to better appreciate the true nature of sexual intimacy. The true nature of sexual intimacy includes these principles:

Intimacy Is Both Emotional and Physical in Nature

The divine purpose of sexual intimacy is to unify spouses and strengthen the marital bond, not simply physical gratification. Therefore, we need to define sexuality in terms of both emotional and physical forms of intimate expressions. Intimacy is connected to *shared vulnerability* where people reveal themselves to each other and feel nurtured and cared for in their interactions. This type of revealing happens when we talk, share, and disclose to others; as well as when we are physically close to them. So, when we talk about sexual intimacy and chastity, we should think about relationship behaviors broadly—not just the physical behaviors typically defined as "sexual."

Chastity Is a Physical Expression of an Inward Condition

As I noted previously, chastity is more than abstinence. It is a spiritual condition. Our thoughts, attitudes, desires, and words are as much chaste or unchaste as are our behaviors. The chastity of our attitudes and behaviors is one of, if not the best, indicator of our spiritual maturity and testimony. It is completely inconsistent to profess a testimony of the gospel and then act in unchaste ways that deny the true purposes of sexual intimacy.

Our Sexual Desire Is Based in a Spiritual Motivation, Not a Physical Drive

Most of us have heard the term "sex drive." What does this phrase mean and do we actually have a sex drive? The term "drive" finds its psychological origins in the work of Sigmund Freud, who hypothesized that the human psyche was made up of uncontrollable drives or motivations. According to Freud, the primary drive of human behavior was a need for sexual gratification or release. In these terms, the need for sexual gratification is seen as being non-agentive, meaning

that people cannot control it. This is how many people today think about the notion of a person's sex drive.

These views are not in harmony with the gospel or modern sciences' view of sexual desire. Correctly understood, our desire for sexual intimacy is connected to belonging and connection, not simply physical sexual gratification. In fact, research shows that people who pursue physical gratification outside of committed relationships often feel depressed, lonely, and hollow. This is because their true desire or need is not met in this type of sexual expression. Our true desire is to love and be loved in lasting relationships—only when sexual intimacy contributes to this end do we feel content or fulfilled.

Teaching on this subject, Elder David A. Bednar emphasized:

> Every appetite, desire, propensity, and impulse of the natural man may be overcome by and through the Atonement of Jesus Christ. We are here on the earth to develop godlike qualities and to bridle all of the passions of the flesh. . . violating the law of chastity is a grievous sin and a misuse of our physical tabernacles. To those who know and understand the plan of salvation, defiling the body is an act of rebellion (see Mosiah 2:36–37; D&C 64:34–35) and a denial of our true identity as sons and daughters of God. As we look beyond mortality and into eternity, it is easy to discern that the counterfeit companionship advocated by the adversary is temporary and empty.
>
> . . .We also are promised that, as we pursue the pathway of virtue, "the Holy Ghost shall be [our] constant companion" (D&C 121:46). Thus, living the law of chastity invites some of the greatest blessings men and women can receive in mortality: appropriate spiritual confidence in the presence of family, friends, Church associates, and, ultimately, the Savior. Our innate longing to belong is fulfilled in righteousness as we walk in the light with hope. (April 2013, We Believe in Being Chaste)

Three Guiding Doctrines

Elder Jeffery R. Holland's talk, "Of Souls, Symbols, and Sacraments" has become the landmark address of our time on the topic of chastity and personal purity. I highly encourage you to read and re-read this talk. In fact, I encourage engaged couples to read this talk each week during their courtship—the principles are powerful and transformative if you will learn them and live them.

What sets Elder Holland's talk apart from so many teachings on sexual intimacy is that he does not just tell us to "be morally clean," he answers the question *why be morally clean*? He provides the answers that the young woman needed as she counseled with Bishop Millet. Specifically, Elder Holland teaches us that there are three primary reasons or doctrines for why we should be chaste—the doctrine of the soul, the doctrine of the symbol, and the sacramental nature of sexual intimacy in marriage.

The Doctrine of the Soul

Even little Primary children can tell you what makes up the human soul—it is the unified state of our spirits and our bodies. This understanding of what makes up our souls is a powerful principle when we consider the topic of sexual intimacy. Elder Holland explains:

> One of the plain and precious truths of this dispensation is that "the spirit and the body are the soul of man" (D&C 88:15.) and that when the spirit and body are separated, men and women "cannot receive a fullness of joy" (D&C 93:34). (Of Souls, Symbols, and Sacraments, BYU Speeches, January 1988, p. 4)

This doctrine teaches us that there is no such thing as casual or just physical sex. Our spirit is always involved—and the consequences of our actions in this aspect of life are always spiritual. This type of understanding helps us see why sexual sin is so important in the eyes of our Father in Heaven. Elder Holland noted:

> So partly in answer to why such seriousness, we answer that one toying with the God-given body of another, toys with the very soul of that individual, toys with the central purpose and product of life. . . In trivializing the soul of another (please insert the word body there), we trivialize the Atonement that saved that soul and guaranteed its continued existence . . . Exploitation of the body is, in the last

analysis, an exploitation of him who is the Light and Life of the world .(Of Souls, Symbols, and Sacraments, p. 5)

Our spiritual progression, and the progression of others, is tied to sexual intimacy. This makes it a reverent and sacred part of life—not something that is trivial or recreational. Our actions related to personal purity will always reflect God's divine purposes if we remember that sexual intimacy is a "soulful" expression, involving both body and spirit.

The Doctrine of the Symbol

In addition to the soulful nature of sexuality, Elder Holland also taught that a sexual union between a man and a woman is intended to be a special and transformative symbol of their relationship.

> Second, may I suggest that human intimacy, that sacred, physical union ordained of God for a married couple deals with a symbol that demands special sanctity? Such an act of love between a man and a woman is—or certainly was ordained to be—a symbol of their total union: union of their hearts, their hopes, their lives, their love, their family, and their future, their everything. (Of Souls, Symbols, and Sacraments, p. 6)

When the symbolic aspect of intimacy is present in a marriage, the meaning of these experiences fulfills our deepest desires to belong and matter to someone else. However, when physical expressions of intimacy are engaged in outside of these commitments and connections, they produce an opposite effect. Elder Holland explains:

> Can you see then the moral schizophrenia that comes from pretending we are one, sharing the physical symbols and physical intimacy of our union, but then fleeing, retreating, severing all such other aspects—and symbols—of what was meant to be total obligation...
>
> If you persist in sharing part without the whole, in pursuing satisfaction devoid of symbolism, in giving parts and pieces and inflamed fragments only, you run the terrible risk of such spiritual, psychic damage that you may undermine both your physical intimacy and your wholehearted devotion to a truer, later love. You may come to that moment of real love, of total union, only to discover to your horror that what should have been saved has been spent, and—mark my words—only God's grace can recover that piecemeal dissipation of your virtue. (Of Souls, Symbols, and Sacraments, pp. 6–7)

Elder Holland also introduced the principles of *counterfeit intimacy* and *sexual fragmentation*. Quoting Dr. Victor L. Brown, he said:

> Fragmentation enables its users to counterfeit intimacy. . .If we relate to each other in fragments, at best we miss full relationships. At worst, we manipulate and exploit others for our gratification. Sexual fragmentation can be particularly harmful because it gives powerful physiological rewards which, though illusory, can temporarily persuade us to overlook the serious deficits in the overall relationship. Two people may marry for physical gratification and then discover that the illusion of union collapses under the weight of intellectual, social, and spiritual incompatibilities.
>
> Sexual fragmentation is particularly harmful because it is particularly deceptive. The intense human intimacy that should be enjoyed and symbolized by sexual union is counterfeited by sensual

episodes which suggest—but cannot deliver—acceptance, understanding, and love. Such encounters mistake the end for the means. . . . (Of Souls, Symbols, and Sacraments, p. 7)

Sexual fragmentation occurs whenever we share ourselves physically in ways that do not integrate physical intimacy with emotional intimacy within the covenant of marriage. This principle does not just pertain to sexual intercourse. Even the uncommitted kiss or so-called "make-out session" (sometimes called a NCMO, short for "non-committed make-out") is a form of sexual fragmentation. We cannot separate expressions of physical affection from their intended

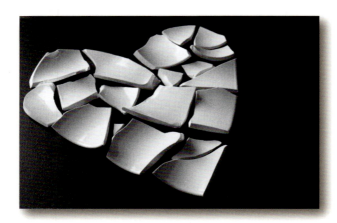

symbolic power and intention. Also note how Elder Holland highlights the premarital risks of such behaviors. Sexual fragmentation can cause young people to "fall in love" and become attached to someone who is not a right person for them in marriage. Or, a couple may never develop the foundation of partnership and friendship needed in a mature marriage if they base their early associations on physical attraction and gratification.

A Holy Sacrament

According to Elder Holland, sexual intimacy is not only intended to unify husbands and wives, it is also intended to unify couples with God and His divine purposes. Elder Holland taught:

Sexual intimacy is not only a symbolic union between a man and a woman—the uniting of their very souls—but it is also symbolic of a union between mortals and deity, between otherwise ordinary and fallible humans uniting for a rare and special moment with God himself and all powers by which he gives life in this wide universe. . .in this latter sense, human intimacy is a sacrament. . . .a sacrament could be any one of a number of gestures or acts or ordinances that unite us with God and his limitless power.

. . . you will never be more like God at any other time in this life than when you are expressing that particular power. (Of Souls, Symbols, and Sacraments, pp. 11–12)

Clearly Elder Holland appreciates that our Father in Heaven is indeed a sexual being when he says that we will never be more like God than when we are appropriately expressing our procreative powers in marriage. When connected with our covenants in the holy temple, sexual intimacy can be a way to invite the Holy Spirit of Promise into our relationships. This literally permits spouses to become one in marriage—one in flesh and one in spirit.

Chastity in Marriage

As we have already discussed, the need to be chaste does not end when we get married. Before marriage we demonstrate our chastity by abstaining from sexual intimacy; while in marriage we demonstrate our chastity by *how* we engage in sexual intimacy. In Doctrine and Covenants we read:

Thou shalt *love* thy wife with all thy heart, and shalt *cleave* unto her and none else. And he that *looketh*

upon a woman to *lust* after her shall deny the faith, and shall not have the Spirit; and if he repents not he shall be cast out (D&C 42:22–23, emphasis added).

This verse is typically regarded as a scripture about marital fidelity; a commandment to be faithful to our husband or wife. While that is not a wrong interpretation of the scripture, that is not what these verses actually says. Notice that this scripture does not say that looking upon a woman, *other than your wife,* denies the faith. It says to look lustfully upon a woman, any woman—including your wife, denies the faith. Clearly, the Lord expects marital intimacy for both husbands and wives to reflect a mutual other-centeredness between them. To repeatedly withhold our affections because we are "not in the mood" or to lustfully pursue physical relations reflects a selfish orientation that will push spouses apart rather than bring them together. During their dating and engagement, couples will start to determine if the physical intimacy in their relationship will be self-centered or other-centered in nature. Other-centered love binds spouses to one another and enables the intimacies of marriage to become a special symbol of their commitment and togetherness.

Notice how the verses contrast *loving* and *cleaving*, with *lusting*. This is why abstinence-based approaches to teaching chastity do not convey the full meaning and nature of sexual intimacy. Not only do we need to wait until marriage to be sexually intimate, we need to make sure that our attitudes and behaviors in marriage express love and demonstrate cleaving. President Joseph F. Smith stated, "Sexual union is lawful in wedlock, and if participated in with right intent is honorable and sanctifying" (Gospel Doctrine, 1919, p. 309, emphasis added).

The intent is the key—marriage is not a license to lust. Sanctifying intimacy in marriage is always other-centered, unselfish, responsive, and loving. We will talk about this principle in greater detail when we discuss sexual intimacy in marriage in a later chapter.

Repentance from Sexual Sin

On a final note, we should discuss the topic of repentance as it applies to sexual sin. Many parents and leaders are sometimes reluctant to teach repentance from sexual transgression because they fear that young people will feel that it is easy to repent of sexual transgressions or that sexual sin is "not a big deal." Hopefully, as you have studied the *Doctrine of the Soul* as taught by Elder Holland the spirit impressed upon your minds the importance of sexual purity and the severity of sexual transgression. When we know the *whys* behind the *whats* of chastity, the importance of sexual purity becomes very clear. We also come to understand why our Father in Heaven considers all forms of sexual intimacy outside of marriage such a serious sin.

Many years ago, there was another object lesson that was used by some church members to teach about the consequences of sin and the nature of repentance. This object lesson involved driving nails into a board and then telling the class, "This is like sinning." Then the teacher would remove the nails and tell the class, "This is like repenting." Then, as the punch line of the lesson, the teacher would hold up the board and say, "But the holes are still there!" Many members of the church were discouraged and hurt by this distorted view of repentance and the Atonement of Jesus Christ.

In contrast, the Savior has told us that ". . . though your sins be as scarlet, they shall be as white as snow; though they be red like crimson, they shall be as wool" (Isaiah 1:5). The Lord does not just remove the nails from our board, nor does he just cover up the holes so that no one will notice they are still there. He gives us a whole new board. He cleans us, restores us, and strengthens us to withstand temptation in the future.

This is true of all our sins—including sexual transgression.

I have always taken hope from the statement—*To repent in the present is to make a new future.* I know that to be true. I encourage you that as you prepare for marriage you will repent of any sins that exist in your past or current behavior. If you are entangled in sexual sin, leave your inappropriate thoughts and behaviors behind you and "come unto Christ and be perfected in Him" (Moroni 10:32). If needed, gather your courage and go confess to your bishop. He will direct you on a path of complete and full repentance. As you do this, you will feel the peace and comfort that comes from being fully pure and chaste. And that restoration of your chastity will be the greatest gift you could every give to a future spouse.

Modern Threats to Marriage

CHAPTER 8

> We call upon responsible citizens and officers of government everywhere to promote those measures designed to maintain and strengthen the family as the fundamental unit of society.
>
> *Proclamation on the Family, ¶ 9*

What do we know about the condition of society during the time of Noah? The scriptures tell us that Noah and his family lived in a time of great wickedness. In fact, the level of unrighteousness was so great at the time of Noah that the Lord commanded him to build an ark to prepare for a purging flood that would cover the whole earth. The Lord did this because His divine purposes could no longer be brought about among a society that had turned to such wicked ways.

Given the state of wickedness at the time of Noah, consider the following scripture from the New Testament:

> But as the days of [Noah] were, so shall also the coming of the Son of Man be. For as in the days that were before the flood they were eating and drinking, *marrying and giving in marriage*, until the day that [Noah] entered into the ark, And knew not until the flood came, and took them all away; so shall also the coming of the Son of Man be. (Matthew 24:36–39, emphasis added)

What does it mean in this scripture when it says the people of Noah were "marrying and giving in marriage" until the flood came?

It means that marriage can exist even in times of great wickedness and that people can distort the true purposes of marriage. Clearly, during Noah's time the reasons why people got married and how they acted in their marriages did not conform to the divine design of marriage. This scripture in the Book of Matthew teaches us that when people use the term *marriage*, it does not always mean the same thing our Father in Heaven means by the word *marriage*.

There is much from this scripture that we can "liken unto ourselves" (1 Ne 19:23). Currently, in the last days, we too live in a time of widespread wickedness. Yet, marriage is still a very prominent part of our society. Over 90% of people in the United States rate "having a happy marriage" as one of their most important goals in life (Waite & Gallagher, *Case for Marriage*, 2000 p. 2). Americans still desire to marry, but social norms about what marriage means have changed in subtle ways that undermine couples' ability to form

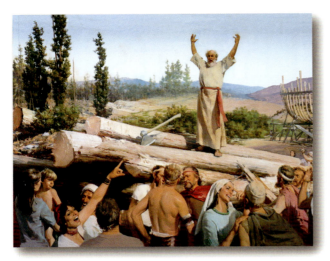

lasting marriages. Our society today is not turning away from or abandoning marriage, but we have witnessed a *distorting of marriage* in recent generations. We have seen the meaning and purpose of marriage change in people's lives and in society as a whole.

The purpose of this chapter is to increase your understanding of the current *context of marriage* and the threats to marriage that exist in our modern society. The marriage culture that exists today is different than the marriage culture that existed when your grandparents married or when Joseph and Emma Smith were married. In order to fully live according to the divine design of marriage as the Lord intends, you must come to understand what the Lord's pattern of marriage is and what it is not. Within our society today, you will be exposed to various lifestyle options that you will be encouraged to incorporate into your dating and marriage relationship. The objective of this final chapter in the Foundations Section is to help you avoid mixing the false notions of marriage in our society with the

divine patterns of marriage revealed by our Father in Heaven to His living prophets.

The Deinstitutionalization of Marriage

In our previous chapter about the institutional nature of marriage, you were introduced to the concept that marriage is a social institution.

In addition to viewing marriage as a divine institu-

Three Views of Marriage

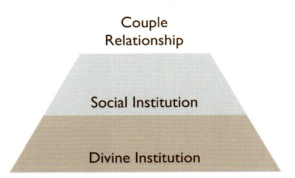

tion, the Lord also ordained marriage as not only the basic building block of the family, but also as the foundational institution of society. In paragraphs one and nine of the Proclamation on the Family we read:

> We...solemnly proclaim that marriage between a man and a woman is ordained of God and that the family is central to the Creator's plan...(1995, ¶ 1). We call upon responsible citizens and officers of government everywhere to promote those measures designed to maintain and strengthen the family as the *fundamental unit of society*. (¶ 9, emphasis added)

In a time when many are seeking to redefine marriage in our society, it is critical for us to consider the implications of such changes on the welfare of our communities. Numerous social trends are redefining the significance and practice of marriage in modern society.

Dr. Andrew Cherlin, a highly regarded sociologist

at John Hopkins University, wrote an article entitled "The Deinstitutionalization of American Marriage" (2004, Journal of Marriage and Family). In his article, Dr. Cherlin argues that marriage has undergone a process of *deinstitutionalization*—a weakening of the social norms that define partners' behavior—over the past few decades. Specifically, he presents examples and data about social trends that indicate that the meaning of marriage has changed in our society from an institution to a private couple relationship. As you learn more about the social trends that Dr. Cherlin discusses in his article, you will come to have a greater appreciation of the modern context of marriage and how dating and marriage today differs from marriage in previous generations.

Six Social Trends

Dr. Cherlin discussed four trends to support his argument that marriage in American society has weakened in recent generations. In addition to the four trends he discussed, I have added two additional trends that are important for you to understand. It is interesting to note that the Proclamation on the Family addresses each of these trends too.

Trend #1: Changing Division of Labor in the Home

According to Dr. Cherlin, the changing division of labor in the home is undermining the institutionalized basis of marriage. The distinct roles of homemaker and breadwinner have faded as more married women have entered the paid labor force. While these

The Deinstitutionalization of Marriage

From Institution to Companionship
Dr. Andrew Cherlin

Four Trends
(Cherlin, p. 851)

- Changing division of labor in the home
- Out-of-wedlock childbirth (above 40%)
- Growth of cohabitation (above 70%)
- Legalization of same-sex partnerships

Other Trends

- Historically high divorce rates (45-50%)
- Declining marriage rate

changes have had some very positive consequences, these changes have also shifted the meaning and importance of marriage in many people's lives, especially for women. In particular, many people now are reluctant to develop a full partnership in marriage where spouses rely on each other and trust each other to work as a team in providing for and nurturing their family. It's not important that couples today divide household labor in exactly the same way as was done in previous generations, but learning to collaborate and rely on each other is critical to enduring marriage. The Proclamation on the Family proclaims,

> By divine design, fathers are to preside over their families in love and righteousness and are responsible to provide the necessities of life and protection for their families. Mothers are primarily responsible for the nurture of their children. In these sacred responsibilities, fathers and mothers are obligated to help one another as equal partners. (¶ 7)

Trend #2: Out-of-Wedlock Childbirth

Dr. Cherlin also points out that the number of children born outside of marriage has dramatically increased during the last fifty years. Today, between 40 to 50% of children born in the United States are born out-of-wedlock. As Dr. Cherlin concludes, "marriage is no longer the nearly universal setting for child-bearing that it was a half century ago" (2004, p. 849). The Proclamation on the Family proclaims,

> Children are entitled to birth within the bonds of matrimony, and to be reared by a father and mother who honor marital vows with complete fidelity. (¶ 7)

Trend #3: The Growth of Cohabitation

Perhaps the greatest change in American family life during the last 50 years has been the increased role of cohabitation in the adult life course. As noted by Dr. Cherlin, only 36% of adults in the 2000 United States General Survey disagreed with the statement, *It is alright for a couple to live together without intending to get married*. Now more than two-thirds of marriages in the United States are preceded by non-marital cohabitation.

One of the main reasons that couples cohabit before marriage is that they believe living together before marriage is a good way to test their relationship and see if they will make a good marriage together. This line of thinking is similar to test-driving a car. The thought may be, *you wouldn't buy a car without test-driving it, would you?!* So, young people reason, *I shouldn't get married without test driving it first*!

Does the research data support this approach to marriage? Do people who test-drive their relationships by living together before marriage have better marriages? The data proves the *test-drive theory* of cohabitation to be completely false. Dozens of studies have shown that couples who live together before marriage actually have higher divorce rates and less satisfying marriages than couples who do not cohabit. This supports the Proclamation on the Family which proclaims:

> We further declare that God has commanded that the sacred powers of procreation are to be employed only between man and woman, lawfully wedded as husband and wife. (¶ 4)

Trend #4: The Emergence of Same-Sex Marriage

According to Dr. Cherlin, the most recent development in the deinstitutionalization of marriage is the current movement to legalize same-sex partnerships. Same-sex marriage has been legalized in parts of Europe and Canada; and now the Supreme Court in the United States has granted legal status to same-sex couples. Nothing could lead to a more dramatic change in the meaning and purposes of marriage than to legally sanction same-sex marriages between persons of the same gender. The Proclamation on the Family proclaims: "...marriage between a man and a woman is ordained of God...marriage between man and woman is essential to His eternal plan "(¶ 1&7).

As we discussed earlier, viewing marriage as a *divine institution* means it is recognized as a sacred system *established by God*, with divinely decreed laws and practices, which bring about His eternal purposes. This is in direct contrast to the modern notion that marriage is simply a private relationship formed by couples for

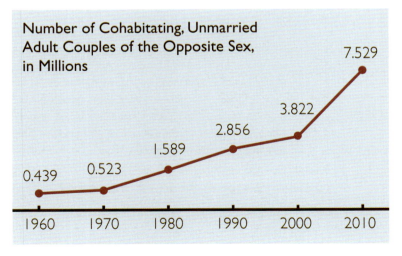

The Growth of Cohabitation
Source: U.S. Census Bureau, Current Population Reports; Analyst: Dr. Samuel Sturgeon

their own purposes and desires. The First Presidency recently taught:

> Marriage is far more than a contract between individuals to ratify their affections and provide for mutual obligations. Rather, marriage is a vital institution for rearing children and teaching them to become responsible adults. Throughout the ages, governments of all types have recognized marriage as essential in preserving social stability and perpetuating life. Regardless of whether marriages were performed as a religious rite or a civil ceremony, in almost every culture marriage has been protected and endorsed by governments primarily to preserve and foster the institution most central to rearing children and teaching them the moral values that undergird civilization. (Divine Intuition of Marriage, p. 2, ¶ 2 & 3)

Marriage is our Father in Heaven's divinely designed means for forming families, both in this life and in the life to come. Therefore, the true order of marriage is inseparably linked to the creation of life and bringing God's spirit children into the world. Procreative marriage, only possible between a man and a woman, is a distinct form of relationship defined by procreation, the sharing of family life, and generational posterity. This why the scriptures and the Church teaches that that sexual relations for all people are only appropriate in this type of marriage.

Trend #5: Historically High Divorce Rates

The American divorce rate today is nearly twice that of 1960, but has declined slightly since hitting the highest point in our history in the early 1980s. For the average couple marrying for the first time in recent years, the lifetime probability of divorce or separation remains between 40 and 50 percent.

The increase in divorce probably has elicited more concern and discussion than any other family-related trend in the United States. Although the long-term trend in divorce has been upward since colonial times, the divorce rate was level for about two decades after World War II during the period of high fertility known as the baby boom. By the middle of the 1960s, however, the incidence of divorce started to increase and it more than doubled over the next fifteen years to reach an

historical high point in the early 1980s. Since then the divorce rate has modestly declined, a trend described by many experts as "leveling off at a high level."

By now almost everyone has heard that the national divorce rate is close to 50% of all marriages. This is true, but the rate must be interpreted with caution and several important caveats. For many people, the actual chances of divorce are far below 50/50. The background characteristics of people entering a marriage have major implications for their risk of divorce. So if you are a reasonably well-educated person who works hard to provide for your family, come from an intact family, are religiously devout, marry after your teenage years, and do not have a child before marriage, your chances of divorce are quite low indeed. In fact, LDS couples who marry in the temple and continue to be temple worthy and active in the Church through their lives may have a divorce rate that is closer to 5% than 50%—so your chances of divorce are not like flipping a coin!

Trend #6: Declining Marriage Rate

There are also some indications that lifelong singlehood may be increasing. The likelihood that adults will marry has declined dramatically since 1960. Much of this decline results from the postponement of first marriages until older ages, but it may also reflect a growing trend toward the single life. In 1960, 94 percent of women had been married at least once by age 45. Currently, nearly 20% of men and 15% of women will never marry in their lifetime in the United States.

Declining Marriage Rate

Source: U.S. Census Bureau, Current Population Reports; Analyst: Dr. Samuel Sturgeon

The Benefits of Marriage

While the social norms of marriage are weakening in American culture, there is a growing body of research that suggests that such changes will have a negative impact on the wellbeing of our society. One area of research that helps us appreciate the need for a strong marriage culture is research on the health benefits of marriage. Scholars have spent the last two decades investigating the impact of marriage on people's health and wellbeing. In their book *The Case for Marriage: Why Married People are Happier, Healthier, and Better Off Financially* (2002), renowned demographers Dr. Linda Waite and Dr. Maggie Gallagher summarize the last two decades of research on the benefits of marriage. Here is a summary of what they found in the research.

Physical Health Benefits

In comparison to their single counterparts, married people live longer, suffer less from illness, and recover quicker from illnesses. Married individuals also exhibit fewer risk-taking behaviors and have the lowest rates of suicide and alcoholism. Because of these findings, many experts are starting to recognize marriage as a public health issue, just like smoking or obesity. The data is clear—forming and maintaining a loving marriage relationship is as important (and perhaps even more important) to your health throughout your life as regularly exercising and eating right.

Mental Health Benefits

Numerous research studies have also found that married people, on average, are happier and enjoy higher well-being in all facets of life. They suffer significantly less from depression and other psychiatric disorders. Many people have heard the false idea that married women have higher depression rates than single women. This is simply not true. Married women, like married men, have lower depression rates and better indicators of mental health, on average, than do single adults.

Financial Benefits

One of the common misconceptions about marriage is that it is a risky financial move to get married. Young people today talk about avoiding marriage to avoid financial risk. The data shows that, on average, marriage benefits people financially—rather than being a risk. Research studies show that married people are better off economically, spend less, and save more. Research also shows that married, two parent families are a powerful barrier against poverty. In fact, children

who do not grow up in a married-parent home are five times more likely to live below the poverty level than children raised by married parents. These research findings have been so convincing that the U.S. Government recently launched a Healthy Marriage Initiative within the Department of Health and Human Services to help promote healthy marriage, particularly among low-income communities.

Sexual Benefits

A common belief in our society is that marriage smothers the sexual passion in a relationship. Hollywood movies show us young attractive people who seem to have incredible passion and chemistry in non-marital relationships. In contrast, marriage is portrayed as a *romance-killer* with raising young kids, the stresses of paying the bills, and expanding waistlines as the antithesis of sexual passion. In fact, media messages about what constitutes "good sex" are so powerful; I know some young people who whenever they see a couple older than 50 years old kiss in a movie say "Oh, gross!" (How did you react to the picture on this page?)

However, the research data do not back up the Hollywood version of romance. In fact, studies prove that married people are more fulfilled in their sexual relations than other sexually active people. They are less likely to be disinterested in or to feel anxiety over sex. In fact, the studies over the years have found that many people in long-term marriages (over 25 years) report some of the highest levels of sexual satisfaction in their relationships (yes, for many of you reading this that would be your parents!). Even with their older, not so perfect bodies, people in long-term, loving marriages often report that they have the best sex! This is one of the best evidences of the *doctrine of the symbol* we learned about from Elder Holland in our foundation chapter about sexual intimacy. They have rich, deep relationships that are based on emotional and spiritual connections—which give their physical connections deeper meaning and pleasure.

It is important to note that research studies show that the benefits associated with marriage do not extend to cohabiting relationships. Couples who are living together have the same lower levels of health, on average, as single individuals. It is also important to note that most of these studies only examined marital status (i.e., married or not) and did not include measures of marital quality. The benefits of marriage increase even more when we examine "happy marriages" or "high quality marriages."

Selection versus causation?

As the research findings proving the benefits of marriage have piled up over the years, some have questioned whether these benefits are best explained by selection effects or causation effects. Let's talk for a minute about what that means.

The Theory of Selection

The theory of selection suggests that the reason why studies find that married people, on average, are better off than people who are not married is because healthier and more successful people are more likely to get married. Therefore, a higher proportion of healthy people select into marriage, thereby skewing the data. The key idea of the theory of selection is that it proposes that the benefits exist before marriage and there is nothing that marriage does to create or produce them.

The Theory of Causation

On the other hand, the theory of causation, suggests that there is actually something about marriage that causes or creates the benefits we have just discussed for married people. Thus, by entering marriage these benefits are gained and by exiting marriage these benefits are lost.

So Which Theory is Right?

So which theory is right? What type of research is needed to tell us if the benefits of marriage are best explained by the theory of selection or the theory of causation? Since we cannot do research studies that randomly assign some people to get married and others to stay single, the only kind of research studies that can help resolve this debate are studies that follows people over time. This kind of research is called longitudinal research.

By following people over several years of their life, researchers can measure a person's health before they get married and then see what happens after they get married. And, unfortunately, because divorce has become so common in our society, researchers can also measure what happens to some people's health when they exit a marriage. After a thorough review of longitudinal research on marriage, scholars have concluded that the benefits of marriage are best explained by the theory of causation. One group of leading marriage researchers concluded,

> ...differences between the married and divorced are sizeable, but may result from the selection of the healthy and successful into marriage and the unhealthy failures out. Many recent studies have addressed this selection by following individuals over time, to assess the relationship between changes in marital status and changes in their well-being. These studies consistently find that selection into or out of marriage does *not* account for the better physical or psychological health of married men or married women. *It appears that there is something about being married, and something about being unmarried that affects health and well-being* .(Doherty, Carroll, & Waite, 2006, Supporting the Institution of Marriage, p. 39, emphasis added)

So, how does marriage actually produce or create the benefits. It has to do with how married people live in comparison to how single or cohabiting people live. In a book chapter that I wrote with Dr. Bill Doherty and Dr. Linda Waite we explained some of the ways that marriage actually causes better health.

> ....in particular, scholars have theorized that there is something about the key features of institutional marriage that promotes health and wellbeing for spouses and children. Permanence, joint production, co-residence, and the social recognition of a sexual and childrearing union are, perhaps, the most important characteristics of the institution of marriage. Because two adults make a legally-binding promise to *live and work together for their joint well-being*, and to do so, ideally, for the rest of their lives, they tend to *specialize*, dividing between them the labor required to maintain the family. This specialization allows married men and women to produce more than they would if they did not specialize. The co-residence and resource sharing of married couples lead to substantial *economies of scale;* at any standard of living it costs much less for people to live together than it would if they lived separately. These economies of scale and the specialization of spouses

both tend to increase the economic well-being of family members living together.

The institution of marriage also assumes the sharing of economic and social resources and co-insurance. Spouses act as a *small insurance pool* against life's uncertainties, reducing their need to protect themselves by themselves against unexpected events. Marriage also connects spouses and family members to a *larger network of help*, support and obligation through their extended family, friends and others. The insurance function of marriage increases the economic well-being of family members. The support function of marriage improves their emotional well-being. The institution of marriage also *builds on and fosters trust.* Since spouses share social and economic resources, and expect to do so over the long term, both gain when the family unit gains. This reduces the need for family members to monitor the behavior of other members, increasing efficiency. (Doherty, Carroll, & Waite, 2006, Supporting the Institution of Marriage, p. 39, emphasis added)

Marriage Benefits for Men and Women

One of the most common myths about marriage is that men benefit from marriage, but women do not. For example, one USA Today headline proclaimed, "*Guys Wed for Better, Wives for Worse*" (October 11, 1993). Many people have heard the idea that marriage protects men from depression and makes women more vulnerable to depression. In academic circles, the origins of the myth that men benefit from marriage, but women do not can be traced back to a book written by Dr. Jesse Bernard in 1972 entitled, *The Future of Marriage*. In her book, Dr. Bernard argued that there are really two marriages: *his* marriage and *her* marriage. She argued that for men, marriage brings health, power, and satisfaction and for women it brings stress, dissatisfaction, and loss of self. Bernard's basic conclusion—marriage is good for men, but bad for women—is still widely repeated not only in popular culture but even in college textbooks and courses.

However, these views are based more in extreme ideology than they are based in empirical facts or research findings. Dr. Linda Waite and Dr. Maggie Gallagher are two of the leading experts in the world on the health benefits of marriage. They have studied the topic for two decades and are familiar with every study that has ever been done on the consequences of marriage for men and women. After extensively reviewing the literature they conclude,

> The evidence is in...both men and women gain a great deal from marriage. True, marriage does not effect men and women in exactly the same ways. Both men and women live longer, healthier, and wealthier lives when married, but husbands typically get greater health benefits from marriage than do wives. On the other hand, while men and women get bigger bank accounts and a higher standard of living in marriage, wives reap even greater financial advantages than do husbands. Overall, the portrait of marriage that emerges from two generations of increasingly sophisticated empirical research on actual husbands and wives is not one of gender bias, but gender balance: A good marriage enlarges and enriches the lives of both men and women. (Case for Marriage, 2002, p. 163)

If Marriage Benefits Both Men and Women, Why Do So Many People Say That Men Benefit More from Marriage Than Women Do?

The answer to this question is because it is true. Can this be possible? Can marriage benefit both men and women, but have a larger benefit for men? The answer is yes. But the reason for this has much more to do with how single men compare to single women than how married men compare to married women (see figure below). Single men have much poorer health and well-being than do single women. This is because single men, on average, engage in much higher levels of risk behaviors (i.e., binge drinking, drug use, criminal behavior, speeding while driving, etc.) and live less healthy lives (e.g., poor eating habits, poor sleep patterns, etc.) than single women. So, on average, men have *more room for improvement* in marriage than women do. Addressing this issue, Dr. Waite and Dr. Gallagher concluded,

> True, by some measures men's health benefits are somewhat more that women's, but that is largely because single men, as a group, are so much more prone to antisocial and unhealthy ways of living, which affects single men's mental and physical health. In other words, the reason getting a wife boosts your health more than acquiring a husband is not that marriage warps women, but that single men lead such warped lives. (Case for Marriage, 2000, p. 164)

In sum, marriage is good for women. But, marriage is salvation for men! Can you see why God ordained

The Benefits of Marriage for Men and for Women

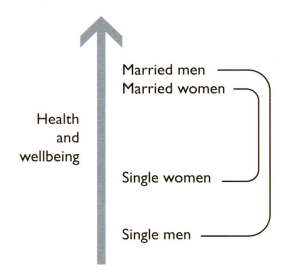

Marriage benefits men more because single men, on average, are so low (sorry guys!)

marriage and said that it is "not good that the man should be alone!" (Moses 3:16–18).

The social institution of marriage matters. It matters to spouses, to their children, and to our society as a whole. That is why the changing meaning and practice of marriage is something to be concerned about in the United States and in other parts of the world. As Dr. Waite and Dr. Gallagher concluded,

> The scientific evidence is now overwhelming: Marriage is not just one of a wide variety of alternative family forms, each of which is equally good at promoting the well-being of children or adults. Marriage is not merely a private relation; it is a public good. As marriage weakens, the costs are borne not only by individual children and families but by all of us. . . . (Case for Marriage, 2002, p. 186)

However, despite the fact that many people in our society will collectively lose the benefits of marriage as they avoid marriage or enter into marriages that do not follow the foundational patterns that have cre-

ated these benefits (e.g., permanence, specialization, partnership, etc.), each of us personally can seek after these benefits in our own lives. The divine design of marriage provides the template to the type of marriage that produces all of the benefits identified in research on healthy marriages.

Paradigms of Modernity

In addition to being knowledgeable about the social trends related to marriage in modern society, we also need to be wise about the ways of thinking in contemporary culture that may undermine our marriages. In this section, we discuss four *Paradigms of Modernity* or common ways of thinking that shape our society today. Each of these paradigms changes the meaning of marriage from God's intended purposes. In later chapters, we will discuss how these paradigms can negatively influence specific parts of dating and marriage relationships.

Secularism

Secularism is the belief that answers to life are found through rationale means. A secular individual or couple turns to intellectual sources of authority and devalues spiritual meanings. *The primary harm of secularism is that it distorts our view of truth.* Secular perspectives deceive people into believing that they can come to know the truth of things by themselves or that modern science will give us complete answers to all of life's questions. Ultimately, secularism disconnects God from all of the aspects of our lives—including marriage.

Is there any evidence that secularism is a growing part of modern society? A recent national survey conducted by the Pew Foundation found that 20% of young people between the ages of 18 and 25 in the United States report having no religious affiliation. This is more than double the number who reported no religious affiliation in previous generations.

The common theme we hear these days is that young adulthood is a time for you to come to know *what you want in life*. This reflects a secular view of life that is not concerned with God's will or purposes. Rather than seeking for what *you* want in life, the better focus of young adulthood is to come to know what *God* wants for your life. As the scriptures teach, "Trust in the Lord with all thine heart; and lean not unto thine own understanding. In all thy ways acknowledge him, and he shall direct thy paths" (Proverbs 3:5–6). The only way to do this is to not buy in to the secular paradigm of modern society.

Individualism

Individualism is the belief or assumption that rights, freedoms, and privileges of individuals should be given higher priority than the rights of society or groups. When taken to extremes, this perspective leads to the idea that families serve the needs of individuals, not individuals serving the needs of families. *The primary harm of individualism is that it distorts our view of progression.* Individualistic perspectives deceive people into believing that growth in this life is an individual pursuit. The individualistic person attempts to build their identity on personal accomplishments and achievements in areas such as school, work, or other activities; believing that such pursuits can provide a sense of meaning in this life. Ultimately, individualism disconnects growth from marriage and family relationships.

Is there any evidence that individualism is a growing part of modern society? In my current research on young adults in the United States, I have found that 67% of young people in our study report that before they will be ready to marry they must "fully experience the single

life." Marriage is frequently viewed by some young people today as something that will limit their potential or make them miss out on opportunities for growth and experience. These views reflect an individualistic view of life. God has ordained marriage for our lives because it is a context for rich spiritual growth and progression. There are very few worthwhile things you can do in life when you are single that you cannot do when you are married. But, there are numerous growth experiences that are experienced in marriage and family life.

The common theme we hear these days is that young adulthood is "a time to find yourself." Notice how this stands in contrast to Christ's teaching that whosoever will "deny himself" and "lose his life shall find it" (Matt 16:24–25). Christ also taught that, ". . . there are many who make themselves first, that shall be last, and the last first" (JST Mark 10: 30). The term *finding yourself* implies that you are somehow missing or lost and need to be found. You are not lost to God! If you truly want to "find yourself," then turn to your Father in Heaven who knows you better than anyone. As President Ezra Taft Benson taught, "Men and women who turn their lives over to God will discover that He can make a lot more out of their lives than they can" (The Teachings of Ezra Taft Benson, 1988, p. 361).

Materialism

Materialism is the belief that material objects, needs, and considerations are the most important parts of a good life and should be given much emphasis. A material approach to life believes that happiness comes from accumulating money and tangible possessions. *The primary harm of materialism is that it distorts our view of money and temporal resources.* Materialistic perspectives deceive people into believing that they will experience deep fulfillment and a high quality life if they can achieve economic success. Ultimately, materialism disconnects our financial decision-making from marriage, causing us to believe that our pursuit of material objects is separate from our marriage and family relationships. For some, marriage becomes simply viewed as a shared partnership in which two people work together to acquire material possessions.

Is there any evidence that materialism is a growing part of modern society? A recent national survey conducted by the Pew Foundation found that young people between the ages of 18 and 25 in the United States report that the top priority of their generation is to "make money." From my research project, my colleagues and I found that 86% of young adults agree with the statement that *It is extremely important to be economically set before you get married,* and 80% agreed with the statement, *Your educational pursuits or career development come before marriage at this time in your life.*

The common idea in society today is that young adulthood is a time for "getting ahead, before getting wed." While preparation for providing and caring for a future family is indeed an important part of young adulthood, many young people today are striving to accomplish financial goals before marriage that their parents and grandparents accomplished after marriage. Some young people today believe that they need to be finished with school, established in a career, and a homeowner before they are ready to get married. These were all seen as milestones of marriage by previous generations, not milestones before marriage. In God's plan, marriage is intended to be a cornerstone, not a capstone in our lives.

Hedonism

Hedonism is the belief that it is the accepted nature of people to seek pleasure and avoid pain.

Within a hedonistic approach to life, experiences that are pleasant, pleasurable, or comfortable are seen as good; while experiences that are unpleasant, require work, or are strenuous are seen as bad. Therefore, a hedonistic lifestyle seeks to emphasize pleasure, typically through physical pursuits related to sex, drugs, food, thrill-seeking activities, entertainment, and sleep. For our purposes in this chapter, *the primary harm of hedonism we will focus on is how it distorts our view of sexual intimacy.* Hedonistic perspectives deceive people into believing that there is no harm in enjoying the physical pleasures of sex outside of marriage.

Is there any evidence that hedonism is a growing part of modern society? Where do we begin?! There are numerous examples of how fixated our society has become on illicit sexual relationships and other hedonistic pursuits. The growth of the pornography industry, the use of sexual content in advertising, and the inclusion of sexual material in media all reflect our society's slide toward hedonistic values.

For many young people today, young adulthood is a time to experiment sexually. The conventional wisdom of the day is that during dating and engagement it is important to test the "sexual chemistry" in your relationship. This is a similar line of reasoning to the test-drive hypothesis of cohabitation we discussed earlier. And the research findings are similar too. Numerous studies have shown that people who have multiple sexual partners before marriage have higher divorce rates than people who begin their sexual experience with their spouse. Studies also show that premarital sex increases divorce rates, it does not lower them.

Modern Threats to Marriage

As you were reading about the paradigms of modernity, I bet you started to identify certain behaviors associated with each perspective that can damage marriages. In fact, because of the rise of the paradigms of modernity and the social tends we discussed at the first of the chapter, I am convinced that forming a loving and lasting marriage relationship in our current society can only be done with intentional efforts to be "in the world, but not of the world." Much of our modern culture is toxic to marriages. The figure below lists examples of the modern risks to marriage that emerge from the paradigms of modernity. We will discuss each one of these in detail in later chapters.

Modern Threats to Marriage

Secularism?	Spiritual waywardness, spiritual apathy
Individualism?	Selfishness, careerism, divorce, delay of marriage, intentional childlessness, narcissism, false self-esteem
Materialism?	Careerism, debt/financial strain
Hedonism?	Sexual immorality (pre-marital sex, non-marital childbirth, cohabitation, infidelity, porn, etc), addictions, excessive, leisure/recreation

Personal Reflection

As you review the list in the figure above, ask yourself if any of these risks are present in your life. If they are, they should be given the highest priority in your preparation for marriage or strengthening your current marriage. Remember that the paradigms of modernity are very pervasive. Each of us has been exposed to them numerous times throughout our lives. At first you may not be fully aware of how materialistic or individualistic you are in your orientation to life.

The old rhetorical question is *Can a fish describe*

water? The meaning of this phrase is that because a fish swims in water every day, and has only known life in water, it may not be aware of what water is. The same can be said of you and me as we live in a secular culture that is becoming so individualistic, materialistic, and hedonistic. It is quite possible that you are not aware of how much you have internalized these values and lifestyles.

When it comes to removing the paradigms of modernity from our lives it is *not a matter of if* the paradigms are a part of our thinking, but *a matter of how much* they are present. As you recognize the damaging effects these attitudes and behaviors can have on your life, you are better prepared to remove them from your dating and marriage relationships.

SECTION 2

Becoming a Right Person

For more than 80 years, researchers have sought to identify what causes some marriages to succeed and others to fail. In this pursuit, researchers have identified a certain number of "common characteristics" of successful couples and marriages. This does not mean that all successful couples are exactly the same, but there are some key behaviors and patterns that are always present in healthy marriage relationships. Of particular note, scholars have found that there are certain personal characteristics or virtues that happily married spouses have developed that help them create healthy marriages. These personal characteristics are developed during adolescence and young adulthood; and continue to be refined during the transition to marriage.

In this section, we will shift our focus to a discussion of becoming a right person for marriage. In particular, you will be introduced to these common factors that researchers have found to be present in loving and lasting marriages. These factors come together to form what we will call *The Ecology of Marriage*—because these personal traits and communication patterns form an inter-connected system that have been found to be different in successful and unsuccessful marriages.

Over many years, marriage prediction scholars have found that a person's readiness for marriage is largely determined by their *ability to love* and the *ability to communicate*. In this section, we will discuss these important areas of becoming. Specifically, we will discuss how the ability to love consists of two aspects—personal security and marital virtues. The term *personal security* refers to a person's sense of self-importance, which involves perceptions of self-worth, the ability to regulate negative emotions (e.g., depression, anxiety, anger), and feelings of secure attachment. You will learn how personally secure people rely on sources of internal validation (e.g., the love of God, a sense of personal worth, personal optimism, etc.) rather than seeking external validation of their worth (e.g., through accomplishment, physical appearance, material possessions, unhealthy relationships, etc.). Personal security is the foundation for several key attributes that are need in dating and marriage relationships. These include courage, vulnerability, and a willingness to trust other people. Without personal security, vulnerability in close relationships becomes threatening and the fear of rejection will often dictate how people behave in dating situations. When this happens, there is less authenticity, disclosure, and mutual reliance in couple relationships—all necessary ingredients to forming an intimate and supportive relationship.

We will also discuss *marital virtues,* which reflect an orientation toward the importance of others and is embodied in traits such as kindness, commitment, fairness, sacrifice, forgiveness, and other personal virtues. As you strive to develop marital virtues, you will create the capacity to care for others and the maturity to allow their needs to become of equal or greater priority to your own. In recent years, marriage researchers have begun to conduct research studies on forgiveness, sacrifice, commitment, and other aspects of marital relationships—principles that most of us have learned about for years in Sunday school classes.

In this section, we will also discuss *effective communication*. While the first two aspects of personal readiness for marriage (e.g., personal security and marital virtues) typically influence our motives and intents in relationships, the third aspect, effective communication, deals more with our behaviors and actions. When our hearts are in the right place, we are ready to learn skills that can help us effectively express our love toward others. We will discuss how effective communication involves two primary skills—empathetic listening and *clear-sending communication.* As you develop these skills, you will be better prepared to establish healthy and productive couple interactions in dating and marriage relationships.

Becoming and Creating

Principles for Courtship and Marriage

CHAPTER 9

> You become what you hope your spouse will be and you'll have a greater likelihood of finding that person.
>
> *Elder David A. Bednar*

In the Foundations Section, we primarily focused on understanding marriage as a divine institution. In the remaining units, we shift our focus to understanding the couple relationship aspects of marriage, such as dating, communication, sexual intimacy, managing conflict, becoming parents, and managing finances in marriage. As you will recall, in the first chapter, I mentioned viewing marriage as a couple relationship is not wrong—it is just incomplete.

We need to base our understanding of the couple relationships aspects of marriage on the principles of God's divine design for marriage. Now that you have studied the foundation principles of discipleship, cleaving, equal partnerships, family stewardships, and chastity; you are prepared to learn about the couple relationship aspects of marriage. By building on these foundation principles, you will come to have a deeper and far richer understanding of marriage than if you had studied the couple relationship aspects by themselves. All of the remaining chapters are best understood as extensions of the principles we discussed in Section I. For example, managing conflict in marriage is ultimately an expression of equal partnership and mutual decision-making in marriage. Following the proper stages of dating is a way that we demonstrate our discipleship and faith in the Lord and His prophets.

This chapter is a brief introduction to the remaining sections in the book. As you understand how the chapters fit together you will be better able to organize and synthesize the material you learn in the book.

Approaches to Dating

As I have studied dating patterns over the last 25 years, I have noticed that different people approach dating in different ways. Some of these "styles of dating" are unique to the individual and others are shared by many people. Among the shared approaches I have witnessed, I believe that there are two common approaches to dating during the young adult years—and which approach you follow will make quite a difference in how you go about the whole dating process.

The "Finding Mr. Right" Approach to Dating

The first approach to dating is what I call the *Finding Mr. Right Approach* to dating (or *Finding Mrs. Right* or *Finding Elder Right*—whichever fits best!). This approach is very popular in the mainstream culture and is quite common among Latter-day Saint young people too. This approach is emphasized in commercials for dating websites that promise to help each of us find "that one special person" who is right for you.

The primary question at the core of this approach to dating is—*How do I find the right person for me?* In sum, the focus in this style of dating is on *finding or matching* with the person you are meant to marry. Not only does this approach often create feelings of anxiety about dating as young people feel overwhelmed with the prospect of finding that perfect match out there (we will talk about this in a future chapter on *soulmates versus eternal companions*), but the implicit message in this approach to dating is that a successful marriage is first and foremost about making a good match with someone who is uniquely suited to us and our needs—someone who will love us just the way we are! If it is all about matching, then finding is the only process that matters.

Approaches to Dating

Finding Mr. Right
Focus = Finding or Matching
"How do I find the right person for me?"

Becoming Mr. Right
Focus = Becoming and Creating
"How do I become ready to form a loving and lasting relationship?"

The "Becoming Mr. Right" Approach to Dating

By contrast, the principles you have been studying in this book set a foundation for a different approach to dating. Within a *Becoming Mr. Right Approach* to dating (or *Becoming Mrs. Right*) the primary question is—*How can I be prepared to form and nurture an eternal marriage?* The primary difference is that this approach primarily emphasizes preparation and readiness. While a becoming-based approach to dating still emphasizes the importance of finding a right person to marry, finding is not the primary focus. Rather, you put your main emphasis on becoming ready for marriage and then creating a right relationship when you have made the decision to marry. In many ways, the mantra of this approach to dating is *The more you become a right person for marriage, the easier it will be to find a right person for marriage*. Successful marriage is seen as much the result of your own becoming and creating as it is finding a right person to marry.

Two Guiding Principles

The two remaining sections in the book are organized to help you practice a becoming-centered approach in your dating, courtship, and marriage. There are two guiding principles to the courtship and marriage process:

1. **Becoming** a right person for marriage
2. **Creating** a right relationship for marriage

There are several overarching lessons that emerge from incorporating these two guiding principles into your approach to dating and forming a lasting marriage, these include:

Becoming Should Precede Finding and Creating in Sequence

Becoming should precede finding in timing and sequence because the more ready you become for marriage, the better you will be able to find a right person for marriage. There are at least three reasons for why this is the case.

The Readier You Become, the More You Will Know Who to Find and How to Create a Relationship

The principles that apply to your readiness for marriage also apply to the readiness of the people you date. Because of this, the principles of becoming are also the principles of finding—they are two sides of the same coin.

The Readier You Become, the Better You Will Be at Finding and Creating

Your level of becoming will influence who you are able to attract or find. It is true that people tend to couple with partners of similar maturity and life goals. The first step to marrying a high quality person is to become a high quality person. You do not want to be in the hypocritical position of seeking to find qualities in another person that you cannot offer in return.

The Readier You Become, the More the Spirit of the Lord Will Guide You

As your spiritual maturity increases, you will be better prepared to seek and recognize the influence of the Lord in your dating experiences. While the Lord does not make dating decisions for you (we'll talk about this more in an upcoming lesson on seeking a spiritual confirmation in our marital decision making), the spirit can direct you to better understand God's purposes for your life.

Becoming Should Precede Creating in Priority

Becoming should also precede finding in priority because becoming continues after marriage, whereas finding occurs before marriage only. In short, becoming and committing are eternal processes, whereas finding is a time-limited experience. Thus, we should focus on the foundation processes that will last long after our dating years.

Marriage as a Couple Relationship

As you begin to study the couple relationship aspect of marriage, it will be important for you to make a distinction between the *common characteristics* of healthy couple relationships and the *personal preferences* each of us has for these relationships. For more than 80 years, researchers have sought to identify what causes some marriages to succeed and others to fail. In this pursuit, researchers have identified a certain number of common characteristics of marriages that last. These common characteristics should be seen as the *essential ingredients* of a loving and lasting marriage. This does not mean that all lasting marriages are exactly the same, but there are some key behaviors and patterns that are *always* present in healthy marriage relationships.

At the same time, each of us has some *personal preferences* in what we would like in a partner and relationship. These preferences may be in appearance, interests, or lifestyle patterns. While personal preferences are good, they are not necessarily essential to the success of a relationship. In upcoming chapters, we will discuss some of the risks of putting too much or too little emphasis on our personal preferences in dating and marriage.

The Metaphor of a Home

One way to distinguish the difference between the common characteristics of healthy marriages and our personal preferences for a relationship is to compare these aspects of couple relationships to the features of a home.

Imagine a large group of people all going house shopping together. What do you think are the chances that they will be able to settle on the same home? Not very likely, right? Someone in the group will want to purchase a house with a large country porch in a rural community; while another person in the group will want to purchase a contemporary home in a suburban neighborhood. Each person in the group will have dif-

ferent preferences for the style and features of the home they want to live in.

However, while each member of the group may have different preference in style, each of them will desire a home with some common features or attributes. No one wants a home with a cracked foundation, a leaky roof, or a furnace that does not work. Everyone wants a home with good mechanical features and a strong structure.

This metaphor fits what experts have learned about successful dating and marriage relationships. *Common factors* are the foundation aspects of a relationship that are needed to form a loving and lasting relationship. Just as all good homes have a solid foundation and a sturdy roof, all good marriages have open communication, forgiving spouses, and appropriate boundaries with extended family members. Personal preferences are more like the color of the paint on the walls or the style of couch in the living room. Personal preferences can matter, but we need to be careful about how much priority we give to these issues in dating and marriage. Clearly it would be a mistake to purchase a house with termites in the walls just because we liked the color of paint in the kitchen! Or to walk away from a very high quality home with a very stable foundation because it does not have every designer feature we may desire. The primary focus of the remaining sections of the

Three Views of Marriage

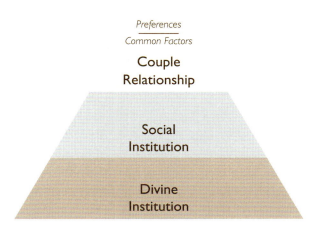

book is to teach you about the common factors of successful marriage so that you can focus your becoming and creating efforts in these areas.

THE ECOLOGY OF MARRIAGE

Marriage scholars have identified four main domains or groupings of common factors that explain why some marriages succeed and others fail (see figure at right; see Holman, 2006, Premarital Prediction of Marital Quality or Breakup). These four domains include:

1. Family of Origin Influences
2. Personal Readiness Characteristics
3. Couple Processes
4. Social Context Factors

Family of Origin factors have to do with your family and peer experiences while growing up. Scholars have found that factors such as the quality of your parents' marriage, whether or not your parents divorced, your relationship with your father, your relationship with your mother, and teen dating experiences can all influence later success in couple relationships.

Personal Readiness for Marriage: Researchers have also found that the individual characteristics and personalities of individuals can influence relationship success. In particular, scholars have identified three subsets of personal readiness factors: level of *personal security* (e.g., secure attachment, self-esteem, regulating negative emotions, etc.), *other-centeredness* (e.g., marital virtues, marital virtues, etc.) and *effective communication* skills (e.g., empathetic listening, clear sending of messages, etc.).

Couple Processes: Over the years, marriage researchers have found that what most distinguishes marriages that last from those that do not is the way that spouses interact with each other. Couple processes such as communication patterns, conflict management, emotional

An Eco-Developmental Model of Marriage
Jason S. Carroll, Ph.D.

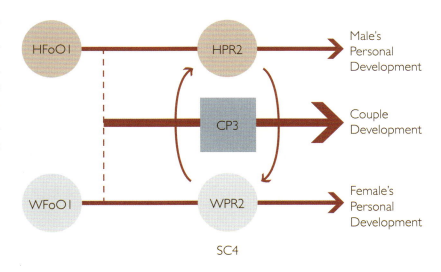

Internal Distal Factors

HFoO1 = Husband's family of origin
WFoO1 = Wife's family of origin

External Distal Factors

SC4 = Social Context

Proximal Factors

HPR2 = Husband's personal readiness
CP3 = Couple processes
WPR2 = Wife's personal readiness

intimacy and sexual intimacy have been found to be particularly important.

Social Contexts: In recent years, marriage researchers have also demonstrated that couple relationships do not exist in a bubble or on a desert island. All couples are surrounded by extended families, friends, neighborhoods, school demands, work schedules, and other environmental factor that can influence their relationship. Social context influences can be positive or they can be negative.

Notice how in the model family of origin influences and social context factors are labeled as *distal factors*. They are labeled this way because scholars have found that they play a more distant or background role in marriage success. They *indirectly* influence couple relationships by influencing individual maturity and couple processes. Family of origin and social context factors are not part of the actual marriage relationship, but they are factors that can influence the inner workings of dating and marriage relationships. Personal readiness characteristics and couple processes are labeled as *proximal factors* because they are the core of couple interaction and relationship dynamics. In simple terms, they are the relationship.

An Organic Model—The Marriage Ecology Tree

While the mechanical model presented on the previous page demonstrates some of the relationships between the four domains of common factors in marriage, it often does not fully convey the ecological nature of these domains. The figure below presents an organic representation of the same four domains as a tree, with family of origin influences represented as the soil, personal characteristics as the roots, couple processes as the trunk, and social processes as the climate or environment. Notice how the *distal factors* are not actually part of the tree (e.g., soil and climate), but they influence the health of the tree. The proximal factors are actual parts of the tree (e.g., roots and trunk). This model will help you keep the domains organized as you study them in coming chapters.

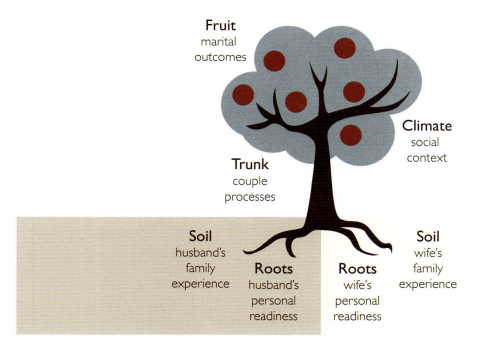

Ecology of Marriage

Family of Origin

BACKGROUND INFLUENCES ON DATING AND MARRIAGE
CHAPTER 10

> A transitional character is one who, in a single generation, changes the entire course of the lineage....Their contribution to humanity is to filter the destructiveness out of their own lineage so that generations downstream will have a supportive foundation upon which to build productive lives.
>
> *Dr. Carlfred Broderick*

In this chapter, we discuss the process of *becoming* a right person for marriage. Of course, the principle of discipleship is the foundation of becoming ready for marriage. In this chapter we will build upon the foundation principle of discipleship.

This chapter also begins a series of chapters in which we discuss the Ecology of Marriage Tree. As you will recall from the previous chapter, this ecosystem of marriage is made up of four primary domains or groupings of factors of common characteristics of successful marriages. In the previous chapter these domains were compared to the components of a tree with two root systems (see figure at left).

In this chapter, we study family of origin influences on becoming a right person for marriage. In the tree model, family of origin influences are compared to the soil that the tree is planted in (in this case "his soil" and "her soil"). This representation can be insightful because the quality of the soil around a tree can impact how the tree grows. Like the relationship between soil and the roots of a tree, family of origin factors (the soil) primarily influence personal readiness levels (the roots) in dating and marriage.

However, unlike real trees, you need to see your *personal readiness roots* as *intentional roots*—which means that you have agency and you can decide which nutrients in the soil to bring into the tree and which toxins in the soil to leave behind. Our focus in this chapter is to help you increase your awareness of how your experiences growing up impact your current attitudes and behaviors related to dating and marriage. With this insight, you can be more intentional about which parts of your family experience you bring forward and which parts you leave behind as you set out to form or maintain a healthy marriage relationship.

The Generational Nature of Married Life

Families are different than any other social organization. Perhaps the most notable difference between families and other social organizations is that families are *generational*, which means they exist over time and across different generations of family members. The generational nature of family relationships has two significant implications for your efforts to become ready for marriage.

Kindred Family

The first implication of the generational nature of families is that every marriage is somehow connected to and embedded in an extended family system. Elder J. Richard Clarke called this extended family system the *kindred family;* he explained,

> In the earliest biblical culture, the family was more than a parent and child unit. It included all who were related by blood and marriage. This kindred family, as I prefer to call it, was strongly linked by natural affection and the partriarchal priesthood. The elderly were venerated for their experience and wisdom. There was strength and safety in numbers and, through love and support, members established solidarity and continuity. (Ensign, May 1989, p. 60)

The old phrase is *No man is an island.* When we understand that all marriages are linked to an extended family system we can also say *No marriage is an island.* Also, notice how Elder Clarke mentions the generational nature of the patriarchal priesthood (i.e., priesthood of the fathers), similar to our discussions about equal partnership and shared decision making in marriage.

The Generational Stream

The second implication of the generational nature of families is that every one of us experiences a "generational stream" where we have certain values, behaviors, and lifestyles that are passed on to us from previous generations; and we in turn pass on these things to an upcoming generation. The metaphor of a stream is appropriate here, because the "current" or "flow" of the generational stream can be powerful in shaping who we are and how we approach our adult lives. Learning to successfully navigate the generational stream is one of life's most important tasks.

Two Key Tasks of Marriage Readiness

Due to the generational nature of marriage, there are two key tasks you must accomplish to become ready for marriage:

First, you must come to understand and appreciate how your family background experiences influence your thinking and behaviors in *current* relationships. This influence can be for good or for bad, or a mixture of both. As you study family of origin factors, you should have a "here and now" focus. The goal is not to understand the past for the past's sake, rather the goal is to understand the past so that you can fully understand the present.

Two Key Tasks of Marriage Readiness

- *Here and Now Focus*
  Come to understand and appreciate how your family background experiences influence your thinking and behaviors in current relationships.

- *Stability vs. Change*
  Finding an appropriate balance between stability and change in relation to your family of origin.

Second, you must find an appropriate balance between *stability* and *change* in relation to your family of origin. All of us have both positive and negative aspects of our families. In some families there is high proportion of positive family patterns and in other families the negative seems to dominate. Whether your family has a 90%—10% ratio or a 10%—90% between positive and negative behaviors, or even a 50%-50% ratio, you'll need to find a balance on what passes on and what does not. We each have to judge what the ratio may be in our particular case, but no matter the ratio, each of us has to seek a balance of *stability* (e.g., the attitudes and behaviors we keep doing and pass on to our children) and *change* (e.g., the attitudes and behaviors we stop doing and do not pass on to our children).

In this chapter, you will be introduced to two principles—a principle of stability and a principle of change.

Stability—"Going with the Flow"

Family scholars have long appreciated the generational nature of families and the *generational stream* into which each person is born. Scholars use the term *intergenerational transmission* to describe the process of how families transmit their lifestyles from one generation to the next. Research has revealed two things about intergenerational transmission. First, that it is universal. All families engage in intergenerational transmission. Some aspects of intergenerational transmission are explicit and intentional, others are implicit and non-intentional. Sometimes parents are very aware of the values and behaviors they are passing on to their children, and other times they are not aware of the messages that are passed on.

The second truth that research on intergenerational transmission has revealed is that the process is wide ranging. There are several aspects of family life

that are passed on from one generation to the next. These include:

- Beliefs (ideologies & values)
- Behavior patterns (ways of doing things)
- Communication (skills & handling differences)
- Emotions (intimacy & handling stress)

Everything from our religious beliefs to the most common of day to day behaviors is influenced by intergenerational transmission. Intergenerational transmission influences just about everything in our lives.

For example, when you load a dishwasher do you put the silverware face up or face down? As I have asked this question to large groups of people and ask them to raise their hands for their preference, I always have a large portion of the group indicate "face up" and another large portion indicate "face down." And, there is always a third group that is a bit puzzled on which to indicate because they put the forks and spoons face up and the knives face down!

If you ask people to explain themselves you will hear two lines of reasoning. The first group will tell you that you should put the silverware face up so that it will be more exposed to the water spray in the dishwasher and get cleaner. The second group will say that you should put the silverware face down because if it is up your hands will touch the part you eat off of when you pull it out—thus erasing the benefit of being cleaner.

Now, this may seem like a silly example of intergenerational transmission, but chances are you have a specific way you load silverware into a dishwasher and chances are you are pretty sure that your way is the right way to do it! In fact, until you saw a neighbor or roommate load a dishwasher differently than you do, you may not have even been aware that there was another way to do it (although your roommate was doing it wrong, right?).

Key Factors: Stability Across Generations

There are several key family of origin factors that researchers have found to have some stability across generations. This means that as you examine how your family of origin influences your current attitudes and behaviors, these are the main factors to look at (see Holman, 2006, Premarital Prediction of Marital Quality or Breakup). These factors include:

The Quality of Your Parents' Marriage

Research has shown that the quality of your parents' marriage can influence how you think about and act in your own dating and marriage relationship. In fact, from as early as the 1930s, scholars have found that how much someone agrees with the statement, *I*

want my marriage to be like my parents' marriage is a reliable predictor of how happy he or she is likely to be in their own marital quality.

The reason why marital quality transmits across generations like this is that children develop positive expectations for marriage and are able to model their own marriage after the healthy patterns they observed in their parents' marriage. Children who do not have this "healthy marriage model" in their home have to intentionally seek other marriage mentors from whom they can model positive interaction.

THE INTERGENERATIONAL TRANSMISSION OF DIVORCE

In addition to studying parents' marital quality, researchers have also studied the impact of parental divorce on the divorce rates of their children. This research has been discussed in the popular media of magazines and television, so many people have heard that people who have divorced parents tend to have higher rates of divorce themselves as adults. Is this true? The answer is yes. Numerous studies have shown that there is an *intergenerational transmission of divorce* (see Amato, 1996, Explaining the Intergenerational Transmission of Divorce). On average, the adult children of divorced parents have higher divorce rates than children whose parents are still married. However, there is a second part to the story—the part that is rarely talked about in the popular media.

If your parents divorced does it mean that you will automatically have a greater chance of getting divorce? The simple answer to this question is no. There are many people who come from divorced homes who go on to have wonderful marriages. Research in the last few years has been trying to better understand the intergenerational transmission of divorce and why it is that some children of divorce have higher divorce rates, but others do not. What they have found is that the relationship between parental divorce and their children's marriages is moderated by *marital commitment* levels in the children (see Amato & DeBoer, 2001, The Transmission of Marital Instability Across Generations). What this means is that only the children

of divorce who have lower levels of commitment have higher divorce rates, those with high levels of marital commitment have as low or lower divorce rates as children from homes where their parents remained married.

To understand this research, you need to remember, as we discussed in a previous chapter, that the divorce rate does not apply to all couples uniformly. While the average divorce rate in the United States is currently at about 50%, this does not mean that every couple has a 50% chance of getting divorced. Some couples have a 90% chance of divorce and others have a 10% chance—the average is 50%. Researchers have found that some children of divorce have very high divorce rates (thus raising the average level for all children of divorce) and other children of divorce have very low divorce rates (as low or lower than children from intact parent homes).

As I just mentioned, the key that distinguishes which group someone falls into is the level of commitment they have in marriage. Because they want to avoid the negative consequences they saw in their parents' failed marriage, some children of divorce are scared about commitment in dating and marriage relationships. These individuals are always planning an *"escape route"* out of relationships—*"just in case"* things do not work out. However, this approach to relationships cre-

ates a self-fulfilling prophecy of sorts as it lowers their willingness to sacrifice in marriage and dramatically raises their chances of getting a divorce.

On the other hand, some children of divorce are very motivated to not follow in their parents' footsteps. They know firsthand the struggles for children when parents' divorce and they are committed to not passing that on to their own children. With this high level of commitment to their marriage, these children of divorce make the needed sacrifices in their marriages and have very low divorce rates. Nothing is determined—anyone can have a loving and lasting marriage. The key is in your current attitudes and behaviors.

The Quality of Parent-Child Relationship

Another important family-of-origin factor is the quality of relationships you had with your mother and your father while growing up. When relationships with parents were warm and supportive growing up, adult children find it easier to be open and trusting in their current relationships. Parents also can influence the sense of self-worth and self-confidence their children have as they move into adulthood.

Childhood or Teen Trauma

Unfortunately, some people have traumatic experiences during their childhood or teenage years such as abuse, poverty, debilitating illness, parental neglect, or other forms of adversity. Sometimes these types of experiences can have lingering effects on a person's sense of self-worth and self-confidence. In cases of abuse, there is often difficulty with the emotional vulnerability and physical closeness involved in exclusive dating and marriage. If you have been the victim of abuse, it will be very important for you to come to terms with this part of your background and make sure that you are able to heal both emotionally and spiritually from these unfortunate events. Some people who have experienced abuse in their past find professional counseling to be helpful in learning to manage their emotions and reactions so that they can have satisfying and healthy adult relationships.

Teen Peer and Dating Experiences

While family of origin factors typically focus on experiences within the family realm, this domain in the ecology of marriage also includes peer and dating experiences in the teenage years. During our teenage years, each of us starts to develop a sense of ourselves in relation to members of the opposite sex. For some, these experiences create a sense of confidence and a positive regard toward dating. For others, they feel unattractive and unsuccessful with dating and carry those feelings into their young adult years. Each of us needs to be

aware of how our dating history influences our current attitudes and behaviors about dating and marriage.

Change—"Altering the Flow"

While intergenerational transmission is a powerful part of every person's life, it is not a deterministic force. We must always understand the principle of intergenerational transmission within the broader lens of the gospel, including the principle of agency. Elder Neal A. Maxwell explains,

> Of course our genes, circumstances, and environments matter very much, and they shape us significantly. Yet, there remains an inner zone in which we are sovereign, unless we abdicate. In this zone lies the essence of our individuality and our personal accountability. . .God thus takes into account not only our desires and our performance, but also the degrees of difficulty which our varied circumstances impose upon us. (Ensign, November, 1996, p. 21)

As you just read about the intergenerational transmission of divorce, not all children of divorce experience the same outcome. Within this *"inner zone"* that Elder Maxwell mentions some choose to maintain a high commitment to marriage in their own lives, while others allowed their parents' marriage decisions to lower their commitment to their own marriages. It is this ability to choose and be sovereign that is the essence of the ability to change generational patterns and form new healthy patterns when needed. This is true of all family of origin factors—the same experience does not always produce the same result.

Transitional Characters

Scholars refer to someone who changes generational patterns a *"transitional character."* This term was coined by Dr. Carlfred Broderick, a highly respected family scholar who was a Latter-day Saint. Dr. Broderick explained,

> A transitional character is one who, in a single generation, changes the entire course of the lineage. The changes might be for good or ill, but they break the mold. They refute the observation that abused children become abusive parents. . .Their contribution to humanity is to filter the destructiveness out of their own lineage so that generations downstream will have a supportive foundation upon which to build productive lives. (Marriage and the Family, 1988, p. 14)

Notice how Dr. Broderick uses the metaphor of filtering impurities out of a stream so that family members downstream will have pure and healthy water to drink.

In addition to examples from research, the scriptures are full of examples of transitional characters. Some, like Laman, Lemuel, and King Noah did not follow the example of their righteous parents. Others were righteous transitional characters. Perhaps the best example we have of a transitional character in all of scripture is the prophet Abraham. He grew up in an unrighteous home where his father worshipped idols and practiced human sacrifice. Abraham records in his

own record that he left his father's house seeking after a better way and seeking the priesthood and thus "holding the right belonging to the fathers" (Abraham 1:2). If you are seeking to be a transitional character in your own life, I highly recommend that you read the first three chapters of the Book of Abraham in the Pearl of Great Price. These chapters provide a wonderful example of a transitional character to shaped his life beyond his background.

Coming to Terms—Intentionality

Family of origin factors are a lot like the quality of the air we breathe. When we are breathing fresh, clean air we rarely think much about the breathing process. However, if the air around us becomes polluted or stagnant we become very aware of it! In fact, if air quality becomes bad enough, nothing else matters until we can restore our breathing.

For some of you, it is probably quite easy to take your family of origin experiences for granted. If you experienced a relatively happy home with well-functioning parents and a supportive family environment, you likely have not given your family background experiences a lot of thought. If this is the case for you, hopefully this chapter has helped you see what a blessing your extended family has been in your life.

Unfortunately, for others of you, you are very aware of your family of origin experiences because they have been hurtful to you in some way. If this is the case for you, then you will need to engage in a process of coming to terms with your family of origin experiences as you increase your readiness for marriage.

As you do this, remember that family of origin factors are *distal factors* in the ecology of marriage. These means that family of origin factors influence your current relationships *indirectly* by impacting other factors—particularly in the domain of personal maturity (the roots). In particular, they influence the root of *personal security*, which involves emotional regulation (e.g., anger, sadness, anxiety, etc.) and a willingness to be vulnerable (e.g., self-worth, trusting, disclosure, etc.). Family of origin factors also influence levels of commitment and communication skills in dating and marriage. These are the areas you should focus on in coming to terms with any negative influences from your family of origin. The next three chapters discuss each of these aspects of personal maturity in detail.

Current Family Relationships

There are two primary source of healing that can be applied in cases where family of origin experiences have been less than ideal. The first is to make intentional efforts to improve current family relationships. Extended family members are unique in the ecology of marriage in that they are a part of two domains in the system. As we have discussed in this chapter, they are an important part of the soil or past experiences; but they are also a part of the current climate or environment that surrounds dating and new marriage relationships. When current relationships can be improved, it benefits the relationship at both levels. It provides a healthier social context for the marriage and changes any negative feelings about the past. You should make every effort possible to nurture positive and mature relationships with your parents, siblings, and other extended family members.

The Atonement of Jesus Christ

The other primary source of healing from negative family experiences is the Atonement of Jesus Christ. As we view our family background as experiences intended to further our eternal development, we posi-

tion ourselves to more fully benefit from the principles of healing found within the gospel of Jesus Christ. A knowledge of our Eternal Father's plan can ease emotions associated with struggles in our past and can provide needed guidance along the often unpredictable journey towards healing. Speaking on the scriptural question the Savior posed to the grieving Mary Magdalene, "Woman, why weepest thou?" President James E. Faust suggests that the Savior was not just speaking to the sorrowing Mary, rather he was also speaking to all of us "for the tears of sorrow, pain, or remorse are the common lot of mankind." He further explains that all of us can "benefit from the transcendent blessings of the Atonement and the Resurrection, through which the *divine healing process* can work in our lives" (Ensign, November 1996, p. 52, emphasis added).

Jesus Christ," which "leads to faith in Him and obedience to His commandments" (Ensign, May 1994, p. 9).

The prophet Alma also provided a crucial insight into the nature of the Atonement and Christ's healing power when he addressed the people of Gideon. Referring to the Savior, Alma taught:

> And he shall go forth, suffering pains and afflictions and temptations of every kind; and this that the word might be fulfilled which saith he will take upon him the pains and sicknesses of his people. . . . And he will take upon him their infirmities that his bowels may be filled with mercy, . . .that he may know according to the flesh how to succor his people. (Alma 7: 11–12)

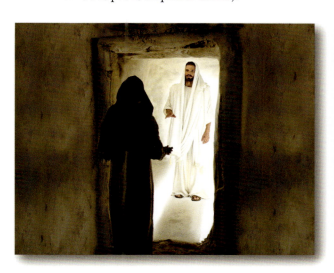

While the specific steps in the process of coming to terms with negative family background experiences are unique for each person's situation, the gospel of Jesus Christ provides a firm directional course for each of us to follow as we move along our own personal pathways to healing. Summarizing the Lord's pathway to healing, Elder Richard G. Scott noted that the surest, most effective, path comes through an application of the teachings of Jesus Christ in our lives. He further noted that such a path begins with an understanding and appreciation of the "principles of the Atonement of

From this scripture, we learn two important truths. First, the Atonement's healing power is not only for overcoming the effects of sin, but also extends to the entire range of mortal suffering and adversity (Bruce Hafen, The Broken Heart, 1989, p. 50). Elder Neal A. Maxwell noted, "Since not all human sorrow and pain is connected to sin, the full intensiveness of the Atonement involved bearing our pains, infirmities, and sicknesses, as well as our sins" (Not My Will, But Thine, 1988, p. 51).

The second truth we learn from Alma's words is that because the Savior has experienced the complete range of human suffering and loss, He is uniquely positioned to comprehend our pain and succor us in our times of personal suffering. As Elder Merrill J. Bateman counseled:

> The Savior's atonement in the garden and on the cross is intimate, as well as infinite. Infinite in that it spans the eternities. Intimate in that the Savior felt each person's pains, sufferings, and sicknesses. Consequently, He knows how to carry our sorrows and relieve our burdens that we might be healed from within, made whole persons, and receive everlasting joy in his kingdom. (Ensign, May 1995, p. 14)

As we realize that the blessings of Christ's Atonement extend to all of life's suffering and that the Lord truly understands our situation, we can more fully turn to the Savior as we come to terms with any negative family of origin experiences we have gone through and accept His invitation: "Come unto me, all ye that labour and are heavy laden, and I will give you rest. Take my yoke upon you and learn of me; for I am meek and lowly in heart: and ye shall find rest unto your souls" (Matthew 11:28–30).

While coming to terms with family of origin experiences, exercising faith in Jesus Christ involves trusting that the Lord knows what is best for us and can direct our lives in those ways that will allow us to reach our fullest potential. Our trust in the Lord must be more powerful and enduring than our confidence in our own feelings and experience. Often this means being willing to obey, even when we do not know the end from the beginning. As the book of Proverbs counsels: "Trust in the Lord with all thine heart; and lean not unto thine own understanding. In all thy ways acknowledge him, and he shall direct they paths" (Prov. 3: 5–6). Surrendering ourselves to God's will is not an easy process, but as we follow the Savior's example and sincerely pray unto the Lord, "Thy will be done" (Matt. 26:39), we

position ourselves to receive of the Lord's divine healing power.

Saviors on Mount Zion

Dr. Broderick wrote about transitional characters in both his scholarly writing, but also in his writings for members of the Church. He explained that within a gospel view, transitional characters act as "*Saviors on Mount Zion*" as they take upon themselves the impurities in a family line and filter them out for later generations. This act is very similar to what the Savior did in His sacrifice for all of us in that the pains that He suffered were from the choices and actions of others. Plus, with the added understanding of vicarious ordinances in the temple, transitional characters may bless their

family lines not only downstream, but also upstream as they receive the blessings of the gospel.

This type of understanding helps us see that the common notion that righteous individuals are always sent to righteous families is not true. That was certainly not the case for Abraham. In fact, the Lord may send many of his most valiant sons and daughters into families where they can be transitional characters and change the direction of the line. The central message of the gospel is the possibility and reality of change through the Atonement of Christ.

Personal Security

Personal Readiness, Part I
CHAPTER 11

> Remember the worth of souls is great in the sight of God. For, behold, the Lord your Redeemer suffered death in the flesh; wherefore he suffered the pains of all men, that all men might repent and come unto him.
>
> (D&C 18:10–11)

The question we set out to answer in this chapter is: *Is the pursuit of self-esteem a good thing?* For most people in Western culture the answer to this question is common sense. Of course we should seek to have good self-esteem. When it comes to dating and marriage the common cliché in the popular culture is *you can't love others until you love yourself.* According to this line of thought, one of the most important developmental tasks of young adulthood is to "find yourself" and come to "love yourself" so that you will be able to love others without "losing yourself." Even among Latter-day Saints it is not uncommon to hear people talk about the importance of developing good self-esteem and positive regard for yourself.

Are these perspectives about self-esteem accurate? Do you need to have high self-esteem to succeed in dating, marriage and family life?

The answer to these questions is both yes and no. Modern philosophies on self-esteem are accurate about the beneficial *characteristics of self-esteem*, such as self-confidence, a positive outlook on life, and optimism; but they are inaccurate in the prescribed *origins of self esteem* (i.e., self-love and achievement). In many ways, the notion that we need to develop a "love of self" sits in direct contrast to the Savior's commandment that we should "love one another; as I have loved you, that ye also love one another" (John 13:34). Christ's love was not a love of self. The example of the Savior is one of other-centered love, not self-centered love.

How then do we achieve the characteristics of self-esteem? What are the true foundations or origins

of self-worth, self-confidence, and emotional security? To answer these questions you must understand two key issues. First, you must understand your true nature. This understanding is based in an understanding of the principles of *Amae*. Second, you must understand the true origins of what Elder Neal A. Maxwell called "justifiable self-esteem" (The Neal A. Maxwell Quote Book, 1997, p. 306). This understanding is based in an understanding of the principle of *belonging*.

You will recall that in our Ecology of Marriage Tree there are three roots that represent the three subsets of personal readiness factors that have been identified as common characteristics in healthy marriages. These sub-factors are *personal security* (root 1), *other-centeredness* (root 2), and *effective communication skills* (root 3). In this chapter, we study the first root—personal security. The root of personal security is the primary way that family of origin influences enter into the marriage system. Personal security also sets the foundation for the other aspects of personal readiness and maturity, namely other-centeredness and effective communication.

Amae: Our True Nature

Elder Bruce Hafen and Sister Marie Hafen have taught about the Japanese concept of a*mae* (pronounced ah-my-a'). They translate this principle to mean "a longing for belonging" that is a fundamental part of our natures. They explain, "People simply desire to be connected with others, especially in close relationships. They are feeling the longing to belong. . . .Both our theology and the feelings of our hearts make us want to belong, now and eternally, to the father of our Spirits, to his Son, and to those we love on earth" (The Belonging Heart, 1994, pp. 9–11).

This longing to belong is a basic human need that is shared by all people. Although an individualistic society such as ours champions independence and not relying on others, this cannot change the fundamental need we each have to be deeply connected to others. Elder and Sister Hafen commented,

> Amae describes the innate need and desire within each person to depend on and feel connected to other people, especially in relationships of love and intimacy. In a sense, amae is the desire to receive love. Through the fulfillment of our amae we find not only security but also freedom and meaning. (Belonging Heart, p. 21)

Notice how Elder and Sister Hafen describe amae as the "desire to receive love." In the language of the gospel, charity is the *giving* of Christ-like love and *amae* is the receiving of Christ-like love. This is why charity is the greatest gift of the spirit (1 Cor 13:13) because it fulfills the deepest and most basic of others' needs—to be loved and cared for.

The At-one-ment of Jesus Christ

Ultimately, the principle of amae gives us insights into the power and promise of the Atonement of Jesus Christ. The Hafens explain, "The gospel's most fundamental promise is the At-one-ment of Jesus Christ, which offers the assurance of returning us to unity with God in eternal satisfaction of our amae" (Belonging Heart, p. 21). Thus, the atonement can make us one with God and with our spouses in marriage—fulfilling our greatest need—to love and be loved in eternal relationships.

It is important to note, that the concept of amae is not unique to the Japanese culture or to the gospel perspectives shared by Elder and Sister Hafen. Similar concepts can be found in the social sciences that use other language systems to describe this basic human need to feel loved and be connected to others. For example, *Attachment Theory*, a highly regarded theory in developmental psychology, discusses the universal need in human infants to develop a secure attachment with their primary caregiver—typically their mother. Hundreds of studies have shown that children who do not develop this type of secure attachment relationship struggle with feelings of anxiety and avoidance in relationships, while children with secure attachment carry forward a sense of personal security and confidence. Whether it is called amae, a need to belong, attachment, a need to be loved, or some other term the concept is the same—it is our basic human nature to need to be loved. In short, we are relational beings and our true nature desires closeness and intimacy in permanent relationships.

Belonging: The Basis of Self-Worth

As we come to fully appreciate amae and our relational natures, we gain insights into the true origins of the type of personal security that will benefit us in dating and marriage. Simply put, personal security is found in the fulfillment of our amae. The fulfillment of our amae is found in belonging to God and to others. It is through this belonging and investment in others that we develop a true sense of freedom and wellbeing. This is why the Hafens explained that perhaps the best translation for the concept amae is found in the German translation of the term *Freiheit in Geborgenheit*, which means "freedom through emotional security." This stands in direct contrast to the common Western notion of seeking freedom through the rejection of dependency.

How can increased investments in others and commitments to care for their needs increase our freedom?

The key to understanding this principle is to remember that there are two types of freedom—*freedom from* and *freedom for*. When we are free *from* commitments to others we have increased independence of time and resources, but we also lack the closeness and intimacy we need. Plus, we feel more distant from our Father in Heaven as we turn our focus on ourselves, rather than serving others. This frequently heightens our sense of anxiety and avoidance in relationships. While committing ourselves to others constrains our time and resources in some ways, it also fulfills our deepest needs—thus freeing us from anxiety or self-doubt. Because this is according to our divine nature, this type of freedom allows us to live for others and God—returning to us a deep sense of personal security and wellbeing.

The Hafens also discussed how belonging is connected to developing a sense of personal identity. They explained, "growth is the conceptual bridge between

belonging and individual identity" (Belonging Heart, p. 63). Thus, the commitments of marriage become an essential context for personal growth and development.

> Marriage is one of the Lord's primary institutions for perfecting us individually, because taking upon ourselves the unlimited commitments of marriage and parenthood will develop our core personality and character to levels that are otherwise almost impossible to find. (Belonging Heart, p. 71)

Self-Esteem = Fruit or Root?

A study of amae and belonging raises questions about how we should view self-esteem, particularly in the context of marriage. An emphasis on self-esteem often contributes to greater selfishness, excessive individualism, and processes that undermine healthy marriage processes. A focus on enhancing self-esteem tends to focus people's attention on their self, and this promotes a certain type of self-consciousness, self-attention, and self-preoccupation (see Burr & Christensen, 1992, Undesirable Side Effects of Enhancing

Self-Esteem). It evaluates the concern people have for their own self to an important and focused on part of their lives, and the net result of this is that it promotes selfishness. Rather than help people become more connected in intimate ways, attention to the self preoccupies them with their own self and thereby focuses their attention less on things such as their care, concern, love, compassion, and connection with others.

Common Factors Related to Personal Security

So why does a deeper understanding of the origins and nature of personal security matter? Quite simply, because people with better personal security have better relationships and marriages (they are better parents too). Over three decades of research has shown that different measures of personal security are predictive of marital success. These include:

Self-Esteem / Sense of Self-Worth

Several studies have shown that people with better self-esteem make better partners in dating and marriage relationships (see Shackelford, Self-Esteem in Marriage, 2001). People with a high sense of self-worth are less anxious in relationships and better at giving attention to other people. Rather than worrying about making a good impression, high self-esteem individuals are able to focus on others and their needs. By contrast, research has shown that individuals with low self-esteem are anxious about being accepted and worry that others are not as interested in them as they are in others. Sometimes low self-esteem can lead people to compromise their standards or values in an effort to get others to like them. Plus, low self-esteem can lead people to stay in dating relationships that are not good for them because they fear that no one else will be interested in them so they might as well settle for what they have.

Secure Attachment

As noted previously, research using attachment theory has shown that people with a secure attachment style (low anxiety and low avoidance in relationships) form romantic relationships more easily and at a deeper level than individuals with insecure styles of attachment (see Sandberg, Busby, & Johnson, 2012, The BARE Scale). Two primary insecure attachment styles have been identified—*preoccupied insecure* and *avoidant insecure*. Preoccupied attachment occurs when someone views others positively, but has a negative image of themselves. Therefore, they seek relationships (low avoidance), but they are very anxious (high anxiety) that they will not be accepted or attractive to others. This creates a form of self-focus that disrupts relationship formation. Avoidant attachment occurs when someone has a positive view of themselves, but a negative view of others. Therefore, they avoid relationships (high avoidance), but profess to have little anxiety (low anxiety) about not being in a committed relationship. Avoidant people are reluctant to rely on others and often struggle to disclose and let themselves be vulnerable in relationships.

Negative Affect Regulation

Marriage researchers have found that people with high levels of personal security are better able to regulate their negative emotions such as anger, anxiety, and depression (see Beach et al., 1990, Depression in Marriage). This is called *negative affect regulation*. This does not mean that individuals with high personal security do not experience anger or sadness, it just means that they are able to keep these emotions from controlling their actions (or reactions). When people experience chronic (lasts for a long time) and/or severe (high intensity) bouts of anger, anxiety, or depression it starts to influence their relationships with other people, particularly their romantic partners or spouses. The old cliché in marriage counseling is that the only thing tougher than being depressed is being married to someone who is depressed. The research proves this to be true—depression and other negative emotions can erode relationships overtime as partners get pulled into patterns of negativity and poor conflict management (we will discuss this more in a later chapter).

If you are struggling with depression, anxiety, or anger management this should become a primary focus of your efforts to become more ready for marriage. Sometimes there are biological or chemical explanations for poor negative affect regulation. For example, there are organic forms of depression that result from a chemical imbalance in the brain. Typically these forms of depression manifest earlier in life and there is often a family history of such symptoms.

Other forms of depression are the result of negative family of origin experiences, poor coping skills, lifestyle management, or unrighteous living patterns. Professional counseling and medical treatment can be helpful for some people as they learn how to manage their depressive or anxious emotions. If this is the case for you, you will benefit from seeking out the help you need so that these patterns will not disrupt your future dating and marriage relationships.

Personal security is needed in dating and marriage

Personal security is the foundation for several key attributes that are needed in dating and marriage relationships. These include courage, vulnerability, and a willingness to trust other people. Without personal security, the vulnerability in close relationships becomes threatening and fear of rejection will often dictate how people behave in dating situations. When

Why is Personal Security Needed?

Personal Security

Courage, Vulnerability, Trust

Authenticity, Disclosure, Mutual Reliance

this happens, there is less authenticity, disclosure, and mutual reliance in couple relationships—all necessary ingredients to forming an intimate and supportive relationship. In fact, vulnerability is the gateway to both intimacy and pain. We can choose to minimize our pain by avoiding vulnerability in dating and marriage, but we will also minimize the intimacy we experience. This is why personal security is such an important part of the personal maturity needed to form and maintain a loving and lasting marriage relationship.

How can you strengthen your personal security?

Given the importance of personal security in dating and marriage, how can each of us strengthen this aspect of our marriage readiness? Again, this is where the principles of amae and belonging can provide some guidance. To develop genuine and lasting personal security you need to ground your sense of self-worth on true foundations of belonging. There are at least three ways you can strengthen your personal security. These include: (1) recognize your *individual worth* and *true identity*, (2) focus on service and self-forgetting, and (3) avoid false notions of self-esteem that are comparison-based and grounded in the paradigms of modernity.

Recognizing Your Worth

A primary foundation of "justifiable self-esteem" (The Neal A. Maxwell Quote Book, 1997, p. 306) is recognizing and remembering our true worth. One analogy I have found helpful in understanding the true worth of each of us comes from the television show *The Antiques Roadshow* on PBS. Are you familiar with this show? If not, it is a program where the crew of the show goes to convention centers in cities all around the country and put out a call for people to bring in all of their antique furniture, paintings, dishes, and other heirlooms to be appraised by expert appraisers. People stand in lines all around the convention center waiting

for their turn to have their items appraised. Camera crews circle through the crowd and show us certain items as they are appraised. After a detailed description of the items by the expert appraisers they tell the person how much the item is worth. And then the person gets to say the famous line from the Antiques Roadshow: "I had no idea!"

Now, how can the Antiques Road show help us understand our personal worth? The key is how the appraisers ultimately settle on the value of the item. In the final analysis the value of the item is not determined by its condition or uniqueness. It is not determined by the maker of the item or the materials that were used to make it. Regardless of the condition of the item, the value is determined by *the price someone would pay* for that item at auction.

Do you see the insight? You already know what price someone would pay for you—that price has already been paid. In the Doctrine and Covenants we read, "Remember the worth of souls is great in the sight of God. For, behold, the Lord your Redeemer suffered death in the flesh; wherefore he suffered the pains of all men, that all men might repent and come unto him" (D&C 18:10–11).

We frequently use this scripture as a missionary scripture to remind us how important it is to share the gospel with others because they are so valuable to God. The scripture applies to you too. The worth of your soul is great in the sight of God. His Son declared your worth to be priceless—as He withheld nothing to pay the price to bring you home. This is the price that was paid for you.

Why Would Christ Do This for You?

Even in your imperfect condition, Christ suffered for you in the garden and on the cross because He understands your *true identity*. He understands who you are, who you can be, and to whom you belong. Because of His perfect love for you and His complete devotion to our Father, He paid this price for you. One of the keys to having personal security in this life is to come to see yourself as Christ sees you. Christ recognizes three key parts of your true identity, each is connected to your past, present, and future:

Your Divine Heritage—The Past: The Proclamation on the Family teaches that each of us is a beloved son or daughter of Heavenly Parents and that we are literally the offspring of Deity. This is who you are—nothing can ever change that.

Your Divine Nature—The Present: The scriptures teach us that we are literally created in the image of our Father in Heaven. Elder Parley P. Pratt described what this means when he said:

> An intelligent being, in the image of God, possesses every organ, attribute, sense, sympathy, affection, of will, wisdom, love, power, and gift, which is possessed by God Himself. But these are possessed by man in his rudimental state in a subordinate sense of the word. Or, in other words, these attributes are in embryo, and are to be gradually developed. They resemble a bud, a germ, which gradually develops into bloom, and then, by progress, produces the mature fruit after its own kind. (Key to the Science of Theology, as quoted in James E. Talmage, Articles of Faith, appendix 8, p. 48)

Do you see yourself as possessing this divine nature? Again, nothing can change this part of your nature. Christ sees you this way and knows who you are capable of becoming in this life.

Your Divine Destiny—The Future: In the Proclamation on the Family we also read that each of us is an "...heir of eternal life" (1995, ¶ 3). Each of us has the potential to live according to the pattern of eternal life and to inherit all of the blessings that our Father in Heaven has Himself. Each of us needs to live for this destiny and remember to see ourselves and others through an eternal lens.

Why Would Christ Do This?

He Understands Your True Identity

Divine Heritage – Past:
- Beloved child of heavenly parents literal offspring of deity

- Divine Nature – Present

- Divine Destiny – Future: Heir of eternal life

-The Family: A Proclaimation to the Word, par. 2-3

Service and Self-Forgetting

The principles of amae and belonging help us appreciate that the true source of self-worth does not come from ourselves—it is not about loving ourselves. It is about the love of others. Ultimately there are two true sources of self-worth: our belonging with God and our belonging with others.

Our Belonging with God

When we consider the intense need we each have for belonging, the Primary song *I am a Child of God* may be one of the most doctrinally profound hymns we have in the Church. The simple, yet profound doctrine that each of us is literally a spirit child of a loving Father in Heaven has the power to transform our lives. In this sense, a sense of belonging is similar to charity—it is an endowed gift from God (see Moroni 7:48).

The most important implication of viewing self-worth as a by-product of belonging with God is that our Father in Heaven loves all people equally. Everyone belongs to God. Thus, this view of self-worth discourages comparisons that are so frequent in traditional views of self-esteem. One of the indicators that someone has a true sense of self-worth is that he or she recognizes the worth of others and treats them accordingly.

Our Belonging with Others

In many ways the pursuit of self-esteem is paradoxical. This means that the less we worry about and directly pursue self-esteem the more likely we are to find it. One of the primary ways to strengthen our sense of self-worth is through service to others and to involve ourselves in the lives of others in meaningful ways. President Spencer W. Kimball said, "The more we serve our fellowmen in appropriate ways, the more substance there is to our souls. We become more significant individuals…Indeed, it is easier to 'find' ourselves because there is so much more of us to find!" (New Era, Sep 1974, p. 4).

Avoid False Notions of Self-Worth

Worth vs. Worthiness

Because our divine worth is connected to the unchanging love of our Father in Heaven and the price paid for our souls by the Savior, worth is an eternal absolute. This means that our worth cannot be enhanced or diminished by our actions. Worth is constant and unchanging. Yes, we can feel worthless, but this feeling denies the eternal truth that each of us is of infinite worth to our Father in Heaven.

In order to get each of us to forget our divine worth, the Adversary tries to get us to confuse the principles of worth and worthiness. As Dr. Lockhart and Dr. Cox explain:

> Worthiness is different than worth. Worthiness is dependent on what we do in our lives, how we use our agency, coupled with the Lord's grace. Worthiness is dependent on our love for the Savior and our obedience to His commandments. But worthiness does not determine worth. Worth is always a part of us, whether we are good or bad. Heavenly Father always loves us, whether or not we are good or bad. Having a testimony of our worth or importance to Heavenly Father does have a great impact on our worthiness. If we feel that we are "no good" or "worthless," and that Heavenly Father couldn't possibly love us, the tendency is to give up or do things that affect our worthiness. If we have a testimony of our worth, when we make a mistake we want to

repent. We are able to distinguish between who we are and what we do. We can view ourselves similarly to the way our Heavenly Father views us. (Strengthening Our Families, 2000, p. 221)

A critical part of maintaining a personal security in this life is to remember our divine worth and turn toward rather than turning away from the Lord in times of unworthiness.

Recognize the Influence of Past Experiences

Some of us struggle with feelings of low self-worth due to discouraging and devaluing experiences in our family of origin experiences. If this is the case, you need to work at coming to terms with these experiences and developing a new positive self-image based in belonging with God and healthy relationships with others.

Beware of Counterfeit Sources of Self-worth

Many of us turn to counterfeit sources of self-worth in an effort to feel good about ourselves. For example, some people focus on academic achievement,

physical beauty, and material possessions as ways to boost their self-esteem and self-image. These sources of self-esteem are temporary and unstable. They also create patterns of comparison with others, and sometimes competition to be better than others. No matter how well we do in school, or how physically fit we become, or how wealthy we are, these things will never fulfill our need to belong and be genuinely loved. Now would be a good time for you to reflect on any counterfeit forms of self-worth that have crept into your ways of thinking and do all you can to remove them from your life. These false foundations of personal identity and self-image can create destructive patterns in dating and marriage as people pursue distorted paths of validating and revalidating their self-worth. Build your sense of self-worth on a true foundation that meets your true needs—belonging with God and with others.

Other-Centeredness

PERSONAL READINESS, PART II
CHAPTER 12

> I would invite all members of the Church to live with ever more attention to the life and example of the Lord Jesus Christ, especially the love and hope and compassion he displayed. I pray that we might treat each other with more kindness, more courtesy, more humility and patience and forgiveness.
>
> *Pres. Howard W. Hunter*

In this chapter, we discuss the *second root* (within the tree model of marriage) of personal readiness—other-centeredness. Other-centeredness is the capacity to care for others and the maturity to allow their needs to become of equal or greater priority to our own. In this chapter we build upon the foundation principle of *charity* (love) and discuss four *marital virtues* that all spouses need to develop for the good of their marriages. Because most of you have participated in gospel-based lessons on forgiveness and love, we focus here on social science research findings related to these topics. In recent years, marriage researchers have begun to conduct research studies on forgiveness, sacrifice, commitment, and other aspects of marital relationships that were previously considered to be the content of Sunday school classes.

MARITAL VIRTUES

Leading marriage scholar, Dr. Blaine J. Fowers, wrote a book entitled, *Beyond the Myth of Marital Happiness* in which he explains what years of counseling and research have taught him to be the foundation of a successful marriage. In simple terms he says, "The best way to have a good marriage is to be a good person" (2000, 23). In particular, Dr. Fowers espouses four *marital virtues* that each of us needs to begin to develop for the good of our future marriages: (1) the *virtue of friendship*—embodied in the characteristics of caring, helpfulness, and companionship; (2) the *virtue of generosity*—exhibited in the way spouses give freely to one another, forgive each other, and see the best in each other; (3) the *virtue of fairness*—fostered when spouses learn to shoulder the work and difficulties of marriage and family life together and rely on the mutual strengths each brings to the relationship; and (4) the *virtue of loyalty*—based in a steadfast commitment to one's relationship in spite of difficulties that inevitably arise over the course of a marriage.

The Virtue of Friendship

The first virtue of marriage is the *virtue of friendship*—embodied in the characteristics of *caring, helpfulness, and companionship*. Far too many spouses today fall into the pattern of *parallel marriage*—where they share a home together, but they do not share a life together. Each of us must make intentional efforts to foster the friendship in our marriage and to find ways to have meaningful and sincere interactions with our spouse. Research has consistently found that one of the strongest predictors of marital happiness is whether or not a spouse feels understood by his or her partner.

The Five Magic Hours

Our efforts in this area do not have to be large to have great benefits. Research by Dr. John Gottman (see Gottman 1999, The Marriage Clinic) has shown that couples who devote an extra five hours a week to their marriage have stronger, more satisfying relationships. During this time, couples attended to four things:

1. Learning about one another's day
2. Having a stress reducing conversation at the end of each day

3. Doing something every day to show genuine affection and appreciation
4. Having a weekly date together

Studies find that lasting marriages are ones in which spouses create a deep friendship through shared activities, values, and conversation. Each of us can work to deepen our capacity to be a good friend, regardless of our current dating status. As we show real concern for others we will experience our other-centeredness deepen and our personal maturity grow.

The Virtue of Fairness

The second virtue Dr. Fowers deems as essential in marriage is the *virtue of fairness*—fostered when spouses are equal partners and share the work of marriage and family life together. The pattern held up for us by the Savior in this regard is one of *equal partnership* and *interdependence*. Perhaps nowhere is the

Marital Virtues
Fowers, 2000

Friendship
Embodied in the characteristics of caring, helpfulness, and companionship

- Feeling understood (love map)
- Avoid parallel marriage

> Studies find that lasting marriages are ones in which spouses create a deep friendship through shared activities, values, and conversation.

Fairness
Fostered when spouses are equal partners and share the work of family life together

- Involvement and participation in housework
- Men—do the water chores!
- Women—support providing efforts

> Studies find that lasting marriages are ones in which spouses feel as sense of partnership and teamwork.

Loyalty
A covenant-based commitment to one's relationship in spite of difficulties that inevitably arise over the course of a marriage

- Commitment and sacrifice
- Transformation of motivation

> Studies find that lasting marriages are ones in which spouses are devoted to each other and are willing to sacrifice for the good of the relationship – a shift from "me" to "we."

Generosity
Exhibited when spouses give freely to one another, forgive each other, and see the best in each other.

- Forgiveness—letting go of offenses
- Transformation of motivation

> Studies find that lasting marriages are ones in which spouses sincerely forgive each other and maintain a positive attitude about life.

and family life. Spouses need to find ways to show their devotion to each other and their family through completing needed tasks and responding to the family's current needs.

If you will permit me, I would like to make a couple of recommendations to foster the sense of fairness in your future marriages. The first recommendation is for the men and the second is for the women.

Husbands—Do the Water Chores!

Most men come to realize that there is a hierarchy of gifts they can give their girlfriends or wives on special occasions. Flowers are nice, but jewelry is better! The same is true when it comes to household chores. Vacuuming is nice, but washing the dishes is better! And scrubbing a toilet is the best of all! One of my primary recommendations to young husbands is to participate in the water chores in your home. Water chores are all of the chores in the home that involve water, such as washing dishes, washing clothes, bathing children, cleaning bathrooms, scrubbing toilets, etc. While washing a car is nice, it does not demonstrate the same commitment to fairness as the inside water chores in a family. Trust me—if you remember nothing else from this book, remember this: *do the water chores!* Nothing will show your wife

degree of fairness more displayed in a marriage relationship than in how husbands and wives share the work of maintaining a household and nurturing a family. In this aspect of family life, spouses must cultivate a loving responsiveness to each other, as they find mutually agreeable ways to balance work

that you see her as a true equal and that you are committed to fully sharing the burdens of household labor.

While I am on my soapbox, I will share one more recommendation for fostering fairness in marriage. Make it a rule that whoever prepares a meal should not clean up after the meal. This encourages all family members to be either a *meal-preparer* (carrying a dish from the counter to the table does not count as preparing!) or a *meal-cleaner-upper*. Mealtime chores are another area were some couples and families struggle with fairness and equality—this simple proscription can help couples find a balance that works for both spouses.

WIVES—RECOGNIZE THE WEIGHT OF PROVIDING

As we discussed in our previous chapter on family stewardships, husbands/fathers are divinely appointed to have a primary stewardship to provide for the necessities of life for their wives and children. For many men, this is a daunting commandment that can feel intimidating. There is frequently very real stress involved in struggling to meet a family's temporal needs. For many husbands, their sense of success or failure in life is tied to their feelings of success in providing. As a fiancée and spouse, always recognize the weight of the provider stewardship and be supportive of you husband's efforts in this aspect of marriage. Show appreciation and do all that you can to lower the financial expectations and demands within your marriage.

Nearly two decades of research studies have shown that lasting marriages are ones in which spouses feel a sense of partnership and teamwork. They have also found that the expression of gratitude and an awareness of what our spouse does for us is an important part of happy marriages.

You can begin now to commit yourself to fairness is your current relationships. Whether it is with your roommates, friends, or family members, do you always strive to do your share of the work that benefits you? Do you express gratitude to those who perform labor on your behalf? Do you have the skills needed to perform a wide range of household tasks and chores? All of these aspects of personal maturity can help you as you prepare to live the virtue of fairness in a future marriage relationship.

THE VIRTUE OF GENEROSITY

Next is the *virtue of generosity*—exhibited in the way spouses give freely to one another, forgive each other, and see the best in each other. President Howard W. Hunter espoused this virtue as well when he said,

> I would invite all members of the Church to live with ever more attention to the life and example of the Lord Jesus Christ, especially the love and hope and compassion he displayed. I pray that we might treat

each other with more kindness, more courtesy, more humility and patience and forgiveness. (Ensign, July 1994, pp. 4–5)

Sister Linda Burton invited each of us to ask ourselves some questions that will show us whether or not we are expressing the virtue of generosity. She said:

> We might test ourselves by asking a few questions. With a little adaptation, these questions can apply to most of us, whether we are married or single, whatever our home situation might be.
>
> When was the last time I sincerely praised my companion, either alone or in the presence of our children?
>
> When was the last time I thanked, expressed love for, or earnestly pleaded in faith for him or her in prayer?
>
> When was the last time I stopped myself from saying something I knew could be hurtful?
>
> When was the last time I apologized and humbly asked for forgiveness—without adding the words "but if only you had" or "but if only you hadn't"?
>
> When was the last time I chose to be happy rather than demanding to be "right"?
>
> . . .the Spirit has taught me, and I have committed to speak words of kindness more often to my cherished companion and about him, to lift the men in my family and express gratitude for the ways they fulfill their divine and complementary roles. And I have committed to follow the proverb "Thee lift me and I'll lift thee, and we'll ascend together." (April 2015, We'll Ascend Together)

Each of us is revealed in our marriage relationship. All of our faults and our virtues are laid open in this most intimate of relationships. As spouses we stand on sacred ground with how we respond and react to the shortcomings and imperfections of our spouse, and they in turn to ours. There is something very powerful when spouses are each other's strongest supporters—when spouses rally to each other's side, rather than turning away; who encourage, rather than criticize; who see the best in each other, rather than the worst; and who lift each other up, rather than push each other down.

FORGIVENESS

Leading marriage scholar Dr. Frank Fincham has said, "The people that we love the most are frequently the people that we hurt and are hurt by" (Fincham, Beach, & Davila, Journal of Family Psychology, 2004, p. 320). Because of the vulnerability associated with intimacy and disclosure, it is inevitable that partners will hurt one another from time to time. Forgiveness is a key part of the virtue of generosity that is needed at these times in a relationship.

Because it is a complex construct, considerable effort has been expended by marital researchers such as Dr. Fincham on conceptualizing forgiveness and how it might best be studied. Dr. Fincham explains,

Although a consensus has yet to emerge, central to various approaches to forgiveness is the idea of a freely chosen motivational transformation in which the desire to seek revenge and to avoid contact with the transgressor is overcome. To forgive entails a struggle to overcome the negative feelings that result from being wrongfully harmed and the magnitude of this struggle will differ across individuals. This view immediately distinguishes forgiveness from related constructs such as forgetting (passive removal of the offense from consciousness; to forgive is more than not thinking about the offense), condoning (no longer viewing the act as a wrong and removing the need for forgiveness), and pardon (granted only by a representative of society such as a judge). Thus the common phrase, "forgive and forget" is misleading as forgiveness is only possible in the face of a remembered wrong. (Fincham, F., Beach, J, & Davila, A., Journal of Family Psychology, 2004, p. 320)

Leading figures in society have also stressed these ideas. Mother Theresa once said, "If we really want to love, we must learn how to forgive." Mahatma Gandhi also stated "The weak never forgive. Forgiveness is the attribute of the strong."

Dr. James Harper and Dr. Mark Butler (*Strengthening Our Families,* 2000) suggest that that there are three types of forgiveness we should foster in our lives and marriages. The first is *seeking forgiveness from God and forgiving ourselves*. A first step in forgiving others is accepting the Atonement of Christ into our lives by repenting and forgiving ourselves. The prophet Joseph Smith taught, "the closer we get to our Heavenly Father, the more we are disposed to look with compassion on perishing souls; we feel that we want to take them upon our shoulders, and cast their sins behind our backs" (Teachings of the Prophet Joseph Smith, 1938, p. 241). The second type of forgiveness is *seeking forgiveness from others*. One of the most needed virtues in married life is the ability to admit we are wrong, sincerely apologize for our actions, and seek forgiveness from our spouse. This virtue fosters healing and helps couples manage differences that emerge between them. The final type of forgiveness is *forgiving others*. Elder Neal A. Maxwell said,

> Faith in the Atonement gives us the strength and love gives us the desire to unlock the prison door through forgiving, that all who will heal may heal, and none of us—neither the offended nor the offender need remain a prisoner of the past. (Ensign, July 1982)

Forgiveness must be sincere and complete. At times, people practice *hollow forgiveness* where they forgive on the surface, but not in their inner feelings or attitudes. Only forgiveness that transforms our motivations, as well as behaviors, will have the lasting benefits needed in marriage and family relationships.

The Virtue of Loyalty

The final virtue is the *virtue of loyalty*—a covenant based commitment to one's relationship in spite of difficulties that inevitably arise over the course of a marriage.

A number of years ago, I was very touched the passing of Sister Marjorie Hinckley, the beloved eternal companion of President Gordon B. Hinckley. I watched fondly the memorials of her remarkable life on TV and I marveled at the simple goodness she brought to all of her life's endeavors. I was particularly struck by one of her statements from an interview. When commenting on the foundation of her loving marriage of over 60 years with President Hinckley, she said that the key to marriage is for spouses to be "loyal, fiercely loyal" to one another. We must also remember that our loyalty and commitment in marriage must be to more than just marriage itself—we must be committed to the wellbeing of our spouse, to his or her happiness, and to having a healthy, high quality marriage. Our commitment must reflect an inward devotion to our spouse and the quality of our relationship, not just an outward commitment to marriage regardless of its condition.

Sacrifice

There is growing empirical evidence that partners' commitment to a future is strongly linked to healthy types of *sacrifice* or mutual giving among partners. This seems to be particularly true for men. According to research by Dr. Scott Stanley and his colleagues, there is compelling evidence that the degree to which males will sacrifice for female partners, without a sense of personal loss and ensuing resentment, is strongly related to how committed they are to a long term future. Dr. Stanley explains,

> The relationship between commitment to a future and sacrifice appears to be strong for men and weak in women—a finding warranting further research. This, along with data from various studies, has led me to hypothesize that women may give their best to men as long as they are attached to them while men may not give their best to women unless they have committed to a future. (2006, p. 21)

Commitment (discussed in Chapter 4) and sacrifice act as twin virtues that hold a marriage together

during times of trouble and give partners a sense of security that it is worthwhile to invest in the relationship for the long term. This type of security leads to a willingness to sacrifice for the good of the couple, thus enriching both partners' lives.

Conclusion

When we practice these four virtues (i.e., friendship, fairness, generosity, and loyalty) in our dating and marriage relationships, we begin to view marriage as more than a means to our own personal happiness, but rather to view marriage as a partnership that invites us to live outside ourselves for the good of our spouse and others. The perspective of one spouse who had been married for 10 years and was interviewed by Dr. Fowers captures this approach to marriage—she said,

> I think a lot less about what I get out of the relationship and more about what I can give to it. I think a lot about how I can keep our togetherness going and about how it is good for our children. We are a couple in love, and we have lived through a lot of difficult times. We work through those problems together and always come back to that love. I've seen it grow stronger and deeper as a result. (Beyond the Myth of Marital Happiness, 2000, p. 79)

Effective Communication

PERSONAL READINESS, PART III
CHAPTER 13

> You need to learn to listen beyond the words, with your heart as well as your ears.... A friend put it this way: "You listened as if you wanted to hear what I was going to say, as if it was really important to you. And that makes me feel good!"
>
> *Dr. Herbert Lingren*

Have you ever heard these statements:

"You're not listening to me!"

"If you will let me finish what I'm saying, I'll tell you!"

"I may as well be talking to a brick wall!"

"You just don't understand!"

"But that's not what I said!"

According to communication expert Dr. Herbert Lingren, these statements are all signs of ineffective communication. Have you ever had someone say one of these statements to you? If you ever hear these types of comments coming from your friends, roommates, parents, co-workers, dating partner, or spouse, it may be a sign that perhaps you are not being an effective communicator.

In this chapter, we discuss the *third root* (within the tree model of marriage) of personal readiness—effective communication. *Effective communication* is a set of skills that is grounded upon the foundation of the first two roots of personal maturity—personal security and other-centeredness. While the first two aspects of personal readiness (e.g., personal security and other-centeredness) typically influence our motives and intents in relationships, the third aspect, effective communication, deals more with our behaviors and actions. When our hearts are in the right place, we are ready to learn skills that can help us effectively express our love toward others. Effective communication involves two primary skills—*empathetic listening* and *clear-sending communication*. As you develop and refine these skills, you will be better prepared to establish healthy and productive couple processes in dating and marriage relationships.

Effective Communication

For many of us, communication means talking. Therefore, we sometimes mistakenly believe that good communication is about being good at speaking or talking. While some forms of communication, such as public speaking or teaching, may emphasize skills in presenting information to others in effective ways, effective communication in personal relationships is based on a different type of skills. Above all, effective communication in relationships is more about listening and understanding than it is about being articulate or well-spoken. Besides, in close relationships such as dating and marriage the goal of communication is to connect, rather than to inform or teach.

Plus, in relationships with family members and friends, the influence of our words is always based on the quality of the relationship we have with each other. The old cliché is true that *people don't care how much you know, until they know how much you care.* Thus, to help you learn some skills that can help you become a more effective communicator this chapter is divided into two primary sections—empathetic listening and clear-sending communication

Empathetic Listening

Empathetic listening is the art of connecting with another person so you fully understand what they are saying and feeling. The goal of empathetic listening is to help another person feel understood and valued. It goes without saying that it is a vital and necessary skill needed in creating and maintaining a marriage. You may think, *What is so important about listening? I listen!* Of course you *hear* other people, but do you really *listen* to them? There is a difference between hearing and listening.

How well you listen largely depends on how you listen to others? To be an effective listener, others must first believe that you really want to listen. They must feel that when they tell you something, you really care about what they are saying. This is why effective listening must be based on the foundation of mature love and marital virtues. If you do not really care what others are saying, then there is no set of skills or techniques you can use to convince them that you do. You may be successful in *pretending to care* from time to time, but in the long run others will always discover the true intents of your heart.

To be an effective listener, communication expert Dr. Herbert Lingren counsels:

> You need to learn to listen beyond the words, with your heart as well as your ears. Observe the signs of the inner feelings such as voice quality, facial expressions, body posture and motions, etc. These actions are revealing, and sometimes may have an opposite meaning from the spoken word. A friend put it this way: "You listened as if you wanted to hear what I was going to say, as if it was really important to you. And that makes me feel good!" (Listening—With Your Heart As Well As Your Ears, 1992, p. 1)

Listening with our hearts, as well as our ears is the foundation to empathetic listening. Let's look at some of the reasons why some people are poor listeners while others are so good at making others feel understood. Then we will examine some suggestions for improving our listening skills. As you read this section, pay careful attention to which suggestions are right for you. This part of the chapter draws extensively from an article entitled "Listening—With Your Heart As Well As Your Ears" written by Dr. Herbert G. Lingren at the University of Nebraska-Lincoln (1997, University of Nebraska Cooperative Extension educational programs).

Ineffective Listening

Why are some people such poor listeners when it is such an important skill in developing and maintaining relationships? According to Dr. Lingren, the first reason is that people are in the habit of *tuning out*—which involves processes of *selective attention* and *selective perception*. When someone does this, they hear what they want to hear and screen out what they don't. Since it is estimated that the average person spends 45 percent of his waking hours listening to someone, no wonder we sometimes tune out what we don't want or don't need to hear. But, in couple relationships, tuning out what our partner has to say almost always has negative consequences for couple communication and intimacy.

Dr. Lingren says that the second reason for poor listening is physiological. He explains:

> People listen about five to ten times as fast as they speak. In the time it takes the speaker to say 100 words, the listener has the capacity to hear 500 to 1,000 words. So, while you are talking, the other person is listening with only a fraction of the capacity for attention. The rest of that person's mind impatiently uses the extra capacity for other things—to plan the next day's work; to fantasize about their future; to think of an excuse for not being home for dinner on time; to reminisce about a vacation, etc. One of the keys to effective listening is to use this excess mind capacity to constantly analyze what is being said, instead of daydreaming or letting your mind wander. (Listening, p. 3)

A third reason for poor listening is the sheer impact of the stimuli from the outside world. People are bombarded with literally thousands of different messages each hour, and the volume of *"noise"* in their communication network makes effective listening difficult. According to Dr. Lingren, the average person speaks 12,500 words per day, and if that is multiplied by five or more persons in their immediate work or family environment, it is no wonder people get tuned out.

Styles of Poor Listening

One reason ineffective listening takes place in couple's communication is because one or both partners have developed bad habits and poor listening styles which prevent them from really hearing others. Dr. Lingren has identified six *poor listening styles*. Which one best describes you?

1. **The Faker.** Fakers only pretend to be listening. They may smile while you talk to them. They may nod their heads. They may appear to be intent, but they are either thinking about something else, or are so intent on appearing to be listening that they do not hear what you are saying. Often their minds wander as they tune in and out of the conversation.

2. **The Dependent Listener.** Some people primarily want to please the speaker. They are so concerned about whether the speaker has a good impression of them that they are unable to listen and respond appropriately. Dependent listeners may agree excessively with what the speaker says, not because they really agree, but because they want to maintain the goodwill of the speaker (nodding head all the time). By trying to please, dependent listeners are frustrating at best.

3. **The Interrupter.** Interrupters never allow the other to finish. They may be afraid that they will forget something important they want to say. Or they may feel that it is necessary to respond to a point as soon as it is made. Or they may simply be more concerned with their own thoughts and feelings than with those of others. In any case, they

barrage the speaker with words rather than offering an understanding ear.

4. **The Self-Conscious Listener.** Some people are concerned more with their own status in the eyes of the other than with the ideas and feelings of the other. Trying to impress the other person, they don't listen with understanding; therefore they may be constantly framing their replies in order to be helpful.

5. **The Intellectual Listener.** Intellectual listeners attend only to the words of the other. They make a rational appraisal of what has been said verbally, but they ignore the nonverbal cues (including the feelings that are communicated nonverbally). The intellectual listener may develop this style because of the type of work in which he or she engages.

6. **The Judge and Jury Listener.** These listeners often become so involved in the judgment of the idea or behavior of others that they don't hear the full story. They may interrupt with a comment about being "wrong" or "incorrect" or may attack the other person without attempting to understand their position. When this happens, they shut their ears so they don't listen.

Effective Listening

Effective listening requires an understanding that it is not just the speaker's responsibility to make sure that he or she is understood. The listener has a major role to play in hearing the complete message. Dr. Lingren suggests the following ideas for making sure that as a listener you are understanding the messages other people are trying to share with you.

1. **Stop talking!:** You cannot listen when you are talking. You will only be thinking about what you are going to say next instead of paying attention to what the other person is trying to say. Consciously focus your attention on the speaker.

2. **Put the speaker at ease:** Relax, smile, look at the speaker and help that person feel free to talk. Look and act interested. Remove distractions: turn off the TV; close the door; stop what you are doing, and pay attention.

3. **Pay attention to nonverbal language:** Physical gestures, facial expressions, tone of voice, and body posture are all important parts of communication. Communication experts have found that about 55 percent of the message meaning is nonverbal, 38 percent is indicated by tone of voice, and only 7 percent is conveyed by the words used in a spoken message. Few people know how to listen to the eyes; what a tapping foot means; a furrowed brow; clenched fist; the biting of nails. These often reveal the key feelings behind the words.

4. **Listen for what is not said.** Ask questions to clarify the meaning of words and the feelings involved, or ask the speaker to enlarge on the statement. People often find it difficult to speak up about matters or experiences that are very important or highly emotional for them. Listen for how the speaker presents the message. What people hesitate to say is often the most critical point.

5. **Know exactly what the other person is saying.** Reflect back what the other person has said in a "*shared meaning*" experience so you completely understand the meaning and content of the message before you reply to it. A good listener does not assume they understand the other person. You, as the listener, should not express your views until you have summarized the speaker's message to his satisfaction.

6. **Be patient. Don't interrupt the speaker.** Interrupting other people is disrespectful and suggests you want to talk instead of listen. Allow plenty of time for the speaker to convey ideas and meaning. Be courteous and give the speaker adequate time to present the full message.

7. **Hold your temper!** Try to keep your own emotions from interfering with your listening efficiency. When emotions are high, there is a tendency to tune out the speaker, become defensive, or want to give advice. *You don't have to agree to be a good listener.* Don't argue! Even if you win, you lose.

8. **Empathize with the speaker.** Try to "walk in the other's person's shoes" so you can feel what that person is feeling and understand the point of view the speaker is trying to convey. Remember, effective listening conveys empathy and makes the other person feel understood.

Payoffs for Effective Listening

When you strive to be attentive and caring in your listening it offers the opportunity for others to share their life with you. Empathetic listening fosters intimacy, heals hurts, and strengthens partnership. When you listen to others and help them feel understood, they are much more likely to trust you, thus opening the gate for more intimate communication.

Dr. Lingren emphasizes that "the first real evidence of effective communication occurring is when each person really understands what the other person has said—the meanings, attitudes, and feelings behind the words." He also notes that this takes time and concentration. Dr. Lingren highlights that there are several positive results results that can be gained from effective listening, these include:

1. **Gaining knowledge.** Each person can learn new information about topics, ideas, and people. Listen for the meaning beyond the words and the context of the communication. Listen to the person—get in touch with emotions, language, habits, and temperament.

2. **Receive better work and cooperation from others.** Showing sincere interest in other peoples' problems, ideas, thoughts, and opinions can bring you more respect and cooperation.

3. **Listening helps to solve problems and resolve conflict.** Only after understanding the other person can you agree or disagree, and then work cooperatively to clarify thinking, seek solutions, and resolve conflict.

4. **Listening can reduce tension.** It gives the other person a chance to *get it off his chest*, to *clear the air*, or *let off a little steam*.

5. **Listening can prevent trouble.** If people can learn to listen before speaking, before sticking their neck out, before taking untenable and unreasonable positions, or making commitments that can't be kept, they will likely avoid many unfortunate experiences.

6. **Listening can help you do a better job.** Try asking your partner or fellow workers for ideas about improving your listening performance. Then listen and try some of their suggestions.

7. **Listening can increase enjoyment in life.** Efficient listening can increase everyone's enjoyment of a movie, a television program, a lecture, a play, music, and even just plain conversation. It may help people to develop higher standards for everything they hear.

8. **Listening can strengthen family relationships.** Marriages are created, maintained, and/or destroyed through effective communication. Most important is our need to listen to each other—with the heart as well as the ears. Empathic listening is the greatest gift parents can give to their children. It is the ability to put themselves in their child's place and understand where the child is coming from without imposing their point of view.

CLEAR-SENDING COMMUNICATION

In addition to empathetic listening, effective communication is built upon clearly sent messages to others. This is the talking part of communication. However, most unclear communication in close relationships has very little to do with partners having actual difficulties in talking or forming words. Messages become unclear because of background issues that cause people to not be direct, open, and authentic in their statements to others.

In order to be an effective communicator, we have to be authentic in our conversations with others. Simply put, we have to *say what we mean and mean what we say*—while respecting the feelings and the perspectives of others. True relationships are built on the communication of the truth. When we won't state our true

Clear-Sending Communication

In order to communicate effectively, we have to be authentic in our conversations with others. Simply put, we have to "say what we mean and mean what we say," while respecting the feelings and the perspectives of others. True relationships are built on the communication of the truth.

Authenticity

- Never fake, deceptive, pretending, etc.
- Authentic human interactions become impossible when you lose yourself in a role
- Requires vulnerability, transparency, and integrity

feelings or perspectives or we lie about them, trust and intimacy cannot develop or be maintained. Warner further explains,

> Learning the truth about a problematic condition in our physical bodies enables us to take steps to find the remedy. But with emotions and relationships, the truth is the cure. . .self-betrayal occurs when we go against acknowledging the needs and feelings in others [or ourselves] when we do to another what we sense we should not do, or don't do what we sense we should. (Bonds That Make Us Free: Healing Our Relationships, Coming To Ourselves, 2001, pp. 83–84)

When the purpose of our communication is to cover up, mislead, deceive, intimidate, threaten, disapprove, hurt, fault-find, or make someone feel guilty we are not being authentic. Furthermore, if we allow our emotions or personal insecurities to overwhelm us, we tend to communicate in less authentic ways—thus sending less authentic messages.

I-Statements

One way to be clear in our message is to use *I-Statements* instead of *You-Statements* in our conversations with others. I-Statements describe your ideas and feelings, and enables you to take responsibility for your thoughts and emotions. They are much more effective than You-Statements, which carry a judgmental tone, and often put a person on the defensive immediately. Examples of I-Statements include: "I don't understand what you are saying," "I missed having your input at the meeting," or "I felt hurt when you showed up so late for our date." Examples of You-Statements include: "You didn't make any sense," "You didn't care enough to come to the meeting," and "You made me so angry when you came late."

I-Statements are an important part of clear-sending communication because they tend to: (a) place responsibility with you, the speaker, (2) clarify your position, feelings, or opinions, (3) build trust by giving others information about yourself, and (4) be less threatening or carry a tone of blame. On the other hand, You-Statements tend to: (a) elicit a negative or defensive response, (b) place blame or put people down, and (c) come off as being accusatory or preachy.

A simple formula for using an I-Statement is:

> I feel _____ (put a name on the emotion and claim it) when _____ (formulate a non-judgmental description of the behavior) because _____ (describe the tangible effects of the behavior).

Speaking in I-Statements helps each of us take responsibility for our own feelings and actions. I-Statements are also an effective conflict management technique because they require individuals involved in a conflict to put space between their action and their reaction. This allows the individuals to take time to get in touch with their feelings and to choose an appropriate response instead of reacting spontaneously. Although using I-statements can be uncomfortable at first, they are effective and using them gets easier with time because you will learn how to adapt the statements so that they sound natural and still incorporate all the necessary elements.

Love Languages

While clear-sending communication involves being as clear and authentic with our messages as possible, it also requires sending messages to others in a way they will understand. Effective communication is more than words.

People like to be shown love and communicate in different ways. These different ways might be thought of as different languages of love. When we really want to communicate well with another person we study what is important to him or her. We customize our messages of love to fit our partner's preferences. Dr. H. Wallace Goddard has summarized some of these *love languages* that we need to develop the ability to utilize if we are going to become effective communicators. He says:

> One language of love is telling. Some people love to hear words of affection. "I love you." "I enjoy being with you." "You mean so much to me." Some people want to hear such words every day, maybe even several times every day. Yet some people think that words are not enough or not a meaningful demonstration of love.
>
> Another language is showing. Some people want to see love in action. "If you love me, help me around the house." "If you love me, make time to be with me." "Show me your love by the way you help with the children." For some people, actions speak much louder than words.
>
> Another language is touching. Some people love to hug and cuddle. They appreciate a part-

ner who holds his or her hand. They may like to sit close. Physical closeness is important to them. Most people do not want love in just one language; we all have a combination of languages of love. One may prefer showing with occasional telling. Another may want lots of hugging with regular doses of showing. We may discover another person's language of love by noticing how that person shows love, by noticing how that person has preferred to receive love, or by asking what that person enjoys.

> There are other powerful languages of love: taking time and showing understanding. . . Gladly accept your partner's efforts to show you love while sending clear messages about your preferences. Sometimes we become impatient with our partner's efforts to show us love. Sometimes our languages are so different from each other that it is hard for either of us to get the message through. We can choose to appreciate our partners' best efforts and we can keep trying to be more effective in our own efforts to show love. (Learning Languages of Love in Marriage, 2008, p. 2)

As you learn to be clear in the messages you send, to use I-Statements, and to focus on sending messages according to other's preferred languages of love, you will grow in your capacity to be an effective communicator. Together with empathetic listening, these skills will allow you to effectively express your love and concern for others in ways that will help them feel understood and connected to you. These are foundation processes in successful dating and marriage relationships.

SECTION 3

Creating a Right Relationship

In this section, we begin our discussion of principles related to *creating* a right relationship for marriage. We will emphasize how marriage relationships are made, not just found. Because of this, each of us can have confidence that we can intentionally create an eternal marriage.

In particular, we will discuss principles that can help you both before and after marriage to create a healthy relationship. We will discuss principles that can help you make wise dating decisions and properly evaluate the characteristics of the people you date. We will also discuss how to evaluate a relationship and the types of common characteristics that are needed to form a lasting and loving marriage relationship.

Building on those principles, we will also discuss how we create an eternal marriage by expressing our commitment to marriage in our daily lives. Specifically, we discuss the topics of: time together, extended family relationships, money and debt, the transition to parenthood, sexual intimacy in marriage, and divorce decision making.

As you begin this section, it is important to remember that you have already learned a lot about creating a marriage when you studied the foundation chapters and the chapters about becoming a right person. Remember, the same principles you learned about becoming ready for marriage, such as strengthening your personal security, developing marital virtues, and effective communication skills, are also the key attributes that make others ready for marriage too. Ultimately, *two right people make a right marriage*. As you develop the attributes of emotional maturity, forgiveness, empathetic listening, other-centeredness, and true friendship you will be able to recognize and expect these attributes in the people you date and in the spouse you eventually marry.

Below is my summary of the key principles we have covered so far. I recommend that you use this list as your "dating checklist" of what you should be seeking for in a spouse. But, don't forget—becoming should precede finding! So, you should also be striving to develop these virtues and skills yourself, not just looking for them in others. Also, don't forget that nobody is perfect in all of these attributes. These attributes are best perfected by spouses together in marriage as you grow together, rather than expecting that they can be fully achieved without the experiences of marriage and family life. Marriage is a means, not just an end—and our progression and growth is a key reason for why marriage is ordained of God.

Dr. Carroll's Becoming/Finding List

- **Discipleship**—Testimony of Christ; Striving to live the gospel; Temple worthy; Personal worship practices; Serving in the Church; Sustains the prophet; Willing to put marriage and family over earthly pursuits, etc.
- **Cleaving**—Desire to be married; A willingness to place spouse above all other people and pursuits; A covenant-keeper; Striving for mature relationships with parents and family, etc.
- **Equal Partnership**—A desire for true partnership; A correct understanding of the pattern of equal partnership in marriage; Someone who listens to and respects others, etc.
- **Family Stewardships**—A desire to live the divine design of marriage; A common view of spousal stewardships across the life course; A man who honors motherhood and womanhood; A woman who honors the priesthood, etc.
- **Chastity**—A respect for God's divine purposes of sexuality; Striving to be self-disciplined in sexual expression; Seeing sexual intimacy as a means to divine ends; rather than an end in and of itself,; An ability to openly discuss and communicate about sexual matters, etc.
- **Family of Origin**—An awareness of how family of origin experiences are influencing current relationship patterns; A willingness to make needed changes, etc.
- **Personal Security**—A sense of belonging with God; Positive and optimistic outlook; Ability to manage negative emotions; Mature and responsible approach to life.
- **Other-Centeredness**—Kind and flexible; Willing to admit mistakes and forgive others; Enjoyable to be with; Thoughtful and considerate; Realistic expectations for self and others.
- **Effective Communication**—A good listener; Make others feel understood; Manages emotions during disagreements; Clear-sender in communication; Authentic and real.

When to Wed?

The Timing of Marriage
CHAPTER 14

> Throughout your life on earth, seek diligently to fulfill the fundamental purposes of this life through the ideal family. While you may not have reached that ideal, do all you can through obedience and faith in the Lord to consistently draw as close to it as you are able.
>
> *Elder Richard G. Scott*

A few years ago I did a media interview with a reporter about dating and courtship among Latter-day Saints. During the interview, the reporter asked me, "Are LDS young people encouraged to get married at an early age?" How would you answer this question? I told the reporter that before I could answer her question, I would need her to clarify what she meant by the word "early." Ultimately, designations of what is "early" and "late" are relative comparisons based on a standard of what is considered "on time."

Since 1950, the median age at first marriage in the United States has increased substantially and is currently at a historic high of 27.4 years for women and 29.5 years for men (see Carroll, 2016, The Economic Consequences of Delayed Marriage). Considered in this context, current LDS courtship patterns could be labeled as "late" compared to the average marital ages of their parents and grandparents. However, compared to their national counterparts some could consider current LDS dating patterns and ages as "early" or "too soon."

So, which perspective is right? Is there a best time or age to get married? Does getting married during your twentysomething years put your marriage at risk? Is it true that older people are more mature and better prepared for marriage than people who are younger?

Answers to these questions can be helpful for each of us as we prayerfully consider the timing of marriage in our own lives. To give you some insight into these issues, we will consider prophetic counsel on timing of marriage in the life course and scholarly research on the

Median Age of First Marriage
Carroll, 2016

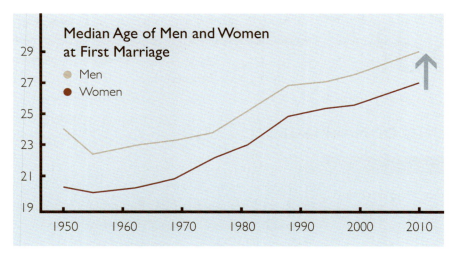

Since 1950, the median age at first marriage has substantially increased in the United States and is currently at a historic high of nearly 30 years for men and 28 years for women.

association between age at marriage and marital outcomes. As you study these principles, remember that like other aspects of finding a right person to marry there are errors of extremes. Moving toward marriage too early or too fast can create problems, as can moving toward marriage too late or too slow.

Prophetic Counsel on Marital Timing

When it comes to counsel about timing related to dating and marriage, our prophetic leaders teach us principles rather than giving precepts or specific age recommendations. However, this does not mean that the ideal timing of marriage is relative to each person. Prophets and apostles have repeatedly emphasized the importance of marriage in God's plan and the priority that should be given to marriage as young people transition to adulthood. A few years ago, President Hinckley came to BYU to give a devotional to the students. During his talk he said:

I remind you that the association you now enjoy as students is probably the best time of your lives to find your own "Beloved Eternal Companion." Do so with a prayer in your heart. It will be the most important decision you will ever make. It will influence your life from now through all eternity (BYU Speeches, October 2006, p. 6).

Elder Dallin H. Oaks has also taught:

It's marriage time. That is what the Lord intends for His *young adult* sons and daughters (CES Fireside for Young Adults, May 2005).

These statements are examples of how prophets have taught us that young adulthood is the ideal time to begin our search for an eternal marriage partner. Young adulthood opens the possibility of marriage for each of us. Marriage may or may not come during this period of life, but we should prepare ourselves for the possibility when a right opportunity presents itself. Trusting in the Lord means that you should prepare yourself to live according to His plan—even if marriage comes into your life sooner or later than you anticipate.

When it comes to the timing and priority of marriage in your life, it is helpful to remember that the Lord has a family ideal that we should strive to fulfill as we transition to adulthood. Elder Richard G. Scott has taught:

> Throughout your life on earth, seek diligently to fulfill the fundamental purposes of this life through the ideal family. While you may not have reached that ideal, do all you can through obedience and faith in the Lord to consistently draw as close to it as you are able. Let nothing dissuade you from that objective. If it requires fundamental changes in your personal life, make them... If you have lost the vision of eternal marriage, rekindle it. If your dream requires patience, give it... Living a pattern of life as close as possible to the ideal will provide much happiness, great satisfaction, and impressive growth while here on earth regardless of your current life circumstances. (Ensign, May 2001, p. 7)

The Lord's servants have counseled us to put marriage as the highest priority in our preparations for adult life—placing it above education, career, and other very important pursuits. The purpose of this counsel is to encourage us to be "anxiously engaged" (D&C 58:27) in finding an eternal marriage companion, not be become "anxiously engaged" by not being careful and deliberate in selecting a future spouse. The counsel of our prophetic leaders is not intended to make us rush the process of dating or to compromise our standards and desires in order to marry at a younger age. Above all, the counsel is to not unduly or selfishly postpone marriage in order to pursue individual pursuits and worldly accomplishments.

Research on Age of Marriage and Divorce

Marriage researchers have conducted several studies to examine the question *Is age at marriage associated with marriage outcomes?* The findings of these studies contradict some of the so-called conventional wisdom of popular culture that labels marriage in the young adult years as "early" or "too young."

When we look at the data from 20 years ago, the argument that being older is better when you get married makes a bit more sense—but not nearly as late into the lifespan as people commonly believe. The bars on the left side of the graph on the next page depict data from the National Survey of Family Growth in 1995 showing the association between the age of marriage and the probability of divorce. From this analysis, we see that as people get older, at least up until the early 20s, there's a significant association between age of marriage and divorce.

Simply put, if one or both of the spouses was a teenager at the time of the marriage the risk of divorce was significantly higher than if both spouses are in their 20s. The risks of teenage marriages have been widely publicized in our culture and we have a pattern of warning young people about the risks of marriage at such an early age. However, we often take this pattern too far and forget to emphasize that the age benefit flattens out dramatically after the early 20s. So, the "older is better" pattern is only true to a point. But, this was a useful conversation to be having when many people we marrying in their teen-

age years—a pattern that is not nearly very common today.

But, now I would like you to see what happens when we fast forward 20 years and look at the new data of what we see in our culture today (see the bars on the right of the graph on this page. The Family Studies Institute released a study recently (Wolfinger, 2015) that analyzed more current data from the National Survey of Family Growth (2006–2010) that examines the trend patterns between age of marriage and the probability of divorce. While the high risk of divorce remains for teenage marriages, they also found that the risks patterns for divorce have changed significantly—particularly for people who marry after the age of 35. What was once largely a linear pattern of association now shows a clear curvilinear pattern, with couples marrying in their 30s starting to have an increased level of divorce compared to couples who married in their twentysomething years. And this is a significant trend given that nearly half of first marriages in the United States are now happening *after* the age of 30. It is clearly time to shift our cultural conversation from the risks of teenage marriage and start to have a more thorough conversation of the potential risks of 30+ marriages.

So, when is the best time to wed? I think the important lesson to learn is that after the teenage years studies have shown that age of marriage is associated with marital outcomes, but it is not a particularly strong predictor of marital satisfaction or divorce proneness. As we have been discussing in the other chapters, we are all better off to gain a greater understanding of the individual and couple factors that are strong predictors of marital quality. We should all encourage young adults to pursue high quality relationships when possible; rather than waiting for an arbitrarily selected age of marriage.

Over 80 years of research on premarital predictors

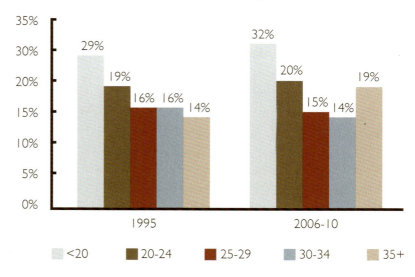

Is Age at Marriage Associated with Marital Outcomes?
Institute for Family Studies – Wolfinger, 2015

Unadjusted estimates of divorce in National Survey of Family Growth in 1995 and 2006-2010

of marriage outcomes have shown that true marital competence or readiness involves helping young people develop the *capacity to love* and the *capacity to communicate* (Carroll et al., 2006, Evaluating the Developmental Domains of Marital Competence). Thus, the foundation factors of personal maturity, emotional readiness, commitment, forgiveness, religious devotion, sexual restraint, communication skills, and the management of conflict are far stronger predictors of marriage trajectories than is age at marriage. We should also stress the "success sequence" of family formation which involves gaining maturity and education prior to marriage and marriage prior to child bearing. It's time for the college-educated segment of our culture to start preaching what they practice when it comes to family formation patterns.

Timing of Marriage

While we have primarily focused on the delay of marriage, for many people the trial of faith they experience related to the timing of marriage is that marriage does not happen as soon as they would like or expect. Our prophetic leaders have frequently addressed this topic. Elder Dallin H. Oaks has stated:

> Our most righteous desires may elude us or come in different ways or at different times than we have sought to plan. For example, we cannot be sure that we will marry as soon as we desire. . .we should commit ourselves to the priorities and standards we will follow on matters we do not control and persist faithfully in those commitments, whatever happens to us because of the agency of others or the timing of the Lord. When we do this, we will have a constancy in our lives that will give us direction and peace. (Ensign, October 2003, p. 10)

Elder Oaks has also taught:

> Singleness, childlessness, death, and divorce frustrate ideals and postpone the fulfillment of promised blessings. . .But these frustrations are only temporary. . .Many of the most important deprivations for mortality will be set right in the Millennium. (Ensign, October, 2003, p. 10)

In the early chapters of this book, we discussed how eternal life is best understood as *God-like life*, which is a way of life centered on marriage and family relationships. The promise of the Lord is that eternal marriage will be a part of celestial glory for all true disciples of Jesus Christ. Therefore, each of us can continue to prepare for marriage with the surety that it will be a part of our eternal destiny and future—even if the realization of that blessing does not happen according to the ideal timing in this life. As we come to understand the assurance of eternal marriage for all true disciples, this doctrine should give us comfort. However, each of us must continue to strive to do all that we can to form an eternal marriage in this life and not become complacent about dating or finding a right person to marry.

Later Marriage

Because I married at 53, I sometimes consider myself the poster child for single adults. I was a participant in the young single adult program, the single adult program, and the older single adult program. You are especially precious to me because I have walked some of the paths you walk, faced some of the concerns you face, and I have enormous empathy and respect for you. Our responsibility is to become the best disciples of Christ we can become.

On one occasion, full of worry and frustration about my single situation and my advancing years, I went to a priesthood leader for a blessing to strengthen me. The words spoken in that blessing stay with me to this day and ring truer to me as time passes. I can still quote them: "If you cannot bear the difficulties and challenges of single life, you will never be able to bear the difficulties and challenges of married life." I sat a bit stunned. Those words were a call to action for me to make my life wonderful regardless of any situation or difficulty I faced. If I made a happy single life for myself, it would determine the happiness I would have as a married woman, and I wanted a happy future.... Life is a challenge, but it will always be a challenge—single or married—and I wanted to be equal to that challenge. I testify from hard-earned experience that the Lord is always preparing us for greater happiness and blessings. We need only try our best and trust in Him with all our hearts.

—Sister Kristen M. Oaks, CES Fireside, 2011

A DEEP AND ABIDING CONCERN

In a recent talk to young adults in the Church, Elder Earl C. Tingey of the Presidency of the Seventy stated:

> The Brethren of the Church have a deep and abiding concern that our young single adults know the doctrine of the Church on marriage. (Ensign, April 2007, p. 37)

I counsel you to always pay close attention to statements by our leaders that begin with the phrase "the brethren of the Church. . ." My experience is that Church leaders are typically very careful to not generalize their statements to include other leaders in the Church unless they have been directly instructed to do so. Elder Tingey is teaching us that the Lord and His ordained leaders are concerned about the trends of our time that encourage young people to delay marriage as they transition to adulthood. They are also mindful that we focus on finding a right person in the right ways as we seek to fulfill this commandment. As you apply the principles of this chapter to your dating attitudes and behaviors you will receive the blessing and promises of the Lord—which will bless your life no matter when marriage occurs for you on your eternal journey.

Who to Wed?

Soulmates vs. Eternal Companions

CHAPTER 15

> Choose a companion you can always honor, you can always respect, one who will complement you in your own life, one to whom you can give your entire heart, your entire love, your entire allegiance, your entire loyalty.
>
> *Pres. Gordon B. Hinckley*

We live in the age of so-called "soulmate marriage," where love is frequently portrayed as a seamless matching with your "other half" and couple relationships are seen as a pathway to personal happiness. In a national survey of single young adults, 94% agreed with the statement that *when you marry you want your spouse to be your soulmate, first and foremost* and 88% also agreed that *there is a special person, a soulmate, waiting for you somewhere out there* (see nationalmarriageproject.org/reports).

Founded on the belief of predestined love (which has many of the same characteristics of *immature love* that we discussed in Chapter 3), marriage today is often portrayed as a *super relationship*—an effortless and conflict-free union, filled with romantic intimacy and emotional togetherness—that can meet our every need and desire. Other bases for marriage, such as a religious covenant, an economic partnership or parenting have generally disappeared from the popular culture's discussion of marriage.

Because of these beliefs, dating and courtship are largely viewed by young adults as a process of finding your "one and only" and matching up with that person who is predestined to be the love of your life. The unspoken assumption of this type of approach to finding love is that people are already personally prepared for marriage or that marriage should not require any personal change, growth, or development. Simply put, love fits itself to you, you don't have to fit yourself to love.

While *soulmate love* may work for scripted Hollywood films or romance novels, most couples making marriage work in the real world will tell you that maintaining their relationship requires work, patience,

A Soulmate Culture
National Marriage Project

Percent of never-married men and women ages 20-29 who strongly or somewhat agree that...

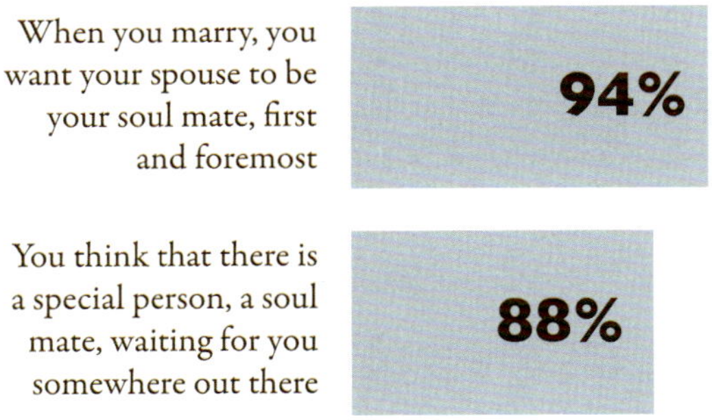

When you marry, you want your spouse to be your soul mate, first and foremost — **94%**

You think that there is a special person, a soul mate, waiting for you somewhere out there — **88%**

personal growth, compromise, commitment, and sacrifice. They will tell you that marriage is definitely worth it, but that what they experience in marriage is not the type of relationship portrayed in popular culture. President Spencer W. Kimball warned Latter-day Saints to not get led astray by the soulmate culture of our day when he said,

> Soulmates are fiction and illusion; and while every young man and young woman will seek with all diligence and prayerfulness to find a mate with whom life can be most compatible and beautiful, yet it is certain that almost any good man and any good woman can have happiness and a successful marriage if both are willing to pay the price. (Marriage and Divorce, 1976, p. 16)

President Boyd K. Packer similarly taught,

> I do not believe in predestined love. . .you must do the choosing, rather than to seek for some one-and-only so-called soulmate, chosen for you by someone else and waiting for you. (Eternal Love, 1973, p. 11)

Soulmates—Fiction and Illusion

"There is a never-failing formula which will guarantee to every couple a happy and eternal marriage; but like all formulas, the principal ingredients must not be left out, reduced, or limited. The selection before courting and then the continued courting after the marriage process are equally important, but not more important than the marriage itself, the success of which depends upon the two individuals—not upon one, but upon two.

"... The formula is simple; the ingredients are few:

    First, there must be the proper approach toward marriage, which contemplates the selection of a spouse ... and then those two parties must come to the altar in the temple realizing that they must work hard toward this successful joint living.

    Second, there must be a great unselfishness, forgetting self and directing all ... to the good of the family,

    Third, there must be continued courting and expressions of affection, kindness, and consideration to keep love alive and growing.

    Fourth, there must be a complete living of the commandments of the Lord as defined in the gospel of Jesus Christ."

—Pres. Spencer W. Kimball

Unrealistic Expectations

Now some may ask, *Does believing in soulmates really do any harm*? There is some evidence that indicates that it does. The trouble lies in the *unrealistic expectations* and *resulting consequences* that arise from approaching marriage this way. When love in dating and marriage is portrayed as perfect and trouble free, many couples are left grasping for answers when they have a major disagreement or when their spouse's lack of responsiveness leaves them feeling hurt and alone. The romantic notions of soulmate love give spouses very little direction on ways to improve, restore, and maintain a marriage in the real world. Unrealistic expectations of one's spouse and married life in general can lead disillusioned partners to believe that their problems lie in having made a "faulty match" and that their only line of recourse is to "unmatch" and "rematch" again with someone else who must be their "real soulmate."

It may be tempting to shrug off these reflections on soulmate culture as merely being a part of popular culture, as something that does not affect Latter-day Saint couples. But, there is some evidence that suggests otherwise. First, popular LDS books and movies presentations portray couple and family relationships as being created in the pre-earth life—with couples coming to earth to find each other and fulfill their pre-earth life promises to each other. Because these portrayals are so widely accepted by members of the Church, Latter-day Saints often have a unique version of soulmate thinking—one that is based in divine destiny and spiritual matchmaking. This line of thought contradicts President Kimball's instruction that soulmates are "fiction and illusion."

What Is the Risk of Soulmate Thinking?

Unrealistic Expectations

- Soulmate = perfect, no compromises
- Soulmate = without effort or change
- Soulmate = know end from beginning

Dating Paralysis

- Finding is hard, "needle in a haystack"
- Fear of making a mistake
- Pass up promising opportunities

Dating Rush

- Rapid courtship
- Lack of careful consideration and personal decision

Even among Latter-day Saints, soulmate beliefs can lead to unrealistic expectations about marriage. In a recent study, LDS marriage counselors were given a list of 29 possible problem areas and were asked to estimate the percentage of LDS couples who have problems or complaints in each area. The problem area entitled "unrealistic expectations of marriage or spouse" was the most frequently reported issue (more than communication, finances, decision making, and sexual intimacy) with these counselors estimating that 71% of LDS couples experience problems in this area (Stahmann & Adams, 1997, p. 26).

One and Only: Made or Found?

Now, if you are like many people, you get a little pit in your stomach when you hear that soulmates are "fiction and an illusion." For many of us, we like the idea of soulmate love and having a one and only. We resonate with the idea that we will be made complete in marriage and have a deep union with our spouse that is emotional, physical, and spiritual in nature.

If you like all of these aspects of so-called "soulmate love," I have good news for you! You do not have to abandon your desires for any of these things. In fact, as we discussed previously, your desire to couple with a special person and experience deep love and belonging with each other is a part of your divine nature (i.e., amae and belonging). Desiring the type of couple unity portrayed in soulmate relationships is a good and righteous aspiration. However, while the goal or outcome of soulmate thinking is a good thing, the way that these relationships come about is presented all wrong in the soulmate thinking of our day.

Our desire should be to become eternal companions with our spouse in this life. Eternal companions are different that soulmates. *While soulmates are found, eternal companions are chosen and made.* The key is to understand that *one-and-only* partners are made, not found. Two people become uniquely suited for each other as they go through the experiences of life with each other and learn to adapt and grow in ways that make them a better fit with their spouse. This type of *one-and-only-ness* is not found or discovered. It is not waiting for you around the next corner—such oneness takes time to fully develop. We cannot see true togetherness in marriage as a simple recipe of matching with the one right person intended to be our spouse.

A Right Person vs. The Right Person

When understood correctly, our focus in finding a marriage partner is to find *a* right person, rather than find *the* right person. This distinction is much more than a semantic difference. If you focus on finding *the* right person, you will either increase your anxiety in dating as you seek out "the one" or you could become complacent about dating, expecting that your pre-chosen partner will be delivered to you without effort or searching on your part.

Understanding prophetic counsel about soulmates and focusing on finding *a* right person brings balance to dating. Anxiety decreases as you realize that there likely will be several people you will meet in your dating who could be a good marriage partner for you. But, these teachings also emphasize that we must do our part in dating to search out an appropriate companion and to commit ourselves to that relationship when the time is right. President Gordon B. Hinckley taught,

> Choose a companion you can always honor, you can always respect, one who will complement you in your own life, one to whom you can *give* your entire heart,

your entire love, your entire allegiance, your entire loyalty. (Ensign, February 1999, emphasis added)

Notice that President Hinckley emphasizes *choosing* and *giving* in finding a marriage companion. This is best done when we understand the difference between soulmate and eternal companion relationships.

EIGHT TRAPS OF SOULMATE THINKING

Now, my experience is that many people who say they do not believe in soulmates, sometimes still allow soulmate thinking to creep into their dating attitudes and behaviors. The following "traps" are examples of how soulmate thinking can affect dating. As you read each of these traps, ask yourself if you think about dating relationships in these ways.

1. THE "LOVE AT FIRST SIGHT" TRAP

This is the notion that when you meet *the* right person—you'll know *immediately* (notice the soulmate nature of the word *immediately*). The trap of this line of thinking is that it might cause you to put too much emphasis on first impressions and not get to know that person well enough before you determine if they could be a marriage prospect for you.

2. THE "OLD BOYFRIEND" TRAP

Soulmate thinking can create anxiety for you as you begin to get serious in a current dating relationship. The question in your mind may be—*Am I supposed to be with someone else*? (notice the soulmate nature of the phrase *supposed to be*). If you believe that there is only one correct path to marriage for you, then you may question if you are in the right relationship. Sometimes people start to think about past relationships or other people they have dated and worry if they are with the wrong person—even when the current dating relationship is going well.

3. THE "ONE TO ONE MATCH" TRAP

Another common trap of soulmate thinking is the notion that *If she is the right person for me, I must be the right person for her*! (notice the soulmate nature of the phrase *the right person*). I have counseled with several individuals who have been quite distressed about the fact that they had found their *one and only*, but there was one problem—he or she did not agree! Soulmate thinking requires a *we-are-the-only-ones-for-each-other* type of mindset. Properly understood, it is quite reasonable that one person can be a right person for the other (able to meet his or her needs) while the other partner is not necessarily a right person for them. Also, two people may both be right for each other, but one is willing to choose that relationship at that time, while the other is not. When you understand this, you can move on and find a partner who is right for you without worrying that you are leaving your soulmate behind.

4. THE "I CAN'T LEAVE HIM" TRAP

Sometimes soulmate thinking causes people to stay in relationships that are not good for them. The thought may be, *I have serious concerns, but we are meant to be together* (notice the soulmate nature of the word *meant*). If you become convinced that you have found your soulmate while dating, what do you do if he or she makes poor choices or you discover serious areas

of incompatibility between you? If they are *the one,* you cannot leave—if they are *a one,* then you can move on to find a healthier and better relationship.

5. THE "SIGNS ARE LINING UP" TRAP

Sometimes couples see their meeting each other and their coming together as being divinely directed and inspired. While I am confident that our Father in Heaven blesses our lives and provides us with opportunities to obtain our divine potential, we must be careful with ascribing too much emphasis to divine matchmaking and spiritually-directed partnering. Such notions are difficult to reconcile with prophetic teachings about soulmates and instructions that dating and marriage decisions are ours to make. Some couples believe that *the spiritual signs are telling us we are meant to be together* (notice the soulmate nature of the phrase *meant*). Perhaps the greatest risk of this line of thinking is couples who become exclusive, and even get engaged, in very short periods of time—without spending more time to get to know each other and one another's families. While many people can point to examples where a couple got engaged a few days or weeks after meeting each other and are still happily married many years later, there are also numerous examples of couples who followed this pattern and had disastrous results. We will discuss prophetic principles about proper dating and engagement in a future chapter on stages of dating.

6. THE "WE FELT THE SPIRIT TOGETHER" TRAP

For some couples, if they feel the spirit together they interpret such feelings as a soulmate-like prompting to partner with that person. The thought may be, *we felt the spirit together—God must intend for us to marry* (notice the soulmate nature of the word *intend*). Clearly you can feel the spirit while being in the presence of a wide number of people—many of whom are not good marriage partners for you. Again, you must do the choosing—God does not make the choice for you and then merely inform you of His choice.

7. THE "LOVE DOESN'T INVOLVE COMPROMISES" TRAP

Soulmate thinking can lead to the unrealistic expectation that a right relationship for you will not involve any struggles or compromises. The thought may be, *when you meet the right person—love is easy* (notice the soulmate nature of the phrase *the right person*). While you should not compromise on matters that are foundational to the divine design of marriage, all good relationships involve flexibility and a willingness to open up space for your partner. Give and take is the reality of marriage, perfect fit is the myth of soulmates.

8. THE "OUR LOVE IS GUARANTEED" TRAP

I have counseled with dozens of young LDS married couples who struggle in the early years of marriage. One of the common areas of struggle I have seen is for spouses who are confused by the fact that they felt a spiritual confirmation about their choice to marry their spouse, yet cannot understand why they are having troubles in their marriage. The line of thinking here is *I don't understand why we are struggling—I felt the Spirit on our wedding day, maybe I made the wrong choice* (notice the soulmate nature of the phrase *the wrong choice*). All marriages require effort and commitment. Spouses will become more and more "fitted to each other" as they strive to manage differences in respectful and loving ways. A spiritual confirmation is not a guarantee, it is a promise that the relationship has the potential to be a right relationship for you—if both people will seek to become all that they can become.

Avoid Dating Paralysis

Sometimes, soulmate perspectives create a sort of dating paralysis among LDS young adults. They know that marriage is a very important decision with eternal consequences, yet they are fearful of making a wrong decision. So, many young people simply "lock-up" in dating—neither moving ahead nor moving back.

One of the misunderstandings that leads to dating paralysis is the notion that prayerful decision making involves determining the path for our lives that God has already chosen. Prophetic leaders have repeatedly taught that decisions about dating and marriage are yours to make. Elder Richard G. Scott counseled about how to properly use the gift of prayer in making important decisions. He said:

> When you are living worthily and your choice is consistent with the Savior's teachings and you need to act, proceed with trust. As you are sensitive to the promptings of the Spirit, one of two things will certainly occur at the appropriate time: either the stupor of thought will come, indicating an improper choice, or the peace or the burning of the bosom will be felt, confirming your choice was correct. When you are living righteously and are acting with trust, God will not let you proceed too far without a warning impression if you have made the wrong decision. (Ensign, May 2007, p. 10)

Elder Scott is teaching us a pattern of *prayerful action*, rather than directive answers to prayers that must precede action on our part. Often our Father in Heaven sustains our choices, thus making what we choose according to righteous desires and principles a good course for us. As we are striving to do what is right, we can proceed with faith.

Compatibility and Attraction

Two of the most common questions I am asked as a marriage educator are: (1) *How do you know if you are compatible with your dating partner?* and (2) *How important is it to be physically attracted to your spouse?* This section discusses each of these important topics in finding a right person to marry—compatibility and attraction.

Compatibility

Compatibility is one of the most commonly used modern terms to describe what people are looking for in their dating and future marriage. In fact, the question *Are you compatible?* might be the best way to sum up what modern dating is all about. While this emphasis on compatibility is understandable, and even desirable, as we strive to form a marriage based in equal partnership, friendship, and shared commitment, we also have to be careful about what it means to be compatible with someone. Typically, when we say compatible we mean "the same" or "similar." While a certain amount of similarity is needed in a partnership like marriage, it may not always be the best indicator of a good fit.

Let's read a quote again that we have already seen from President Hinckley:

Choose a companion you can always honor, you can always respect, *one who will complement you in your own life*, one to whom you can give your entire heart, your entire love, your entire allegiance, your entire loyalty. (Ensign, February 1999, emphasis added)

Notice that President Hinckley encourages us to choose a marriage companion who will *complement* us. Is complement the same as compatible? There is a key insight here that can help us better understand what creates true compatibility in marriage.

Compatibility vs. Complementarity

Consider the following definitions:

Com-ple-ment (n.)

1. That which completes or brings to perfection
2. The amount or number needed to fill or complete
3. A complete set
4. Something added to complete a whole; either of two parts that complete each other

Com-ple-men-tary (adj.)

1. Acting as a complement; completing
2. 2. Making up what is lacking in one another

Com-ple-men-tar-ity (n.)

1. The state or fact of being complementary; necessary interrelationship or correspondence.

Notice that the emphasis of complementarity is the process of *completing* something or making it whole. This process may involve similar parts, but often it also involves different talents and capacities that augment and strengthen each other because they add something new, above and beyond what already exists. As you search for a right person to marry, be mindful that a person who is right for you is going to have an appropriate balance of similarity and difference from you.

Common Factors, Complementary Characteristics and Personal Preferences

You have already been encouraged to distinguish between common characteristics of successful marriages and personal preferences you may have in a partner or future relationship. Making distinctions between these types of issues will help you make wise dating decisions. Sometimes people become attracted to and involved with someone who meets their personal preferences, but is lacking in foundation aspects of a healthy relationship. Others pass up on potential dating partners who have a wonderful foundation to be compatible partners, but lack on certain preference issues such as physical attributes, interests in hobbies, or other minor matters. Elder Richard G. Scott counseled:

> There are several essential attributes which we should look for in a potential mate: a deep love of the Lord and of His commandments, a determination to live them, one that is kindly, understanding, forgiving of others, and willing to give of self, with the desire to have a family crowned with beautiful children, and a commitment to teach them the principles of truth in the home.
>
> I suggest that you not ignore many possible candidates who are still developing these attributes, seeking one who is perfect in them. You will likely not find that perfect person, and if you did, there would certainly be no interest in you. These attributes are best polished together as husband and. (Ensign, May 1999)

Elder Scott and other prophetic leaders have counseled you to put first things first in your dating priorities. Seek someone with whom you can be partner disciples in this life. However, make sure you distinguish between finding someone who is on a righ-

teous track versus someone who is perfect. Marriage is one of the most important contexts of growth in this life—when two people are on a righteous trajectory and are striving to follow the Lord, then they will grow together in their marriage relationship.

Compatibility—Beyond Discipleship

A common question I hear is, *Can two people who are both striving to be disciples not be right people for each other*? I believe the answer to this question is yes. You should seek for a goodness of fit in complementary characteristics, as well as principles of discipleship.

What are some examples of these types of possible *Complementary Characteristics*? Examples of such characteristics include: age and experience levels, personality and temperament, cultural backgrounds and environments, living arrangements (location, type, etc.), and interests and hobbies. For example, one person may desire to live in a rural community, while the other may desire to live in an urban setting. A person can have righteous desires and can still desire to live in either type of community, but two spouses not being in alignment with an issue such as this could be disruptive to their marriage. Similarly, spouses may want to consider how having similar or different interests in hobbies and leisure interests will impact their future relationship. These types of preferences can become quite important to some people and sometimes require investments of money and time, which could lead to disagreements in the future over purchases and time patterns.

Criteria of Compatibility

Preference to Preference — "Personal Choice"

Personal Preferences
Differences that you can live with (all marriages have these!)

Complimentary Characteristics
Compatibility and Complementarity
Differences that will make a difference (struggle at the extremes)

Healthy to Unhealthy — "True Principles"

Foundation Factors
Discipleship
Faith, repentance, cleaving, spousal preeminence, equal partnership, spousal stewardships, chastity
Becoming
Personal security, mature love, marital virtues, empathetic listening, clear-sending communication

> "...become what you hope your spouse will be."
> -Elder Bednar

> "I suggest that you not ignore many possible candidates who are still developing these attributes, seeking one who is perfected in them."
> -Elder Scott

> "I'm not suggesting you lower your standards and marry someone with whom you can't be happy."
> -Elder Uchtdorf

Some Cautions about Compatibility

Ultimately, finding a companion requires each of us to balance several principles, without making the error of sliding to the extreme in either direction. For example, it is important for you to determine the things that matter the most to you in a partner and future marriage and to not compromise on those things that are central to your identity. However, you must also be cautious in determining the length of this "must have" list. When people are unwilling to be flexible and compromise, the size of their "eligible pool" for dating candidates goes way down and some people discover that they cannot find anyone who meets their extensive list of criteria. The best way to know if you are being too picky is to look at how many eligible candidates you are finding to date. If the criteria are too narrow, dating will feel like finding a needle in a haystack. The Lord did not intend for finding a marriage partner to feel like winning the lottery!

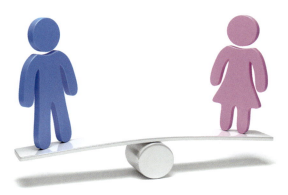

Another area that must be balanced is determining between partners being *compatible now* versus *compatible later*. Some couples are very compatible as dating partners, but struggle as married partners and co-parents. Make sure that you emphasize compatibility for the future relationship you desire to have, not just the enjoyable boyfriend or girlfriend you have now. For example, being spontaneous and carefree can be very endearing while dating, but cause contention in later family life as these same attributes are seen as lazy or unproductive. I encourage you to partner for the future, not just the here and now. President Spencer W. Kimball encourages us to seek a compatibility that is lasting. He says:

> In selecting a companion for life and for eternity, certainly the most careful planning and thinking and praying and fasting should be done to be sure that of all the decisions, this one must not be wrong. In true marriage there must be a union of minds as well as of hearts. Emotions must not wholly determine decisions, but the mind and the heart, strengthened by fasting and prayer and serious consideration, will give one a maximum chance of marital happiness. (Marriage and Divorce, 1976, p. 11)

Physical Attraction

As I mentioned previously, a common question about dating is *Is physical attraction important*? As I have pondered on and researched this question, I am convinced that there are two answers to this question, a simple answer and a more complex one.

The Simple Answer

The simple answer is yes. Physical attraction between spouses is important as it fosters forms of closeness and belonging that foster emotional and sexual intimacy. If one or both partners in dating are not physically attracted to each other, this may cause them to hold back and not fully invest in the relationship as they should. This can disrupt cleaving, spousal preeminence, and other important aspects of becoming one in marriage.

Because physical attraction matters, each of us should strive to be as physically fit and attractive as we can be. In this regard, the Word of Wisdom is a principle of dating and marriage. Eating well, exercising, getting proper amounts of sleep, and seeking to dress and groom ourselves in an attractive manner are important parts of becoming and finding a right person to marry, and creating a marriage afterwards.

Clearly our emphasis on physical attractiveness in ourselves and others must be tempered and balanced. This does not require us to spend a lot of money on designer clothes, spa makeovers, and exercise equipment to achieve the *salon look* or *modern chic* that is prevalent today. Yet at the same time, patterns of spouses "letting themselves go" after marriage or stating that only *spiritual beauty* matters will not serve our purposes in dating or marriage either. A proper attention to our physical health and appearance is appropriate both before and after marriage.

The Complex Answer

While we are given some insight and direction into the matter of physical attraction by the simple answer that yes it matters, there are deeper issues involved with attraction that deserve our consideration. These include:

- What is physical attraction?
- Why is physical attraction important?
- Will our physical traits change during this life?
- Are there other traits that influence our attraction to someone?
- Is attraction to others agentive?

As you ponder on these questions, the answer to the question of how important is physical attraction in dating and marriage requires a mature outlook and perspective. Clearly, attraction is more than physical. You can be attracted to someone because of their character, their personality, their sense of humor, their family situation, their money, their possessions, and numerous other traits and attributes. Some of these bases for attraction are more important than others. Some are appropriate sources of attraction and others are not.

You must also address the question of why being with someone we find physically attractive is important to us or not. What is the motivation? Is it so you feel better about yourself because you have a beautiful boyfriend or girlfriend? Also, we all know that ours' and others' physical traits will change during our lifetimes. What happens if you prioritize physical traits in dating that change after you are married. Hairlines recede, wrinkles appear, bodies lose their youthfulness—this

happens for everyone. Are you attracted by features that will endure, such as character and discipleship, or are you attracted by the latest fashions or trends?

Over all of these issues is the question about agency and attraction. Too often we talk about attraction as if it is something that happens to us, something we cannot explain or control. But how much can you choose who you are attracted to? My experience is that each of us tends to find desirable the people who have the traits we have our own hearts set upon. Each of us clearly influences who we are attracted to and to be mature we must recognize our own contribution to attraction.

Cautions about Attraction

Similar to compatibility, we must be cautious about fostering a mature and gospel-centered perspective about attraction. Here are several cautions to be aware of as you think about your own views of attraction.

Beware of the "Supermodel Phenomenon"

Each of us needs to be careful about the images and messages we are bombarded with in the media about physical attractiveness. It seems like everywhere we turn we are exposed to images of movie stars, models, and music performers who have perfect bodies, dress in the latest fashions, and live exciting lifestyles. The more we see these images, the more normal they seem and we begin to compare ourselves and others to these standards. The risk in this is that we forget that the images we see are typically distorted, manufactured, and anything but typical.

For example, consider what I call the *supermodel phenomenon*. When you see a picture of a beautiful woman on the cover of a magazine, what are you really looking at? What you see is a picture of a woman who was selected out of tens of thousands of women for her facial features and body type. She is literally a *one-in-a-thousand* woman when it comes to these features (and often she has dieted, altered her looks, and used plastic surgery to conform to this ideal). Next, this "one-in-a-thousand woman" takes part in a photo shoot where

over 1,000 pictures are taken of her and the best one is chosen. The picture is literally a "one-in-a-thousand" picture (and great effort is given to manufacturing the picture with make-up, lighting, poses, and other techniques of creating attractive pictures). Next, the one-in-a-thousand picture of the one-in-a-thousand-woman is sent to the production shop where it is airbrushed and photoshopped to remove any undesirable features. This is the image we ultimately see. If you want to test how un-real this image is, take a picture of supermodel to a crowded downtown street corner and stand there until someone who looks like the picture walks by. You could be there for days, if not weeks, waiting for anyone who resembles this "normal picture" to pass by. In fact, you may never leave that corner, because chances are that even if the woman who is in the picture walked by she would not look anything like the picture you are holding.

Can you see why adopting popular cultural standards of beauty can be so damaging? These images can make us overly critical of ourselves and others, warping our sense of physical attractiveness.

Premarital vs. Post-Marital Attraction

I have been perplexed at times by the contradictory standards of physical attraction I hear people express when it comes to dating versus marriage. For example, if a guy is talking to his friend about a girl he has dated and he says, "I'm not sure if I should date her anymore, she's a little overweight and I'm not that physically attracted to her." His friend is likely to say, "*That makes sense, you have to be physically attracted to her.*" Many of us nod our head at this exchange and agree with the views expressed. But, if a married guy says to his friend, "My wife just had a baby and she put on some weight during the pregnancy, I'm not very attracted

to her anymore," most of us want to whack him with a heavy object! His views of physical attraction in marriage seem immature, insensitive, and lacking an eternal perspective. Why then are we accepting of such views in our own and others' attitudes during dating? We should foster a mature view of attractiveness that will be appropriate across all stages of life.

Trait-Based vs. Person-Centered Love

While it is flattering to be with someone who thinks we are physically beautiful, such foundations of a relationship can also be anxiety producing as we all get older and change physically. Being loved as a person, rather than for our traits or appearance is what gives us comfort and security.

Don't Restrict the Size of Your "Eligible Pool"

Similar to compatibility, having very high expectations for physical attractiveness will narrow your eligible pool of potential marriage candidates. Again, the best way to know if you are being too picky is to look at how many eligible candidates you are finding to date. If the criteria are too narrow, dating will feel like finding a needle in a haystack. Plus, make sure you are not expecting in others what you yourself do not offer—unrealistic expectations will make dating a frustrating and unproductive experience.

The Power of Pairing and the Stages of Dating

CHAPTER 16

> The successful marriage depends in large measure upon the preparation made in approaching it...One cannot pick the ripe, rich, luscious fruit from a tree that was never planted, nurtured, nor pruned.
>
> *Pres. Spencer W. Kimball*

In this chapter we discuss the topic of dating. This is the *how* part of finding a right person for marriage. As you begin this chapter, I would like you to consider some important questions. *Is there a "divine design" for dating? Does the Lord have a specific pattern for how we should date and find a marriage partner? Are there right ways to date and wrong ways to date? Will a couple's pattern of dating influence their relationship later in marriage?*

If your answer to these four questions is yes, then—*what is the Lord's plan for dating*? Unfortunately for many young people in the Church, if you ask them to explain the Lord's plan for dating they will tell you— "Don't date until you are 16 years old!" Perhaps even more concerning is that some parents in the Church can only articulate this one principle too. The Lord's pattern for dating is a little more detailed than this!

In this chapter we discuss the Lord's *divine design* for dating and finding an eternal companion. Doesn't it make sense that if the Lord has a divine design for marriage, that He also has a divine design for how to form one? In fact, our loving Heavenly Father has revealed a step-by-step pattern for dating. This is important to understand, because it means that there are actually *correct approaches* and *incorrect approaches* to dating. As you come to better understand the Lord's pattern and plan for your dating experiences in this life, you will have greater success in dating and deeper happiness in your later marriage.

The Erosion of Traditional Dating and Courtship

Many sweeping demographic shifts have taken place over the last fifty years that have contributed to changing views about becoming an adult and what is needed to be ready for marriage. One of the most dramatic changes impacting marriage preparation in the United States during the last quarter century has been the emergence of a new period in life between adolescence and adulthood that has been labeled "emerging adulthood" (Arnett, 2000).

This life stage has emerged as a result of the substantial increase in the last 30 years in the median age at first marriage for both men and women. Since 1970, the median age of marriage in the United States has risen from about 21 years for females and 23 for males, to 28 and 30 for females and males, respectively (see Carroll, 2016, The Economic Consequences of Delayed Marriage). This tendency to delay marriage has created an extended period of nearly 10 years in the family life cycle where most young adults have left adolescence and are beginning to view themselves as adults, but have not yet entered into the commitments and lifestyle patterns of married adult life.

With the emergence of this new life stage, a growing question for the rising generation is: *What impact does this new period of "extended singleness" have on adult development and emerging adults' preparation for later marriage and family life?*

Modern Dating Pitfalls

One of the best places for us to turn in understanding how the period of emerging adulthood is influencing preparation for later marriage and family life is to look at the defining characteristics of the current dating and courtship culture among young adults today. Numerous scholars have noted that the culture of dating that young adults experience today is markedly different than the one experienced by their parents and grandparents. In particular, these family professionals have noted an erosion of traditional courtship patterns and a dating culture that lacks any socially defined norms, rituals, and relationship milestones to guide young people toward marriage.

As a result of these changes a number of pitfalls exist in our current dating and courtship culture, including: (1) a growing pessimism about marriage, (2) a focus on personal independence before and after marriage, (3) hanging-out versus dating, (4) widespread sexual permissiveness, (5) high rates of couples living together before marriage, and (6) changing parental attitudes about marriage.

Pessimism about Marriage

Despite the growing trend to delay marriage, recent research indicates that having a successful, life-long marriage is still a highly valued goal for the majority of young adults. In fact, 92% of young adults in the United States rate "having a good marriage" as quite or extremely important to them (National Marriage Project, 2001). However, having grown up in a society saturated with divorce, many young people are becoming increasingly pessimistic about their chances of having a happy marriage. In 1975, 1 in 4 young adults agreed with the statement *One sees so few good or happy marriages that one questions it as a way of life.* However, in 2005, the number of young adults agreeing with that statement has risen to 1 in 3. Simply put, when it comes to marriage, many young adults today have high aspirations, but low expectations (see nationalmarriageprojet.org/reports/).

Getting Ahead before Getting Wed

In past generations, events such as marriage and parenthood marked the entrance into adulthood. The central responsibilities of adulthood in past generations centered on caring for one's spouse, providing for a family, and nurturing children—all of which involve duties toward others. However, recent research reveals that young people no longer consider marriage and parenthood as criteria for adulthood (Nelson et al., 2007, Journal of Family Psychology). In contrast they report that they believe they have reached adulthood when they accept responsibility for one's self, achieve financial independence, and become independent decision makers. For the most part, these new markers of adulthood carry a theme of self-sufficiency and self-reliance compared to the traditional, other-oriented criteria of the past. Coupled with a sense of pessimism about their chances for marital success, it appears that many young adults see their 20s as a time to pursue their personal interests and become independent financially. Simply put, young adult culture today fosters an attitude that one's duty lies first and foremost to one's self.

Hanging Out vs. Dating

One of the most dramatic changes in the dating culture is the disappearance of dating. Put another way, the "dating" culture has become a "hanging out" culture. Several studies have found that traditional dating, where a man asks a woman out on a date and pays for the evening's events is becoming rare. Only 50% of college women report that they have been asked out on 6 or more dates, and one-third said they had been asked on two or fewer dates. The common pattern these days is for young women and men to informally hang out—in a group or with just each other—rather than go on planned dates. With these patterns becoming widespread and accepted, young adults frequently report that even when they have hung out with a friend of the opposite sex for a long period of time, they still do not know whether they are a couple. This type of ambiguity in dating leaves young adults with few widely recognized norms to guide and support them as they try to move forward toward love, commitment, and marriage.

Hook-ups and Sexual Permissiveness

Along with hanging out, today's dating culture is one characterized by casual attitudes toward sexual relationships. Even though premarital sexual behavior has been shown to be a significant risk factor for future marital success (Heaton, 2002, Factors Contributing to Increasing Marital Stability in the United States), single life in American culture has become synonymous with sexual experimentation in non-committed romantic relationships. A study of 1,000 college young women showed that a form of getting together, called "hooking up," is wide-spread and accepted on college campuses today. Hooking up occurs when a young man and woman get together for the sole purpose of some kind of physical encounter, often full sexual expression, with nothing further expected of the relationship. A group of scholars concluded:

> ...the culture of courtship, a set of social norms and expectations that once helped young people find the

pathway to marriage, has largely become a hook up culture with almost no shared norms or expectations. Hooking up, hanging out, and fast-moving ("joined at the hip") commitments are logical, though we believe seriously flawed, responses to this disappearance of a culture of courtship. (Glenn & Marquardt, 2001, Hooking up, Hanging out, and Hoping for Mr. Right, p. 4)

Another research team characterized today's dating and mating culture as "sex without strings, relationships without rings" (see nationalmarriageproject.org/reports). Women are accusing young men of being "commitment phobic," and there is evidence to support that view. One study of young men suggested several reasons so many are unwilling to marry. Some of these reasons are: (1) they can get sex without marriage, (2) they can enjoy the benefits of having a wife by cohabiting rather than marrying, (3) they want to avoid divorce and its financial risks, (4) they fear that marriage will require too many changes and compromises, (5) they are waiting for the perfect soul mate and she hasn't yet appeared, (6) they face few social pressures to marry, and (7) they want to enjoy single life as long as they can.

Acceptance of Cohabitation

Recent research also indicates that emerging adults are increasingly embracing the idea that a couple needs to live together before marriage to test their relationship and see if they are ready for marriage. Recently, 62% of young adults reported that they believe that living together before marriage is a good way to avoid eventual divorce and more than half of all marriages in America today are preceded by cohabitation (National Marriage Project, 2001). The core ideas among these young adults is that cohabitation is a way to take the risk out of marriage and assure themselves that they won't get divorced. However, research shows that this is a paradoxical belief. Studies on cohabitation and later marital success have consistently found that couples who cohabit before marriage are *more* likely to divorce than couples who do not cohabit before marriage (see Kuperberg, 2014, Premarital Cohabitation and Marriage Dissolution). Sadly, a positive attitude toward premarital cohabitation is widespread even among many professionals who either don't know or choose to ignore the research showing that cohabiting before marriage is actually related to less success in future marriages.

Parental Attitudes About Marriage

One final trend worth mentioning is the shifting views parents are offering their young adult children when it comes to marriage preparation. Because of the rise of divorce during their own generation, many parents today may be encouraging their children to prepare for the possibility of divorce by delaying marriage to pursue education, develop in their careers, and gain economic independence. This espousal of a *personal independence ethic* of adult living may be encouraging emerging adults to develop self-focused identities and sends the message that marriage is an unstable foundation for adult life and happiness. Furthermore, the encouragement of delayed marriage by parents may be exposing their children to additional martial risk factors such as cohabitation and premarital sexual behavior. Simply put, *parents may be preparing their children for divorce, rather than marriage* and this may be acting as a self-fulfilling prophecy in their adult children's marriages.

Dating Patterns Among Latter-day Saints

As distressing as the modern trends of dating are in the broader society, perhaps even more distressing is the rising evidence of this kind of thinking and behaving taking hold among young adults in the Church. Given the messages young adults in the Church are receiving from our culture, and even from families and friends in the Church, it is not surprising that many young adults are confused, afraid to make commitments, and too often turning their ears to the messages of the world. For example a recent study of unmarried BYU students showed that "fear of making a mistake" was a factor influencing nearly 60% of those who are delaying marriage. Other studies have shown that hanging out patterns have increased among LDS young people, although such patterns are not as prevalent as they are among other samples of young adults. There is also some evidence that some LDS young people are "hooking-up" outside of committed relationships by engaging in NiCMos (Non-Committed Make-out) or other forms of non-committed physical intimacy.

The Lord's Divine Pattern of Dating

In recent years, our prophetic leaders have warned young adults about the erosion of courtship in our society and have counseled young people to follow a divinely directed approach to dating and courtship. In this section of the chapter we examine prophetic teachings about dating and courtship. Specifically, we discuss some key principles of dating, the power of pairing, and the stages of dating. We conclude the chapter by discussing prophetic counsel related to engagement and planning a wedding.

Principles of dating

Dating Is a Means, Not an End

A key principle you need to remember when it comes to dating is that in the Lord's plan dating is not the end goal—it is a means to another end or goal. That goal is temple marriage. In the *For the Strength of Youth* pamphlet written by the First Presidency we are taught that proper dating is about marriage preparation. Remember the quote from Elder Bruce R. McConkie you read at the first of the book—

> Everything we have in the whole gospel system is to prepare and qualify us to enter that holy order of matrimony which makes us husband and wife in this life and in the world to come. . . .There is nothing in this world as important as the creation and perfection of family units. (Improvement Era, June 1970, pp. 43–44)

Whether marriage is close for you or still several years away in your life trajectory—never lose sight that God's pattern for dating is based in the purpose of creating eternal marriages and families. When we understand this, we can see why the Lord's pattern of dating is so important. Proper dating is a key part of one day having a temple marriage and eternal family. Life's greatest joys are found in these relationships when we follow the Lord's plan. Unfortunately, some of life's greatest heartaches are possible when we do not follow this plan. Live for the marriage and family you desire to have some day—that begins now with proper dating.

Timing and Sequence Matter

In the Lord's plan for dating, sequence and timing matter. Ecclesiastes 3:1 says, "To everything there is a season, and a time to every purpose under the heaven." President Spencer W. Kimball applied this teaching to dating when he taught,

> There is definitely a time for the dance, for travel, for associations, for the date, and even for the steady date that will culminate in the romance which will take people to the holy temple for eternal marriage. But it is the timing that is so vital. It is wrong to do even the right things at the wrong time in the wrong place under the wrong circumstances. (New Era, November 1980, p. 39)

I want to emphasize what President Kimball said—"It is wrong to do even the right things at the wrong time." It could also be said that it is wrong to *not* do the right things at the right time. The Lord's pattern of dating involves doing the right things at the right times—this is the path of safety and peace.

The Power of Pairing

Although I have referred to these principles as the Lord's pattern for dating, perhaps the best label for

them is a *pattern for pairing*. While much of the focus of discussion on this subject refers to dating, the Lord's servants have actually provided counsel about how and when to pair off or couple with others, whether you are on a formal date or not. Prophetic counsel to youth and young adults in the Church reflects an understanding of the power of pairing and the natural processes that emerges as two people begin to spend time together and eventually become a couple. In fact, the power of paring is recognized as being so powerful, that teens are counseled to not pair off or form couple relationships. On the other hand, young adults are encouraged to properly use the power of pairing to move forward in the courtship process when the time is right. As you study the stages of dating in the next section, notice how the stages are about pairing and coupling, not just the type or timing of formal dates.

Stages of Dating

As I noted at the first of the chapter, for many young people in the Church, if you ask them to tell you what the prophetic principles of dating are, all they can say is—"Don't date until you are 16 years old!" If this is the case, then appropriate dating has only two stages—the "No Stage" and the "Go Stage."

As I have studied prophetic teachings about dating, I am convinced that there are at least *five stages* in the Lord's divine pattern of dating. These stages are not rigid step-by-step prescriptions as much as they are life stages with purposes and developmental goals. These stages start early in life and are developmental in nature. This means that each stage is meant to build upon the stage before it. There are purposes and

Stages of Dating
Jason S. Carroll, Ph.D. Brigham Young University

	Pre-Dating *Relationship*	Group Dating *Friendship*	Paired Dating *Companionship*	Exclusive Dating *Partnership*	Engaged Dating *Courtship*
Age	12-16	16-18	18+	18+ (post mission)	Age varies
Purposes	■ Learn standards ■ Develop social skills and talents ■ Strengthen self-worth ■ Counsel with parents	■ Improve social skills and talents ■ Develop respect, self control, courage, etc. ■ Counsel with parents	■ Refine social skills and talents ■ Experience a range of potential partners ■ Experience self with others	■ Explore a potential marriage relationship ■ Move forward or backward	■ Confirm a marriage partnership ■ Make wedding preparations ■ Form new family relationships
Practices and Capacities	■ Combined YM/YW ■ Supervised mixed group activities ■ Ages 14+ non-date dances	■ Non-couple status ■ Date a variety of people ■ Group dates ■ Date dances	■ Non-couple status ■ Date a variety of people ■ One-on-one and group dates	■ Couple status ■ Steady dating ■ Hanging-out as a couple ■ Merge schedules	■ Engagement ■ Forsake others (spousal pre-eminence) ■ Hanging-out as a couple ■ Merge lives

practices in each stage that help us develop the competencies we need to form and maintain a loving and lasting marriage relationship. We miss out on needed experiences when we move through the stages too quickly or too slowly. As you learn about these stages, you'll better understand the Lord's principles for how we should go about finding a right person for marriage.

PRE-DATING STAGE

The first stage of dating is the *pre-dating stage* which is intended to help young people ages 12 to 16 develop the capacities needed to form and maintain relationships. The *purposes* of the pre-dating stage are to develop basic relationship skills and competencies. In this stage, junior high age teens begin having structured social interactions with members of the opposite sex and to learn about the principles of appropriate dating. These experiences help them develop social skills, strengthen their self-worth, and learn standards of dating. Describing this stage, a Church youth manual states:

> Of course, socializing with people of the other gender doesn't start when you go on your first official date. Sometimes, usually during the early teenage years, young men and young women start noticing each other more. They socialize at church and school related activities. And many get together with friends in informal, non-dating settings. Some good things can come from these associations, such as making new friends and learning social skills. (Church manual, 1992)

Appropriate *practices* of the pre-dating stage involve attending combined young men and young women activities in Church youth groups, participating in mixed gender activities at school and with friends, and attending non-date dances when one turns 14 years old. At these dances, young people pair off for the duration of the song in a supervised setting.

GROUP DATING STAGE

The second stage of dating is the *group dating stage* which is intended to help young people ages 16 to 18 develop the capacities needed to form and maintain friendships. The *purposes* of the group dating stage are to improve social skills and to develop personal maturity in the areas of respect for others, self-control, and courage. In this stage, high school age teens begin having actual dating experiences and to begin to practice the principles of appropriate dating. However, this stage is called the group dating stage because prophetic leaders have repeatedly instructed that early dating experiences should be limited to group dates and should avoid pairing-off to become a couple. Consider the following quotes:

> Do not date until you are at least 16 years old. Dating before then can lead to immorality, limit the number of other young people you meet, and deprive you of experiences that will help you choose an eternal partner... When you begin dating, go in groups or on double dates. Avoid going on frequent dates with the same person. (For the Strength of Youth Pamphlet).

> When are you old enough? Maturity may vary from individual to individual, but we are convinced that dating should not even begin until you are 16. And then, ideal dating is on a group basis. Stay in group activities; don't pair off. Avoid steady dating. Steady dating is courtship, and surely the beginning of courtship ought to be delayed until you have emerged from your teens. (Boyd K. Packer, *Liahona*, June 2004, p. 27)

Appropriate *practices* of the group dating stage involve continuing to attend combined young men and young women activities in Church youth groups, continuing to participate in mixed gender activities at school and with friends, and attending date dances when one turns 16 years old. At these dances, young

people pair off for the duration of the evening, in the presence of other couples.

An important part of the group dating stage is to maintain a *non-coupled status* in our dating. One of the serious errors young people make during the group dating stage is to become exclusive with one person and to begin to spend a lot of time alone with him or her. Elder Dallin H. Oaks counseled young adults about hanging out instead of going on traditional dates (we'll discuss this counsel in just a minute). In his comments, Elder Oaks was warning about hanging-out as a way to avoid pairing off. With teens, there is a different form of hanging out and they do it so they *can* pair off. What this involves is young people telling their parents they are just "hanging out" with a group of friends and then when the group is out of sight of parents the young people pair off into their boyfriend and girlfriend pairs.

Some teens in the church think it is ok to pair off exclusively because they call it hanging out instead of dating. Don't play with definitions. No matter what you call it, it still leads to spending time alone with one person and identifies you as a *coupled* person. If you pair

off, the attractions and feelings you will have for that person are the same whether you call it dating, going out, going steady, or hanging out. When our prophetic leaders talk about relationships, they talk about principles and practices that apply no matter what words we use to label or define those relationships. President Kimball taught,

> Early dating, especially early steady dating, brings numerous problems, much heartache, and numerous disasters. The early date often develops into the steady date. . .Dating, and especially steady dating, in the early teens is most hazardous. It distorts the whole picture of life. It deprives the youth of worthwhile and rich experiences. It limits friendships and reduces acquaintances which can be so valuable in selecting a partner for time and eternity. Going steady too young oftentimes leads to intimacies which are encouraged by dating with one partner only. (New Era, November 1980, p. 39)

The sad reality in today's dating culture is that too many young people have boyfriends or girlfriends before they have boy friends or girl friends. This limits social experiences and friendships in ways that hinder proper preparation for marriage. Plus, premarital sexual intimacy can distort your sexual conditioning and attach feelings of guilt, shame, and regret to sexual expression. These are feelings that can negatively impact proper sexual intimacy later in marriage.

Paired Dating Stage

The third stage of dating is the *paired dating stage* which is intended to help young people ages 18 and above develop the capacities needed to form and maintain companionships. The *purposes* of the paired dating stage are to refine social skills, to allow young people to gain experience with a range of potential marriage partners, and to experience interactions with different companions. In this stage, post high school age teens and young adults can broaden their dating experiences and deepen their understanding of the types of people that best complement them in relationships. This stage is called the paired dating stage because young people

begin to pair off and spend time one-on-one getting to know one another. Elder LeGrand R. Curtis explained,

> As you go out on dates, you may think you are simply out to have a good time and to share the company of someone you like, doing things you both like to do. That is not wrong or inappropriate in any way. But you should also remember that in your own way, you are searching for the one you will eventually marry, the one with whom you will spend your lifetime and all eternity. It seems to me that this dating, courtship, and marriage process is like baking bread: it needs careful measuring, sifting, and mixing. Then it needs time to rise. Then, finally, it's ready for the oven. (New Era, June 1993, p. 4)

Within this analogy, paired dating is the "measuring, sifting, and mixing" that occurs before the "rising" of exclusive dating and the "baking" of engagement. President Harold B. Lee counseled young people to remember that the ultimate goal of paired dating is to prepare ourselves for marriage and find a future spouse. He taught,

> The purpose of dating which leads to courtship and ultimately to marriage is a social process by which young people ultimately find their mates in marriage. It is a truism that we find our husband or wife among that company we frequent the most. (Ye Are the Light of the World, Deseret Book, 1974, p. 72)

Appropriate *practices* of the paired dating stage involve going on traditional dates, attending a young single adult ward, attending Institute or religion classes, and participating in mixed gender activities and group dates. In traditional dating, couples pair off for the duration of the evening or activity and may go out with one another on multiple occasions.

While paired dating involves one-on-one pairing and involvement, in this stage of dating young people still maintain a non-coupled status. When someone becomes exclusive with one other person paired dating ends and exclusive dating begins. As we will discuss later, this changes the dating context dramatically. The purposes of the paired dating stage can only be accomplished when young people pair off with multiple people without becoming couples.

Paired Dating and Missionary Service

Prophets have repeatedly taught that paired dating is the most committed form of dating a young man or woman should enter into before his or full-time missionary service. This counsel is provided for the benefit of young people entering the mission field, as well as young women and men who are "waiting" at home. In an address to young women of the Church, President Ezra Taft Benson counseled,

> The Lord wants every young man to serve a full-time mission. . .a young man can do nothing more important. School can wait. Scholarships can be deferred. Occupational goals can be postponed. Yes,

even temple marriage should wait until after a young man has served an honorable full-time mission for the Lord. Now, why do I mention this to you young women this evening? Because you can have a positive influence in motivating young men to serve full-time missions. Let the young men of your acquaintance know that you personally want them to serve in the mission field, because you know that's where the Lord wants them. *Avoid steady dating with a young man prior to his mission call.* If your relationship with him is more casual, then he can make that decision to serve more easily and also can concentrate his full energies on his missionary work instead of the girlfriend back home. And after he returns honorably from his mission, he will be a better husband and father and priesthood holder, having served a full-time mission. (Ensign, November 1986, p. 81)

When young people keep their dating relationships at the paired dating stage before missionary service, the person at home is able to continue dating while the one in the mission field can focus on service. This gives them both valuable experience that will benefit them immensely in choosing a spouse and being ready for marriage. A young man and young woman can continue to "pair-date" while one of them is in the mission field by writing to each other and maintaining contact. In this way, both individuals can continue to mature and grow during this period.

Paired dating is the most endangered stage in the modern context of dating. It is the stage that has disappeared the most in the contemporary erosion of courtship. Because of this, our prophetic leaders have begun to counsel young adults in the Church about paired dating that can lead to exclusive dating.

The most recognized talk on this subject was given by Elder Dallin H. Oaks at a CES Fireside in May of 2005 (Dating Versus Hanging Out). Let's summarize a few of his main points about paired dating.

Dating (vs. Hanging-Out) Is the Best Way to Initiate and Sustain a Mature Relationship

Simple and more frequent dates allow both men and women to "shop around" in a way that allows extensive evaluation of the prospects. The old-fashioned date was a wonderful way to get acquainted with a member of the opposite sex. It encouraged conversation. It allowed you to see how you treat others and how you are treated in a one-on-one situation. It gave opportunities to learn how to initiate and sustain a mature relationship. None of that happens in hanging out.

Plan Your Dates

"If you don't know what a date is, perhaps this definition will help. I heard it from my 18-year-old granddaughter. A "date" must pass the test of three p's: (1) planned ahead, (2) paid for, and (3) paired off."

Men Have Been Counseled to Show Initiative When It Comes to Dating

"Men, if you have returned from your mission and you are still following the boy-girl patterns you were counseled to follow when you were 15, it is time for you to grow up. Gather your courage and look for someone to pair off with. Start with a variety of dates with a variety of young women, and when that phase yields a good prospect, proceed to courtship. It's marriage time. That is what the Lord intends for His young adult sons and daughters. Men have the initiative, and you men should get on with it".

Young Women Should Encourage Simple, Inexpensive, and Frequent Dating

"Young women, resist too much hanging out, and encourage dates that are simple, inexpensive, and frequent. Don't make it easy for young men to hang out in a setting where you women provide the food. Don't subsidize freeloaders. An occasional group activity is okay, but when you see men who make hanging out their primary interaction with the opposite sex, I think you should lock the pantry and bolt the front door. If you do this, you should also hang out a sign, "Will open for individual dates," or something like that. And, young women, please make it easier for these shy males

to ask for a simple, inexpensive date. Part of making it easier is to avoid implying that a date is something very serious. If we are to persuade young men to ask for dates more frequently, we must establish a mutual expectation that to go on a date is not to imply a continuing commitment."

Practice Dating Patterns That Have the Potential to Mature into Marriage

"My single young friends, we counsel you to channel your associations with the opposite sex into dating patterns that have the potential to mature into marriage, not hanging-out patterns that only have the prospect to mature into team sports like touch football. Marriage is not a group activity—at least not until the children come along in goodly numbers."

Notice how Elder Oaks is encouraging the exact same behaviors that he and other leaders have discouraged for teens, namely pairing off and spending time one-on-one with each other. During young adulthood there should be enough maturity to handle these situations and take advantage of the power of pairing. So the message about pairing to young daters is *slow down*, while the message to older daters is *get going!*

Also notice that Elder Oaks is encouraging frequent and simple dates. The goal in these dates is conversation and interaction, not just entertainment. It is nice to have fun together and do things that are enjoyable, but paired dating should also follow a pattern that allows for meaningful conversation and dialogue. Elder Oaks also encourages all of us to resist the cultural trend where there are only two kinds of dating—hanging-out or exclusive (some young people in the mainstream culture call this "messing around" or "altar bound"). Proper dating needs the middle ground of paired dating. For this to happen, we cannot jump to the conclusion that because two people have gone on a couple of dates that there must be something serious going on. Allow yourself and others the freedom to pair date without being confronted with questions about commitment and marriage.

Exclusive Dating

The fourth stage of dating is the *exclusive dating stage* which is intended to help young adults develop the capacities needed to form and maintain a partnership. The *purposes* of the exclusive dating stage are to explore a potential marriage relationship with a specific person and to come to a decision whether you should move forward with the relationship toward engagement and marriage or move back to a paired dating stage to explore relationships with other people. The *practices* of this stage involve young adults initiating a steady dating experience with one person to explore the full potential of the relationship for marriage. This involves maintaining a relationship with someone above and beyond dates and social activities.

The transition to an exclusive dating status makes two people a couple to each other and to other people. This is an important developmental milestone in a relationship that changes the social and developmental context of the relationship. This transition opens a new social reality that often involves extended families, friends, and others. This transition should happen with open discussion between the partners and a clear understanding by both partners that the relationship has entered an exclusive stage of dating. This transition should not be entered lightly or unintentionally. Nor should the transition to exclusive dating be rushed. Elder Hugh B. Brown remarked,

> Infatuation may be romantic, glamorous, thrilling, and even urgent, but genuine love should not be in a hurry...Time should be taken for serious thought, and opportunity given for each partner to gain physical, mental, and spiritual maturity. Longer acquaintances will enable both to evaluate themselves and their proposed companions, to know each other's likes and dislikes, habits and dispositions, aptitudes and aspirations. (You and Your Marriage, Bookcraft, 1960, p. 38)

While rushing into exclusivity can be problematic, so can unduly delaying or avoiding exclusivity when the relationship is ready for it. All relationships that appropriately progress toward marriage reach a point where they need to become exclusive to continue progressing. If this step does not happen at the right time, the relationship often stalls and anxiety replaces confidence. If this happens, even a very promising relationship can begin to falter.

The power of pairing requires reciprocity and mutuality to thrive. One of the pitfalls in today's dating culture is what I call the *half-a-boyfriend-is-better-than-no-boyfriend* phenomenon. This occurs when one partner (often the woman) has entered the exclusive dating stage, but the other partner (often the man) is still in the paired dating stage (or he is going back and forth from exclusive dating to paired dating). Clarity needs to be the rule when it comes to exclusive dating—both when entering the stage or when exiting the stage to return to paired dating with other people. Learn to be mature and open with these matters—it is one of the best indicators that someone is ready for the deeper commitments of engagement and marriage.

Engaged Dating Stage

The fifth stage of dating is the *engaged dating stage* which is intended to help young adults make preparations for marriage and develop the capacities needed to form and maintain a courtship.

The *purposes* of the engaged dating stage are to confirm a decision to marry someone, to make wedding preparations, and to strengthen new extended family relationships. When a couple becomes engaged they promise to "forsake all others" as the couple finalizes their plans to marry. The *practices* of this stage involve

strengthening relationships with extended family members, meeting regularly with priesthood leaders, preparing for a wedding, and making specific plans for early married life. President Spencer W. Kimball has commented,

> The successful marriage depends in large measure upon the preparation made in approaching it…One cannot pick the ripe, rich, luscious fruit from a tree that was never planted, nurtured, nor pruned. (The Miracle of Forgiveness, 1969, p. 242)

By and large, couples will be better served by having longer periods of exclusive dating, followed by shorter engagements. Remember what we just read from Elder Brown, "genuine love should not be in a hurry." Be mature and allow your relationship to grow and deepen. Involve family and friends in ways that will help them feel comfortable with your relationship and demonstrate to them that you are being deliberate and wise in your decision making.

The exclusive dating stage is the primary period in which to make the decision whether or not to marry your boyfriend or girlfriend. Engagement provides a chance to confirm the decision to marry and any red flags that come up during engagement should be addressed before moving forward with the wedding. While engagement is an important relationship milestone that should be respected by the couple and by others, it is not yet a stage of covenant. While it is common to experience some anxiety and nervousness as a wedding approaches, you should not move forward with a wedding if you have serious reservations and concerns about foundational aspects of the relationship. A pre-marriage breakup is always preferable to a post-marriage divorce. Even if the reservations have been made or the invitations sent out, if there are serious and valid concerns about your partner or the relationship, you should address them before going forward with the marriage.

Wedding Planning

As an engaged couple and their families plan for a wedding, there are two key questions they should ask themselves. First, *what are the typical parts of an LDS wedding?* (Parents may hear this question as—what are the typical *expenses* associated with an LDS wedding?). The list gets pretty long, right? A sealing ceremony, reception, luncheon, honeymoon, rings, wedding dress, pictures, flowers, food arrangements, bridesmaid dresses, tuxedos, invitations, and the list goes on. Now, the second question that must be asked is—*what parts of a wedding are required of the Lord to be sealed in the temple*? This list is much shorter. Ultimately all that is essential to the Lord, is a worthy couple who is willing to commit themselves to each other and to Him, some witnesses, and a state marriage license. Even the rings are not a part of a temple sealing ceremony—although sealers allow couples to exchange rings in the sealing room after the ordinance is preformed.

What can we learn from examining these two lists? Is one list the "bad list" and the other is the "good list?" No, there are many things on the first list that can be good and appropriate. These two lists are best thought of as the *essential parts* of a wedding and the *discretion-*

ary parts of a wedding. This means that couples and families can make choices and decisions about how to best structure the wedding plans to meet the needs and resources of the families.

There are very few *shoulds* and *must-dos* when it comes to wedding planning. Many couples today are structuring their wedding days in ways that are different than in the past. Rather than having what I call a "Big-Three Wedding" where the couple runs from a *sealing ceremony* to a *luncheon* to a *reception* and departs on a honeymoon late in the night; some couples are having receptions the night before the sealing ceremony and luncheon or are holding a reception after the couple returns from a honeymoon trip. You should use discretion when making decisions about the events and expenses associated with your wedding. Couples and families should avoid going into debt to buy expensive wedding rings or hold elaborate receptions or go on exotic honeymoon trips. While the billion dollar wedding industry in the United States is more than happy to tell you that such expenses are justified because this is a "once in lifetime event," such messages are typically more about getting money into the pockets of wedding retailers than building a lasting marriage.

Be mindful of nurturing the spiritual aspects of your wedding day. Elder Cree-L Kofford of the Seventy gave some specific advice to couples as they plan their weddings. Your wedding experience will be more meaningful to you personally and have a more lasting impact on your future marriage if you follow his counsel. In particular, he advised couples to focus on the spiritual in your plans for that day. He said,

> Plan the activities of the temple day such that they focus on the spiritual. I realize that is extremely hard to do when you're talking about being sealed. There are many times when people come from out of town who want to express their best wishes. Sometimes there is a meal; usually there is a reception. All too often you are so exhausted you are unable to comprehend the significance of what you have experienced.
>
> Frequently you become so caught up in the things of the world that it becomes difficult, if not impossible, to fully appreciate the things of God. Realizing that sometimes it simply can't be done—do everything you can to move as many social commitments off that day as possible. Often we cheat ourselves out of the greatest spiritual experiences of our lifetime by being too wrapped up in temporal things. Remember that your wedding day is not a social experience with a tinge of the spiritual, but rather a spiritual experience with a tinge of the social. (Ensign, July 1998, p. 15)

We live in a time when many couples spend more time planning their wedding than they do planning

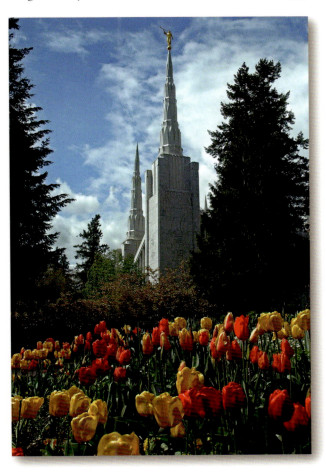

their marriage. Careful and intentional planning of a wedding can make it one of the most special days of your life as you form a unique covenant with both your chosen spouse and God. This ordinance can endow your relationship with the Holy Spirit of Promise as you cherish and live your sealing covenants every day of your marriage. This type of pattern is most likely to occur as you strive to make your wedding day a spiritual day that focuses on the essential parts of a wedding—with some well chosen discretionary parts to complete the day.

Key Principles to Remember

In conclusion, let's summarize some of the key principles we each need to learn that are associated with the stages of dating.

Optimal Courtship Is Built on the Foundation of Other Relationship Experiences

Ultimately, the capacities and skills needed to form a healthy marriage relationship are the result of an ongoing developmental process involving our capacity to form various types of relationships. Striving to be responsive and other-centered in all of our relationships will strengthen our capacity for intimacy in marriage when the time comes.

Dating Experience Is Helpful

One of the main risks in today's dating culture is that young people often lack much dating experience before they get involved in an exclusive dating relationship and, sometimes, quickly engaged. As you gain greater experience with paired dating and other young adult social experiences you will learn more about yourself and the type of people who complement you in life. This will lead to wiser decision making about a marriage partner and foster greater preparation for marriage. Dating and other social experience will provide you with greater self-awareness, greater appreciation of the range of potential partners, and greater confidence in later courtship.

It Is Possible to Back Up in Stages

Although we discussed the stages of dating as a progressive sequence, you should remember that it is possible to go backwards in the stages too. Oftentimes, the best path for your marriage preparation will involve backing up in your dating stage. Clearly, teen couples who have become exclusive in their dating will be best served if they back up to a group dating stage. Also,

Stages of Dating
Jason S. Carroll, Ph.D. Brigham Young University

Pre-Dating	Group Dating	Paired Dating	Exclusive Dating	Engaged Dating
				Confirmation
			Examination	Preparation (Couple)
		Identification	Devotion	
		Experimentation		
	Initiation			
Preparation (Self)	Maturation			
Expectation				

sometimes we learn things about ourselves or our partner during exclusive dating that indicate that the relationship should end and you should return to paired dating status. Perhaps an engagement needs to be called off. Sometimes it takes courage to alter or end a relationship that we feel needs to move back to an earlier stage of dating, but sometimes this is the best thing that can be done for the marital futures of both people involved.

Pairing Is Powerful and Couple Status Is Very Influential—Use It Wisely

The Lord's pattern for dating is as much about how and when we pair off with other people, as it is about formal dating behaviors. As teens, pairing off is risky as young people lack the maturity to handle the emotions and intimacies involved with increased attachment and commitment. For young adults, however, pairing off creates the ideal dating environment to get to know potential partners and to evaluate the prospect of your relationship. Also, be very wise about the decision to enter into an exclusive relationship with someone. Exclusive dating should always involve an intentional decision, not just waking up one day and "finding" yourself in a committed relationship. When you become a couple with someone, you change the nature of the relationship between the two of you and the nature of your interactions with others. You stop dating others and no longer gain dating experience of that sort. Make sure that you intentionally choose to become exclusive with someone and that both of you have a similar commitment to move the relationship to that level.

Conclusion

In Proverbs 3:5–6 it reads,

Trust in the Lord with all thine heart; and lean not unto thine own understandings. In all thy ways acknowledge him, and he shall direct thy paths.

This scripture teaches us that we may not always understand the Lord's pattern or the pattern may be quite different than the patterns of others around us—especially those outside of the Church. We should never set aside the patterns of the Lord because we do not fully understand them. This is the essence of faith—to trust the Lord, even when we do not completely understand why he tells us to do something.

When it comes to dating, seek to develop your own testimony and understanding of the Lord's pattern of dating. However, even if you are struggling to understand or accept some of the Lord's teachings about dating, have faith in the Lord's plan. Trust the Lord, trust your parents, trust your bishop, trust your prophetic leaders. They will teach you the pattern and the standards you should follow in your dating relationships. As you do this and come to trust the Lord enough to follow Him, you will come to see that He knows you better than you know yourself and that He knows better than you do what will make you happy in this life.

Chastity in Dating

CREATING THE FOUNDATION FOR MARITAL INTIMACY

CHAPTER 17

One of the primary goals of dating and courtship is for couples to develop deep levels of emotional and affectionate intimacy, which will serve as the ongoing foundation for passionate intimacy after they are married.

One of the most common questions, although often unspoken, about dating and premarital relationships is: *How far can you go?* When we hear this question we all know immediately that this question is asking about sexual intimacy before marriage and how far can a couple go before they have "gone too far."

Before we answer this question, we should step back for a minute and ponder what exactly is being asked when someone asks the question "how far can I go?" The counter question is "How far until what?" Is the question, "where is the line before I need to confess the behavior to my bishop?" The assumption of this question is that it is okay to be physically intimate with someone before marriage as long as it will not get you "in trouble" with the Church or keep you from being able to go on a mission or go to the temple.

Upon deeper analysis, the question "how far can you go?" is a question that reveals a lack of thoughtful understanding about the principles and purposes of sexuality in God's plan. This question is perhaps the quintessential example of focusing only on the precepts or actions, and not on the principles or doctrines of sexuality in our eternal progression. As we discussed in our foundation chapter on chastity, sexuality in God's plan is always intended to be a means to other ends, never an end in and of itself.

When we step back and view physical intimacy in dating as contributing to or detracting from divine purposes, the correct questions become:

How far should I go in order to build a foundation for complete intimacy in marriage?

and

How well does the physical intimacy in our relationship symbolize the emotional intimacy in our relationship?

These are the questions we set out to answer in this chapter. Our goal in this chapter is to apply the principles from our foundation chapter on chastity to dating relationships *before* marriage, and then in a later chapter we will apply the principles to sexual intimacy *after* marriage.

The purpose of this chapter is to help you gain a better understanding of complete intimacy in couple relationships and the types of intimacy needed in dating and courtship to prepare you and your future spouse for sexual wholeness in marriage. Ultimately, as you come to understand these purposes, you will see why living with personal purity and sexual integrity are essential aspects of marriage preparation in your dating and engagement relationships. For married readers, these principles can help you reflect on the foundations of sexual intimacy in your marriage.

Three Levels of Chastity in Dating

Where is the line when it comes to sexual expression before marriage? There are actually at least three answers to this question. Each answer is associated with a deeper and more mature level of understanding of what it means to be chaste and pure in romantic relationships. The first level is what can be called *behavioral chastity*. The second we will refer to as *spiritual chastity*, and the third can be called *sexual wholeness*. Let's discuss each of these levels of chastity.

Behavioral and Spiritual Chastity

Consider the following quote from the *For the Strength of Youth* pamphlet issued by the First Presidency of the Church:

Physical intimacy between husband and wife is beautiful and sacred...God has commanded that sexual intimacy be reserved for marriage....

When you are sexually pure, you prepare yourself to make and keep sacred covenants in the temple. You prepare yourself to build a strong marriage and to bring children into the world as part of an eternal and loving family....

Never do anything that could lead to sexual transgression. Treat others with respect, not as objects used to satisfy lustful and selfish desires. Before marriage, do not participate in passionate kissing, lie on top of another person, or touch the private, sacred parts of another person's body, with or without clothing. Do not do anything else that arouses sexual feelings. Do not arouse those emotions in your own body. Pay attention to the promptings of the Spirit so that you can be clean and virtuous.

Do you see the first two levels of chastity discussed in this quote? The first level, *behavioral chastity*, is conveyed in the final paragraph which lists some specific behaviors each of us should avoid before marriage. These behaviors include passionate kissing (i.e., "making-out" or "french kissing"), lying on top of another person, touching the sacred parts of another person's body above or beneath clothing. The First Presidency also teaches us in this statement that we should not allow others to do these behaviors to us and we should strive to resist engaging in these behaviors with our own bodies (i.e., masturbation or self-stimulation).

Our prophetic leaders provide us with such clear instructions about non-chaste behaviors before marriage because many youth and young adults only have the spiritual maturity to understand such basic behavioral prescriptions. Don't forget, we give the For The Strength of Youth Pamphlet to 12 year olds! Even then, many young people with an immature view of physical intimacy start to play games with the definitions of behaviors on the list by asking questions such as *How passionate does kissing have to become to be labeled "passionate kissing"?*

Other young people treat the list as if it was meant to be a comprehensive list of all of the possible unchaste behaviors and, therefore, label behaviors that are not listed as "ok" or "not prohibited." This line of thinking causes some young people to think things like *The statement says lie on <u>top</u> of another person, but it doesn't say lie <u>next</u> to another person!* or *The list doesn't include <u>sexting</u> so that must be ok.* Such self-justifying attitudes demonstrate an immaturity about a very sacred topic and will ultimately create difficulties with sexual intimacy in dating and later marriage relationships. Sister Elaine Dalton also taught:

> Cherish virtue. Your personal purity is one of your greatest sources of power. When you came to the earth, you were given the precious gift of a body. Your body is the instrument of your mind and a divine gift with which you exercise your agency. This is a gift that Satan was denied, and thus he directs nearly all of his attacks on your body. He wants you to disdain, misuse, and abuse your body. Immodesty, pornography, immorality, tattoos and piercings, drug abuse, and addictions of all kinds are all efforts to take possession of this precious gift—your body—and to make it difficult for you to exercise your agency. Paul asks, "Know ye not that ye are the temple of God, and that the Spirit of God dwelleth in you?" (April 2013, Be Not Moved)

If you pay careful attention to this quote from the First Presidency you will see that they also teach us a higher level of chastity than behavioral chastity, a level of chastity we will refer to as *spiritual chastity*. When we commit ourselves to the standard of spiritual chastity, we come to understand that the behavioral list at the end of the statement is merely illustrative, not comprehensive in nature. Our desire is to foster chaste interactions in our dating and courtship relationships, not to merely avoid certain behaviors or get as close to them as possible.

The second level of chastity is contained in the parts of the quote that emphasize the conditions of our hearts—the motivations, intentions, and reason for why we express our sexuality. Notice the phrases, "treat others with respect, not as objects to satisfy lustful and selfish desires" and "pay attention to the promptings of the spirit." These principles encourage each of us to purify our motivations and seek to link sexual expression to charity and discipleship. Chastity is not just *what* we do before (and after) marriage; but is also *why* we do it.

In our foundation chapter on chastity, Elder Jeffry R. Holland taught you about the *doctrine of the soul* of sexual intimacy. Simply stated, this doctrine reminds us that our bodies and spirits are eternally united, and thus all expressions of physical intimacy involve both our bodies and spirits. The First Presidency counsels to not engage in behaviors that "arouse sexual feelings." Now of course, having sexual thoughts and emotions in our minds are a natural part of coming of age and no one should feel wrong about experiencing these natural feelings. So what exactly is the First Presidency counseling here. How do you know if you are arousing emotions that should be reserved for marriage?

The doctrine of the soul tells us that if you arouse powerful feelings in your spirit, you will also arouse changes in your body and in the body of your partner. Any behavior that initiates the sexual response cycle in your body or your partner's body before marriage is moving toward sexual relations that the Lord's prophets have taught should only be expressed as part of the sacred symbol shared between spouses who have committed themselves to one another and to God. The key is to learn to be aware of and to intentionally manage your state of arousal. Learning to pay attention to your body will help you make good decisions in dating. If you begin to experience the bodily changes involved in the sexual response of your body, you should pay attention of your arousal state and change your behaviors if you are progressing towards behaviors in ways that don't maintain the standard of spiritual chastity. (We will discuss the stages of the sexual response cycle in detail in our chapter on sexual intimacy in marriage).

To be clear, I don't think experiencing the sexual response of our bodies constitutes sin. It's common and normal for each of us to experience attraction, and even some degree of physical arousal to others while dating—particularly when we pair-off and move into exclusive and engaged dating. This is not wrong or inappropriate. In fact, such experiences will help you know that you are properly sexually attracted to their future spouse one day. As you develop greater body awareness and pay attention to your physical arousal states you will be able to make decisions of when to stop or discontinue behaviors that may lead to transgression. A recent Family Home Evening lesson developed by the Church taught this principle well when it said,

> When we often focus on the negative consequences of breaking the law of chastity, it can sometimes be challenging for children to understand that sexual feelings are good. It is important to teach that these feelings are wonderful and can help us develop healthy relationships when they are expressed appropriately. Help your children understand the relationship between the sexual feelings they have or will develop and the sexual behavior that should be reserved for married couples. Teach that sexual feelings are a gift from our Heavenly Father and should be treated with respect.

Sexual Wholeness in Marriage

As each of us grows in spiritual maturity, we should progress from the behavioral level of chastity to the spiritual level of chastity in our paired dating experiences. These two levels of chastity capture the essence of personal purity and the type of preparation each of us should bring to the later stages of exclusive and engagement dating.

As you move into the stages of exclusive and engaged dating, there is an additional level of chastity that builds upon the other two. We will refer to this highest level of chastity as *sexual wholeness in marriage* because it involves creating a foundation for complete intimacy in later marriage. While the first two levels of chastity (behavioral and spiritual) are primarily about our personal level of chastity across relationships, developing sexual wholeness in marriage is primarily about the level of connection and chastity in the relationship.

Individuals who approach their dating relationships with this highest level of chastity always remember that one of the primary purposes of dating is to develop a relationship that is capable of complete marital intimacy. They view their intimacy in dating and engagement as a foundation or stepping stone for the intimacies they will share later in marriage.

In order to fully understand the foundation that is needed for complete marital intimacy, each of us needs to appreciate that there are at least three types of intimacy that are needed components in a loving and lasting marriage. Let's discuss these three types of intimacy and how these principles help us make decisions about intimacy in our dating relationships.

Three types of intimacy

It is helpful to think of intimacy in marriage as involving at least three types intimacy:

1. Emotional Intimacy
2. Affectionate Intimacy
3. Passionate Intimacy

These types of intimacy are overlapping in most marriages and spouses tend to have personal preferences for the relative ratio or amount of each type of intimacy that is experienced in marriage. By gaining a deeper understanding of these three types of intimacy, you will more fully appreciate the *Doctrine of the Symbol* that Elder Holland spoke about in our foundation chapter on chastity. Ultimately, loving and lasting marriages involve all three of these types of intimacy, with passionate intimacy being a deep physical symbol of the emotional intimacy and affectionate intimacy shared between the spouses.

One of the primary goals of dating and courtship is for couples to develop deep levels of emotional and affectionate intimacy, which will serve as the ongoing foundation for passionate intimacy after they are married.

Let's talk about each of these types of intimacy and how they help us see the importance of chastity in dating and courtship. We spend more time here discussing emotional intimacy, because we will focus on affectionate and passionate intimacy more in our later chapter discussing sexual intiamcy in marriage.

Emotional Intimacy

Emotional intimacy exists in a relationship when two people experience a sense of *security, support, trust, comfort, and safety* with one another. Emotional intimacy is deeply connected to our innate need to belong and be loved by others and by God. You can experience this type of intimacy with a wide range of people, such as a parent, a sibling, a friend, boyfriend or girlfriend, or spouse since emotional intimacy is not restricted to a single person. In fact, emotional intimacy and appropriate expressions of affectionate intimacy (hugging a friend, kissing a child goodnight, holding a grieving family member, etc.) can occur in multiple relationships in our life, while passionate intimacy is reserved for only our covenant spouse. However, the principles of spousal preeminence and cleaving help us understand that the depth of emotional intimacy involved in marriage will be unique to any other relationship save our relationship with God.

In dating, a couple's level of emotional intimacy can be measured by each partner's ability to be emotionally open, allowing themselves to be vulnerable and allowing the other to understand them on a deeper level. When partners develop emotional intimacy in a relationship, they do not have to edit or filter their true thoughts and feelings. Both partners are able to show their true feelings and express their

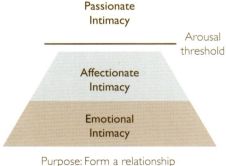

Preparing for Sexual Wholeness in Marriage

Three types of couple intimacy

Purpose: Form a relationship capable of complete marital intimacy

full opinions and thoughts. In short, they are able to be authentic and real. In dating, the person with whom you become emotionally intimate comes to know you from the inside out, not just outside in.

Acceptance

One of the first steps towards building emotional intimacy is *acceptance*. In a relationship, both of the partners need to accept each other as they are. Expecting the other person to change or to be more like you will typically create barriers to developing true connection and trust. Learn to value the other person for who he or she is, rather than evaluating or critiquing what he or she is not. Remember, acceptance is not the same as agreement. You may decide as you come to know someone else that an ongoing relationship is not a good fit for you—but this does not mean you cannot still accept the other person for who they are and appreciate their willingness to be real and authentic with you.

At the same time, accept yourself for who you are and do not try to be someone else. An important part of developing emotional intimacy is to know and accept yourself deeply. Until you know your own thoughts, feelings, strengths, and weaknesses, you cannot accurately convey them to another. And until you accept yourself, you will likely be afraid of risking rejection by sharing yourself with someone else. Finally, the process of knowing and accepting yourself will make you better able to accept others, and will make you a safe person to whom they can reveal their own inner selves. As we discussed in a previous chapter, the foundation of acceptance of self and others is our belonging with God and the testimony that we are of infinite value to Him as one of His beloved spirit sons or daughters.

Trust and Trustworthiness

Getting to know people is a different experience for different people. Many people are eager to share their thoughts, feelings, and beliefs with people they meet and go on dates with. As a relationship starts to form, these types of people feel that the new relationship is exciting, and being open and vulnerable is fun. For others, sharing their thoughts and feelings with others, particularly new acquaintances, can feel awkward or threatening. Fear of rejection or worries about saying something that will not be accepted prompt some people to "play it safe" and keep their inner feelings and thoughts to themselves.

These two types of approaches to relationships— *eager and disclosing* verses *cautious and closed* both have strengths and challenges when it comes to forming emotional intimacy in dating relationships. Disclosing personal details prematurely in a relationship can disrupt emotional intimacy, as well as create lopsided disclosure that is one-sided where one person is very open and the other is closed. However, at the same time, not disclosing and sharing of ourselves will also limit your ability to develop emotional intimacy. Being too guarded will not allow others to feel comfortable and safe in disclosing to you.

Ultimately, emotional intimacy is based on developing trust with each other. *Trust* should be developed hand-in-hand in a relationship with *trustworthiness*. To trust when someone has not yet proven trustworthy can be as much of a problem as not trusting when someone has proven to be trustworthy. This is why emotional intimacy needs to be developed overtime and should involve mutual disclosure and vulnerability between both people.

STAGES OF EMOTIONAL INTIMACY

In dating, there are at least three stages or levels of emotional intimacy. These stages are primarily determined by the level of disclosure and commitment in the relationships. For relationships to progress with a healthy foundation, it is important for commitment and disclosure to be connected to one another and to not become out of sync with each other. It is not healthy for a relationship to progress to higher levels of commitment, without the corresponding levels of disclosure and vulnerability, but it is also problematic when one or both partners overly discloses in a relationship that lacks reciprocal commitment. Both extremes should be avoided. The stages of emotional intimacy include:

The Talking Stage

When we first meet someone, we typically engage in conversations that are safe and nonvulnerable in nature. This is appropriate when we are first getting to know someone. In the talking stage of emotional intimacy, two people spend time with each other either alone or in the company of other people. The conversation at this level of emotional intimacy is primarily informative in nature and centers on what could be called "surface talk." This type of conversation is comfortable in a public setting and involves getting to know more of the *facts* about someone you have met or are interested in. The talking stage of emotional intimacy is the hallmark of paired dating we talked about in our discussion of the stages of dating.

Do not underestimate the importance of the talking stage of emotional intimacy. Too many couples today become committed to each other and then learn the details about one another. Being "friends first" is more than a cliché—enjoying someone's company and becoming relaxed around someone are very important aspects of intimacy. The talking stage of intimacy allows you to evaluate if you have common fundamental beliefs and core values with others before moving to deeper levels of disclosure and emotional intimacy.

In the talking stage of emotional intimacy, asking questions casually while you spend time together is the best way to get to know someone, but do not disclose a lot at a time, especially in the beginning. Do not disclose prematurely. Such disclosures can make relationships uncomfortable as the other person is not sure if similar disclosures are now required of them. Sometimes premature disclosure does elicit disclosure from the other person and the two people plunge quickly into the intimate details of each others' lives. If this happens too quickly, the relationship often lacks the foundation to appropriately handle such revelations. Couples become quickly attached to each other and know intimacies about each other, yet lack an understanding of some of the basic facts or foundations a couple needs. Disclosure should progress developmentally as both partners move to deeper levels of disclosure and commitment to one another.

The Sharing Stage

The next level of emotional intimacy involves the sharing of personal ideas and feelings with another person. Sharing thoughts, feelings and needs is the best way to become emotionally close to someone. Spending time together and having meaningful conversations are the keys to building emotional intimacy in a rela-

tionship and are the hallmarks of the sharing stage of intimacy. As a relationship progresses from the talking to the sharing stage, it is important to never shy away from your feelings. Sharing and discussing your feelings, opinions and thoughts will not only help you become more intimate with a person, but also let you see things from another person's perspective. How a person reacts to your inner thoughts and feelings is an important part of seeing if the relationship has potential for you to pursue it.

The sharing stage of emotional intimacy typically occurs in one on one interaction and should be an important milestone before moving a relationship from paired dating to exclusive dating. The idea of becoming exclusive in a relationship where one or both people struggle to share their ideas and feelings with each other does not make sense. In fact, one of the later parts of the sharing stage is the maturity to share with one another your thoughts and feelings about each other and the relationship. The infamous *DTR Talk* (i.e., "Determining the Relationship") is a form of deep sharing. Couples need to develop the ability to discuss their authentic feelings with each other in order for a relationship to develop the emotional intimacy needed in later engagement and marriage.

The Revealing Stage

The highest level of emotional intimacy involves a deep and vulnerable connection with another person that involves disclosing our whole self, including our fears, faults, and struggles. This type of disclosure should typically only occur in a setting of commitment and mutual support. Both partners should disclose at this level, rather than one who discloses while the other does not.

The intimate talk involved in the revealing stage of emotional intimacy should be a milestone before a relationship is taken from the exclusive stage to the engagement stage. This type of disclosure involves deep trust and faith in the other person. Being suspicious or cautious all the time will erode emotional intimacy in the relationship. Although you should not disclose prematurely and it takes time to build trust, some relationships stumble in these later stages of emotional intimacy because one or both partners is too apprehensive and guarded. Before engagement, both partners should feel that they are able to be real in the presence of their partner, without withholding their true thoughts and feelings.

How Far Have You Gone?

While the question, "how far have you gone?" is typically a question about the degree of physical intimacy in a relationship, the question is far more appropriate as a question about the level of emotional intimacy in a relationship. Understanding the current level of emotional intimacy in your dating relationships will help you know what types of physical intimacy are appropriate between partners.

DEVELOPING EMOTIONAL INTIMACY

Below are several suggestions for deepening the emotional intimacy in your dating relationships, particularly relationships that may be moving toward exclusivity and engagement.

1. Spend More Time Together

Some dating relationships begin with the couple seeing each other once or twice a week. This works while initially both people are managing other responsibilities and dating other people. Over time, however, you may decide that you want to know more about the other person, and that involves spending more time together through the week or on weekends so that you can observe each other

more often and experience a variety of lifestyle situations. This should be a shared decision, not one person demanding more time than the other wants to give. Work out the details of when and how often you will get together, and for what purpose.

2. Share More of Your Lives

The type of lifestyle events you share can make a difference in the direction of your relationship. For example, you may decide to introduce your dating partner to the family and even to invite him to dinners or parties with friends. These types of social gatherings are different than running errands together, like getting a haircut or washing the car. Whichever direction you go, taking the other person along can help you grow closer as you experience each others daily schedules or special events.

3. Cultivate intimate conversation

Special discussions or time spent conversing about meaningful things helps to foster a relationship. Set a

few minutes aside during your time together to talk over each other's day, to share political or religious views, or to exchange opinions on current events. You may want to solicit advice or air a viewpoint. Perhaps you just seek a listening ear. Being these things for each other can deepen your value as a couple.

4. Discuss Problems Openly

Sometimes we need to ignore petty irritations. But do not sweep major problems under the rug. Issues dealing with commitment, extended family, time schedules, and future expectations can have serious ramifications for many relationships, especially if you are thinking about getting married. Thoughtfully explore these issues and other problems that rise to the surface of your relationship. Be an empathetic listener and make sure you understand your partner's position before trying to express your own. Then together, work on finding a suitable solution.

Affectionate Intimacy

As a dating relationship progresses through the stages of emotional intimacy it is natural and appropriate that couples will desire to share physical expressions of their affection for one another. Affectionate intimacy involves any form of physical touch that communicates care, concern and affection that *does not arouse* the sexual response of our souls (body & spirit). Holding hands, sitting close to each others, and hugging each other are all appropriate forms of expressing affection to someone in a romantic relationship.

Also, mature couples know the difference between the kiss of affection and the kiss of passion. Not only do the two differ in terms of length and intensity, but they primarily differ in intent and purpose. Affectionate kissing conveys tenderness and intensifies bonding. Passionate kissing triggers the mental and physical arousal parts of the sexual response cycle. It is natural and appropriate for expressions of affectionate intimacy to be a part of exclusive and engaged dating relationships. It is appropriate to foster this type of intimacy because it continues to play an important part in mar-

riage. A common error for some marriage partners is to believe that in marriage passionate intimacy replaces affectionate intimacy. In healthy marriages, this is not the case. Passionate intimacy is added to the foundation of emotional and affectionate intimacy that was created in dating.

Passionate Intimacy

Passionate intimacy involves any form of physical touch that communicates love, commitment, and passion that *does arouse* the sexual response of our souls (body & spirit). To this point, we have indirectly talked about passionate intimacy as the behaviors premarital couples should not engage while dating. However, this should not be interpreted to mean that these are wrong or inappropriate behaviors in and of themselves.

As you will recall, in the quote we read from the *For the Strength of Youth* pamphlet the First Presidency stated: "Do not have sexual relations with someone outside of marriage, and be completely faithful to your spouse after marriage." Within God's plan, being chaste is best understood as engaging in sexual behaviors at the right time and for the right reasons, rather than avoiding or abstaining from sexual behaviors. When the time is right, sharing passionate intimacy with your spouse will be an expression of your commitment to purity and chastity, not an act that is contrary to it. We will discuss the sexual response cycle and principles for effectively sharing passionate intimacy in marriage in our marital intimacy chapter.

Where is the Line?

We started the chapter discussing the question of *where is the line?* when it comes to physical intimacy before marriage. One thing is certain, we are deceiving ourselves if we believe that the line is fuzzy or not well defined. The prophet Nephi taught that the Lord "doeth nothing save it be plain unto the children of men" (2 Ne 26:33), and such is the case when it comes to chastity in dating. By pulling all of the principles together that we have discussed thus far, we come to some very clear principles about intimacy in dating relationships. Here are the principles that emerge:

Principle #1

Dating involves developing emotional and affectionate intimacy, but expressions of passionate intimacy must be expressed only in marriage.

Where is the line in dating? The line is expressions of passionate intimacy that arouse powerful emotions and physical changes in our souls. This principle is pure and simple and has been given to us as a safeguard by a loving Father in Heaven, not because He wants to restrict our sexual fulfillment, but because He desires us to experience it to its truest and fullest extent in our later marriage relationships.

Principle #2

Emotional intimacy should be the focus of dating.

Too many couples allow expressions of physical intimacy to be the focus and foundation of their dating

Preparing for Sexual Wholeness

Emotional Intimacy

Talking
- Spend time together
- Surface talk

Sharing
- Share ideas
- Share feelings

Revealing
- Intimate talk
- Disclose fears and faults
- Share struggles

Note: Commitment should increase at deeper levels

Affectionate Intimacy

- Holding hands
- Affectionate kissing

———— "The Line" Before Marriage ————

Passionate Intimacy

- Passionate kissing
- Lie on/next to each other
- Light petting (breast)
- Heavy petting (genitals)
- Sexual Intercourse

relationship. In order to fully experience the doctrine of the symbol in the sexual intimacy in our marriages, we must build an unshakable foundation of emotional intimacy. That foundation begins before marriage and is determined by how we conduct ourselves in dating—this is the core of the doctrine of the symbol in marital sexuality within marriage.

Principle #3

Emotional intimacy needs to progress with disclosure and commitment.

Too many relationships today are marked by incongruent levels of commitment and disclosure. In particular, there is a pattern where women become fully committed, while they wait to see if the man will reciprocate the commitment. This asymmetrical commitment pattern is destructive to the confidence and trust that is needed to form a loving and lasting marriage. Trustworthiness should be coupled with trust, and commitment should be coupled with disclosure.

Principle #4

Emotional intimacy needs to be mutual.

Relationships become lopsided when one partner has disclosed and allowed themselves to be vulnerable, while the other does not share their thoughts and feelings with their partner. Vulnerability needs to be shared to be safe.

Principle #5

Expressions of affectionate intimacy should be symbolic of the depth of emotional intimacy in the relationship.

It should go without saying that expressions of physical intimacy in relationships that do not have an appropriate level of emotional intimacy are harmful to your soul and future relationships. These type

Stages of Dating and Chastity

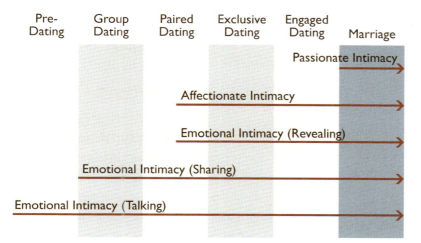

of *hooking up, friends with benefits,* or *NiCMO* (non-committed make-out) behaviors are what Elder Holland called "sexual fragmentation" because they pretend that we can engage in physical intimacy with just our bodies, not our whole souls. Even in ongoing dating relationships, couples should make sure that their expressions of affectionate intimacy are congruent with the level of emotional intimacy in the relationship.

Principle #6

Engaged couples should desire passionate intimacy in marriage.

Passionate intimacy is powerful. Our bodies and spirits are designed to attach and bond with our chosen spouse through sexual bonding. As we will discuss in our future chapter on marital intimacy, couples should

look forward to sharing passionate intimacy with each other once they are married—and it is normal that they will experience arousal and anticipation as they approach their wedding date. Learning to recognize and appropriately manage your arousal states during exclusive and engaged dating sets the proper pattern for managing and sharing passionate intimacy in marriage.

Research on Sexual Restraint in Dating

The current dating culture in our society often emphasizes that two people should test their "sexual chemistry" before committing to each other. This type of compatibility is frequently mentioned as an essential characteristic for people to seek out in romantic relationships, particularly ones that could lead to marriage. Thus, couples who do not test their sexual chemistry prior to the commitments of exclusivity, engagement, and marriage are often seen as being at risk for getting into a relationship that will not satisfy them in the future—thus increasing their risk of later marital dissatisfaction and divorce.

While we have looked at the teachings from the prophets about the importance of premarital chastity, what do research studies tell about living a chaste life. A growing number of published studies call into question the validity of testing "sexual chemistry" early in dating. For example, my colleagues and I published the first study a few years ago in the American Psychological Association's *Journal of Family Psychology* (see Busby, Carroll, & Willoughby, 2010, Compatibility or Restraint?: The Effects of Sexual Timing on Marriage Relationships). This study involved a nationally selected sample of 2,035 married individuals. The study found that the longer a couple waits in dating to have sex the better their relationship is after marriage. In fact, couples who wait until marriage to have sex com-

Sexual Timing in Dating and Later Marital Quality

Busby, Carroll, & Willoughby
(2010) Journal of Family Psychology

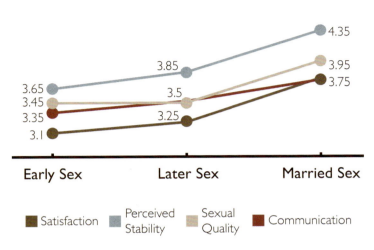

Note: Responses from 2,035 married individuals

pared to those who started having sex early in their dating report higher relationship satisfaction (20% higher), better communication patterns (12% better), less consideration of divorce (22% lower), and better sexual quality (15% better) (see the figure below).

Another study was done by Dr. Sharon Sassler and her colleagues at Cornell University who also found that rapid sexual involvement has adverse long-term implications for relationship quality (Sassler et al., 2012, Tempo of Sexual Activity). Their analyses also suggest that delaying sexual involvement is associated with higher relationship quality across several dimensions. They also found that the negative association between sexual timing and relationship quality is largely driven by cohabitation; meaning that sexual involvement early in a romantic relationship is associated with an increased likelihood of moving quicker into living together.

So, why does sexual restraint benefit couples during dating and later in marriage? Evidence points to two primary explanations for why couples benefit from waiting to become sexually involved—*intentional partner selection* and *sexual symbolism*.

INTENTIONAL PARTNER SELECTION

A primary reason why sexual restraint benefits couples is that it facilitates *intentional partner selection*. Simply put, you have a better chance of making good decisions in dating when you have not become sexually involved with your dating partner. Leading marriage expert, Dr. Scott Stanley has proposed a concept of dating that he calls "relationship inertia" (Stanley et al., 2006, Sliding vs. Deciding: Inertia and the Cohabitation Effect). The central idea of inertia is that some couples end up married who otherwise would not have married partly because they become *prematurely entangled* in a sexual relationship prior to making the decision to be committed to one another. Inertia suggests that it becomes harder for some couples to veer from the path they are on, even when doing so would be wise. Thus, some couples are "sliders," while others are "deciders" (Stanley et al, 2006).

For many young adults, single life has become synonymous with hook-ups and sexual experimentation. The problem with these patterns is that proper partner selection is often skewed for sexually involved couples who experience strong physical rewards with each other, thereby causing them to ignore or minimize deeper incompatibilities in the relationship. The human brain and body do not just experience pleasure during sex; they also experience strong sensations of attachment and bonding. Simply put, we are hard wired to connect. Rapid sexual initiation often creates poor partner selection because these intense feelings of pleasure and attachment are confused for true intimacy and lasting love. This is exactly why Elder Holland taught that early sex creates a sort of *counterfeit intimacy* that makes two people think they are closer to each other than they really are. This can cause people to "fall in love" with, and possibly even marry, someone who is not a good choice for them in the long run.

SEXUAL SYMBOLISM AND LASTING LOVE

Sexual restraint also benefits couples because it requires partners to prioritize communication and commitment as the foundation of their attraction to each other. This gives couples a different type of foundation than couples who build their relationship on physical attraction and sexual gratification. This difference becomes particularly critical as couples naturally move past an initial period of intense attraction and excitement into a relationship more characterized by companionship and partnership. As Dr. Mark Regnerus, author of "Premarital Sex in America," explains:

> Couples who hit the honeymoon too early—that is prioritize sex promptly at the outset of the relationship—often find their relationship underdeveloped when it comes to qualities that make relationships stable and spouses reliable and trustworthy. (see news.byu.edu/news/good-things-come-couples-who-wait)

Couples who do not wait to have sex often develop lopsided commitment levels (i.e., the woman is more committed than the man), less developed communication patterns, more constraint to leaving the relationship, and less ability to manage differences and conflict.

Ultimately, loving and lasting marriages are ones where the sexual intimacy is a *meaningful physical symbol* of the emotional intimacy shared between the spouses. Without this, sex is just physical and lacks the meaning needed to be truly satisfying and lasting. In dating, couples should focus on developing a foundation of friendship and communication that will serve as the ongoing foundation for sexual intimacy in their marriage. By practicing sexual restraint, couples allow themselves to focus on a true foundation of intimacy—acceptance, understanding, partnership, and love. So, while true love does indeed wait, it may actually work the other way around—waiting helps create true love.

Pornography in Dating

Our discussion of the different types of intimacy and building a foundation for later sexual wholeness in marriage should help each of us better appreciate why our prophetic leaders have repeatedly warned us about the harms of pornography. Having a lasting marriage is all about having *the right kind* of relationship. Researchers and therapists have found that marriages that last have *two important bonds* or types of connections in their relationship—a strong *emotional bond* as well as a strong *physical bond* between the two spouses.

As we appreciate the needed emotional and physical bonds of healthy relationships, we can see that porn undermines love. And it does it by eroding these key relationship bonds of love, trust, and attraction between spouses. How does pornography do this? Pornography can harm our us in *three main ways* that hurt their chances of having a loving and lasting marriage in the future.

1. Unrealistic Expectations

First, pornography teaches myths about sex, people's bodies, and relationships. Simply put, pornography is a really bad form of sex education. People who view pornography get tricked into believing that when they see pornography they are watching real experiences with real couples; when they are actually seeing a staged, choreographed presentation with people who are strangers to each other. Pornography is not like a real relationship at all. We need to understand that if we use pornography we will likely develop *unrealistic expectations* about what their future romantic relationships and marriage will be like.

Plus, pornography encourages objectification. *Objectification* means treating a person as a thing or object, without regard to his or her thoughts or feelings. We are objectifying others when we: (1) think or talk about others' body parts, (2) treat others as a tool or object for making ourselves feel good, (3) treat others as if they are replaceable and don't mean anything to us, (4) believe it is ok to hurt or mistreat others, and (5) believe there is no need for us to worry about the feelings and preferences of others. These five characteristics of objectification are a laundry list of what pornography portrays about sex. Pornography teaches that both men and women aren't worth anything more than the sum of their body parts and how much physical pleasure they can offer. Whether pornography users like it or not, those perceptions often start creeping into how they see themselves and other people in real life. The harder it becomes for the user to see themselves and others as anything more than sexual objects, the harder it is to develop real relationships.

2. Keeping Secrets

A second way that pornography harms relationships is that it often happens in secret. Users of pornography typically hide, or at least minimize, their use of pornography from everyone, including their dating partners and spouses. Studies have found that when people engage in this type of *self-concealment*—which is when they do things they are not proud of and keep them a secret from their friends and family members, it not only hurts their relationships and leaves them feeling lonely, but also makes them more vulnerable to depression, poor self-esteem, and anxiety.

Keeping secrets damages trust. When spouses keep secrets from each other their trust in each other erodes and their confidence is their relationships starts to struggle. Studies with women who are spouses or romantic partners of habitual pornography users have found that they feel they "can't trust" their partner and worry about whether he will be faithful to their relationship. On top of creating secrecy in the relationship, pornography also creates expectations and behaviors that place it on a collision course with commitment and exclusivity in the relationship. Research studies have found that people who use pornography are more accepting of cheating on their partners. It is not surprising, then, that the deterioration of trust is the most significant negative impact of pornography use. When teens and young adults are getting involved with pornography they rarely think about these types of long-term consequences that can result if they persist in hiding pornography use.

3. Distorted Attraction Template

A third way that pornography harms relationships is that it distorts what scientists call our "attraction template." Our attraction template is our personal preferences for who we find physically attractive and what types of behaviors we find exciting. *In short, it is who we find good looking and what turns us on.* Although some people think we simply "have" these preferences, scientists are discovering that we "develop" and "shape" these preferences—and what we look at and watch can shape who and what we are attracted to.

This is where the fantasy and myth of pornography becomes a big problem. Not only does pornography offer a fictional version of sex education, but also that education is being delivered in a way perfectly tailored to how our brains learn. Images are an especially powerful teacher, since they can pack in a whole lot of information that the viewer can understand very quickly. And while words are often interpreted as opinions, our brains are more likely to interpret images as facts; after all, it's a lot harder to argue with something you're seeing happen in front of you. Our brains also learn better when they're aroused. When you add in the focused concentration of searching through pornographic images to find exactly what the user is looking for, and reinforcing what's being taught with physical pleasure, it creates the perfect conditions for wiring new beliefs and behaviors into the brain.

As a result, users who grow up on porn wire their sexuality to looking at 2D images of unrealistic, surgically altered bodies. Instead of learning to build relationships with real people, it often feels more natural and arousing to them to be alone in front of a computer. Of course, this erodes the level of attraction in a real romantic relationship.

Couple Differences

Stepping Stones or Stumbling Blocks

CHAPTER 18

> True love is not so much a matter of romance as it is a matter of anxious concern for the wellbeing of one's companion.
>
> *President Gordon B. Hinckley*

After nearly three decades of research on couple processes in marriage there has been one finding that has been replicated over and over again. This finding is that numerous studies have shown that what distinguishes marriages that succeed from those that do not *is not the amount of differences* in the relationship, rather it is the *way that differences are handled* by the couple. What does this research finding tell us about managing differences in dating and marriage? It tells us that differences and some degree of conflict (e.g., frustration, negativity, disagreements, etc.), are normal in couple relationships. In fact, some degree of conflict should be expected in dating and marriage and when expressed in appropriate ways it can be the sign of a healthy, safe, and caring relationship.

Consider another research finding: Nearly 70% of the problems couples report in their relationships can be labeled as *perpetual problems*, meaning that they often never get fully resolved (see Gottman, 1999, The Marriage Clinic).

What does this research finding tell us about managing differences in marriage? It tells us that if many of the differences in marriage are perpetual in nature; our goal in handling conflict cannot always be to "resolve the problem." The goal in these cases is often to establish a dialogue around perpetual problems that communicates acceptance, affection, and collaboration to our partner. Without these "gentle dialogues" about these perpetual issues, couples can enter a state of "gridlock" that is hurtful and destructive to their relationship. Research has also found that for the conflicts that are resolvable, there are certain communication skills that can help couples strengthen the intimacy

in their relationships and help partners maintain their sense of partnership.

In this chapter, we discuss how to manage differences in dating and marriage relationships. These are a critical part of the couple processes domain in the "marriage ecology" (e.g., trunk of the tree model). Because of their importance to marital success or failure, couple conflict patterns have been the primary focus of marriage research for the last 30 years. This research has discovered *what not to do* and *what to do* in handling differences and conflict as a couple. We'll discuss both of these in this chapter.

The foundation principle for this lesson is equal partnership. Ultimately, how we handle conflict in marriage is an expression of how committed we are to maintaining an equal partnership with our spouse. In our equal partnership chapter, we discussed the *principles* of shared decision making in marriage. In this chapter, we discuss the *practices* of shared decision making by examining how you can make that happen in your day-to-day relationship with your dating partner or spouse.

Differences in Marriage

Elder Bruce C. Hafen once told the story of a young woman on her wedding day. Sighing blissfully, she said "Mom, I'm at the end of all my troubles!" "Yes," replied her mother, "but at which end?" (Covenant Hearts, p. 26). Like this young woman, some young people envision marriage as a conflict free relationship without differences or problems. In fact, some people mistakenly believe that the purpose of dating is to find someone they will never have an argument with or a disagreement about a decision with. Occasionally, couples claim that they have never had an argument or difference of opinion. Commenting on this type of claim, Elder Joe J. Christensen remarked,

> If that is literally the case, then one of the partners is overly dominated by the other or, as someone said, is a stranger to the truth. Any intelligent couple will have differences of opinion. Our challenge is to be sure that we know how to resolve them. That is part of the process of making a good marriage better. (Ensign, May 1995, p. 65)

As we noted in the introduction, differences and conflict are a normal, even essential, part of married life. Listen to what President Gordon B. Hinckley said about conflict in marriage:

> Marriage requires a high degree of tolerance, and some of us need to cultivate that attribute. I have enjoyed these words of Jenkins Lloyd Jones, which I clipped from the newspaper some years ago. Said he:
>
> "There seems to be a superstition among many thousands of our young [men and women] who hold hands and smooch in the drive-ins that marriage is a cottage surrounded by perpetual hollyhocks to which a perpetually young and handsome husband comes home to a perpetually young and [beautiful] wife. When the hollyhocks wither and boredom and bills appear the divorce courts are jammed....
>
> "Anyone who imagines that bliss [in marriage] is normal is going to waste a lot of time running around shouting that he has been robbed.
>
> "[The fact is] most putts don't drop. Most beef is tough. Most children grow up to be just people. Most successful marriages require a high degree of mutual

Couple Differences: Stepping Stone's or Stumbling Blocks?

Differences between spouses are:

- The norm of married life
- Should be expected
- Are a sign of a healthy marriage
- Are an important stepping stone to increasing intimacy and closeness in marriage

> A great marriage is not when the perfect couple comes together. It is when an imperfect couple learns to enjoy their differences.

> Why are differences an important part of developing intimacy in marriage?

toleration. Most jobs are more often dull than otherwise....

"Life is like an old-time rail journey-delays, sidetracks, smoke, dust, cinders and jolts, interspersed only occasionally by beautiful vistas and thrilling bursts of speed.

"The trick is to thank the Lord for letting you have the ride" ("Big Rock Candy Mountains," Deseret News, 12 June 1973, A4). (Ensign, March 1997, p. 58)

Approaching marriage with realistic expectations prepares you to learn how to manage differences in ways that will turn them into *stepping stones of intimacy* rather than *stumbling blocks of contention*. The figure above summarizes some of the key perspectives each of needs to have about conflict in marriage.

WHERE DO DIFFERENCES IN MARRIAGE COME FROM?

By now we have discussed several principles that can help us understand why differences are a normal and expected part of marriage. Differences arise because we are all unique individuals with personal talents, strengths, gifts, perspectives, challenges, and struggles. Differences also arise from the process of intergenerational transmission that instills in each of us a different set of values, priorities, and ways of doing things. Also, there are differences in the unique but complementary natures of men and women. These gender differences, when recognized and appreciated, can strengthen marriages and families.

WHY IS THE EXPRESSION OF DIFFERENCES A SIGN OF A HEALTHY MARRIAGE?

When we properly understand differences in marriage, we come to see that differences of opinion, and even arguments, can be a sign of a healthy marriage. If I was to go home today and my wife said to me: "There is something in our marriage that has been bothering me for the last 10 years, but I haven't mentioned it because I was afraid you would get mad." Would that comment be the sign of a strong relationship or a poor one? Most of us express our frustrations when we feel safe and are expecting our thoughts to be heard. Every couple should strive to form a dating and marriage relationship where both partners feel comfortable sharing their opinions and frustrations. This helps create a supportive and mutually beneficial relationship for both partners.

WHY ARE DIFFERENCES AN IMPORTANT PART OF DEVELOPING INTIMACY IN MARRIAGE?

One of the main lessons I hope you will remember from this book is this—*Differences are not problems in relationships, they are opportunities!* This is because when your partner expresses a complaint or frustration with your relationship, you have an opportunity to be responsive to his or her needs and desires. Plus, when you choose to do something for your partner or spouse that you would not choose for yourself, you express a powerful form of other-centeredness. President Gordon B. Hinckley said,

Respect [for one's spouse] comes of recognition that each of us is a son or daughter of God, endowed with something of His divine nature, that each is an individual entitled to expression and cultivation of individual talents and deserving of forbearance, of patience, of understanding, of courtesy, of thoughtful consideration. *True love* is not so much a matter of romance as it is a matter of anxious concern for the wellbeing of one's companion. (Ensign, June 1971, p. 71)

Differences and conflict provide us with opportunities to be truly responsive and selfless toward our spouse. When both partners do this, they can achieve more deep and meaningful levels of intimacy. This is an important part of becoming eternal companions for each other as we change and grow in order to better fit what our spouse needs us to be.

in contention. The Lord taught that "he that hath the spirit of contention is not of me, but is of the devil, who is the father of contention" (3 Nephi 11:29). While management of conflict is the key part of handing differences in a couple relationship, there are some factors that "set the stage" for success or failure in the earlier parts of the process. Let's examine each of these aspects in more detail.

DIFFERENCES: PREFERENCES OR IDENTITY

Although differences are to be expected in all marriages, not all differences are of the same magnitude or have the same consequences for relationships. Similar to our discussion of the *home metaphor* to distinguish between foundation issues and personal preferences, there are two primary types of differences. There are *preference differences* that all couples have. These include everything from how we use our time, what activities we engage in, and what color of couch we should buy. We all have preferences on these matters and it is inevitable that we will have differences of opinion in our marriage about these things. With preference differences there is room for negotiation and compromise. We understand that we will not always get what we want all of the time and we sacrifice some of what we may want personally for the good of the

PATTERNS OF COUPLE CONFLICT

The figure at right shows a graphical representation of the major parts of couple conflict patterns. The sequence of conflict starts with *differences*, then *complaints*, and then *conflict*. Notice in the figure how up until the point of conflict the general pathway is the same for all couples. However, at the point of conflict, there is a critical crossroad where some couples manage their conflict well and increase their intimacy; while other couples manage their conflict poorly and engage

Patterns of Couple Conflict

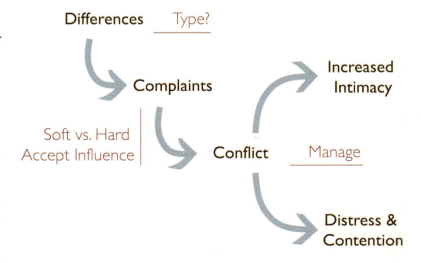

relationship. These sacrifices strengthen our relationship and help us be less selfish in life.

However, there is also another kind of difference called *identity differences*. These differences are about core aspects of who we are and what is most important to us in life. For example, if one partner wants to have children and the other does not, there is not much room for negotiation or compromise. There is no way to have children on Tuesdays and Wednesdays, but not on the other days of the week! There is no middle ground and this is an issue that is likely a core part of each spouse's sense of meaning in life. Identity issues are very difficult to manage in marriage. The best solution to identity differences is to engage in a thoughtful, searching dating process that makes sure that spouses are "on the same page" when it comes to these central aspects of marriage.

Complaints: Startup and Accepting Influence

Research shows that over 90% of the time the way a discussion begins is the way it will end. When one partner begins the discussion using a *hard startup*, such as being negative, accusatory, or using criticism, the discussion is basically doomed to fail. On the other hand, when one partner begins the discussion using a *softened startup*, the discussion will most likely end on the same positive tone (see Carrere & Gottman, 1999, Predicting Divorce Among Newlyweds). *Now, sisters this principle is particularly important for you to pay attention to because research shows that women bring up issues about 80% of the time in couple relationships!* The choice of using a hard or softened startup can set the stage to how responsive your partner will be to your complaint. Research shows that women who soften their startup during conflict discussions have partners who are significantly more responsive to the conversation, whereas hard startup increases the likelihood that men will reject the message.

While startup is an important part of complaints, another important part of the process is how responsive or accepting partners are of the message. Partners set the stage for a positive conversation when they accept a partner's influence and respectfully listen to the complaint, rather than "batting it back" at their partner. *Now, brothers this principle is particularly important for you to pay attention to because if research shows that women bring up complaints 80% of the time, this mean you will be the receiver of these messages 80% of the time!* How husbands accept influence from their wives is a major predictor of whether a relationship will last. The failure of boyfriends and husbands to accept influence from their partners can happen by disengaging from the conversation or minimizing the issue; or in more hostile ways of becoming contentious and belligerent (see Gottman et al., 1998, Predicting Marital Happiness and Stability From Newlywed Interactions). Remember, good relationships are characterized by *dialogue* rather than *gridlock* with conflict issues.

Conflict Patterns

Much of the principles we have been talking about in this chapter come from the research of Dr. John Gottman at the University of Washington. Dr. Gottman has spent his whole life studying marriages—both marriages that have endured, and marriages that have eventually ended in divorce. The primary focus of his research on marriages is to identify why some marriages succeed and why others do not. After studying marriages for more than two decades, Dr. Gottman has identified some key patterns that predict which couples will eventually divorce and which will remain married. In fact, he can make this prediction with very

The 4-Horsemen of Negative Conflict

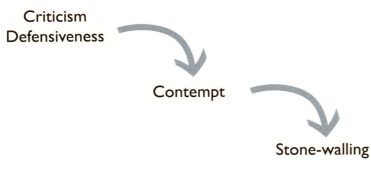

high accuracy based on the ways couples argue, after listening to the couple for just five minutes.

According to Dr. Gottman, the presence of anger and conflict is not what causes relationships to fail. As I mentioned previously, conflict can actually be good if it helps partners clear the air and open channels of communication. Conflict can be a problem, however, if the anger or conflict involves *Criticism, Contempt, Defensiveness,* and *Stonewalling*—what Dr. Gottman calls the "Four Horsemen of the Apocalypse" (see figure above; see Gottman & Gottman, Why Marriages Succeed or Fail, 2005).

THE FOUR HORSEMEN OF NEGATIVE CONFLICT

CRITICISM

The first of the horsemen is *Criticism*. Having complaints in dating and marriage is normal; however, the way one goes about expressing those complaints is most important. The problem arises when complaints turn into criticisms. Unlike complaints, *criticism* tends to overgeneralize, and entails attacking your partner's personality or character, rather than focusing on specific behaviors you do not like. Complaints, on the other hand, are specific statements of disagreement about a specific behavior. Criticism makes one partner right and one partner wrong, and leads to blame and shame. Criticism uses phrases like: *You never, You always, You should, Why don't you ever?* and *Why are you always?* Criticism inevitably puts people on the defensive and invites in the Horseman of Defensiveness, because the other partner feels they need to defend their character.

DEFENSIVENESS

Typically, when one partner uses criticism, the other partner becomes defensive, which is the second horseman. *Defensiveness* is a very common reaction to being treated with criticism and contempt (the third horsemen). Many people become defensive when they are being criticized, but the problem is that it never helps solve the problem at hand. Defensiveness is really a way of blaming your partner. You're saying, in effect, the problem isn't me, it's you! As a result, the problem is not resolved and the conflict escalates further.

When you get defensive, you experience anxiety or a flooding of emotions, which makes it difficult for you to tune in to what your partner is saying. *Defensiveness* also leads to escalation. When couples get defensive and it escalates, couples can get out of control. Defensiveness includes matching anger with anger, blame with blame, hardening your stance, making excuses, or denying responsibly. Verbal examples include, *Yes, but . . . ; So; It's not my fault I . . . ; It wouldn't have happened if you didn't . . . ; That's not true, you're the one who . . . ; That's not fair, at least I didn't . . . ; That may be true, but you do the same thing;* and *I wouldn't have that problem if you didn't. . . .* Even if you feel like a "victim" being "victimized," or even if you feel that you are right in defending yourself, or even if you are right—instead of helping, defensiveness prevents you from solving the problem at hand and further impedes communication.

Contempt

The third horseman, *Contempt*, often follows criticism and defensiveness. Contempt is a more severe form of negative behavior and is a sign that a couple is starting to come apart. Because of this, Dr. Gottman considers contempt to be the most destructive of all the horsemen of negative conflict behaviors. When criticism escalates it can lead to contemptuous comments directed at one's partner. Some examples of contempt are when a person uses sarcasm, cynicism, name calling, eye-rolling, sneering, mockery, and hostile humor. Contempt includes openly insulting your partner, disrespecting them, and tearing down their sense of self-worth. Verbal examples of contempt include putdowns, insults and name calling, yelling and screaming, mocking, sarcasm, ridiculing, and hurtful teasing. Phrases like *You are such a piece of work, There's something wrong with you, You are so selfish,* are examples of contempt. Name calling like: *lazy, fat,* and *stupid* are also examples. Contempt is the worst of the four horsemen because it communicates disgust and a lack of respect. Issues do not get resolved and partners feel hurt and angry towards each other. Contempt behaviors usually lead to one partner tuning out the other, and is the sign that the fourth horseman, stonewalling, will arrive soon.

Stonewalling

When a partner finally tires of the seemingly never-ending *Criticism, Contempt,* and *Defensiveness* in their relationship, they shut down and refuse to respond. This is when the fourth horseman of *Stonewalling* enters the picture. Stonewalling is withdrawing from the relationship in order to avoid conflict. Stonewalling is more common in men than in women. It is a way for them to avoid the feeling of being flooded that usually occurs when a conflict escalates. The stonewaller tends to ignore his partner and does not give any signs of responsiveness, which makes his spouse even angrier. This behavior tends to enter relationships and marriages later, once couples have had a significant period of poorly managing conflict in their relationship.

Stonewalling can happen in the middle of a discussion, when one partner just shuts down and stops responding to their partner. With their silence, the stonewaller is sending a message to their partner that they want to disengage and avoid any meaningful interaction. Stonewalling can also happen when you remove yourself physically without communicating to your partner.

Examples of stonewalling include silence, changing the subject, talking or muttering to ourselves, and removing ourselves physically. Sometimes partners have the misconception that they are calming things down by stonewalling, but stonewalling suggests displeasure, disconnection, division, compliancy, arrogance, and self-righteousness. When a person stonewalls, they are exiting the relationship and avoiding solving the problem at hand. Also, when a person stonewalls, they are not listening, the conflicts become silent and withdrawing becomes a hostile act. This can lead to the other partner attacking or telling the other partner that they are feeling shut out. When stonewalling becomes a predictable pattern, the relationship can be near its end and is need of immediate intervention.

Covert conflict

As I mentioned, the study of couple conflict patterns has been a central focus of studies on marriage. As you have been reading, in this line of research Dr. John Gottman and other scholars have used observational methods to watch couples interact with each other in clinical lab settings. While these studies have proven very successful in identifying negative conflict behaviors such as the Four Horsemen of Negative Conflict, observational methods do not capture all of the kinds of negative conflict behavior that can be destructive to couple relationships.

Some partners use indirect or *covert forms of aggression*, thus avoiding detection in an observational protocol. These covert conflict behaviors are called *relational aggression* (see Carroll et al., Relational Aggression in Marriage, 2010). If you want a simple way to understand what relational aggression is, think back to your high school days. Now think about what boys did to boys when they wanted to hurt each other. You probably thought about boys pushing, fighting, yelling, and directly confronting each other. This is traditional verbal and physical aggression. Now, think about what girls did to girls when they wanted to hurt each other. If you are like most people, you are thinking about behaviors such as excluding someone from the group, spreading rumors and gossip, threatening to not be friends anymore, silent treatments, and other forms of harming a person socially. This is relational aggression.

In research studies, *relational aggression* is defined as behaviors that harm others through damage, or the threat of damage, to relationships or feelings of acceptance, friendship, or group inclusion. This type of covert conflict behavior can involve sharing negative information and gossip about our partner to third

party individuals outside the relationship such as children, extended family members, friends, or co-workers. Generally speaking, relational aggression refers to behaviors in which a partner uses relationships as the vehicle of harm, and this may occur in indirect or direct ways. Indirect relational aggression includes behaviors such as spreading rumors or gossip and subtle forms of social exclusion. In contrast, direct relational aggression includes actively withdrawing interaction and confrontational behaviors such as when an individual threatens another individual with dissolution of the relationship unless certain demands are met.

Research has found that even children as young as preschoolers use relational aggression behaviors. *Research has also found that women are more likely to use relational aggression than men.* Studies show that the long term effects of relational aggression are often worse than the effects of direct verbal or physical aggression. Studies have also shown that relational aggression lowers marital satisfaction and increases the likelihood of divorce (see Archer & Coyne, 2005, An Integrated Review of Indirect, Relational, and Social Aggression).

Learn to handle differences constructively

Research points to three simple questions couples can ask themselves to evaluate if they are handling differences constructively.

1. "When Discussing Differences, Do We Stay Focused on Resolving the Problem?"

Often when couples discuss problem areas in their relationship—such as balancing the budget, dealing with extended families, or disciplining children—they begin to argue and their conversations veer into other topics and areas of complaint. When the focus of the discussion has faded, discussing problems has more of a chance to hurt your relationship than to bring you together. Begin now, before marriage, to set the pattern of discussing differences in ways that focus on finding solutions, not winning arguments.

2. "Do We Manage Our Emotions During Conflictual Exchanges?"

Research has shown that when spouses allow themselves and their partners to become flooded with emotions during discussions they rarely address their differences in a positive way. *Emotional flooding* typically triggers physiological changes in the body such as an increased heart rate, the secretion of adrenalin, and an increase in blood pressure. These physiological changes in the body make it almost impossible for partners to maintain a positive discussion. When you are emotionally flooded, your ability to process information is reduced, meaning it's harder to pay attention to what your partner is saying. A problem solving discussion that leads to one or both partners becoming flooded is doomed to fail.

The cure for flooding is softened startup and soothing. Partners need to learn to bring up concerns in the relationship in non-blaming ways and to find ways to soothe themselves and each other during discussions so that negative emotions stay in check.

3. "Do We Maintain Respect and Concern for One Another during an Argument?"

Marriage scholars have found that successful marriages are ones where spouses maintain high lev-

els of respect and mutual regard for one another—even during an argument. Sometimes spouses allow arguments to degrade into episodes of criticism and personal attack. This type of negative blaming and criticism can have lasting detrimental effects on couple unity, prompting some spouses to withdraw emotionally from the relationship. Maintaining respect and concern for one another sends the message that your relationship is more important than the problems you are currently facing and that you are on the same side in finding ways to constructively deal with your differences.

Managing differences

So far, we have been discussing what not to do in handling conflict. This is important because it helps you understand the behaviors you must avoid and it helps you identify any "red flags" in your dating relationships. However, the absence of negative is not the same as the presence of positive. Not only do you need to avoid doing the wrong things, you must also learn how to do the right things.

Solution-Focused Conversations

Couples need to learn how to have solution-focused conversations, rather than slipping into negative conflict patterns. This involves knowing what to do, not just knowing what not to do. Having solution-focused conversations is not about using the "right" phrases or having to move through specific steps in an exact order. Instead, it is about focusing on solutions instead of problems. Communication experts emphasize key features of positive conflict discussions. These include:

1. *Get on the Same Page:* Couples do better when both partners have the same goal for the conversation. One of the primary problems for couples is when one or both of the partners don't stay focused on the intended purpose of the conversation. Try to keep your conversation focused on finding a solution to the issue being focused on.

2. *Learn Each Other's Point of View:* As a couple, strive to understand each other before you strive to influence each other. This is best done by asking questions and letting the other person talk. This is the perfect time to use your empathetic listening skills we discussed earlier. At the right times, you should share your opinions and ideas too—this is where you use "I-statements" and own your thoughts and feelings, without blaming each other.

3. *Encourage Brainstorming:* It is helpful to use reflective listening—or telling each other what you think the other person is saying. This will let each of you clarify any misunderstandings and let each other know how much you are listening. Then you can brainstorm together solutions and new ways of doing things in your relationship. Spend time together thinking of solutions to the current disagreement. Choose a solution that both partners think can work and will work on together.

4. *Evaluate and Adjust the Plan:* None of us come up with perfect solutions with our first ideas. Plan to regularly discuss your progress and make adjustments that will help your changes work. If you find that your first solutions are not working like you planned, it might be necessary to brainstorm new ideas.

Positive Communication

In his research, Dr. Gottman has also identified the positive relationship skills that help a couple manage conflict well. According to Dr. Gottman, these skills are based in *gentleness* in conversation. In addition to using softened startup and accepting influence from one another, successful couples maintain about a 5-to-1 ratio of positive-to-negative interactions during conflict interactions (see Gottman & Gottman, Why Marriages Succeed or Fail, 2005). During conflict discussions, the ratio of positive to negative interactions in relationships headed for divorce is 0.8:1, not 5:1, as it is in stable and happy couples. The presence of positive affect itself during conflict resolution (and in everyday interaction) is, in fact, crucial. This is why couples need to foster the friendship in their relationship and practice the five magic hours each week. These types of positive interactions go a long way in helping a couple stay positive when handling issues of difference and conflict. Positive communication also involves high levels of disclosure and openness between partners. Openly sharing our inner thoughts and feelings fosters understanding and belonging in marriage.

Meta-Communication

One of the most important types of communication a couple needs to engage in in their relationship is called "Meta-communication." *Meta-communication is communication about communication* (see Fincham & Beach, 1999, Conflict in Marriage). In other words, meta-communication is talking about communication. For example, if two married people sit down to talk about an argument they just had, they are meta-communicating because they are talking about the communication that happened in the argument.

Each partner needs to be willing to talk about how he or she communicates within the relationship and be willing to listen to and respect the other partner. There will be times when partners can come to an agreement without directly talking about the relationship, but at other times, this will be necessary. To find a shared vision, to establish rules, and to agree upon a work ethic, each person must be willing to create an atmosphere that enables both persons to share their feelings and concerns about the relationship. This type of "relationship talk" is a critical part of mature relationships. In fact, regular and productive meta-communication is one of the main characteristics that couples should develop before they become engaged or married.

Protecting Marital Resources

Time and money

CHAPTER 19

> You can never get enough of what you don't need, because what you don't need can never satisfy you.
>
> *Dr. Bernard Poduska*

Although we tend to focus on commitment in relationships as a matter of the heart and mind, it is also a matter of how we act. In fact, commitment is best shown, not simply stated.

In this chapter, we look at critical commitment behaviors related to marriage resources—time and money. When couples struggle, these are two of the most common problem areas. On the other hand, when couples live according to some key principles and following proven patterns in how they use their time and manage their finances, these become strengths that protect marriage and family closeness.

It's About Time

We live in a culture that has accelerated our perception of time. Almost all individuals and families report that they do not have enough time and that their daily life feels frantic and rushed. In fact, reports of being "squeezed for time" are so widespread that family scholars have coined the phase *time famine* to describe our modern culture (see Perlow, 1999, The Time Famine).

Research has linked the experience of time famine to people spending more time at work and in activities outside the home and less time with family members. For example, on average, parents are spending more time in work related activities than in the past. Recent studies show that workers around the world are working more and more hours in paid labor. This pattern is compounded by the fact that even when people are not officially working they continue to attend to emails and texts about work related matters. Many people today never truly go home from the office - they take their work with them wherever they go.

How well does the term "time famine" describe your life? Are you among the millions of people who describe their life as fast-paced, hectic, and rushed? If

you are, you should carefully evaluate how well your lifestyle, now and in the future, will fit with the needed commitments of marriage.

Efficiency over Connection

The frantic pace of our lives is causing many of us to approach family life with a business mentality, emphasizing efficiency and production over connection and experience. Furthermore, many essential aspects of family life, such as family worship, parent-child conversations, and marital dates are increasingly slipping out of many of our lives. Our prophets have repeatedly counseled us to protect our time and make sure that we put first things first. In particular, the Proclamation on the Family clearly instructs that we should make our marriages and families our highest priority and make sure that other pursuits do not seriously detract from these covenant relationships.

> **In choosing how we spend time as a family, we should be careful not to exhaust our available time on things that are merely good and leave little time for that which is better or best.... The amount of children-and-parent time absorbed in the good activities of private lessons, team sports, and other school and club activities also needs to be carefully regulated. Otherwise, children will be overscheduled, and parents will be frazzled and frustrated. Parents should preserve time for family prayer, family scripture study, family home evening, and other precious togetherness and individual one-on-one time that binds a family together and fixes children's values on things of eternal worth. Parents should teach gospel principles through what they do with their children.**
>
> -Elder Dalling H. Oaks (2007)
> *Good, Better, Best*

Prioritize Your Marriage

There are multiple threats to dating and marital time, including: work schedules, school assignments, over-scheduling of children, church callings, extended family commitments, hobbies and recreational pursuits, television and media, and other activities. Because of these pursuits, many individuals do not make their dating and marriage relationships enough of a priority in their daily life. Our prophetic leaders have counseled us to make our marriage relationships our highest priority and to make sure that our commitment to them is demonstrated not only in our words, but also in our daily and weekly schedules. The appointments we have with our spouse are sacred and we should give them the same priority in our schedule that we give to work or church appointments. In counsel given to husbands, President Ezra Taft Benson taught,

> . . .nothing except God himself takes priority over your wife in your life—not work, not recreation, not hobbies. . .what does it mean to "cleave unto her?" It means to stay close to her, to be loyal and faithful to her, to communicate with her, and to express your love for her.(Ensign, November 1987, p. 48)

Our efforts to prioritize time for our marriages do not have to be large to have great benefits. Remember our discussion of the *Five Magic Hours* in our discussion of the marital virtue of friendship? As you will recall, couples who devoted *five extra hours a week* to their marriage reported having a better relationship than couples who did not spend this time together. During these five hours, couples primarily attended to four things: (1) learning about each other's life that day, (2) having a stress-reducing conversation at the end of each day, (3) doing something every day to express genuine affection and appreciation, and (4) having a weekly date together.

Committing to Dating and Marriage

Within the Church, we have all heard the phrase *Choose the right*. For children and teens this phrase typically refers to choosing those things that are good and avoiding those that are bad. However, as we grow older we soon discover that not all decisions in life involve choices between things that are clearly good or clearly bad—sometimes we "choose the right" by learning to prioritize and find balance between two good things. Put another way, to succeed in life we must learn to dis-

Family Time & Media Use

Sadly, some young men and women in the Church today ignore "things as they really are" and neglect eternal relationships for digital distractions, diversions, and detours that have no lasting value. My heart aches when a young couple—sealed together in the house of the Lord for time and for all eternity by the power of the holy priesthood—experiences marital difficulties because of the addicting effect of excessive video gaming or online socializing. A young man or woman may waste countless hours, postpone or forfeit vocational or academic achievement, and ultimately sacrifice cherished human relationships because of mind- and spirit-numbing video and online games. As the Lord declared, "Wherefore, I give unto them a commandment... Thou shalt not idle away thy time, neither shalt thou bury thy talent that it may not be known" (D&C 60:13)

—Elder Bednar, CES fireside, May 3, 2009

How we choose to spend our time is a moral decision that reflects our commitment to our marriage and family. These decisions also influence our growth and development and the quality of our lives both here and hereafter.

—Dr. Mark Widmer et al (2001)

tinguish between things that are *important* and *desirable* and those that are *essential* and *needed*. This type of prioritized decision making is what couples face in balancing dating and marriage with schooling, work, recreation, and other responsibilities. To "choose the right" when it comes to work-family balance requires righteous desires, prayerful decision making, and a commitment to make our dating and marriage relationships the central priority in our lives.

"According to the Desires of Their Hearts" (D&C 137:9)

Balancing work and family life begins with righteous desires and goals. How we prioritize our time is an indicator of what we value most in life. Fostering an eternal perspective in our thinking and decision making helps us put our families first. Work and other commitments are merely *means* to more important ends—whereas our marriages and families are eternal *ends*. Although prioritizing time for dating and marriage can be challenging, the Lord will bless us in our efforts if we are prayerfully striving after righteous goals together as a couple.

Marital rituals

The key to managing time in a way that fosters a loving couple relationship is to be intentional about how you use time. One way to be intentional is to build a couple relationship that is ritualized. Nationally recognized family therapist William Doherty has researched what he calls *marital rituals*. According to Dr. William Doherty, "rituals are social interactions that are repeated, coordinated, and significant" (Take Back Your Marriage, 2013, p. 125). He goes on to say,

> Rituals can be everyday interactions, or they could be once a year, but they are repeated. They are also coordinated. You have to know what is expected of you in a ritual; you can't have a meal ritual together if you don't know when to show up for it, and you can't dance together if you don't know what kind of dance you are going to do. You're not going to have much of a sexual life if you don't end up in the same space at the same time. Rituals are not only repeated and coordinated, they are significant. A ritual is something that has positive emotional meaning to both parties. The matter of significance is what distinguishes ritual from routine. A marriage routine is something you do over and over in a coordinated way, but that does not have much emotional meaning. (Take Back Your Marriage, p. 126)

Dr. Doherty identifies five different types of marital rituals: *Connection Rituals*, *Talk Rituals*, *Love Rituals*, *Intimacy Rituals*, and *Celebration Rituals*. Remember that rituals do not have to be elaborate to be effective. Many of the most significant rituals are daily or weekly expressions of love through prioritizing our time to make sure we talk and connect with our partner. Marital rituals demonstrate our commitment to our marriage and our desire to cleave unto our spouse over all other things.

Extended family relationships

In our discussion of time and couple relationships, we should briefly discuss the subject of extended family relationships. While parents and extended family members can be a rich resource to dating couples and newlyweds, they can also be an area of struggle for the developing relationship. Many of these struggles center around the issue of time and how much time will or will not be spent with partner's extended families. The principles we discuss here are an extension of the principles of *cleaving* and *spousal preeminence* we discussed in the foundations unit. Remember that in that chap-

ter we discussed the importance of confiding in and counseling with your spouse, seeking and considering outside counsel together, honoring the private aspects of the stewardship of marriage, and practicing self-reliance by establishing your own home in marriage.

As you will recall, President Spencer W. Kimball counseling young couples about their relationships with parents and extended family members said,

> . . .you love them (parents) more than ever; you cherish their counsel; you appreciate their association; but you live your own lives, being governed by your decisions, by your own prayerful considerations after you have received the counsel of those who should give it. (Ensign, March 1977)

Extended Families and Dating

The topic of time with extended families is an important one to discuss and observe during dating. This is an area where couples should evaluate if they are a good fit for one another and can complement one another in this aspect of life. While dating, you should come to know what the expectation of your partner is in two important areas. First, *what are his or her expectations for the amount of time they will spend with their extended family after marriage?* Some extended families have very flexible expectations about the amount of time that should be spent together, while other families have very high expectations for time together. Some families, unfortunately, are aware that someone is marrying into their family, but they are less sensitive to the fact that their child or sibling is also marrying into another family too. This can create a time imbalance where the couple spends a lot of time with one extended family and very little with the other. This can create tension within your relationship, and with other family members.

Second, *where does each of you plan to live?* It is important for dating couples to come to an understanding of where each of them plans to live after marriage. Some people are very flexible about this issue, while others have very set plans. The first issue to discuss about living location is the type of community each of you would like to live in. Do you want to live in a rural, suburban, or urban neighborhood? These each represent a lifestyle that may fit or not fit for different people.

You should find out how close you and your partner plan to live to extended family. This issue of proximity is what I refer to as the "*doughnut principle.*" Most of us have a preferred distance that we would like live from our parents and other relatives. Like a doughnut, there is a minimum distance that we would like to be away from our parents (like the inside hole of a doughnut) and there is a maximum distance as well (like the outside of a doughnut). Our *doughnut zone* is the *not-too-close, not-too-far-away* distance we would prefer to live in relation to extend family members. Some people want to live within 10 minutes of their parents so that they can eat Sunday dinner together and see each other multiple times each week.

Others prefer a distance of about a half an hour—close enough to see each other regularly, but not close enough to bump into each other at the grocery store. Others like to be a couple of hours away—close enough to get together for big events, but far enough away to spend more time together as a couple and immediate family. Others prefer to live at some distance, with only occasional visits to see extended family members.

Now, this issue is more complex than I have discussed here, because there are at least two families involved. Moving away from one family may be moving

toward the other. Plus, where couples live is not always a matter of personal choice. Sometimes schooling opportunities or work offers take precedence and family patterns have to be set around them. During dating and engagement, couples need to be mindful to discuss expectations and set patterns that will be mutually agreeable to both spouses. This may be an area to use the principles of solution-focused conversations to successfully manage any differences or conflict.

ADULT-TO-ADULT RELATIONSHIPS

When children marry, a fundamental shift needs to occur in their relationship with their parents. And this shift should be manifest in their use of time. In addition to establishing marital boundaries (as we discussed previously), young people need to strive to incorporate the principle of *reciprocity* into their relationships with their parents. According to Dr. Rick Miller, the former Director of the School of Family Life at BYU, children and parents never develop adult-to-adult relationships until there is reciprocity in their relationships. He explains,

> Relationships develop an equal footing when both people give to each other, but when only one party gives and the other takes, an unequal relationship develops...the relationship between adult children and their parents needs to shift toward an adult-to-adult relationship in which children give back. (Ensign, January 2006, p. 29)

As young couples set their patterns involving time and money, they should avoid the *Santa Claus Syndrome*. Dr. Miller defines the Santa Claus syndrome

as "viewing Mom and Dad as Santa Claus figures who shower love and gifts on their children with little expectation of reciprocity" (Ensign, January 2006, p. 29). When this happens, young couples are often unable to develop mutually satisfying relationships with their parents.

POSITIVE EXTENDED FAMILY RELATIONSHIPS

Thus far, we have discussed how involvement with parents, in-laws, and extended family members can be a risk to marital time and connection. While extended family time must be careful monitored and intentionally chosen, couples should also be mindful of the positive influence extended family relationships can have on their marriage. Elder L. Tom Perry has taught,

> To build a foundation strong enough to support a family in our troubled world today requires the best effort of each of us—father, mother, brother, sister, grandmother, grandfather, aunts, uncles, cousins, and so on. Each must contribute energy and effort in driving piles right down to the bedrock of the gospel until the foundation is strong enough to endure through the eternities. (Ensign, May, 1985, p. 23)

For example, grandparents have been found to be influential in some fundamental aspects of their grandchildren's lives, namely helping them form identities, and in transmitting values, ideals, and beliefs to them. Grandparents and other extended family members can act as family historians, mentor-teachers, nurturers, role models, and playmates to grandchildren. Because of these benefits, couples should seek patterns of interaction that nurture and foster these types of interac-

tions. The key is to find balance between marital time, immediate family time, and extended family time.

Many newlyweds also experience a shift in their relationships with siblings when they get married. For some, there is a collapsing of "sibling distance" as siblings who were once quite distant because of an age gap now find that they have more in common as they are married and raising families. Couples should find ways to appropriately nurture sibling relationships across the marital life course.

Money Issues and Marriage

Another primary resource that must be managed wisely in marriage is money. In fact, financial decision making before and after marriage has become one of the most important ways each of us expresses how committed we are to marriage. Perhaps this is why President Brigham Young taught,

> We cannot talk about spiritual things without connecting with them temporal things, neither can we talk about temporal things without connecting spiritual things with them. (Address in Journal of Discourses 10:329, 1864)

Similar to the topic of time, our prophetic leaders have provided us with principles to guide our decision-making related to money and finances. In this section we will discuss some of these principles and how they make a difference in dating and marriage relationships.

What have the prophets taught us about managing family finances?

Prophets and apostles have repeatedly taught principles for managing our finances. All of these principles are spiritual in nature, but have direct application to how we earn, save, and spend money. President N. Eldon Tanner, a member of the First Presidency, once summarized prophetic teachings about managing our finances. He taught that there are at least five key principles to follow, including:

1. Seek Ye First the Kingdom of God
2. Pay an Honest Tithing
3. Live on Less than You Earn
4. Distinguish Between Needs and Wants
5. Develop and Live Within a Budget

Commenting on these principles, President Tanner commented,

> I have discovered that there is no way that you can ever earn more than you can spend. . .those who structure their standard of living to allow a little surplus, control their circumstances. Those who spend a little more than they earn are controlled by their circumstances. (Ensign, October 1979)

The foundation principle of sound financial decision making is *self-reliance*. We should live in a way that maintains our self-reliance, and only turn to other sources of support when it is absolutely needed. The counsel of Church leaders is that if we cannot meet our temporal needs, we should first turn to extended family for support, then to church or social forms of support.

Now, my experience is that nearly all of us have heard all of these principles before. Are you hearing about any of these financial principles for the first time? Chances are probably not. Chances are that you have heard that you should "pay an honest tithing" and should "live within your means" for most of your life. So, if this is the case, *why can following these principles be so hard to do*? The answer to this lies in our current culture of materialism and the practice of living on credit.

Provident Living
providentliving.lds.org

Pay Tithes and Offerings
Successful family finances begin with the payment of an honest tithe and the giving of a generous fast offering. The Lord has promised to open the windows of heaven and pour out great blessings upon those who pay tithes and offerings faithfully.

Avoid Debt
Spending less money than you make is essential to your financial security. Avoid debt, with the exception of buying a modest home or paying for education or other vital needs. Save money to purchase what you need. If you are in debt, pay it off as quickly as possible.

Use a Budget
Keep a record of your expenditures. Record and review monthly income and expenses. Determine how to reduce what you spend for nonessentials. Use this information to establish a family budget.

Build a Reserve
Gradually build a financial reserve, and use it for emergencies only. If you save a little money regularly, you will be surprised how much accumulates over time.

Teach Family Members
Teach family members the principles of financial management. Involve them in creating a budget and setting family financial goals. Teach the principles of hard work, frugality, and saving. Stress the importance of obtaining as much education as possible.

Materialism and Marriage

As we noted in our chapter on modern threats to marriage, we currently live in a culture that is saturated in materialism. Research studies have shown that materialism can have a negative impact on dating and marriage relationships. A study that my colleagues and I did found that highly materialistic spouses are about 40 percent more likely than nonmaterialistic spouses to experience high levels of financial problems, which consequently harm their marital satisfaction. What's more, materialism was a better predictor of financial problems than income levels—which means that even when people have a lot of money, materialism still creates problems in their marriage relationships (see Carroll et al., 2011, Materialism and Marriage).

This study further found that financial problems have as much to do with how we think about money as they do with how we spend money. For a highly materialistic spouse or couple, it takes less financial disturbance to trigger a financial problem. This is a problem because the study found that about 35 percent of spouses can be classified as *"highly materialistic."* This study suggests that spouses set their own threshold for what they view as a money problem. If spouses are overly materialistic, their threshold will be quite low, thereby increasing the likelihood that finances will be a problem in their marriages. Materialistic expectations may cause a spouse to interpret a financial situation negatively, leading to more complaints and conflicts, even when another couple with similar financial resources won't have such conflicts because of lower expectations.

Four recommendations emerge from the findings of this study:

1. *Separate needs from wants.* It is often said, *Yesterday's luxuries have become today's necessities.* In today's consumer culture, it is important for couples to carefully distinguish between their "needs" and their "wants" when it comes to family spending.
2. *Check financial benchmarks.* Many people do not see their financial expectations as too high because they compare their spending habits to others who have more. Couples who typically compare themselves to others who have more than they do frequently develop a sense of entitlement and resentment, while couples who see their situation through the eye of those who have less are more likely to foster a sense of gratitude in their lives.
3. *Focus on the simple.* The saying goes, *The most important things in life are not things.* While easy to say, this phrase is much harder to live. Financial strain in marriage, brought on by high materialistic expectations, often causes couples to not fully appreciate the simple aspects of their relationship that money cannot buy.
4. *Lower expectations.* Financial problems in marriage are as much about expectations as they are about behaviors. Lowering financial expectations can benefit marriages in two ways. First, spouses will be more willing to avoid making purchases that create debt and stress in their relationship and, second, spouses will be more inclined to interpret their current situation with more gratitude and optimism.

What Have the Prophets Taught Us about Acceptable Debt?

Another reason why so many couples struggle with financial strain is because they do not use debt according to prophetic principles. *What have the prophets taught us about debt? Is there such thing as acceptable versus unacceptable debt?* In order to answer these questions, you need to have a basic understanding of the different types of debt.

If you look at someone's credit report, the debt is typically listed in three categories. The first type of debt is *real estate debt*. For the vast majority of people this is their home mortgage. Mortgage debt is tied to an asset—your home. Typically, home values appreciate over time and people acquire *equity* in their home. This happens when you home is worth more than you owe on it. If a person with real estate debt experiences financial troubles, he or she can typically sell their home and remove this debt, if needed.

The second kind of debt on a credit report is called *installment debt*. This is a broad category of debt that involves anything a consumer purchases on credit that has a fixed payment period and payment amount. For example, cars, student loans, furniture, exercise equipment, boats, and other items can all be bought with installment debt. Installment debt is tied to assets—but the value of these assets almost always depreciates. The moment you drive a new car off the dealer's lot it depreciates in value. Even if you only drive it 10 feet—it is now a used car, instead of a new car.

The third type of debt is called *consumer debt*. Consumer debt is items and services purchased with credit cards (or store cards). Consumer debt is different than other forms of debt because the debt is not tied to an asset such as a home or car. The credit is extended to the consumer to purchase whatever they want to purchase. Movie tickets, clothes, eating out, gas, groceries, downloaded music, textbooks, plane tickets and many other expenses can all be purchased with a credit card. However, none of these items

retain their value after purchase (or only have a very minimal value). You cannot sell back the movie you watched or the gas you used last week in your car.

Our prophetic leaders have repeatedly taught us that we should *be modest and cautious in our use of real estate debt*. Nearly all of us will need to use credit to purchase a home, but we should only buy enough home to meet our true needs. Many couples today are getting into financial trouble because they are stretching to buy large, elaborate, and designer homes (not to mention all the money that is then spent on decorating and furnishing such homes). Plus, many couples find themselves "house poor" when they have to put so much of their income to their mortgage payment, leaving little money for savings, vacations, family activities, or other enjoyable parts of married life. Be wise in your purchasing of a home.

Some uses of installment debt are in harmony with prophetic counsel and other uses of installment debt are not. Education loans and car loans are examples of acceptable debt that many people will need to make use of in their lifetimes. These kinds of *install-*

ment loans can be used to meet legitimate needs to get trained in a profession or to have reliable transportation to get to work and other commitments. However, we should be modest and cautious in our use of installment debt for school or car loans. Transportation is a true need. Driving fast or impressing others with the type of car we drive is not. *Other uses of installment debt, such as purchasing furniture, are more like consumer debt* purchases and should be avoided. As couples save for these types of purchases, they provide a safeguard in times of need. For example, money being saved for a couch can be used for car repairs, if needed.

Our prophetic leaders have always counseled us to *avoid consumer debt*. In all cases, consumer debt is a form of living today on tomorrow's earnings. This is contrary to the principle of living within your means. Plus, consumer debt purchases typically have very high interest rates on them, meaning that you can pay two to three times the value of an item purchased with a credit card by the time it is finally paid off.

Money Problems vs. Behavior Problems

Highly regarded family finance expert Dr. Bernard Poduska is fond of saying, "Financial problems are usually behavior problems, rather than money problems" (Strengthening Our Families, 2000, p. 99). This quote reminds us that how we think about and use money reveals a lot about what is most important to us in life and what we are prioritizing. As you strive to improve your readiness for marriage, your behaviors with money will demonstrate your commitment to marriage or your commitment to other things. Dr. Poduska has also said, "You can never get enough of what you don't need because what you don't need can never satisfy you" (Strengthening Our Families, 2000, p. 99).

Similar to our use of time, successful management of finances begins with righteous desires and goals. How we prioritize our expenses is an indicator of what we value most in life. Fostering an eternal perspective in our thinking and decision making helps us put our marriages first. Money and financial resources are merely *means* to more important ends—whereas our marriages and families are eternal *ends*. Although prioritizing money management in marriage can be challenging, the Lord will bless us in our efforts if we are prayerfully striving after righteous goals together as a couple.

Intimacy in Marriage

SELFLESSNESS AND SEXUAL UNITY

CHAPTER 20

> ...love and concern for one's partner shifts the focus away from the self in a sexual relationship and toward the other person. This selfless approach to sex, paradoxically, is far more likely to bring sexual satisfaction to both men and women.
>
> *Linda Waite and Maggie Gallagher—The Case for Marriage*

In this chapter, we discuss sexual intimacy in marriage. As with other topics in the book our focus will be primarily on principles of marital intimacy, rather than a discussion of practices or techniques. There are three primary reasons why we will approach the topic of sexual intimacy in marriage with a principle based approach.

First, principles are what matter most. One of the greatest myths of in our popular culture about sexual intimacy is that sexual fulfillment in a couple's relationship is primarily the result of proper technique or behavioral practices. While a proper understanding of men's and women's bodies and the human sexual response cycle can be helpful in fostering pleasurable sexual experiences, sexual fulfillment is primarily about the quality of our relationship with our spouse. The principles we discuss in this chapter are focused on how to have a fulfilling sexual *relationship*, not just stimulating pleasurable sexual *responses*.

The second reason why we will discuss principles, rather than practices, is that the specific patterns of rewarding sexual intimacy vary from couple to couple; and the only couple you need to be familiar with when it comes to the specifics of sexual intimacy is your own marriage! It will do you no good to learn about the specifics of intimacy in other people's marriages—they are not you and your spouse. And, in fact, learning too much about the details and specifics of other couple's intimacy patterns may be detrimental to your own sexual relationship in marriage as you strive to mimic the patterns of others, rather than be responsive to the needs and desires of your partner. Nothing is more personal than our sexual preferences and patterns. Therefore, your sexual relationship in marriage needs to be tailored to your spouse, not to outside expectations or comparisons.

The third, and perhaps most important, reason for focusing on principles with this topic is that some parts of marital intimacy are meant to be learned together as a couple. This chapter is designed to give you a foundation upon which to build as you one day explore and discover the fullness of sexual intimacy in your marriage. The Lord intended for it to be this way—and He knows best how to guide us toward complete sexual fulfillment and intimacy in this life and in the eternities. (A fuller discussion of the principles presented in this chapter can be found in the book, *Sexual Wholeness in Marriage,* which I wrote with my colleagues, Dr. Dean Busby and Dr. Chelom Leavitt.)

Intimacy in marriage

Previously, you have studied generally principles of chastity and the importance of personal purity in dating and courtship. In both of these previous chapters, it was emphasized that proper restraint of sexual desire during dating and courtship sets the foundation for proper expressions of sexuality in marriage. The purpose of this chapter is to bring together all of the principles you have studied and to discuss how they culminate in fostering sexual unity and belonging within the marriage covenant.

In the foundations section, you were introduced to foundation principles of marriage relationships that now act as the foundation for understanding the sexual part of a husband and wife's relationship. In fact, all of the principles we have discussed in this book can be re-analyzed and interpreted as principles of forming a loving and lasting sexual relationship in marriage. For example, principles such as (1) *Equal Partnership*, with an emphasis on true partnership involving equal counsel and equal consent, (2) *Cleaving*, demonstrated in spousal preeminence, and (3) the *Divine Triangle of Marriage*, teaching us of the need for alignment between spouses and with God.

In our previous chapters on *chastity* and *purity* you were introduced to essential principles of sexual unity in marriage. This included: (1) *The True Purposes of Sexual Intimacy*, which means understanding sexual intimacy as a means toward divine purposes such as procreation and marital unity, not an end in and of itself, (2) *The Doctrine of the Soul*, reminding us that all sexual experiences involve both our body and our soul, (3) *The Doctrine of the Symbol*, reminding us of how true sexual intimacy must founded upon deep emotional intimacy, and (4) *The Doctrine of the Sacrament*, reminding us that when properly expressed, sexual intimacy unites us with not only our spouse but also with God and His eternal purposes.

Ponder on all of these principles as you begin this chapter. They provide the needed foundation for approaching the sexual dimension of marriage with the proper heart, mind, and behaviors. This chapter is divided into three main parts. First, we will discuss the human *sexual response cycle* as traditionally understood. Building on this foundation, I will introduce you to the *sexual relationship cycle*—which adds two additional phases to help us emphasize sexual unity in marriage. Second, we will discuss the *anatomy of the sexual response* which will include a discussion of the physical anatomy of men's and women's sexual responses, as well as issues related to *sexual conditioning* that may influence sexual responsiveness. The final section will discuss *spousal differences* in sexual preferences and principles to foster sexual unity in marriage.

Moving from Sexual Response to a Sexual Relationship

The Sexual Response Cycle

Traditionally understood, the human sexual response cycle is discussed as having three phases—the *Desire Phase*, the *Arousal Phase*, and the *Orgasm/Climax Phase*. Sometimes experts add an additional phase that is called the *Afterglow period* or phase that follows reaching orgasm. Although some experts do not label the afterglow period as a phase in the sexual response cycle, many experts do consider this to be a phase in the sexual response cycle. We will discuss it this way. Thus, the sexual response cycle has traditionally been understood to have four phases.

The Desire Phase

Desire is understood as the strong emotional urges to initiate and respond to sexual stimulation. Desire is understood to be a complex phenomenon impacted by biology, past experiences, current marital dynamics, and other factors.

The Arousal Phase

The level of sexual stimulation required to cause sexual arousal varies considerably from person to person and with each sexual experience. Some people (especially adolescents and young adults) experience arousal with little physical or mental stimulation, and others require physical stimulation and/or a certain level of emotional intimacy to achieve sexual arousal. Typically, men are sexually aroused more easily than women.

Sexual excitement may or may not be expressed, either verbally or through actions or behavior. Physical signs of arousal include increased heart rate, breathing, and blood pressure; muscle tension; and reddening of the skin of the face, neck, back, and chest (called flushing).

In their marital intimacy book for Latter-day Saints, Drs. Lamb and Brinley describe the arousal phase this way:

> When accompanied by stimulating sensations or memories, sexual desire leads to sexual excitement or arousal. Arousal involves physiologic and anatomic changes that are accompanied by sensations of pleasure . . . the physical changes are most noticeable in the genital area, but other areas of the body, such as the breasts and brain are affected as well. The primary physiologic event that occurs during arousal is "vasocongestion," which literally means "congestion of the blood vessels." During vasocongestion the superficial and deep veins of the pelvis dilate and fill with blood, causing the male penis and the female labia and vagina to enlarge. This vascular engorgement produces pleasant sensations of warmth and fulness." (Between Husband and Wife, 2008, p. 40–41)

The Orgasm or Plateau Phase

During what experts call the "orgasm or plateau phase" of sexual response, a high level of sexual excitement may occur, be lost, and then recur several times. Physical signs of this stage include a further increase in heart rate, breathing, blood pressure, muscle tension, and flushing. In men, the ridge of the glans penis (the head of the organ) becomes more prominent, pre-ejaculatory fluid is secreted, and the testicles are pulled even closer to the body. In women, the clitoris becomes more sensitive and withdraws under the clitoral hood, vaginal lubrication increases, and the vagina and labia continue to swell and tighten.

At the peak of the plateau stage, orgasm occurs. During orgasm, sexual tension is released. The physical signs of orgasm include flushing throughout the body and muscle spasms. In men, the urethra (tube that carries urine and semen out of the body through the penis) and muscles in the pelvic floor and anus contract quickly several times, resulting in ejaculation. In women, muscles in the pelvic floor, the vagina, the uterus, and the anus contract quickly several times.

The Afterglow Phase

Afterglow or resolution is the final stage of the sexual response cycle. During this phase, the body returns to normal. Heart rate, breathing, and blood pressure slow, muscles relax, and blood flow to the pelvis and reproductive organs decreases. Many people experience sweating and drowsiness during the resolution.

Women are physically capable of returning to the plateau phase of the sexual response cycle immediately following orgasm, but men are not able to achieve an erection until they complete a refractory period and enter the resolution phase of sexual response. The length of the refractory period varies from man to man and with each sexual encounter. This period of time ranges from minutes to hours and often increases with age.

Shifting From a Phase Model to a Threshold Model

Now, as you read about the sexual response cycle, as I have just summarized it (which is a very typical example of how the sexual response cycle is typically discussed), what stands out to you? What insights does it give you about sexual intimacy in marriage? As I have asked these questions of students over the years, they almost always comment on how the sexual response cycle only focuses on the physical or biological aspects of the sexual experience. In some ways, it makes sexual intimacy sound medical, technical, or mechanical in nature.

While learning about the traditional phases of the sexual response cycle can be helpful, they do not provide a full understanding of sexual intimacy in marriage. In fact, one of the pitfalls some young married couples fall into is the notion that sexual intimacy is first and foremost about getting their bodies to proceed physically through the four phases of the sexual response cycle. Remember, in God's plan, sexuality is a means to divine ends, not an end in and of itself. It is helpful to gain an understanding of the sexual response cycle, but the phases it describes should be seen as means to relationship ends.

To be clear, the biological processes described in phase models such as vasocongestion and orgasm are accurately described and can be a valuable part of understanding sexual response and functioning. Nevertheless, any benefits that may be gained from learning about these biological processes will be significantly counteracted if they are not connected to the spiritual and emotional aspects of sex. In fact, when presented in isolation, phase models will likely promote common myths about marital sexuality. The sidebar on the opposite page lists several common myths associated with the typical phase models used to teach human sexuality. The best way to view the phases of the sexual response cycle is as thresholds of arousal, rather than prescribed stages—and each spouse has different personal phases of arousal and orgasm response."

The Sexual Relationship Cycle

In previous chapters, we discussed the principles of *amae* and the *doctrine of the soul* related to sexual intimacy. As you will recall, amae is the innate need each of us has to belong to others and to God. The fulfillment of our amae is found in the receiving of Christlike love that communicates to us that we are loved, valued, and needed. Elder Jeffery R. Holland taught us that the doctrine of the soul requires us to acknowledge the spirit and body as a part of all sexual experiences in this life.

Building on these principles, an important question for each of us to answer is: *How can we better understand the sexual response cycle when we view it through the "doctrine of the soul" and the principle of amae?* When we ponder on these principles, we begin to see the shortcomings of the sexual response cycle as it is traditionally understood. This is because our sexual

Myths & Misunderstandings of Phase Models

"It's All About the Physical" Myth: At their core, phase models fail to integrate the emotional and relational aspects of sexual intimacy with the physical response of our bodies. They do not incorporate the human capacity for intimacy and the emotional meanings that can accompany sexual experience.

- Physical stimulation is the amount of "external stimulation" experienced during sex and is the function of the quality and quantity of physical touch and the capacity of the body to experience it.

- Psychological stimulation is the amount of "internal stimulation" experienced during sex. It refers to the emotions and thoughts spouses have during sex and is influenced by spouses' attitudes and approaches to sexuality, as well as the quality of the overall relationship surrounding a particular sexual experience. Together, physical stimulation and psychological stimulation create the total level of stimulation experienced in a given sexual experience.

"One Right Way" Myth: Phase models present sexual experience in a linear, progressive fashion that conveys that there is a "right way" to be sexual.

"Orgasm is the Goal" Myth: Orgasm is often portrayed as the goal of sex and the "completion" of the cycle is seen as the primary marker of sexual quality.

"Individual Experience" Myth: Phase models describe a process of one person progressing through the phases of desire, arousal, and orgasm. There is rarely the vision of two people being present and the common pattern of husbands' and wives' experiencing sexual response with different pace, intensity, and completion.

---

response is only one part physical, it is also emotional and spiritual. True sexual fulfillment originates in the spirit, not in the body. And most importantly, these principles help us see that sexual fulfillment is fundamentally about loving and being loved, the sense of belonging in our marriage, and the profound meaning sexual intimacy can come to have as it allows us to fulfill the amae needs of our eternal companion.

As displayed in the figure "The Sexual Relationship Cycle" on the next page, we need to add two additional phases to the sexual response cycle to appropriately understand how sexual interactions between spouses are embedded in and influence the larger relationship in marriage. In particular, the sexual relationship cycle adds a *Foundation Stage,* consisting of the quality of the emotional intimacy and partnership in the marriage and a *Outcome phase,* which consists of the emotional outcomes of sexual interactions in marriage. The red arrows in the cycle diagram the patterns of sexual intimacy in loving marriages. In this setting, the phases of the sexual response are means to celebrate and strengthen the marital bond and fulfill each part-

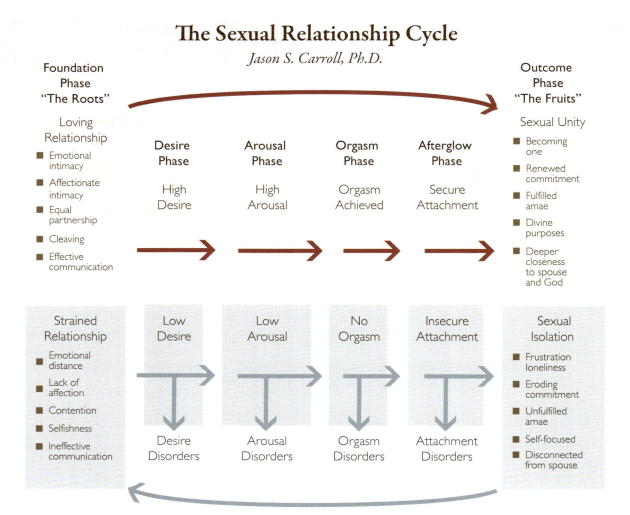

ner's desires to be loved and valued as a whole person. The blue arrows in the diagram represent the patterns of sexual intimacy in strained or distressed marriages. When the quality of emotional intimacy, partnership, and communication erode in a marriage, the couple will inevitably struggle with sexual intimacy in their marriage. At best, they will complete the phases of the sexual response cycle in their lovemaking, the quality of the experience will be marginal and the outcomes will be those associated with sexual isolation rather than sexual unity. At worst, when emotional intimacy is strained in a marriage, many couples struggle with even being able to progress through the phases of the sexual response cycle. Notice the second set of blue arrows that represent different types of sexual disorders associated with one or both spouses not progressing through various aspects of the sexual response cycle—thus adding to the sense of sexual isolation in the relationship. The addition of these two added stages should remind you to focus on developing a full and meaningful sexual relationship in your marriage, not just on creating pleasurable sexual responses in your body.

The Anatomy of the Sexual Response

None of what we have discussed to this point should be interpreted to mean that learning how to progress through the phases of the sexual response cycle together as a couple is not an important part of marriage. In fact, knowing how to help your partner achieve orgasm is an important part of the sexual adjustment to married life. Sharing orgasm and afterglow together as a couple can be a very vital part of bonding in marriage and meeting one another's needs for amae. The focus of this section is to help you better understand how to foster arousal and orgasm as a couple in marriage. As I noted in the introduction, our focus is on principles not practices. The only person who can teach you the specifics of this process will be your spouse as you learn to be responsive to him or her within your marriage relationship.

CREATED IN THE IMAGE OF GOD

Each of us is a beloved spirit son or daughter of God and was created in the image of Him. As literal offspring of God, our bodies have been created so that we are fully equipped to experience all that our loving Father in Heaven intended for us to experience in this life—which includes sexual pleasure and fulfillment. Because of this, it can be helpful in your preparation for marriage to come to have a better understanding of the anatomy of the sexual response in women and men. This topic requires a special reverence and sense of sacredness, particularly in a modern culture such as ours that uncovers and reveals the human body in ways to titillate and arousal carnally-minded attitudes about sex. A discussion of our bodies should inspire an awe and reverence for the majesty of our loving Father in Heaven and a profound appreciation that we have been blessed with a tangible body that can allow us to progress and experience a fullness of eternal life.

Diagrams of men's and women's sexual anatomy are provided below. As you study these diagrams, you will become familiar with the parts of your body and the body of your future spouse that initiate arousal and orgasm during sexual intimacy.

The top of the diagram shows how involved the various organs are in sexual response. As you can see, the most important sexual organ for both women and

The Anatomy of the Sexual Response

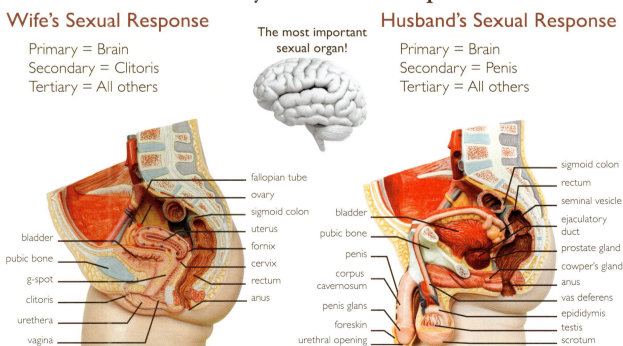

men is the brain. The sexual response that occurs in our bodies is as much about emotional and psychological arousal as it is about physical arousal. Unless the brain becomes aroused, the body typically will not become aroused, or will not become aroused enough to reach orgasm. This is especially true for women. Appreciating the pivotal role our brains play in our sexual response gives us insight into understanding why emotional intimacy and relationship quality must be the foundation of sexual intimacy in marriage. The first step toward orgasm involves each partner arousing their partner's brain. This comes from helping our spouse feel loved, cared for, and respected in the relationship. It stems from empathetic listening and open disclosure in the relationship. It is based in loving responsiveness and a sense of fairness in household tasks and work. This is the whole purpose of the first stage of the sexual relationship—the foundation phase.

A Wife's Sexual Response

As a fetus develops in the womb, it progresses through an initial phase of development before it manifests whether or not it is a male or female child. During this initial period of development, a cell mass develops that eventually becomes the sexual organs of the fetus. The developmental foundation for the sexual organs of females is exactly the same as the developmental foundation for the sexual organs of males. In fact, in adulthood men's and women's physical anatomy mirror one another, with husbands and wives having *anatomical counterparts* that are similar in form and function to one another.

For women, the clitoris is the physical counterpart that has similar sexual functions to the penis for men. The clitoris is a part of a woman's external genitalia (see figure on previous page) and, similar to a man's penis, plays a critical role in sexual arousal and orgasm for women. Dr. Tim LaHaye, explains:". . .*the clitoris has the same number of nerve endings as does the penis, but is only one-tenth the size. . .the walls of the vagina [are] not endowed with sensitive nerve endings*" (The Act of Marriage, 1995, pp. 113 & 159). Dr. Robert Stahmann, former director of the Marriage and Family Therapy program at BYU and a certified sex therapist explains:

> For a woman, the key to orgasmic success is the clitoris. Every orgasm that occurs in a woman is clitoral. Women are unable to climax without direct or indirect stimulation of the clitoris. (Becoming One, 2004, p. 18)

Thus, for married couples, learning how to successfully stimulate the wife's clitoris is a needed part of sexual fulfillment for her and ultimately for the couple. Proper arousal of a woman's clitoris often requires patience as the clitoris can be very sensitive, initially requiring light or indirect stimulation. A husband must be very responsive to his wife as he helps build her sexual arousal. This process should also involve tender caressing and touching of other parts of the body which become more sensitive to touch as arousal progresses.

It is important to understand that the clitoris has no other physical purpose than to provide physical pleasure and arousal for wives. This helps us understand how God created us to for his divine purposes—which include the experience of sexual pleasure in marriage.

A Husband's Sexual Response

Similar to a women's clitoris, men's primary sexual arousal comes from stimulation of the penis. Dr. LaHaye explains:

> After fifteen to sixty seconds, the male becomes fully aroused . . . for the man [achieving orgasm] is quite simple and easily detected. When sufficient stimulation is applied to the nerve endings in the penis, a chain reaction is begun by creating muscular contractions in the prostate gland, forcing seminal fluid and sperm cells through the urethra. (The Act of Marriage, p. 95)

Although men and women have similar anatomy and phases in the sexual response, the timing of progression through these phases is typically an area of difference. We will discuss this in more detail in the last section of the lesson on couple differences.

COMMON PHYSICAL QUESTIONS

As we are discussing the anatomy of the sexual response, it is helpful to discuss some other issues that may create anxiety for brides and grooms as they approach their honeymoon. Anxiety or fear is not a good foundation for sexual responsiveness. The more comfortable you can feel about sexual intimacy the better you will be able to relax and enjoy your initial sexual experiences with each other.

PAINFUL INTERCOURSE

As I have counseled with young adults and couples over the years, I have come to understand that a common concern for many soon-to-be brides is that sexual intercourse will be painful. Occasionally, women have heard stories from family members or friends about intercourse being painful and uncomfortable; and that they should not expect to enjoy their honeymoon experience. My experience is that the anxiety that these stories create frequently acts as a self-fulfilling prophecy as the bride is so anxious about sexual intimacy that she cannot relax, thus inhibiting her sexual response and arousal.

Is sexual intercourse painful for women? Some women experience pain with their first experiences with sexual intercourse. Medical professionals have discovered that there are two primary reasons why this occurs—both of which are preventable.

The first, and most common, reason for discomfort during intercourse for women is *insufficient arousal*. During arousal, a woman's body produces a natural lubricant that coats the vaginal opening and canal preparing a wife's body for intercourse. Without sufficient arousal and lubrication, intercourse can feel abrasive and irritating. For this reason, I counsel young couples to remember the "Great Salt Lake" when it comes to honeymoon intimacy. The initials GSL can also stand for "Gentle, Slow, and Lubricated"—all important parts of making intimacy comfortable for both partners. Even with careful attention to the wife's arousal, sometimes a wife's natural lubrication will not be enough to facilitate comfortable intercourse. At these times, a personal lubricant can be very helpful for many couples, particularly during their first few sexual experiences. A tube of personal lubricant is a "must have" item for honeymoon packing and can be purchased at most pharmacies.

The second reason why some women experience pain or discomfort during intercourse is the stretching or tearing of hymen tissue. Drs. Lamb and Dr. Brinley explain:

> The hymen is a membrane or ring of skin that partially covers the vaginal opening. The first time sexual intercourse is undertaken, it is normal for there to be stretching and tearing of the hymenal skin. This can cause mild discomfort or, in some cases, severe pain. Bleeding can occur as well.
>
> Even from birth, all hymens are not the same. Some women have very little hymenal tissue, while others have near complete blockage of the vaginal opening by a thick band of tissue. This means that some women have very little difficulty with their first sexual experience, while others may have significant problems. Obviously, if a problem is not discovered until the honeymoon, there will be pain, frustra-

tion, and embarrassment for the couple as they try to engage in their first sexual experiences together. (Between Husband and Wife, 2008, p. 48–49)

It is important for the bride-to-be to have a gynecologic exam several weeks before the wedding date. . .the vast majority of women learn that everything is normal and that sexual intercourse can take place without serious problems. Occasionally, however, the doctor may recommend dilation of the hymenal ring in order for sexual intercourse to proceed properly. Minor surgery to correct an anatomical problem is occasionally necessary. By having this exam several months before the wedding day, there will be sufficient time to get everything done—even if minor surgery is required. (Between Husband and Wife, 2008, p. 42)

Pelvic Floor Muscles

Some young women have heard about exercises that can make sexual intercourse more comfortable and enjoyable for them and their partners. So, the question I often hear is "do these exercises actually exist?" The answer to this question is "yes." Many doctors and other professionals recommend that women strengthen their pelvic muscles by beginning to do *Kegel exercises* several weeks before their wedding. These exercises involve contraction and relaxation of the muscle that helps support the vagina, bladder, and urethra. Women can voluntarily contract this muscle if they tighten up the same muscle they use to stop the flow of urine. Kegel exercises consist of contracting the pelvic floor muscles five to ten times, holding each contraction for ten seconds—repeating the sequence three to four times a day. These exercises can increase the tone of the vaginal canal, and therefore, increase enjoyment of sexual intercourse for some women. This is particularly true for women who have had children resulting in a relaxation of the vaginal canal. However, results from Kegel exercises will usually not be noticed until after several months of exercise, and, unfortunately, some women do not experience improvement form these exercises.

Male Enhancement

It is hard to watch TV these days without seeing a commercial or infomercial program about so-called male enhancement. These ads promote the idea that a simple tablet taken daily can enhance the size of a man's penis, thus making sexual intercourse more enjoyable for both partners. In addition to these advertisements is the ongoing references in movies, TV programs, and other media that "size matters" and that sexual fulfillment for couples is directly related to the size of a man's penis. In fact, in our modern culture, there is no greater way to insult a man than to "question his manhood" by suggesting that he has a small penis, thus insinuating that he is undesirable to women in such a compromised condition.

Needless to say, our society's fascination with the size of men's penises has created a fair amount of anxiety among young men about their bodies and sexual intercourse. The two main questions I hear on this topic are *Do male enhancement procedures work*? and the proverbial question *Does size really matter*? The limited research on male enhancement procedures has found that most male enhancement tablets are ineffective and a waste of money; while other forms of male enhancement are downright dangerous. Many doctors question whether the benefits of male enhancement procedures outweigh the risks. Many professionals feel that men who are overly preoccupied with penis length tend to have unrealistic expectations and should seek counseling instead of physical treatments.

To answer the second question, it is important to understand some basic norms about penis size. First, studies have found that the average penis size is around 3 ½ inches when flaccid or not aroused and between

5.5 to 6.2 inches when erect. Studies also find that the vast majority of men fall within the normal range. In fact, concerns about penis size are typically more imagined than real. In one study, researchers interviewed 92 men who considered themselves "poorly endowed" and found that not a single one had a penis that was smaller than the normal range.

Also, it's ironic that the male preoccupation with enhancement seems to be independent of the needs of women, the supposed benefactors of these so-called improvements to sexual performance. First, the average length of a woman's vaginal cavity is 3 to 4 inches, thus making additional penis length greater than this not as significant to the sexual experience as is often portrayed. Perhaps this explains why a recent study found that the overwhelming majority of women are pleased with their partner's penis proportions. Plus, there is plenty of debate on whether size matters as much as we are often led to believe. The most sensitive nerves in the vagina are found close to the surface and, as we have already discussed, the clitoris, an external sexual organ, has been found to be the most important organ for the sexual arousal of wives. So there should be plenty of ways to arouse and satisfy your partner that have nothing to do with enhancement pills, creams, surgeries, or devices.

Sexual conditioning

In addition to understanding the physical anatomy of sexual functioning, it can be helpful for each of us to evaluate our attitudes and feelings about sex. Our attitudes about sexual intimacy are what experts call "*sexual conditioning.*" Sexual conditioning refers to the attitudes and feelings each of us have toward sexual relations. How you learned about sex and chastity while growing up can contribute to your sexual conditioning.

As Latter-day Saints, there are at least two types of negative sexual conditioning we must guard against as they may disrupt the sexual intimacy in our marriages. Laura Brotherson, an LDS sex educator, has labeled the first type of negative sexual conditioning as "*Good Girl Syndrome*" (And They Were Not Ashamed, 2004, p. 2). Although both men and women can have developed this type of conditioning, it has been found to be more common among women. This type of conditioning occurs when as an individual commits themselves to chastity and purity before marriage they come to see sexuality as a negative or sinful behavior—even after marriage. Brotherson has identified several signs for Good Girl Syndrome, these include:

- Negative conditioning about sex and our bodies
- Discomfort or embarrassment in discussing sexual matters
- Underlying belief that sex is bad, wrong, dirty, or sinful
- Inability to relax and "let go" within the sexual experience
- Inappropriate inhibitions, guilt, shame, or awkwardness associated with sexual relations
- Lack of understanding of the divine purposes of sex

Given our discussion of the important role our brains play in initiating and sustaining the sexual response cycle in our bodies, it is clear that Good Girl Syndrome can be disruptive to marital intimacy.

Our prophetic leaders have repeatedly taught us that sexual intimacy is a good and righteous part of married life. President Spencer W. Kimball taught:

> Husband and wife are authorized, in fact, they are commanded to have proper sex when they are married for time and eternity. (Teachings of Spencer W. Kimball, 1995, p. 312)

> Sex is for procreation and expression of love. It is the destiny of men and women to join together to make eternal family units. In the context of lawful marriage, the intimacy of sexual relations is right and divinely approved. There is nothing unholy or degrading about sexuality in itself, for by that means men and women join in a process of creation and in an expression of love. (Teachings, p. 312)

While chastity before marriage involves abstaining from sexual involvement, chastity in marriage involves initiating, enjoying, and nurturing sexual intimacy with our spouse. Sexual intimacy is one of the rites of marriage we take upon ourselves when we are sealed together as a couple. Each of us needs to develop an abiding testimony of the divinely approved nature of sexual intimacy in marriage. For some people, they have had negative experiences in their premarital years that foster their negative conditioning about sex. Experiences with abuse, pornography, and premarital sexual transgression often create negative emotions of shame, regret, and low self-worth that become associated with sexual intimacy. In these cases, counseling with your bishop or a professional counselor may be helpful in working through these emotions and developing a positive conditioning about appropriate marital intimacy.

A second type of negative sexual conditioning is the antithesis of Good Girl Syndrome. I call it *Bad Boy Syndrome*. This type of conditioning is fostered in popular media that objectifies women and portrays men as "players who score with hot girls." In these messages, sex is seen as a physical drive, particularly for men, and women are viewed as objects to fulfill or meet the sexual desires of men. Signs of Bad Boy Syndrome include:

- Internalized sexual conditioning of mainstream society
- Involvement with pornography
- Judgment of women based on physical features (objectification)
- Intimacy detached from relationship outcomes
- Marriage seen as a "license to lust"
- Belief in a marital finish line of chastity—anything goes after marriage

Our prophetic leaders have warned both men and women about the sexual messages of our day that are incompatible with the true sexual union we should seek in marriage. President Howard W. Hunter has taught:

> Any domineering, indecent, or uncontrolled behavior in the intimate relationship between husband and wife is condemned by the Lord. . .keep yourselves above any domineering or unworthy behavior in the tender, intimate relationship between husband and wife. . .tenderness and respect—never selfishness—must be the guiding principle in the intimate relationship between husband and wife. Each partner must be considerate and sensitive to the other's needs and desires. . .marriage is like a tender flower, brethren, and must be nourished constantly with expressions of love and affection. (Ensign, November 1994, p. 51)

More recently, Sister Linda Reeves taught:

> One reason we are here on earth is to learn to manage the passions and feelings of our mortal bodies. These God-given feelings help us want to marry and have

children. The intimate marriage relationship between a man and a woman that brings children into mortality is also meant to be a beautiful, loving experience that binds together two devoted hearts, unites both spirit and body, and brings a fulness of joy and happiness as we learn to put each other first. (April 2014, A Christ Focused Home)

Key to Marital Intimacy: Managing Differences

Consider the following quote from Dr. Lamb and Dr. Brinley:

> One of the great challenges surrounding the sexual experience relates to the fact that husbands and wives often have very different perspectives about sex. They may struggle to understand and respond to one another's needs and desires. They may have different expectations or may not know how to make intimacy an enjoyable experience for their spouse. These differences can obviously create problems, but they can be overcome as the husband and wife work together to find the ways to provide a positive and fulfilling experience for one another. (Between Husband and Wife, p. 39)

One of the keys to whether or not sexual intimacy will be a stumbling block or a stepping stone in your marriage is how well you manage differences between you and your spouse. Similar to our previous chapter on differences in marriage, differences in preferences for sexual intimacy provide an opportunity for couples to draw closer to each other.

Perhaps the most common difference between spouses is a variation in the desired frequency of sexual intimacy. It is very common in marriage for one spouse to have a higher desire for sexual closeness than the other. Typically, the husband is the higher desire spouse and the wife is the lower desire spouse, but sometimes this pattern is reversed. This pattern requires sensitivity and responsiveness between spouses. Let's discuss some of the most common types of differences in marital intimacy that contribute to this *lower desire spouse/higher desire spouse* pattern and some principles on how to address these differences.

Different Intimacy Preferences

Husbands and wives typically have different preferences when it comes to intimacy. Some spouses place a very high value on emotional intimacy, which involves conversation and shared time together. Other spouses value affectionate intimacy, or physical intimacy that is not focused on initiating sexual arousal or orgasm. Holding hands, cuddling, hugging, kissing and other behaviors that create a physical closeness are deeply meaningful to many spouses. Other spouses value passionate intimacy that involves sharing sexual arousal, orgasm, and afterglow as spouses. Most people value all of these types of intimacy in marriage, but they may differ in the degree or relative ratio of these types of intimacy.

If your goal is to foster sexual unity in your marriage, you will carefully learn the intimacy desires of

your partner. Remember, orgasm is not the goal of intimacy, unity and belonging are the goal. Achieving orgasm does not equal intimacy. Feelings of love and respect are the foundation of intimacy. Also, couples should not become fixated on achieving orgasm and view orgasm as the primary indicator of successful intimacy. Some new wives do not experience orgasm initially during marital intimacy and there are times where one or both partners may desire sexual closeness without experiencing orgasm.

Pace of Arousal

Another area of difference between husbands and wives is the pace of arousal in the sexual response. In fact, some research suggests that for some couples, the wife's sexual arousal may take up to ten times longer than the husband's. This means that if the husband is able to reach full arousal in 2 to 3 minutes, it is not uncommon for the wife to need 20 to 30 minutes to reach a comparable level of arousal. This finding reminds us of the importance of foreplay in marital intimacy in order to make sure that intimacy is an enjoyable and fulfilling experience for both spouses. In fact, perhaps we ought to change the term from "foreplay" to "ten-play" to remind ourselves to be patient and sensitive to the arousal process of both spouses.

When it comes to marital intimacy you must remember the first rule of hiking. When you go hiking with a group the first rule of hiking is that you can only go as fast as the slowest hiker in your group—or else someone will get left behind. The same is true of sexual intimacy in marriage—you can only go as fast as the slowest spouse—or else someone will get left behind!

Sequence of Arousal

Recent research suggests that some spouses, particularly wives, may go through the phases of the sexual response cycle in a different sequence than outlined in the traditional sexual response cycle. In particular, these studies suggest that some people need to begin the arousal process before they experience desire for sexual contact. What this means is that in some marriages

one spouse (typically the husband) becomes aroused visually and mentally, thus creating a stronger desire for sexual closeness; while the other spouse (often the wife) is aroused by touch. When this difference in arousal sequence is not recognized or appreciated, it can lead to misunderstanding and hurt feelings. Wives are seen negatively for "not being in the mood" and husbands feel rejected and hurt by their wife's apparent lack of interest in sexual intimacy. Husbands are seen negatively for "only wanting one thing" and wives feel objectified or obligated to respond to their husband's initiations. The key is for each spouse to recognize the differences in arousal between them and their spouse and to make choices for each other.

Proper Sources of Revelation

Some of the most common questions I am asked by young adults and married couples pertain to inquiries about Church doctrine on specific aspects of marital sexuality. These questions are often phrased in a way that the individuals want to know the "Church's official stance" on a certain sexual practice or another specific part of marital sexuality. Examples of these questions include, "What is the Church's official stance on oral sex?," "Does the Church approve of wearing lingerie?," and "Do you have to put your temple garments back on right after sex or is it ok to sleep together naked after sex?"

When I am asked these types of questions it is very common for some couples to express that they have been searching for the official church position related to their question, but they have been unable to find one. I often explain that while there are principles that have been revealed by prophets that couples should keep in mind while making personal marital decisions, there is rarely an official church position or doctrine that directs couples in the specifics of such intimate and personal decision making. As the Doctrine and Covenants teaches, "These things remain with you to do according to judgment and the directions of the spirit" (D&C. 62:8). It is important to note that this is the exact same pattern within the Church for matters such as birth control and family planning, frequency of temple worship, specifics of Sabbath day observance, calculating tithing, time spent in church callings, and other specific aspects of personal and family decision making.

While there may be Church teachings or professional information that can inform a couple's decision making around the specifics of their marital sexuality, questions regarding the official stance of the Church on these matters reflect a common misunderstanding in the proper pattern of marital decision-making. When spouses ask these types of questions they are revealing that they believe that the answers to these personal decisions lie outside of themselves, rather than inside their relationship. Proper sexual decision-making in marriage is fostered when couples have confidence in the fact that the best answers to these questions come from *within* their relationship, rather than from *outside* of it. This "turning toward" each other pattern fosters responsiveness and attentiveness between spouses and encourages couples to make choices based on their own personal needs, desires, and experiences, rather than outside comparisons. It also helps spouses not just focus on behaviors, but rather focus on the motives and intents of their sexual desires and expressions—focusing on not only *what* they do, but also on *why* they do what they do.

In a recent conference address, Elder Dallin H. Oaks emphasized to church members the need to turn to proper sources of revelation and instruction in their personal decision-making. He taught,

The personal line is of paramount importance in personal decisions and in the governance of the family. Unfortunately, some members of our church underestimate the need for this direct, personal line. Responding to the undoubted importance of prophetic leadership—the priesthood line, which operates principally to govern heavenly communications on Church matters—some seek to have their priesthood leaders make personal decisions for them, decisions they should make for themselves by inspiration through their personal line. Personal decisions and family governance are principally a matter for the personal line...

We must use both the personal line and the priesthood line in proper balance to achieve the growth that is the purpose of mortal life. If personal religious practice relies too much on the personal line, individualism erases the importance of divine authority. If personal religious practice relies too much on the priesthood line, individual growth suffers. The children of God need both lines to achieve their eternal destiny. The restored gospel teaches both, and the restored Church provides both. (Ensign, Nov 2010, pp. 83 & 86)

Marital sexuality is perhaps the ultimate example of the type of personal decision and aspect of marital governance that should be primarily guided by the personal line of instruction. My experience as a sex educator and therapist is that too many young adults and married couples are seeking to have their priesthood leaders, both living and dead, make these decisions for them. As couples foster a personal pattern of making decisions within the divine triangle of their marriage, they will focus on the reasons and motives of their choices, rather than seeking a one-size-fits-all, pre-

scribed pattern of marital sexuality that has never been given by our prophetic leaders. These types of decisions have always been left between the husband and the wife, as they counsel with the Lord.

This personal approach to decision making also encourages couples to maintain proper boundaries around the specifics of their marital sexuality. Comparisons with other couples are typically not helpful in marriage. It will do you no good to learn about the specifics of sex in other people's marriages—they are not you and your spouse. In fact, learning too much about the details and specifics of other couple's sexuality patterns may be detrimental to a couple's sexual relationship as they strive to mimic the patterns of others, rather than be responsive to the needs and desires of each other. Nothing is more personal than your sexual preferences and patterns. Therefore, your sexual relationship needs to be tailored to your spouse, not to outside expectations or comparisons.

Sexual decision making in marriage

In our book, *Sexual Wholeness in Marriage,* my colleagues and I suggest four principles for couples as they make decision about intimacy in their marriages. I summarize them here. Each principle is paired with a question that couples can reflect on and discuss as they share in the ongoing decisions in their marriage about sexuality and intimacy. Each principle and question can be used to examine a specific sexual decision or experience or to examine broader sexual patterns that exist in the relationship.

Principle #1—Marital Unity

Does this strengthen our relationship with each other and with God?

As we discussed in our foundation chapter on chastity, the two divine purposes for sex are procreation and the strengthening of unity between spouses. As spouses focus on this in their sexual expressions with each other, they will also deepen their sense of alignment with God and his divine plan of happiness. The principle of the divine triangle helps couples appreciate the importance of making intimacy and unity the primary focus of their sexual expression in marriage. At times, marital unity will be strengthened by sexual exploration, creativity, fun, passion, and enjoyment of the sexual response in our own and our spouse's body. However, at other times, marital intimacy is strengthened by expressions of sexual restraint as spouses share emotional and non-arousing forms of intimacy, rather than arousing sexuality.

Principle #2—Couple Consensus

Do we agree about this aspect of our marital sexuality?

The divinely prescribed patterns of cleaving and equal partnership require couples to seek a mutually agreeable and satisfying pattern of sexuality in their marriages. Spouses should never manipulate or force their partner to engage in sexual patterns that they are uncomfortable with or do not consent to. Spouses should seek to understand differences in their sexual preferences and make decisions that reflect a commitment to their spouse's happiness and preferences, as well as their own. This principle puts a high premium on couple communication during and after sex as couples negotiate and find consensus in the specific aspects of their marital intimacy.

Principle #3—Positive Attitudes

Does this reflect a positive and healthy attitude about sexuality?

Whenever spouses encounter differences between themselves about the specifics of their sexuality, it often invites one or both spouses to ponder on why they are uncomfortable with or do not desire something that their partner desires. When this happens, it is helpful for spouses to ponder on the origins of their discomfort or lack of desire. Sometimes these preferences are merely situational, such as not being in the mood, being tired, sick, or preoccupied with something else.

Other times these preferences are ongoing and enduring. Many spouses have developed negative attitudes about sexual expression that stem from family background experiences or other sources that are outside of the marriage relationship.

I believe that it is helpful for spouses to distinguish between healthy inhibitions and unhealthy inhibitions. *Healthy inhibitions* are tied to a spouse's personal preferences and desires for sexual experience, and represent his or her personal values about sexuality. Healthy inhibitions are balanced with positive attitudes about sexuality and a willingness to engage in desired forms of sexual experience and arousal. *Unhealthy inhibitions* are typically an expression of negative sexual conditioning and are tied to past experiences or outside perspectives, rather than true personal preferences. Spouses with unhealthy inhibitions avoid creativity in sexual experience and are often uncomfortable with their sexual response regardless of the specific forms of arousal or stimulation experienced.

Principle #4—Sexual Potential

Does this foster the sexual needs of my spouse and myself?

In sexual decision-making, couples should also recognize that sexual preferences originate from innate sexual needs, not just personal desires or choices. As we have highlighted in our model of sexual wholeness, each of us has an innate sexual nature that gives each of us the capacity and desire for deep and meaningful sexual experience. In a marriage, each spouse and the couple itself have a divinely created *sexual potential*. Healthy sexuality is fostered in marriage as spouses seek to share this sexual potential together. This requires openness, vulnerability, and creativity as spouses learn to share the sexual part of themselves with each other. This is part of a rich, whole, and satisfying marriage.

Becoming one

Becoming one in marriage is based on fostering a selfless approach to sexual intimacy in marriage. Marriage researchers Dr. Linda Waite and Dr. Maggie Gallagher have stated:

> Selfless intimacy can "literally double your sexual pleasure: You get satisfaction not only from your own sexual response but from your partner's as well. . .love and concern for one's partner shifts the focus away from the self in a sexual relationship and toward the other person. This selfless approach to sex, paradoxically, is far more likely to bring sexual satisfaction to both men and women." (The Case for Marriage, 2001, p. 89)

This type of selflessness is similar to the promise the Lord makes to us in the New Testament that if we will lose our life for another, we will find it.

Two Become Three

MARRIAGE AND THE TRANSITION TO PARENTHOOD

CHAPTER 21

> The first commandment that God gave to Adam and Eve pertained to their potential for parenthood as husband and wife. We declare that God's commandment to multiply and replenish the earth remains in force.
>
> *Proclamation on the Family, ¶ 6*

In our society today, we often emphasize the extremes of parenting. On the one hand, the terms people use to describe what it is like to be a parent, particularly a parent of young children, are "crazy," "overwhelming," "exhausting," and "hard." The phrases that accompany this type of talk emphasize that in parenting you have no time for yourself and that being a parent is very time consuming. My experience is that because so many people talk about parenting in these ways, many young people have reservations about becoming a parent some day and are often uncertain if they are up to the challenges of having a baby.

On the other hand, some of the other terms you can hear people use to describe parenting are "rewarding," "meaningful," "life-altering," and "fun." The phrases that accompany this type of talk about parenting include—"I love my kids more than anything in the world" and "becoming a parent is the best thing that ever happened to me!" My experience is that some young people are very excited about becoming a parent and feel confident that it will be a wonderful and fulfilling experience.

The truth of the matter is that both perspectives are right and both perspectives are wrong, too. They are correct in that parenting is both demanding and hard, but it is also rewarding and fulfilling. However, both perspectives are wrong if they are seen as the only perspective of parenting. In fact, there are a number of pitfalls that may arise from seeing parenthood in all negative or all positive ways. The all negative view of parenting may create an avoidance of parenting and, thereby, foster a lack of preparation. The all positive view may create a false sense of confidence

that sends the incorrect message that preparation for parenting is not needed. Either way, a young couple may be ill prepared for the transition to parenthood if they adopt either extreme view of becoming parents.

In God's divine design for families, all "marriage partnerships" should also seek to be *parent partnerships*. This perspective teaches us that when we choose a marriage partner we are also choosing a parenting partner—in the gospel plan these two stewardships are intertwined and interconnected. In this chapter, we consider the impact of the transition to parenthood on marriage relationships. We discuss some aspects of parenting that you should consider in your dating relationships and examine prophetic counsel on topics such as birth control, timing of children, number of children, and infertility treatments. We also consider some foundation principles of optimal parenting that can guide you in forming a healthy co-parent marriage.

Marriage as a Co-Parenting Stewardship

Consider the following quote from the Proclamation on the Family:

"Children are an heritage of the Lord" (Psalms 127:3). Parents have a sacred duty to rear their children in love and righteousness...husbands and wives—mothers and fathers—will be held accountable before God for the discharge of these obligations. (Proclamation, 1995, ¶ 6)

Notice how that in the language of the Proclamation, the stewardship of marriage (i.e., husbands and wives) is interconnected with the stewardship of parenthood. As we noted in the foundations section, one of the key parts of our Father in Heaven's plan is the ongoing process of creation. Marriage is God's ordained institution to bring children into this world and further His plan.

As you come to understand marriage in these sacred terms, then your preparation for marriage should include some consideration of your own and your selected partner's readiness for parenthood.

There are two main co-parenting areas to consider while dating. First, it is important to consider each partner's expectations for parenthood. These expecta-

Devote Your Best Efforts

In February of this year, the First Presidency issued a call to all parents "to devote their best efforts to the teaching and rearing of their children in gospel principles which will keep them close to the Church. The home is the basis of a righteous life, and no other instrumentality can take its place or fulfill its essential functions in carrying forward this God-given responsibility."

. . . by teaching and rearing children in gospel principles, parents can protect their families from corrosive elements. They further counseled parents and children "to give highest priority to family prayer, family home evening, gospel study and instruction, and wholesome family activities. However worthy and appropriate other demands or activities may be, they must not be permitted to displace the divinely-appointed duties that only parents and families can adequately perform."

—Elder Robert D. Hales (Ensign, May 1999)

tions would include personal views about the timing and spacing of children, number of children, work and family patterns after children are born, and other issues related to being co-parents together.

The second part of co-parenting to consider is each partner's level of child-centeredness and the type of parent he or she will likely be in the future. This chapter presents some principles to guide your preparation and dating discussions in each of these areas.

Expectations about Parenthood

Consider another statement from the Proclamation on the Family:

> The first commandment that God gave to Adam and Eve pertained to their potential for parenthood as husband and wife. We declare that God's commandment to multiply and replenish the earth remains in force. (Proclamation 1995. ¶ 6)

The Proclamation on the Family teaches us that God invites all married couples to become co-creators with Him in bringing children into this world. Thus, within God's plan, the focus for couples should be *when* and *how often* they will become parents, not *if* they will become parents. However, some people do marry with the expectation that they will not become parents. If this is the case, this should be clearly communicated while dating to assure that both partners have a common expectation about parenthood.

There are two primary questions all couples must address related to their stewardship over procreation. These questions are—*How many children should we have?* and *When should we have children?* Modern prophets have given couples some important principles to prayerfully consider as they make these decisions together as a couple. On the lds.org Index of Topics website it states:

> Children are one of the greatest blessings in life, and their birth into loving and nurturing families is central to God's purposes for humanity. When husband and wife are physically able, they have the privilege and responsibility to bring children into the world and to nurture them. The decision of how many children to have and when to have them is a private matter for the husband and wife. (lds.org, Index of Topics, Birth Control)

This statement teaches that a married couple's stewardship over procreation is a privilege and responsibility. Bringing children into the world and nurturing them in the gospel is one of the central purposes of the Lord's divine design of marriage. This statement also helps us see how this is a private matter between the couple and the Lord. The Index of Topics on the lds.org website also teaches:

> Those who are physically able have the blessing, joy, and obligation to bear children and to raise a family. This blessing should not be postponed for selfish reasons...Husband and wife are encouraged to pray and counsel together as they plan their families. Issues to consider include the physical and mental health of the mother and father and their capacity to provide the basic necessities of life for their children. (lds.org)

It is the responsibility of each couple to prayerfully decide what constitutes a "selfish reason" for postponing having children or limiting the number of children

they will have. Each couple will be accountable for how they answer this question—but ultimately it is a sacred issue between a couple and the Lord. Elder Dallin H. Oaks counseled:

> How many children should a couple have? All they can care for! Of course, to care for children means more than simply giving them life. Children musts be loved, nurtured, taught, fed, clothed, housed, and well started in their capacities to be good parents themselves. Exercising faith in God's promises to bless them when they are keeping his commandments, many LDS parents have large families. Others seek but are not blessed with children or with the number of children they desire. In a matter as intimate as this, we should not judge one another. (Ensign, November 1993, p. 75)

Birth Control

Associated with a couple's stewardship of procreation is the decision about using birth control. The Index of Topics on the lds.org website teaches:

> Decisions about birth control and the consequences of those decisions rest solely with each married couple. Elective abortion as a method of birth control, however, is contrary to the commandments of God. (lds.org, Index of Topics, Birth Control)

Again, decisions about birth control are a sacred and private matter between the couple and the Lord. There are *three key step*s a couple should take in making these types of decisions. *First,* seek reliable health information in order to make an informed decision. *Second,* counsel together as a married couple in making decisions about when to have children and how many children to have. This is one of the most important aspects of marriage where couples need to be equal partners and seek mutual revelation. The *third* step is to seek inspiration and guidance from the Lord. As couples seek to be aligned with each other and with the Lord in these decisions, they will find greater happiness and meaning in their experiences as a parent.

Dealing with Infertility

In the Garden of Eden, the Lord instructed Adam and Eve to "be fruitful, and multiply, and replenish the earth" (Genesis 1:28). The Proclamation on the Family teaches that "the first commandment that God gave to Adam and Eve pertained to their potential for parenthood" (1995, ¶ 4). Within God's divine design, participating in the ongoing process of creation is intended to be a central part of marriage and family life. However, some couples struggle with infertility and pregnancy loss. Infertility is often a silent and solitary struggle, since it is not visible or life-threatening. In fertility, standing by each other as spouses and making decisions about how to handle infertility issues can be one of the most poignant aspects of a couple's stewardship over procreation.

In medical terms, a couple is considered to be experiencing infertility when they have been trying to conceive for at least 12 months without becoming pregnant. It is estimated that at least 10% of couples in the United States experience infertility. Because of this, it is not uncommon for couples to have to make decisions related to infertility as part of their stewardship over procreation.

In our modern society, there are now options such as in-vitro fertilization, infertility medications, and protocols to assist couples with insemination and conception. Many of these procedures offer hope to couples who are having a tough time getting pregnant. However, in the *Church Handbook of Instructions* couples are "strongly discouraged" to avoid fertility treatments that do not maintain the husband and wife relationship. This means that infertility procedures should only utilize the sperm and egg from the father and mother themselves, and not involve a sperm donor who is not the father or a "surrogate mother" who will not raise the child herself. These types of fertility treatments introduce ambiguities into the parent-child relationship that can be problematic as the child comes of age. Of course, many couples choose adoption as a way to establish an eternal family. Adopted children who are sealed to married couples receive all of the blessings of the temple.

Child-Centeredness and Parenting Principles

As you ponder on your own readiness for being a parent and upon the readiness of anyone you become involved with while dating, you should remember that there are two types of parenting behaviors. The first is what can be called *direct parenting*—this is what we typically think about when we think about being a parent. Direct parenting involves direct interactions with a child such as nurturing, teaching, playing, and disciplining.

The second type of parenting is called *indirect parenting*. Indirect parenting refers to how a parent conducts their life when he or she is not in the physical presence of their child. In simple terms, it is a parent's example to their child. When each of us becomes a parent, we are a parent 24 hours a day, seven days a week. What we do with our time, how we treat people, our dedication to the gospel, and how we take care of our spouse will all influence our children. Also, do not forget that your children will not just pay attention to your example beginning on the day they were born. Your children will also want to know about your choices and actions when you were a teenager and young adult. In a very real way, you are already a parent—because you are already making choices that will set an example to your children in the future. Live for the day that you can say to your child—*do as I did* and *do as I am doing*, not *do what I am saying* or *do what I wish I had done*. Parenting is best understood as a lifelong process and experience.

Parenting Styles

Developmental psychologists and family scholars have been interested in how parents influence children's development for nearly 100 years. One of the most validated research findings in this line of research is the concept of *parenting styles* developed by Dr. Diana Baumrind. Of all the research findings we study in this whole book, parenting styles is perhaps the most validated and researched. Learning about parenting styles can help you as you strive to become and find a right person for successful parenting.

Dr. Baumrind's model of parenting styles is based on two central dimensions of parenting behavior: parental warmth and parental control. *Parental warmth* (also referred to as parental responsiveness or supportiveness) refers to "the extent to which parents intentionally foster individuality, self-regulation, and self-assertion by being attuned, supportive, and acquiescent to children's special needs and demands" (Baumrind, 1991, The Journal of Early Adolescence). *Parental control* (also referred to as behavioral control or demandingness) refers to "the claims parents make

on children to become integrated into the family whole, by their maturity demands, supervision, disciplinary efforts and willingness to confront the child who disobeys" (Baumrind, 1991, pp. 61–62).

Categorizing parents according to whether they are high or low on warmth and control creates a typology of four parenting styles: *permissive, coercive, authoritative,* and *uninvolved*. Each of these parenting styles reflects different naturally occurring patterns of parental values, practices, and behaviors and a distinct balance of warmth and control.

1. *Permissive Parents* (also referred to as "indulgent" or "nondirective") are warm and supportive, but struggle to set limits and help their children regulate their behaviors. According to Dr. Baumrind permissive parents are "nontraditional and lenient, do not require mature behavior, allow considerable self-regulation, and avoid confrontation" (Baumrind, 1991, p. 62).

2. *Authoritarian Parents* are highly demanding and directive, but not warm and responsive. "They are obedience- and status-oriented, and expect their orders to be obeyed without explanation" (Baumrind, 1991, p. 62). Authoritarian parents provide well-ordered and structured environments with clearly stated rules. However, there is less expression of affection with little involvement in the lives of their children.

3. *Authoritative Parents* combine warmth with high expectations and regulation. According to Dr. Baumrind, authoritative parents "monitor and impart clear standards for their children's conduct. They are assertive, but not intrusive and restrictive. Their disciplinary methods are supportive, rather than punitive. They want their children to be assertive as well as socially responsible, and self-regulated as well as cooperative" (Baumrind, 1991, p. 62).

Baumrind's Parenting Typology

	High Warmth	Low Warmth
High Control	Authoritative	Coercive (Authoritarian)
Low Control	Permissive (Indulgent)	Uninvolved (Neglectful)

4. *Uninvolved Parents* are low in both warmth and control. In extreme cases, this parenting style encompass neglect and abandonment. Thankfully, research has shown that this parenting style is not as common as the other three. Because of this, Baumrind's model is sometimes presented as having only three styles.

In addition to differing on warmth and control, parenting styles also differ in the extent to which they are characterized by a third dimension: *psychological control*. Psychological control "refers to control attempts that intrude into the psychological and emotional development of the child" (Barber, 1996, p. 329) through use of parenting practices such as guilt induction, withdrawal of love, or shaming. According to Dr. Darling,

> One key difference between authoritarian and authoritative parenting is in the dimension of psychological control. Both authoritarian and authoritative parents place high demands on their children and expect their children to behave appropriately and obey parental rules. Authoritarian parents, however, also expect their children to accept their judgments, values, and goals without questioning. In contrast, authoritative parents are more open to give and take with their children and make greater use of explanations. Thus, although authoritative and authoritarian parents are equally high in behavioral control, authoritative parents tend to be low in psychological control, while authoritarian parents tend to be high. (Darling, 1999, Parenting Styles and Its Correlates)

Parenting styles have been found to predict child wellbeing in the domains of social competence, academic performance, psychosocial development, and problem behavior. Dr. Darling found that research based on parent interviews, child reports, and parent observations consistently finds:

> Children and adolescents whose parents are authoritative rate themselves and are rated by objective measures as more socially and instrumentally competent than those whose parents are nonauthoritative. (Baumrind, 1991; Weiss & Schwarz, 1996; Miller et al., 1993)

Children and adolescents whose parents are uninvolved perform most poorly in all domains. In general, parental responsiveness predicts social competence and psychosocial functioning, while parental demandingness is associated with instrumental competence and behavioral control (i.e., academic performance and deviance). These findings indicate:

> Children and adolescents from authoritarian families (high in demandingness, but low in responsiveness) tend to perform moderately well in school and be uninvolved in problem behavior, but they have poorer social skills, lower self-esteem, and higher levels of depression.
>
> Children and adolescents from indulgent homes (high in responsiveness, low in demandingness) are more likely to be involved in problem behavior and perform less well in school, but they have higher self-esteem, better social skills, and lower levels of depression. (Darling, 1999)

Parenting styles provide a simple, yet insightful way to think of parenting behaviors that predict child wellbeing across a wide range of outcomes. Both parental warmth and parental control are important components of good parenting. Authoritative parenting, which balances clear, high parental demands with emotional responsiveness and recognition of child autonomy, is one of the most consistent family predictors of competence from early childhood through adolescence.

THE TRANSITION TO PARENTHOOD

Research has shown that the transition to parenthood can impact a couple's relationship. The most current research shows that the transition to parenthood impacts different marriages in different ways. For about 1/3 to 2/3 of couples they experience a decline in relationship satisfaction after they become parents. However, the other 1/3 to 2/3 of

couples report stable or increased levels of marital satisfaction (see Roy et al., Transition to Parenthood, 2014). So, what determines if a couple will struggle with the transition to parenthood or if their relationship will stay strong as they bring a baby into their home? Research studies point to three main factors:

1. The Quality of the Pre-Parent Relationship

The best predictor of how a couple will handle the transition to parenthood is the quality of friendship and partnership in their relationship prior to the birth of their child. Becoming parents tends to accentuate the positive or negative aspects of a relationship. If a couple communicates well and practices marital virtues such as forgiveness and sacrifice before the child comes, they will likely continue to do these things after a child is born.

On the other hand, if spouses do not manage conflict well or struggle with making decisions together, it is likely that these problems will be compounded as they add co-parent roles to their relationship. It would be unwise to view having a baby as a way to "save a troubled marriage" or that parenting will make a couple closer and more responsive to each other. It is far better to address these issues early in a relationship and not allow them to linger into the co-parenting stage of marriage.

2. The Quality of the Marital Friendship and Communication

Even in the best of situations, becoming new parents can be stressful for a young couple. Lack of sleep and the demands of caring for a new child alter life in dramatic ways. Babies also tend to bring new concerns about finances, daily schedules, interactions with in-laws, and other aspects of parenthood. Because of these new expectations, researchers have found that couple communication is particularly important during the transition to parenthood. In particular, couples need to practice *meta-communication* as they talk about how they are doing as a couple and find new ways to do things that will work for both partners and their baby. Because of the stress that can accompany this stage of life, couples should also pay close attention to the level of friendship in their relationship. Couples should find ways to nurture their relationship with each other. Making sure that there are still moments of closeness, communication, and caring in the marriage has special symbolic meaning during the early parenting years.

3. Successful Establishment of Work-Family Patterns

Research also finds that couples who can establish agreeable patterns of work, school, housework, and childcare report more positive experiences with the transition to parenthood. While dating, couples should see if they are in alignment about work-family

patterns when they become parents. Will the mother stay at home full-time? How will one or both parents finish schooling? How will family expenses be handled? When couples have similar expectations for these patterns, it helps them find consensus of how to enact these values when a child is actually born.

Marital Distress

Divorce Decisions and Marital Turnarounds
CHAPTER 22

> Divorce is not an all-purpose solution, and it often creates long-term heartache... under the law of the Lord, a marriage, like a human life, is a precious, living thing. If our bodies are sick, we seek to heal them. We do not give up... The same should be true of our marriages, and if we seek Him, the Lord will help us and heal us. Latter-day Saint spouses should do all within their power to preserve their marriages.
>
> *Elder Dallin H. Oaks*

In this final chapter, we discuss the topic of marital distress and divorce decision making. You should study this chapter with two purposes. First, apply the principles of this chapter to your own marriage. If you ever find yourself in a distressed marriage and considering divorce, the principles discussed in this chapter can help you as you make a prayerful and informed decision. As you have learned throughout this book, your chances of being in a distressed marriage are very low when you and your spouse embrace the Lord's divine design for marriage, which includes all of the principles you have learned in this book. However, it is important for each of us to have a sound understanding of what our prophetic leaders have taught us about divorce and healing distressed relationships.

The second purpose of this chapter is to prepare you to counsel and assist others who stand at the crossroads of divorce. While the likelihood of your own marriage ending in divorce may be quite low, the likelihood that you will at some time interact with a family member, relative, friend, work colleague, ward member, or another person considering divorce in their own marriage is quite high. What principles will guide your counsel in these conversations? Should divorce be avoided in all circumstances? If there are situations that warrant divorce, what are they? Can distressed marriages become happy marriages again? These are the critical questions each of us must confront when we ourselves or someone we know stands at the crossroads of divorce.

This chapter has three main sections. In the first section, we discuss prophetic teachings about divorce. Of course, this discussion builds upon the foundation principles of *cleaving, covenant* and the *divine triangle of marriage*. This chapter also builds upon the marital virtue of *loyalty* and the couple processes of *managing conflict* and *solution-focused conversations*. When couples are confronted by the wolf of possible divorce, they determine more clearly than at any other time if they will act as a shepherd or a hireling. Furthermore, the triadic nature of the marriage relationship (i.e., God, ourselves, and our spouse) reminds us that our marriage covenant is not only with our spouse, but is also with our Father in Heaven.

The second section of this chapter draws from an article entitled, *Marriage Crossroads: Why Divorce Is Often Not the Best Option* written by Dr. Brent Barlow for the Utah Marriage Commission. Dr. Barlow was the lead instructor for the Preparation for Marriage course at BYU for more than 30 years. In his article, Dr. Barlow has pulled together numerous sources of research information for couples to consider before they decide to divorce. This information is presented in a way that is in harmony with the principles our prophetic leaders have taught us about divorce decision making.

The final section briefly discusses new research on *marital turnarounds*. When most spouses reach the crossroads of divorce, they tell themselves that

they have only two options—stay in the marriage and be miserable or get out and be happy. However, new research findings show that there are two other possibilities that are far more likely to occur if a couple divorces. These are "get out and be miserable" and "stay in and be happy." We'll discuss what these findings mean for couples considering divorce and the hope they offer for distressed marriages.

Prophetic teachings about divorce

A key question for each of us to answer is *What does the Church teach us about divorce*? Despite the importance of this topic, I have been surprised over the years at how many members of the church struggle to appropriately answer this question. It is important for each of us to give prayerful consideration to the counsel of prophets on such an important matter. President Gordon B. Hinckley has said,

> There may be now and again a legitimate cause for divorce. I am not one to say that it is never justified. But I say without hesitation that this plague among us, which seems to be growing everywhere, is not of God, but rather is the work of the adversary of righteousness and peace and truth. (Ensign, May 1991)

President David O. McKay taught,

> There may be circumstances which make the continuance of the marriage state a greater evil than divorce. But these are extreme cases—they are the mistakes, the calamities in the realm of marriage. (Conference Report, 1964, p. 5)

Both of these quotes emphasize that there are errors of belief at both extremes when it comes to divorce. First, there is the error of being too accepting of divorce. Prophetic leaders have repeatedly taught that divorce is a growing evil in society and that spouses should not consider it lightly. This is particularly true of temple marriages where couples have entered into sacred covenants with each other and with God. However, in the context of stressing the sacred importance of marriage covenants, prophetic leaders have also taught that there are some marital circumstances that may warrant divorce. These circumstances are "the calamities in the realm of marriage," as President McKay stated. They are not the typical ups and downs of married life.

What Is "Just Cause" for Divorce?

Given these prophetic statements, what constitutes an "extreme case" that creates a legitimate cause for divorce? As with most aspects of the gospel, prophets and apostles have taught us principles, rather than precepts about what types of circumstances "make the continuance of the marriage state a greater evil than divorce." There is not list of behaviors or sins that justify divorce. Rather it is a principle-based decision that should be made with confirmation from the Holy Spirit. Elder Dallin H. Oaks said,

> The kind of marriage required for exaltation—eternal in duration and godlike in quality—does not contemplate divorce. In the temples of the Lord, couples are married for all eternity. But some marriages do not progress toward that ideal…There are many good Church members who have been divorced…many of you are innocent victims—members whose former spouses persistently betrayed sacred covenants or abandoned or refused to perform marriage responsibilities for an extended period of time. Members who have experienced such abuse have firsthand knowledge of circumstances worse than divorce. (Ensign, May 2007, p. 70)

Notice that Elder Oaks defines eternal marriage in both terms of length ("eternal in duration") and quality ("godlike in quality"), thus to keep our covenants in marriage is to continually strive to create a high quality marriage that is pleasing to both spouses. It is not enough to merely "endure to the end" in low quality marriages. Our covenant to live according to the rites and laws of eternal marriage is a commitment to how we live, not just how long we will live.

Perhaps the most insightful teaching we have on the question of what may constitute a legitimate cause for getting divorced comes from Pres. James E. Faust. He said,

> Those marriages performed in our temples, meant to be eternal relationships, then, become the most sacred covenants we can make… What, then, might be "just cause" for breaking the covenants of marriage? … In my opinion, "just cause" should be nothing less serious than a prolonged and apparently irredeemable relationship which is destructive of a person's dignity as a human being.
>
> At the same time, I have strong feelings about what is not provocation for breaking the sacred covenants of marriage. Surely it is not simply "mental distress," nor "personality differences," nor "having grown apart," nor having "fallen out of love." This is especially so when there are children. (Ensign, May 1993, pp. 36–37)

According to President Faust, one must consider the *consequences* of marital distress, as well as the *causes* for the distress when making a decision about divorce. When interactions between spouses become "destructive of a person's dignity as a human being" the marriage is bringing about negative and unrighteous consequences, rather than divine and righteous purposes. This is a perversion of the divine institution of marriage—an evil greater than divorce.

Notice also how President Faust refers to a "prolonged and apparently irredeemable relationship" as part of the criteria for legitimate divorce. *How can someone know if a relationship is irredeemable?* The only way to know this is after spouses have done everything within their power to try to redeem the relationship. Only when all options have been exhausted could this criterion be met. Thus, divorce should only be considered after a prolonged and extensive effort to save the marriage. In many ways, divorce can be viewed like an amputation—to be prevented and avoided with all vigor and persistence and only embraced after all other solutions have been attempted—but sometimes unavoidable for survival.

The metaphor of an amputation is helpful, because it helps us see that divorce should never be the first option for a distressed couple. If we have an infected foot or leg, we would try medication, therapy, surgery, and any other viable medical option before we would turn to amputation. Every effort would be made to save the leg. The only time that medical professionals turn to the option of amputation is to save the life of the individual. The same should be true of divorce. Plus, the metaphor of an amputation reminds us that even when an amputation is necessary, there are still long term consequences of the procedure. Amputees must adapt and adjust to their lost limb for the rest of their lives. The same is true of divorce, particularly when a couple has children. You can end your marriage to someone, but you cannot end your parenting partnership. You will continue to associate and interact throughout the rest of your lives as you co-parent your children. This requires long term adaptation and a change of life.

> "Those marriages performed in our temples, meant to be eternal relationships, then, become the most sacred covenants we can make ... What, then, might be "just cause" for breaking the covenants of marriage? ... In my opinion, "just cause" should be nothing less serious than a prolonged and apparently irredeemable relationship which is destructive of a person's dignity as a human being.
>
> -President James E. Faust

At the Crossroads

In his article *Marriage Crossroads: Why Divorce Is Often Not the Best Option*, Dr. Brent Barlow summarized some key advice from relationship experts for couples contemplating divorce. First, in support of the teachings of the prophets, experts have emphasized how important of a decision this is for couples—one that should never be taken lightly. Therapist and author Michele Weiner Davis has noted:

> The decision to divorce or remain together to work things out is one of the most important decisions you will ever make. It is crucial for those considering divorce to anticipate what lies ahead in order to make informed decisions. Too often the fallout from divorce is far more devastating than many people realize when contemplating the move. (Divorce Busting, 1992, p. 25)

Dr. Barlow also emphasized that while advocating marriage, we must be sensitive to those who have chosen to terminate their marriage. There are legitimate reasons or grounds for divorce. An estimated 30 percent of the divorces in the U.S. involve marital rela-

Chapter 22: Marital Distress

tionships with a high degree of conflict. Sometimes violence, physical and mental abuse and/or threat of life to spouse and children are also present in these highly conflicted relationships. As such, divorce in these situations is most often in the best interest of those involved. Chronic addiction or substance abuse, psychosis or extreme mental illness, and physical or mental abuse are also situations or conditions that experts site as fitting this type of situation. Dr. Barlow taught:

> Couples who divorce, particularly for the reasons noted, often need the help and support of family, friends, neighbors, religious leaders and others in their respective communities. This is particularly so where children are involved. The adjustment to divorce is often difficult and apparently lasts for a considerable period of time. Legal assistance is needed, and sometimes couples may need counseling or therapy before, during and after the separation for themselves and their children, if they have them. Competent counselors and therapists are available to assist in this transition. Many couples today are also utilizing the services of divorce mediation organizations that can often help lessen the trauma of divorce both before and after it occurs. (Marriage Crossroads, 2003, p. 22)

Together with Dr. Barlow, I offer my sincere hope for the future for husbands and wives who have chosen to divorce. But, with him I also offer my encouragement to the numerous married couples at the crossroads to try to stay together, where possible, and work through their differences and difficulties.

Points to Ponder

If you are married and trying to decide whether to divorce or stay married; or are counseling someone in that situation, Dr. Barlow recommends that you carefully consider the following eight items before you make your informed decision:

1. The Other 70 Percent of Divorces

When we note that 30 percent of divorces involve couples in highly conflicted marriages, a question arises about the other 70 percent: Should they divorce or stay married? There are, perhaps, legitimate reasons for separating in about 10 percent of these relationships as well.

One study reported that the major reasons marriages fail are (in rank order) (1) infidelity, (2) no longer in love, (3) emotional problems, (4) financial problems, (5) sexual problems, (6) problems with in-laws, (7) neglect of children, (8) physical abuse, (9) alcohol, (10) job conflicts (11) communication problems, and (12) married too young (Olson and DeFrain, p. 522). It is interesting to note that "physical abuse" was ranked as number eight in reasons for divorce, and "no longer in love" ranked as number two. Many marriages seem to end from burn-out rather than blowout. A significant number of these couples could work through their problems, revive their love, and stay married if they desired and worked at it. Only the husband and wife involved in a particular marriage, however, can make the decision whether to stay married or divorce since they are the ones who must ultimately abide by the consequences of the decision.

It is becoming increasingly evident, however, to

those who study marriage trends in the United States, that an estimated 50 to 60 percent of divorces could, and perhaps should, be avoided in the best interests of those involved. Consider the following statements:

> The divorce revolution—the steady displacement of a marriage culture by a culture of divorce and unwed parenthood—has failed. It has created terrible hardships for children, incurred insupportable social costs, and failed to deliver on its promise of greater adult happiness. The time has come to shift the focus of national attention from divorce to marriage and to rebuild a family culture based on enduring marital relationships. (Marriage In America: A Report to the Nation, 1995, p. 4–5)

After acknowledging the necessity for some divorces, therapist Diane Medved wrote the rest of her book stating her case against divorce, thus the title of her book—*Case Against Divorce*. At the beginning she makes the following observation and suggestion:

> It is finally time to renounce—openly and clearly—the self-serving platitudes about independence and fulfillment and look at the reality of divorce. We act too frequently as if every infirm marriage deserves to die, based simply upon the emotional report of one distressed partner. Rather than viewing a separation first with alarm, we're full of sympathy for a divorcing friend, and we offer understanding of the temporary insanity involved in severing old ties. Still influenced by the "do your own thing" era we don't act constructively. We don't take a husband (or wife) by the shoulders and shake him. We don't shout in his ear that he might be making a disastrous mistake. Even if we care immensely about him, we feel it's too intrusively "judgmental" to do more than step back and say, "Okay if that's what you want," and close our eyes to the consequences. My research suggests that this is more cruelty than friendship (The Case Against Divorce, 1989, p. 8).

Medved also notes:

> If you hear someone for whom you have any feeling at all hinting at separation, instead of tacitly endorsing the move, instantly protest. Nearly every marriage has something worth preserving, something that can be restored. Revitalizing a relationship brings triumph and ongoing reward. . . Avoiding divorce spares those concerned from the greatest trauma of their lives. (Case Against Divorce, p. 11)

2. What Are the Benefits of a Stable Marriage?

Several researchers and authors have reported the importance of a stable marriage for adults. In his book *Why Marriage Matters*, Glenn T. Stanton has written:

> As the researchers have gone to press with their work and produced an enormous literature, one of the most consistent findings is that men and women do markedly better in all measures of specific and general wellbeing when they are married, compared to any of their unmarried counterparts. Married couples are healthier—physically and mentally—and they live longer, enjoy a more fulfilled life, and take better care of themselves (and each other). This has been shown consistently over decades, but it is rarely mentioned in the popular debate on the family. One of social science's best kept secrets is that marriage is much more than a legal agreement between two people. Marriage truly makes a difference in the lives of men and women. (1997, p. 73)

Three other authors, David Larson, James P. Swyers and Susan S. Larson, also noted the following in their book, The Costly Consequences of Divorce:

> What would you say if someone told you that a particular social bond could add years to your life and ensure your children a better education and economic livelihood? Furthermore, what would you say if you also found out that breaking this social bond was only slightly less harmful to your health than smoking a pack or more of cigarettes per day and could significantly increase your risk of depression, alcohol abuse, and committing suicide? And what would you say if you found out that this social

bond that was potentially so beneficial to you and your children's health and personal wellbeing was marriage? Truly, the research is striking. For decades, studies have shown that the married live longer and have a lower risk of a variety of physical and psychological illness than the unmarried. (1995, p.1)

3. WHAT CAN BE THE IMPACT OF DIVORCE ON CHILDREN?

It is obvious that a large number of children of divorced parents survive the experience and later become capable and stable adults. But it is also becoming increasingly evident that many children of divorce are at risk for developing detrimental behaviors, personality disorders and disruptive lifestyles. Some of the variables in adjustment of children to parental divorce are (1) age of child at divorce, (2) amount of conflict in the marriage, (3) access to both parents after the divorce, (4) adjustment to a step-parent, if there is one, and (5) access to other nurturing adults during the childhood years.

In the executive summary of the forty-nine page report released June 5, 2000, titled "The Effects of Divorce on America," authors Patrick F. Fagan and Robert Rector of the Heritage Foundation observed the following:

> Each year, over 1 million American children suffer the divorce of their parents; moreover, half of the children born this year to parents who are married will see their parents divorce before they turn 18. Mounting evidence in social science journals demonstrates that the devastating physical, emotional, and financial effects that divorce is having on these children will last well into adulthood and affect future generations. Among these broad and damaging effects are the following:
>
> Children whose parents have divorced are increasingly the victims of abuse. They exhibit more health, behavioral, and emotional problems, are involved more frequently in crime and drug abuse, and have higher rates of suicide.
>
> Children of divorced parents perform more poorly in reading, spelling, and math. They are also more likely to repeat a grade and to have higher dropout rates and lower rates of college graduation.
>
> Families with children that were not poor before the divorce see their income drop as much as 50 percent. Almost 50 percent of the parents with children that are going through a divorce move into poverty after the divorce.
>
> Religious worship, which has been linked to better health, longer marriages, and better family life drops after the parents divorce.
>
> The divorce of parents, even if it is amicable, tears apart the fundamental unit of American society. Today, according to the Federal Reserve Board's 1995 Survey of Consumer Finance, only 42 percent of children aged 14–18 live in a "first marriage" family—an intact two parent family. It should be no surprise to find that divorce is having such effects on society.

Recent research indicates that the majority of children of divorced parents do not manifest the identified problems that can be outwardly noticed or measured. But the absence of an observable behavior disorder does not mean an absence of emotional distress. A significant number of children of divorce apparently do experience a variety of emotional problems that often go undetected until late adolescence or early and even later adulthood. One of the most prevalent sources of distress reported was the children's distant relationship or infrequent contact with

their fathers. Many children blamed their fathers for the divorce, and some were still angry with their fathers later in their adult lives. One-third of the children studied doubted their fathers even loved them. (Laumann-Billings and Emery, pp. 671–687)

In their book, *The Case For Marriage,* Linda J. Waite And Maggie Gallagher make this summary observation:

> Less than a third of divorces are ending angry high-conflict marriages. Here's what the best evidence suggests: most current divorces leave children worse off, educationally and financially, than they would have been if their parents stay married, and a majority of divorces leave children psychologically worse off as well. Only a minority of divorces in this country are taking place in families where children are likely to benefit in any way from their parents' separation. (2000, pp. 147–148)

4. Many Later Regret Divorce

Many who divorce are satisfied with the decision to end their marriage. But it is becoming increasing evident that a significant number, as many as one-third, later regret their divorce. This is particularly so when the long-term consequences are experienced or actually encountered. Seriously consider not only the apparent immediate benefits of divorce but also the long-term consequences many others have experienced. Divorce is a decision that many make but later regret. And most divorces are forever.

Once people have made the decision to divorce, how do they later feel about the choice? There may be some immediate relief in many instances right after the divorce, but how do husbands and wives feel months or even years later? Many studies show that many divorced people report that they regret their decision and wish they had done more to save their marriage.

5. Should Couples Work on Their Marriage?

If a large number of couples who do divorce later regret the decision, the logical question arises: Should couples try to restore what they once had in their marriage? The answer to this question is a simple "yes," in a large number of cases. Many have learned to do so as reported by Michele Weiner Davis in her book Divorce Busting:

> It appears that more and more couples are beginning to take a skeptical view of divorce. . . I believe that people are beginning to realize how devastating divorce is—emotionally, financially, and spiritually—for everyone involved. With enough time under our

belts to have observed the results of rampant divorce, we are beginning to recognize the price we have paid for the freedom of disposable marriages. (1992, p. 27)

Nearly all, if not all, marriages go through peaks and valleys, times of highs and lows. Most of married life, however, is spent cycling between these two extremes. During difficult times, between 40 and 50 percent of currently married spouses seek divorce and follow through with it. And, as previously noted, about 20 percent of those who stay married consider leaving a marriage partner but later choose not to do so.

Apparently many married couples seriously contemplate divorce, may even see a lawyer or file for divorce, and then decide not to proceed with the terminating process. Dr. Barlow in his article reports that in Utah, for example, in the year 2000, 12,574 couples filed for divorce, but only 10,138 divorces were actually granted (CORIS Database, 2000). Thus, for various reasons, one in five couples who filed for divorce decided not to continue the termination process. Their decision may be well-founded. The vast majority of unhappily married couples in the United States apparently do improve their relationship if they stay married.

Seek to Heal Your Marriage

In a landmark conference talk, Elder Dallin H. Oaks counseled Church members to seek the healing power within the Atonement of Jesus Christ if they find themselves in a distressed marriage.

> Now I speak to married members, especially to any who may be considering divorce. I strongly urge you and those who advise you to face up to the reality that for most marriage problems, the remedy is not divorce but repentance. Often the cause is not incompatibility but selfishness. The first step is not separation but reformation. Divorce is not an all-purpose solution, and it often creates long-term heartache...under the law of the Lord, a marriage, like a human life, is a precious, living thing. If our bodies are sick, we seek to heal them. We do not give up. While there is any prospect of life, we seek healing again and again. The same should be true of our mar-

riages, and if we seek Him, the Lord will help us and heal us. Latter-day Saint spouses should do all within their power to preserve their marriages. (Ensign, May 2007, p. 71)

My experience as a marriage counselor is that there are two benefits for spouses who "do all within their power to preserve their marriages." First, the most likely benefit is that you will be able to heal and restore your marriage. I have seen numerous cases where spouses have emerged from troubled marriages to have strong and resilient relationships. I have witnessed couples such as these have a deep confidence in their relationships because they have withstood such troubles. It is like a raft on a river that has already endured Class-4 rapids without tipping over. There is not much to fear because they have already withstood the worst the river has to offer.

The second benefit of striving with all diligence to preserve our marriages comes in the case that the marriage does end in divorce. My experience is that

spouses who have done all that they can do to save their marriage are able to find a deeper sense of peace after their divorce than individuals who have not made such efforts. Many ex-spouses are troubled by doubts that they did not do all that they could have done to preserve their marriage. Sometimes these doubts create a crisis of faith as these individuals question whether or not God approves of their actions. When we seek to know and do the will of the Lord in these matters, we can have the confidence that our choices will be accepted by the Lord.

Marital Turnarounds

I want to make sure that you pay careful attention to what Dr. Barlow talked about with couples seeking to repair their marriage—this is what marriage experts call *marital turnarounds*. The Institute of American Values published a study entitled "Does Divorce Make People Happy?: Findings from a Study of Unhappy Marriages" (2002). Using a large national sample, this study found that on average unhappily married adults who divorced were no happier five years after the divorce than were equally unhappily married adults who stayed married when rated on any of 12 separate measures of psychological wellbeing. *Moreover, two-thirds of unhappily married people who remained married reported that their marriages were happy five years later. Even among couples who had rated their marriages as very unhappy, 80 percent said they were happily married five years later.* The data suggests that if a couple is unhappy, the chances of their being happily married five years later are 64% if they remain together but only 19% if they divorce and remarry. The report seems to crumble the myth that divorce typically makes unhappily married adults happier.

So how did the unhappy couples become happy five years later? The study found three underlying principles. The first is *endurance*. For some couples, if they can merely stick it out through the rough times, chances are things will eventually improve. Another section of couples were more aggressive. They *actively sought out help* from others, including therapists, parents, in-laws, or other relatives, or even by threatening divorce. In the third section, individuals were found *seeking their own happiness* in other ways, even if they could not improve their marital happiness.

The following are additional highlights of the report.

- Divorce did not reduce symptoms of depression for unhappily married adults, or raise their self-esteem, on average, compared to unhappy spouses who stayed married.
- The vast majority of divorces (74 percent) happened to adults who had been happily married five years previously.
- Unhappy marriages were less common than unhappy spouses. This means that most divorces occur when one spouse still wants the relationship to continue.
- Staying married did not typically trap unhappy spouses in violent relationships.
- Spouses who turned their marriages around seldom reported that counseling played a key role.

Most marriages simply outlasted their problems and restored their relationship.

In their book, *The Case For Marriage*, Waite and Gallagher, conclude:

> Decades of social science research have confirmed the deepest intuitions of the human heart: as frightening, exhilarating, and improbable as this wild vow of constancy may seem, there is no substitute. When love seeks permanence, a safe home for children, who long for both parents, when men and women look for someone they can count on, there are no substitutes. The word for what we want is marriage. (2000, p. 203)

Sometimes people fall into the trap of believing that marriages are like fruit, if they go bad all you can do is throw them out. This highly regarded study has challenged this belief. Marriages are not like fruit—they can and do turn around. These findings add a second witness to what Elder Oaks and other prophetic leaders have taught about healing our marriages. Particularly with the help of the Savior, we can heal our marriages if needed. In a world of disposable marriages, these principles give us hope even in the face of the hurt and anger of a troubled marriage. Let us all contribute to a culture of marriage by doing all that we can to preserve our own and others' marriages.

Figure Credits

The following figures were illustrated by April Martin:

Intro-1, 1-2, 1-3, 1-6, 1-16, 1-18, 2-8, 2-9, 2-14, 3-4, 3-10, 3-12, 4-8, 4-13, 4-18, 5-6, 5-17, 6-3, 6-9, 6-17, 6-19, 6-23, 7-6, 7-11, 7-12, 8-4, 8-6, 8-7, 8-9, 8-15, 8-20, 9-3, 9-6, 9-7, 9-8, 10-2, 10-5, 11-8, 11-10, 12-4, 13-3, 13-10, S-3-2, 14-2, 14-6, 14-7, 15-2, 15-3, 15-5, 15-15, 16-7, 16-22, 17-6, 17-15, 17-16, 17-19, 18-4, 18-6, 18-9, 19-4, 19-6, 19-13, 20-5, 20-7, 20-9, 21-3, 21-10, 22-5, ,

The following images are courtesy lds.org:

Intro-3, Intro-4, Intro-5, 1-5, 1-9, 1-10, 1-12, 1-14, 1-15, 1-17, 2-1, 2-3, 2-4, 2-5, 2-6, 2-7, 2-10, 2-15, 2-16, 2-17, 3-1, 3-5, 3-9, 3-14, 4-1, 4-3, 4-4, 4-5, 4-6, 4-7, 4-10, 4-22, 5-5, 5-7, 5-10, 5-13, 5-14, 6-5, 6-6, 6-11, 6-22, 6-24, 6-26, 7-17, 7-22, 8-2, 8-17, 9-1, 9-4, 10-15, 10-17, 10-18, 10-20, 10-21, 11-1, 11-6, 11-11, 11-12, 12-1, 12-3, 12-12, S-3-1, 14-5, 14-8, 15-6, 15-7, 15-14, 16-6, 16-8, 16-9, 16-10, 16-11, 16-14, 16-19, 16-20, 16-21, 16-23, 16-25, 17-1, 20-19, 20-20

The following images are courtesy stockphotosecrets.com:

Preface-2, 20-12

The following images are courtesy adobestock.com:

Preface-1, Preface-3, Preface-4, Preface-5, Intro-2, Intro-6, Intro-7, 1-1, 1-4, 1-7, 1-8, 1-11, 1-13, 2-2, 2-11, 2-12, 2-13, 3-2, 3-3, 3-6, 3-7, 3-8, 3-11, 3-13, 4-2, 4-9, 4-11, 4-12, 4-14, 4-15, 4-16, 4-17, 4-19, 4-20, 4-21, 5-1, 5-2, 5-3, 5-4, 5-8, 5-9, 5-11, 5-12, 5-15, 5-16, 5-18, 5-19, 6-1, 6-2, 6-4, 6-7, 6-8, 6-10, 6-12, 6-13, 6-14, 6-15, 6-16, 6-18, 6-20, 6-21, 6-25, 7-1, 7-2, 7-3, 7-4, 7-5, 7-7, 7-8, 7-9, 7-10, 7-13, 7-14, 7-15, 7-16, 7-18, 7-19, 7-20, 7-21, 7-23, 8-1, 8-3, 8-5, 8-8, 8-10, 8-11, 8-12, 8-13, 8-14, 8-16, 8-18, 8-19, 8-21, 9-2, 9-5, 10-1, 10-3, 10-4, 10-6, 10-7, 10-8, 10-9, 10-10, 10-11, 10-12, 10-13, 10-14, 10-16, 10-19, 11-2, 11-3, 11-4, 11-5, 11-7, 11-9, 12-2, 12-5, 12-6, 12-7, 12-8, 12-9, 12-10, 12-11, 12-13, 12-14, 12-15, 13-1, 13-2, 13-4, 13-5, 13-6, 13-7, 13-8, 13-9, 13-11, 13-12, 13-13, 13-14, 14-1, 14-3, 14-4, 15-1, 15-4, 15-8, 15-9, 15-10, 15-11, 15-12, 15-13, 15-16, 15-17, 15-18, 15-19, 15-20, 15-21, 15-22, 16-1, 16-2, 16-3, 16-4, 16-5, 16-12, 16-13, 16-15, 16-16, 16-17, 16-18, 16-24, 17-2, 17-3, 17-4, 17-5, 17-7, 17-8, 17-9, 17-10, 17-11, 17-12, 17-13, 17-14, 17-17, 17-18, 18-1, 18-2, 18-3, 18-5, 18-7, 18-8, 18-10, 18-11, 18-12, 18-13, 18-14, 18-15, 18-16, 19-1, 19-2, 19-3, 19-5, 19-7, 19-8, 19-9, 19-10, 19-11, 19-12, 19-14, 19-15, 19-16, 19-17, 19-18, 20-1, 20-2, 20-3, 20-4, 20-6, 20-8, 20-10, 20-11, 20-13, 20-14, 20-15, 20-16, 20-17, 20-18, 21-1, 21-2, 21-4, 21-5, 21-6, 21-7, 21-8, 21-9, 21-11, 21-12, 21-13, 21-14, 22-1, 22-2, 22-3, 22-4, 22-6, 22-7, 22-8, 22-9, 22-10, 22-11, 22-12, 22-13, 22-14, 22-15, 22-16, 22-17, 22-18, 22-19, 22-20, 22-21, 22-22